Praise for *Hands-On Microsoft Access*

"Life at the cutting edge of Access development is exciting and very challenging. The knowledge and experience gained over many years of research and trial-and-error has been hard won. But Bob's new book encapsulates the knowledge we now take for granted, and for the first time the beginner is afforded the opportunity to bypass all that hard work. In this his latest work, Bob has distilled the essence of database design and Access development into a highly valuable and easily understandable resource that I wish was available when I first started out."

—Graham R Seach, MCP, MCAD, MCSD, Microsoft Access MVP, author

"This is an excellent book for beginners, with an easy reading style. It is now on my recommended list of books that I hand out in every Access class that I teach."

—M.L. "Sco" Scofield, Microsoft Access MVP, MCSD, Senior Instructor, Scofield Business Services

"If you've been using Access with that typical uncertainty, asking yourself 'Just how could I do that?' or 'Why isn't this working?', or if you'd like to know what you're doing before you hit the wall, this book is perfect for you. Access is a tremendous product and a database is created using a few clicks; but without at least some theoretical background you're bound to encounter problems soon. I wish a book like this one would've been available when I started getting deeper into working with Access some ten years ago."

—Olaf Rabbachin, CEO, IntuiDev IT-solutions

"This book is for any level DB developer/user. It is packed full of *real-world* examples and solutions that are not the normal Northwind database that most Access books use. The examples and the technical content surrounding them are the real strength of the book. Schneider uses real-world scenarios that make for excellent reading. It made me want to go and redo a lot of my older Access DBs that were not written as well as they could have been. This book taught me different approaches to doing some routine tasks."

—Ron Crumbaker, Microsoft MVP – SMS

"While a very powerful application (or perhaps because of its power), Microsoft Access does have a steep learning curve and can be intimidating to new users. Bob Schneider has managed to write a book that's both understandable and enjoyable to read. His examples should be understandable to all readers, and he extends them in a logical manner. This book should leave the reader well equipped to make use of what many consider to be the best desktop database product available."

—Doug Steele, Microsoft Access MVP

"The author takes what is potentially a very dry subject and adds fantastic color through entertaining analogies and metaphors. For instance, his examples using the NBA, the Beatles, and Donald Rumsfeld help us 'get it' without realizing we have just traversed what could be very stale database theory. Brilliant!"

—Kel Good, MCT, MCSD for Microsoft.NET, Custom Software Development Inc. (www.customsoftware.ca)

HANDS-ON MICROSOFT ACCESS

Hands-On Microsoft Access

A Practical Guide to Improving Your Access Skills

Bob Schneider

Addison-Wesley

Upper Saddle River, NJ • Boston • Indianapolis • San Francisco
New York • Toronto • Montreal • London • Munich • Paris • Madrid
Capetown • Sydney • Tokyo • Singapore • Mexico City

The publisher offers excellent discounts on this book when ordered in quantity for bulk purchases or special sales, which may include electronic versions and/or custom covers and content particular to your business, training goals, marketing focus, and branding interests. For more information, please contact:

U. S. Corporate and Government Sales
(800) 382-3419
corpsales@pearsontechgroup.com

For sales outside the U. S., please contact:

International Sales
international@pearsoned.com

Visit us on the Web: www.awprofessional.com

Library of Congress Catalog Number: 2005926950

ISBN 0-321-24545-8
Text printed in the United States on recycled paper at R.R. Donnelley in Crawfordsville, Indiana.
First printing, August 2005

To my brother Randy, who provided calculable financial support and incalculable moral support to the writing of this book.

Contents

PREFACE

This book teaches you basic relational database principles so you can run Microsoft Access successfully. It explains commonly used Access features that can be difficult to grasp, particularly those that present a theoretical or conceptual problem. It analyzes key Access wizards so you understand what they actually do and how you can modify their output. Overall, the book is aimed at readers who have run Access a little or a lot, but who still feel they don't "get" how the program works. It uses a relaxed, conversational style; imperfect but helpful analogies; loads of hands-on, step-by-step, annotated examples; and a little humor to teach you relational database theory, describe the program's essential features, and unravel Access mysteries that can cause you much grief.

How Will This Book Help Me Use Access More Effectively?

My good friend Butler is a computer whiz. For hundreds of PC users in the San Francisco area, the solution to any computer problem is "Call Butler." Need more memory? Call Butler. Have a virus? Call Butler. Cauliflower growing in your hard drive? Butler can solve that, too.

Not long ago, he said to me, "I'd like to inventory my book collection. Could you show me that trick again in Access? You know, where you take fields from some tables and stick them in other tables, and somehow you get everything to work together?"

Now, there's very little I can tell Butler about Windows, or memory, or routers. But in this one area, I could help him. Because what Butler was really asking me was: How does a relational database management system (RDBMS) such as Access work, and how can I exploit that knowledge to use Access effectively?

Other programs in the Microsoft Office Professional suite make no such demands. Certainly, they can be baffling. Why did Word decide to change the font midsentence? Why is this column in Excel including calculations you don't want? Why can't you convert this PowerPoint slide to a web page?

But most of us somehow manage to get a letter written in Word, work with budgets in Excel, and get some sort of presentation out of PowerPoint. These tasks can be challenging, but they require far less extensive theoretical underpinning for you to be able to produce something (that's less true of Excel than Word or PowerPoint, but true nonetheless). What you might produce could flout every best practice and might have been designed far more effectively, yet you can get something out that will more or less serve your purposes.

You can't use Access successfully, however, unless you have a framework in your head of how a relational database works. Oh, sure, you can create a table and add a bunch of contact info to it. But other Office programs serve equally well, if not better, for simply putting data in little boxes. Only when you adopt the principles of relational database design to your data does Access fulfill its potential to manage information.

Many new Access users, if not most, don't come to the program armed with that crucial knowledge. That's not surprising. Unless you specifically take a course or read books in database design, you're unlikely to have gained the understanding of relational database principles necessary to use Access effectively.

Another challenge is exclusive to Access. Open Word, and you get a blank document; open Excel, and there's a blank spreadsheet; open PowerPoint for a blank slide. For the most part, these are the only interfaces you work in. In Access, however, you work in many interfaces. You'll frequently use at least four objects—tables, forms, queries, and reports—and each of those has two or more views. For new users, just figuring out what they're looking at—is this a form in Datasheet view? A query in Design view?—is a challenge.

This practical but relatively mundane problem begs a much larger question: Just how do all the objects and interfaces in Access interact and work together? When should you use a query instead of a table to build a report? If you add groups to a report, will it affect the values in the underlying table? If you delete a form, will it affect a report that uses the same records?

If you have a framework of how Access works embedded in your head, the answers to these questions are obvious (well, somewhat obvious). But learning the relational database model is a hurdle that many Access users never clear.

Is This Book Meant for Me?

I wrote this book so that, equipped with a knowledge of relational database theory, you can successfully use all the key objects in Access—both individually and together—to manage your business and personal information needs.

This book is aimed at readers who have run Access before but don't feel confident using it. Perhaps you've read one of the "for-morons" books. You have created some databases and entered data into them. But you work in Access with hesitation, even trepidation. You don't have a good idea of how you should organize fields into tables. You have read about primary keys and relationships, but you really don't understand how they work or why they're so important. You have created a form or query or report, but you don't recognize how each interacts with its underlying table(s) and with each other. You've used wizards to create forms and reports, but when you want to modify them, you're stumped. You want to enter data easily, retrieve it freely, manipulate it successfully, and publish it with a little panache.

I don't want to oversell. This book should be sufficient if your Access needs extend to inventorying Butler's book collection, or perhaps even running a small, simple business or association. If you are using Access for a company or organization of some size and complexity, however, this book won't tell you all you need to know to design robust Access databases on your own. But it will give you the broad understanding of the major issues that need to be addressed. If you do require the services of database designers and Access programmers, you'll be much better able to understand what they are doing. You'll ask good questions and provide good answers to those posed to you. In short, you'll be a much better client, which means you're much more likely to get a more effective and productive database.

Why Is Understanding Database Principles So Essential for Using Access?

Although this book includes a multitude of explanations and exercises for performing essential, everyday Access tasks, its overriding objective is to instill in you the relational database framework.

My sense of the importance of having the relational database model in your head parallels my experience of learning and teaching accounting.

The basic accounting equation, as every accounting student soon finds out, is Assets = Liabilities + Owner's Equity. As I watched students struggle with the vagaries of accounting—such as why an increase in cash *and* an increase in insurance expense both require debits to their respective accounts—it occurred to me that their main problem was they didn't understand this basic equation. Oh, sure, they could repeat it back on a pop quiz. But they hadn't internalized it to the extent that it had become second nature to use with accounting problems.

But once you are able to see all accounting transactions as affecting assets, liabilities, or owner's equity, accounting's mysteries become solvable. Of course, accounting poses some very thorny theoretical and practical questions, and merely knowing a very simple equation won't solve most of your problems. Without having that model in your head, however, it's difficult to tackle them at all.

Relational database theory can't be reduced to a simple equation. But the need to have an underlying theoretical framework is, if anything, as important in using a relational database program such as Access as it is in accounting.

Because a table is the only object that you actually have to use in Access, it is also the object new users learn about first. So there is a tendency for novices to use a table for all sorts of tasks and functions—entering data, viewing it, printing it, and so on—when other objects are much more effective. Knowledgeable Access users will recognize the central importance of tables to a database, but they actually spend little time working in them. The relational database framework, as manifested in Access, requires that you know not only how to relate tables to one another, but also how the various objects interact with and change each other.

How Is This Book Different from All Other Access Books?

Several Access books on the market accurately describe its many features. A few (not enough) books make database theory accessible to the average user. But no book I've seen spends the time or real estate required for you to gain a basic understanding of relational database theory and then builds on that knowledge to explain key Access objects and features.

I also think some Access books repeat much material that is available in the program's Help files. The motives are perfectly understandable, even laudatory: Access Help has lots of great charts that present information succinctly, and authors want their books to be comprehensive. It's impossible to know which user will need what information, and no author wants his readers running to the Help screen because they can't find what they need in his book.

But in my view, the true mission of a computer book is to explain difficult concepts in innovative ways so that readers learn and remember them. Thus, I have tried to focus on Access features and issues that pose some intellectual or theoretical problem. For topics that do not raise any thorny theoretical issues but are nonetheless still confusing, I try to give detailed explanations or hands-on examples that illustrate the problem and disclose the solution.

For the sake of completeness and convenience, I have included some essential topics that do not pose any great theoretical issues, nor are they bewildering. In these areas, I have attempted to add some value by providing a hands-on exercise, a neat tip, an interesting take, or simply a better presentation than that available in Access Help. I do not deny that you could have gleaned a certain amount of material in this book simply by pressing F1 in Access, but I think it represents a relatively small proportion of the total content.

How Much Access Do I Need to Know to Use This Book?

This book assumes that you have a little—not a lot of—Access knowledge. You should know how to open an Access database and get to work in it. You should feel comfortable navigating the Database window. You should be able to do simple data entry in a form and a datasheet. You should recognize, in a general way, the difference between the Design view of objects (that is, the blueprint) and the object itself (most commonly, Datasheet view for tables and queries, Form view for forms, and Print Preview for reports). I have not been overly fastidious in providing screenshots with callouts (labels) for every toolbar button and Access element; I assume you are familiar with (or can easily find out about) the most common icons.

Let me emphasize, however, that I believe many beginners can profitably use this book. Importantly, in the exercises I've created, I've attempted to fully describe every step needed to complete it. For example, I have mostly avoided instructions such as "Create a new query in Design view and add the Products and Suppliers field lists," which would require you to know how to execute several commands (although I imagine such directions would cause little unhappiness for many readers and would be preferred by some). Instead, each command is clearly stated; for example, the first step here would be "In the Database window, click the Queries button," and you would proceed from there.

What Topics Does (and Doesn't) This Book Cover?

This book emphasizes understanding how Access works. It does not include many topics (some of them important) that the more encyclopedic Access texts contain. I have mostly ignored subjects such as customized toolbars and changing fonts, not because these are not useful, but because they don't pose any conceptual or theoretical issues. There is little on topics that are mostly of use to specialized audiences, such as data access pages. And recognizing the admonishment that "a little knowledge is a dangerous thing," I have almost nothing to say about security issues, such as protecting your data from malevolent forces.

More questionably, the book also does not touch upon the computer language Visual Basic for Applications (VBA), despite its centrality to doing advanced work in Access. VBA gets very complicated very quickly. I wanted to avoid content that, in effect, says, "You don't have to understand this—just type this code here, and it will work." In every topic discussed, I want you to understand fully what you're doing and why you're doing it.

This commitment is particularly applicable to Access wizards. Creating objects in Access often involves many steps, and the program provides numerous wizards to produce them. The wizards are effective and efficient, and usually (although not always) easy to use; however, they only intermittently enhance the user's understanding of relational databases and Access. They can become a crutch, and users who rely too heavily on them will often be at a loss when they need to make even minor modifications to the wizard's output. I want you to use the wizards, but I also want you to know what the wizards are actually doing.

Here is a chapter-by-chapter breakdown of the book's contents:

Chapter 1, "Getting Started," introduces basic database terminology, such as *table*, *field*, and *value*. It describes the various data types and tackles the issue of null values and zero-length strings.

Chapter 2, "Database Design," is devoted to database theory. It explains the shortcomings of nonrelational database models for storing data of some size and consequence. It discusses basic relational database design principles. It takes you from the start of the database creation process (developing a mission statement for the database) to the initial distribution of fields into tables. The essential topic of primary keys and their use in resolving multivalue fields is discussed at length. To illustrate the issues posed in the chapter, I introduce the Classic TV database, which contains data about hit TV shows from the past. I also utilize a traditional order-entry model, like Northwind, to help make some of the points.

I continue to develop the Classic TV database in Chapter 3, "Understanding Relationships," where the focus is on relationships. One-to-many, many-to-many, and one-to-one relationships are analyzed, and numerous examples of each relationship type are offered. You learn how to use a linking table to resolve many-to-many relationships. At the end of the chapter, I describe and simplify the first three rules of the normalization process for relational databases.

Chapter 4, "Establishing Relationships," teaches you how to formally establish in Access the relationships you learned in Chapter 3. I discuss the system of relationship rules known as referential integrity, including two options that mitigate these restrictions: Cascade Update Related Fields and Cascade Delete Related Records.

Tables are the subject of Chapter 5, "Building Tables." It begins with a discussion of lookup fields, a confusing and minor topic that nonetheless serves as an excellent vehicle for reviewing the database design principles covered in Chapters 1–4 and gives you insight into the true nature of tables. The chapter then looks at the various methods of table creation. Most of the discussion, however, focuses on field properties—`Field Size`, `Format`, `Validation Rule`, and so on—which have an extraordinary impact on your database. Table properties are also considered.

Data entry is the focus of Chapter 6, "Entering, Editing, and Displaying Data." Forms are introduced and distinguished from tables. The tricky topic of how controls in forms inherit (and disinherit) field properties assigned in tables is considered. Data-entry tools and features such as input masks and the Undo command are also described.

Chapter 7, "Find and Filter," begins a section of three chapters devoted to finding and retrieving data from your database. In this initial chapter, the Find command is dissected, and the varying filter methods are discussed at length. AND and OR criteria, and related topics such as expressions and operators, are described and examples are offered.

Chapter 8, "Queries," introduces queries, perhaps the most interesting and enjoyable topic in relational databases. You'll learn about calculated fields and the `Top Values` property. The topic of multitable queries is particularly important because these queries reveal the true power and elegance of a relational database. Joins are introduced, and inner joins are distinguished from outer joins. Structured Query Language (SQL) is discussed, if only briefly; it's sufficient, however, to demystify the topic.

Chapter 9 has the unimaginative title of "Queries, Part II." It builds on the knowledge you acquired in Chapter 8, but the queries are not all that advanced, nor are they particularly difficult to use. These include parameter, total, crosstab, and action queries; you'll find them extremely useful.

Chapter 10, "Reports," is dedicated to giving you a more in-depth understanding of reports. Although you can create a fairly sophisticated report using a wizard in a few seconds, understanding what you created or how it was accomplished is another matter entirely. To fill the gap, I take you through the entire process of creating a report in Design view—manually, step by excruciating step, with no help from a wizard. At the end of the chapter, you create a report with the same specifications using a wizard and then compare the results, to demonstrate how each element of the wizard's output would be accomplished manually. Armed with this knowledge, you will be able to edit and add to wizard-created reports, which inevitably you will need to do.

What Chapter 10 did for reports, Chapter 11, "Forms/Subforms," accomplishes for forms. The various elements of forms—combo boxes, subforms, option groups, and so on—are discussed in detail, and you have the opportunity to add them to an existing form. At chapter's end, you'll use a wizard to create a form with the same specifications. As in Chapter 10, I compare the wizard's output with the object created by hand to note differences. Again, the aim is to help you understand what the wizard accomplishes automatically and how you can modify the results.

Chapter 12, "Form/Report Design Elements," covers a multitude of topics on report and form creation that were not covered in Chapters 10 and 11. The approach these chapters took was useful for deconstructing wizards, but there was a major drawback: Many useful report-/form-creation features were glossed over or simply were not covered. This chapter seeks to make amends and fill in the gaps. The result is a discussion that ranges from bound and unbound controls to linking and embedding, from conditional formatting to special effects, from macros to snaked column reports. It is a hodge-podge, but not an unruly one.

Chapter 13, "Importing and Exporting," is all about getting data into Access from external sources, and its opposite, putting Access data into external environments. I show various techniques that can accomplish these transfers: export and import wizards, but also cut/copy/paste as well as drag-and-drop. Because this is an Access book, the focus is on using Access features to move data. But I haven't been draconian in excluding non-Access features, especially when they accomplish the data transfers more successfully than Access tools. For example, I describe Microsoft Word's mail-merge feature at length because you are far more likely to begin and execute mail merges in Word.

Pivot tables are the topic of Chapter 14, "Pivot Tables and Pivot Charts." Although crosstab queries have their uses for slicing and splicing data, pivot tables are a far more powerful and effective tool for data analysis. In earlier versions of Access, pivot tables relied heavily on Microsoft Excel for their execution. But pivot tables are now fully and powerfully integrated in Access. You will have to endure some learning curve to use them effectively, but the investment should yield a high return.

How Should I Read This Book?

This book is designed to be read chapter by chapter, in order, from cover to cover. But I know readers have varied needs and limited time, and many will probably dip in and out of its pages. If you know little about relational databases, I encourage you to you read Chapters 1–4 before tackling other areas. These pages will give you the underpinning in relational database design that is necessary to work with Access successfully.

If you do read the book page by page in sequential order, you might find it useful to know that the subject matter of the rest of the book breaks down into primarily three parts. If I had to give these sections names, Chapters 5–6 would be titled "Building Tables and Getting Data into Them"; Chapters 7–9, "Finding and Retrieving the Data You Need"; and Chapters 10–12, "Building Forms and Reports." Chapters 13 and 14, which cover exporting/importing and pivot tables/charts, stand individually.

What Teaching Devices Does This Book Use?

It's trite, I know, but the best way to learn is by doing. I'd much prefer that all of this book give you hands-on practice in each topic area. Unfortunately, in the first three chapters on database design, I ask you to sit and read patiently as I develop the Classic TV relational database. There just didn't seem any way to usefully involve readers in the action.

In the rest of the book, however, and to the greatest extent possible, I use step-by-step exercises to illustrate key concepts. Most of the examples are based on the Nifty Lions database I built, which is in broadly accessible Access 2000 format. It closely resembles Access's sample database, Northwind.mdb, because I wanted you to use a database that is probably already somewhat familiar. But Nifty Lions is simpler than Northwind; it contains far fewer records, and (for Americans, at least) the supplier names are simple and familiar. In a few exercises, I have used Northwind where the example called for a database with more records. In some of the later chapters, you use other databases and files (Excel, Word, PowerPoint, picture files, text files, and so on) that I've created. All of these files are available online at http://www.awprofessional.com/title/0321245458. Under More Information, click Example(s).

Before the first exercise in each chapter, I ask you to copy the relevant database or file to your hard drive. At the end of the chapter, assuming you've done all the exercises in order, you can compare your results against the solution database or file, which is available from the same Addison-Wesley website. (For example, `NiftyLionsChap7End.mdb` is the Nifty Lions database at the end of Chapter 7.) For each exercise, you will also find one or more screenshots printed in the book against which you can compare your results at intermediate or final stages.

This book uses numerous analogies to help you understand important database principles. William Safire, language maven, says there is no such thing as a bad pun. Maybe that's true, but there is certainly such a thing as a bad analogy. Some database principles are so difficult to get your arms around, however, that I have erred on the side of incaution and included less-than-perfect analogies where I thought they might provide some illumination.

Which Version(s) of Access Does This Book Cover?

The examples in this book were written and designed for readers using Microsoft Access 2003 within the Microsoft Office Professional Edition 2003. But the book reflects little bias toward any particular version: There is no "What's New in Access 2003?" chapter. In the few cases in which Access 2003 differs markedly from Access 2002, I have tried to provide special instructions for users of the earlier version. Nearly all chapters center on crucial issues that Access users have faced for years (well, at least since the introduction of Access 95 and 97).

I do recognize that several examples will not work exactly as advertised with Access versions earlier than 2002. But users with some knowledge of the program can scale this hurdle and still use the book profitably.

What's So Great About an Access Database Anyway?

Some years ago, there was an article in *The New Yorker* about two brothers, both mathematicians, who were on a dubious mission. They had built a homemade supercomputer, lodged in one brother's apartment near Columbia University on Morningside Heights, to find the value of the constant pi to as many decimal places as possible. Pi was already known to millions of places (now it's known to billions), and many scholars questioned just what was being accomplished by generating millions more. One Columbia professor fumed, "This is about as interesting as going to the beach and counting sand.... Mathematics is mostly about giving pleasure."

I love that remark: It conjures up the image of an "adventuress" in an exotic seaport sidling up to a sailor and saying, "Hey, big boy, how about a Pythagorean theorem?" But the professor's comment is also startling: For most of us, *pleasure* is the last word we associate with our own experiences of computing the areas of rhomboids and resolving quadratic equations.

I find higher mathematics as baffling as most people, and I'm not exactly sure what the professor was getting at. But I *think* he was saying that *real* mathematicians find elegant solutions to problems, which cannot help but give pleasure to those who can contemplate such beauty.

I'm not willing to state that you'll ever find the creation and manipulation of an Access database mostly about giving pleasure. But I will say that a well-designed relational database can indeed be elegant, beautiful, *lovely*. Like the best mathematical solutions, an Access relational database is spare and minimal—data is never repeated twice when once will do. In a desirable contradiction, the better integrated its foundation, the more flexible and powerful an Access database becomes. And like all well-designed systems, an Access database is secure and stable: It vigorously denies entry to data that is unsuitable or even harmful.

First and foremost, I want this book to educate. But I also hope it will give you pleasure as you discover the elegance and beauty of a well-designed Access database. I know that if you experience just some of the joy in reading it that I had in writing it, you will have a grand time indeed.

Acknowledgments

Although *Bob Schneider* might be slapped on the cover, the making of this book has been a team effort with many key players. I'd like to thank the members of the editorial group at Addison-Wesley. In the face of a brutal workload, my editor Joan Murray always made time to confer and console. She intelligently steered the book's creation and got it out the door. Acquisitions editor Stephane Thomas encouraged my proposal and commissioned the book. The difficult task of boosting my flagging spirits and confidence, as well as parrying my delaying tactics, fell to three assiduous editorial assistants: Jessica D'Amico, Elizabeth Zdunich, and Ebony Haight. Development editor Chris Zahn provided high-level guidance, project editor Lori Lyons, with the help of Rebecca Storbeck, shepherded the book through production, and copyeditor Krista Hansing edited my prose.

I greatly appreciate the thoughtful criticisms and excellent suggestions I received from my reviewers. Kel Good deserves special recognition for slogging through all the examples, step-by-step, and being generous with both his time and expertise. Doug Steele, Bob Reselman, John Viescas, and Richard Banks all made valuable, thoughtful remarks. I appreciate the warm encouragement of Ron Crumbaker and Arvin Meyer, as well as the comments of Paul Kimmel, David Hayden, and Christa Carp. Whatever the book's shortcomings, they would have been multiplied severalfold had it not been for the well-reasoned abuse of the review group.

About the Author

Bob Schneider has been a writer and editor for more than 25 years. Since 2001, he has been writing about Access for *Smart Computing*, one of the nation's leading computer magazines. For three years he served as editor-in-chief of *Working Smarter with Microsoft Access*, a biweekly newsletter that helps office staff use Access more productively. Prior to that, he was development editor for Access 95, 97, and 2000 textbooks published by Glencoe/McGraw-Hill. He is based in San Francisco, CA.

CHAPTER 1

GETTING STARTED

This short introductory chapter has limited but important objectives.

First, it presents basic database terminology, which lays the groundwork for the detailed discussion on database design in Chapters 2, "Database Design"; 3, "Understanding Relationships"; and 4, "Establishing Relationships." The most important of these terms are table, field, record, value, and relational database.

Second, the chapter offers a brief overview of data types, which gives you some idea of the kinds of items—names, numbers, dates, pictures, hyperlinks, and so on—you can enter in an Access database.

Third, it explores two important areas—primary keys and null values—that often give new users trouble. Ideally, I'd like to delay discussing these topics until I give you a broader understanding of database theory. Unfortunately, it's hard to avoid these thorny subjects early in your Access work, and a lack of understanding of these crucial concepts can become a roadblock to learning the program.

Key Terms

It's always easier to learn theory when it's directly related to something tangible—especially a detailed, real-world example you can use. But there are a few essential database terms I want you to know right away, so let me introduce them using a make-believe example.

Table

A *table* is a grid of rows and columns. Often there are gridlines to distinguish the columns and rows, but the lines themselves merely provide visual clarity. Table 1.1 is a table of contact information for the members of the Hoops Club of Littletown, Georgia, which each Sunday gets together to watch an NBA game on TV.

Notice that the data in any particular column is of the same kind. For example, the Last Name column has only last names, and the Phone column has only phone numbers. Also, each row contains data about just one person—you won't find any information about George Harrelson in the Helen Michaelson row.

Table 1.1 Table of Contact Information

Last Name	First Name	Address	Phone
Michaelson	Helen	659 Kareem Abdul-Jabbar Ave.	555-6548
Harrelson	George	42 Karl Malone Dr.	555-9834
Hendricks	Maury	1178 Michael Jordan Cir.	555-9846
Isaacs	Heather	462 Wilt Chamberlain Ctr.	555-7666
Crandall	Orlando	378 Moses Malone St.	555-1209
O'Connell	William	463 Elvin Hayes Ave.	555-8736
Benton	Elizabeth	355 Oscar Robertson Way	555-0234
O'Connell	James	536 Dominique Wilkins St.	555-9065
Bradley	Milton	1111 Hakeem Olajuwon Towers	555-0036
Ordell	Sally	125 John Havlicek Ave.	555-4609

Field, Record, and Value

On the first day of my high-school bookkeeping class, my teacher asked us to define *debit* and *credit*. Many students had had some exposure to accounting, and they produced a range of definitions. Each was quickly dismissed by the CPA standing before us, who easily produced counter-examples and exposed logical errors for all attempts. Finally, he said, "Just remember: Debit means left side, and credit means right side." It was the most useful thing anybody ever told me about accounting.

Database theory and accounting theory might have little in common, but in this one sense, they are alike: A simple definition can sometimes serve best. So I ask you to think of a *field* as a column in a table, even though a more informative definition might be "a single trait or characteristic about the subject of a table." In Table 1.1, `Last Name`, `First Name`, `Address`, and `Phone` are all fields.

In the same way, it's best to think of a *record* as simply a row in a table, even though a more comprehensive description might be "a group of traits about a particular item." In the table, the data in the first row beginning with `Michaelson` and extending through `555-6548` is a record.

A *value* is the actual data entered at the intersection of a row and column. In the table, `Helen` is a value in the `First Name` field, and `42 Karl Malone Dr.` is a value in the `Address` field.

Relational Database

The next four chapters—indeed, most of this book—are an attempt to answer the question "What is a *relational database*?" So I don't try to define it now. But I ask you to remember three things:

- A database is a collection of data.
- A relational database stores its data in tables.
- Access is a relational database, so its data is stored in tables.

Data Types

The *data type* is a characteristic you designate for an Access field when you create it. It determines what kind of data can be entered into the field. Data types are determined primarily by the nature of the data and the amount of data that can be stored in a particular field.

The selection of data types and how the different types are variously used will make more sense when you start building tables. All data types receive much more treatment in Chapter 5, "Building Tables." But I introduce them now because it gives you an excellent idea of the kinds of data you can enter and manipulate in Access.

Let's say you're a big fan of the Beatles. You want to create a database of their music, personnel, and activities, as well as the CDs, DVDs, and memorabilia you own. You'll include things such as their biographies, song lyrics, and top websites. The following discussion describes the various data types you might use and the kinds of items included in each type.

`Text`

`Text` is the most common data type. It is a string of alphanumeric characters—that is, letters of the alphabet and numbers. You can include strings of up to 255 characters in a field with the `Text` data type.

The names of the Fab Four—`John Lennon`, `Paul McCartney`, and so on—are `Text`. The names of their wives—such as `Yoko` and `Linda`—are also `Text`. Their albums—`Rubber Soul`, `Abbey Road`—are `Text`, and so are their songs—`Let It Be`, `Yesterday`, `Norwegian Wood (This Bird Has Flown)`.

`Number`

You use the `Number` data type to store numeric data that will be used in calculations.

Suppose the Classic Rock Music Store orders nine CDs of *Sergeant Pepper's Lonely Hearts Club Band* for its inventory. The 9 can be added to the 18 the store purchased last month and the 87 bought back in January to find the total number of *Sergeant Pepper* CDs purchased for the year. You use the `Number` data type to store data about the number of CDs in stock.

On the other hand, Beatles fans will recall that the last song on *The White Album* is "Revolution 9," where John gets to repeat his favorite digit over and over: "number 9, number 9, number 9, number 9...."

The 9s in both the song title and the lyrics represent a completely different use for 9 than the number of *Sergeant Pepper* CDs purchased. The `9`s for the song are `Text` because you have no reason to perform arithmetic operations with them. The same logic applies to phone numbers and ZIP codes—they're `Text`.

NOTE A field with the Number data type accepts only numbers—no letters, dashes, ampersands, and so forth are allowed.

When you select a `Number` data type, you have many other choices to consider. For example, should the field contain only integers (that is, whole numbers) or numbers with decimal places? If you do include decimal places, how are they stored and how are they displayed? These issues are considered in Chapter 5.

`Currency`

Another data type available for the entry of numeric data is `Currency`. You use this data type to record, say, the $69.50 you paid for a *Revolver* LP album in good condition, or the $1,150 it cost you for an original *Yellow Submarine* movie poster. An advantage of the `Currency` data type is that it avoids rounding errors and can match values to the penny.

`Date/Time`

The `Date/Time` data type offers several advantages for entering dates and times. First, it makes it easy to convert dates from one format to another. Thus, a date displayed as `12/8/80` can be easily made to appear as

`December 8, 1980`. Second, using the `Date/Time` type enables you to find records that occurred during a specific time period, such as between `11/10/04` and `01/02/05`, or after `8/10/05`.

This data type also enables you to do calculations on your data. For example, suppose your company has a policy that all orders must be shipped within seven days of order placement. You could easily add 7 to each of a list of dates to find the deadlines.

Memo

The difference between a `Text` field and a `Memo` field is primarily a matter of size. `Text` fields can store a maximum of 255 characters. If you wanted to include all the lyrics to the song "Revolution 9" in a `Text` field, you might get to the line "Then there's this Welsh Rarebit wearing some brown underpants." But after that, Access would not allow you to enter any more lyrics. To make sure you can fit in "block that kick!" repeated 16 times, you'd want to use a `Memo` field, which stores up to 65,536 characters.

Yes/No

The `Yes/No` field contains only two possible values: `Yes` (or `True`) and `No` (or `False`). You use this data type to state that a condition either does or does not exist. For example, the Beatles Memorabilia Company might have an `Overnight` field in a products table that indicates whether an item can be shipped overnight. If it can be shipped overnight, the value is `Yes`; if not, the value is `No`. There are no `maybe`, `perhaps`, or `it depends` values in a `Yes/No` field.

OLE Object

Suppose you want to include in your database an image of Ringo's autograph, or a sound file of the song "Lady Madonna," or a Word document containing the letter you wrote Yoko in 1992. All of these are objects created in another program that can be stored in an Access database. An OLE object can be as large as a gigabyte (assuming, of course, you have all that room on your hard disk to store it).

NOTE OLE objects can be either embedded or linked. The differences between these methods are discussed in Chapter 12, "Form/Report Design Elements."

`Hyperlink`

Hundreds, probably thousands, of websites are devoted to the Beatles. You can use a hyperlink to store their addresses. You can also use a hyperlink to store a path to a file on your hard drive or network. If the hyperlink is for a website, clicking it opens the site in your default browser; if the path is for a file, it opens in its associated program.

A hyperlink address has three parts, each of which can contain up to 2,048 characters:

- **Text to display**—The text that appears in the field
- **Address**—The path to a file or a page
- **Subaddress**—A location within the file or page

POP QUIZ ON DATA TYPES

Fauna Emporia is a small chain of pet shops that sells exotic pets and supplies. It uses several tables to store data about its customers, products, suppliers, and other subjects. Match each kind of data to its most likely data type—`Text`, `Number`, `Currency`, `Date/Time`, `Memo`, `Yes/No`, `OLE Object`, or `Hyperlink`.

1. Customer salutation (Mr., Mrs., Ms.)
2. Supplier names
3. Whether a customer is a nonprofit organization and, therefore, tax-exempt
4. The words to the song "You Light Up My Life," which Oliver the parrot knows by heart
5. A sound file of Oliver singing "You Light Up My Life"
6. How many white mice you have available for sale
7. The list price for Aloysius the aardvark
8. The address of the website of Professor Robin Swan, linguist and bird authority
9. The suite number of the chain's feed supplier
10. The date Cleopatra the Persian cat had kittens

Answers

1. `Text` 2. `Text` 3. `Yes/No` 4. `Memo` 5. `OLE Object` 6. `Number` 7. `Currency` 8. `Hyperlink` 9. `Text` 10. `Date/Time`

Primary Keys

A key is a field that serves a specific function within a table. Several types of keys are important, but for now, I want to focus on the *primary key*. In the next few chapters, I discuss the primary key at length, and you will spend a great deal of time selecting and using primary keys. But I introduce the concept now for three reasons:

- It exposes you to fields with the `AutoNumber` data type, thus rounding out our discussion of data types.
- It hints at what distinguishes Access tables from other tables you've worked with.
- I want to make sure that you don't get hung up on the primary key concept.

The last objective most concerns me. Early on, new Access users are exposed to primary keys and usually find them confusing. Here's a typical scenario:

1. You begin to create a table in a database.
2. You begin to enter fields and select data types in Design view (see Figure 1.1).
   As you enter fields, you also likely choose field properties and provide descriptions. These topics are covered in Chapter 5.
3. After you've created the table, you attempt to save it.
   Access issues a message that says you have not defined a primary key. It also says that, although a primary key isn't required, it's "highly recommended" (see Figure 1.2).
4. You click Yes and Access creates a table with a primary key with the `AutoNumber` data type.

You now have a new table with a primary key. But the message doesn't explain much about primary keys. Without some further background, it's almost impossible not to be confused by it.

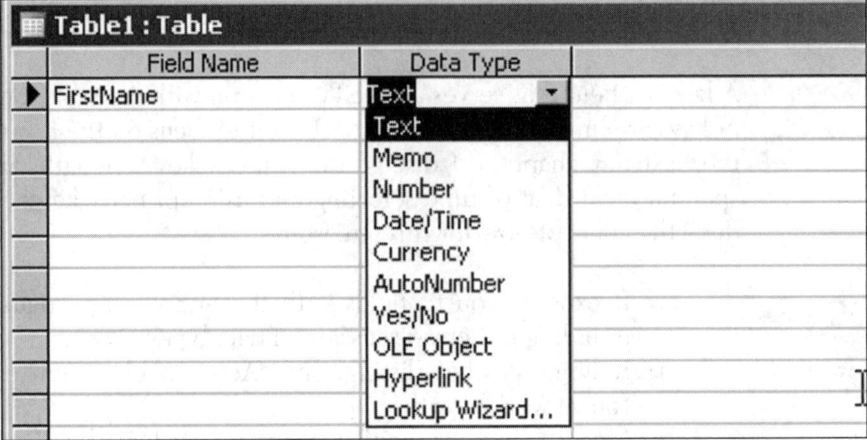

Figure 1.1 A table in Design view. The Data Type drop-down menu displays the various data types. (The last selection, Lookup Wizard, is not a data type and is discussed in Chapter 5.)

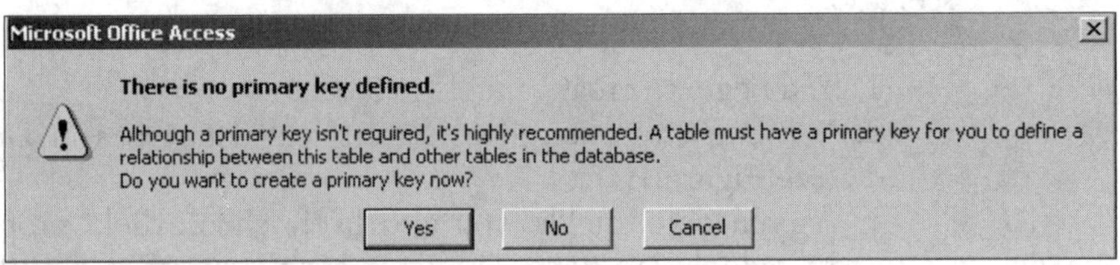

Figure 1.2 Access recommends that you define a primary key.

How Primary Keys Work

One requirement for a relational database is that each record in each table be uniquely identified by a primary key. That means that in a field that is the primary key, there can never be duplicate data.

Let's see what that means in practice. Take a look back at Table 1.1. Each of the fields either currently has a duplicate or has the potential of having a duplicate. For example, in the `Last Name` field, `O'Connell` appears twice. You cannot use the `Last Name` field as a primary key because it's possible that two people will have the same last name. Indeed, even the smallest possibility that a field might have duplicate data disqualifies it as a primary key.

NOTE Primary keys can be more than one field. For now, let's keep the discussion simple by assuming a single field for the primary key.

To repeat: When I say that there can't be any duplicates in the primary key, I mean there can be *no* duplicates. Unless a key is an absolutely unique identifier, it cannot be a primary key.

This obviously sets a very high standard. In everyday life, real uniqueness is highly unusual. Nearly all of us have the same last name as someone else. So finding a field of actual real-life values that describe something that can also be used as a primary key is often difficult.

One solution to the primary key puzzle is to include a field with an `AutoNumber` type. When you use this data type, each time you add another record, the value in the field increases by 1. Take a look at Table 1.2. It is the same table as Table 1.1, but it includes a `Member ID` field as a primary key. It has the `AutoNumber` data type. Each time you add a record, the primary key increases by 1. Each record is thus uniquely identified by the `Member ID` field because each of its values is different.

Table 1.2 The Table of Contact Info Now Includes a Primary Key

Member ID	Last Name	First Name	Address	Phone
1	Michaelson	Helen	659 Kareem Abdul-Jabbar Ave.	555-6548
2	Harrelson	George	42 Karl Malone Dr.	555-9834
3	Hendricks	Maury	1178 Michael Jordan Cir.	555-9846
4	Isaacs	Heather	462 Wilt Chamberlain Ctr.	555-7666
5	Crandall	Orlando	378 Moses Malone St.	555-1209
6	O'Connell	William	463 Elvin Hayes Ave.	555-8736
7	Benton	Elizabeth	355 Oscar Robertson Way	555-0234
8	O'Connell	James	536 Dominique Wilkins St.	555-9065
9	Bradley	Milton	1111 Hakeem Olajuwon Towers	555-0036
10	Ordell	Sally	125 John Havlicek Ave.	555-4609

Gaps in the Primary Key

Now let's assume that Mr. Maury Hendricks (ID# `3`) and Mr. James O'Connell (ID# `8`) have dropped out of the club and you have deleted their records (see Table 1.3). You also added a new member, Charlie Moriarty.

If you already had doubts about the usefulness of an `AutoNumber` field as a primary key, they now intensify. There are gaps in the primary key—there is no record with ID#3 or ID#8. When you added the Moriarty record, its ID wasn't `3`—it was `11`, one more than the last `AutoNumber` used. The breaks in the primary key order seem inelegant, at best, and simply wrong, at worst. You can't renumber the primary key for all the records without a great deal of work.

Table 1.3 Table of Contact Info with Deleted Records

Member ID	Last Name	First Name	Address	Phone
1	Michaelson	Helen	659 Kareem Abdul-Jabbar Ave.	555-6548
2	Harrelson	George	42 Karl Malone Dr.	555-9834
4	Isaacs	Heather	462 Wilt Chamberlain Ctr.	555-7666
5	Crandall	Orlando	378 Moses Malone St.	555-1209
6	O'Connell	William	463 Elvin Hayes Ave.	555-8736
7	Benton	Elizabeth	355 Oscar Robertson Way	555-0234
9	Bradley	Milton	1111 Hakeem Olajuwon Towers	555-0036
10	Ordell	Sally	125 John Havlicek Ave.	555-4609
11	Moriarty	Charlie	522 Walt Frazier Turnpike	555-4889

But here's what you need to remember: You don't want to close the gaps. You are completely indifferent about whether there are breaks in the order of IDs.

Think of it this way: Say you've just entered some swanky restaurant. You give the hat-check guy your new trench coat and your spouse's mink. He gives you two tags, numbered 7 and 9, for the two coats.

Does it bother you in the least bit that there's no 8? Do you spend the entire meal thinking, "Whoa, the first tag was 7, so why wasn't that next tag an 8? Isn't that suspicious?"

Maybe hangar 8 was broken or had guacamole on it; who knows and who cares? All you're worried about is that your coats are checked and they can be found when you leave. In the same way, your only concern is that Access can find records 7 and 9 when you need to view them.

From another viewpoint, the value `8` in an `AutoNumber` field doesn't mean the number that's between `7` and `9`—that is, a number in a sequence that is going to be missed if it's not there. Although the primary key has the `AutoNumber` data type because the values increase one by one, the numbers in it are being used like text; they simply identify the record. Just as the number on a claim ticket is meaningful only as part of the storage system of the cloak room, a primary key with an `AutoNumber` data type exists only to serve the storage system of Access. Indeed, if you were going to print the table and give it to a new member, you might well want to exclude the primary key (as you can easily do) precisely because it has no meaning to fellow members.

It's About Nothing: Null Values and Zero-Length Strings

At a press conference in 2003, Donald Rumsfeld, Secretary of Defense in the Bush Administration, made the following statement:

> Reports that say something hasn't happened are always interesting to me because, as we know, there are known knowns, there are things we know we know. We also know there are known unknowns; that is to say, we know there are some things we do not know. But there are also unknown unknowns—the ones we don't know we don't know.

No doubt unknowingly, Mr. Rumsfeld has provided us with a superb introduction to the topic of nulls and zero-length strings.

Thus far, we've been dealing with values that are "something"—`Helen`, `coffee`, `378`, `10/11/97`, and so on. But what about situations in which we don't have any "something"? Telling Access that we don't have anything to put into a table—and just why we don't have a "something" to put in—is, in some ways, as important as storing those "somethings."

Let's look at a concrete example. The Acme Company makes widgets. It has a database with a Customers table that has contact info, including a field for the fax number. Table 1.4 presents a few facts about four of its customers.

Table 1.4 Customer Facts

Company Name	Has Fax Machine/ Software?	Fax Number
Williams Brothers	Yes	213-555-3678
Dalton Inc.	No	Does not exist
Hellman International	Yes	Exists, but we don't know it
Morgan Company	Don't know	Don't know if there's one

The fax number for Williams Brothers causes no problems. It is a known known—we know there's a fax number, and we know the number. We can simply enter the number in the fax number field.

But what values should we enter in the fax number field for the other companies?

Zero-Length Strings

For Dalton Inc., we know they don't have a fax. Because we know they don't have a fax, we also know there is no fax number. It's also a known known. We can tell Access that we know there is no fax number by entering a zero-length string, represented by two double-quotation marks with no space between them (`""`).

NOTE Only `Text`, `Memo`, and hyperlink fields can accept zero-length strings.

Null Values

Next is Hellman International. We know they have a fax machine. We also know that we don't know the fax number. We have a known unknown. In this case, the fax number is merely missing. Perhaps Acme's clerk forgot to ask Hellman what the fax number is or deleted it by accident. In this case, we would use a null value; we would just leave the field blank. A null value isn't `0`; it isn't a "we know it doesn't exist." It's just nothing, empty, zilch.

Finally, there's Morgan Company. We don't know whether the company has a fax. So we don't know whether Morgan Company has a fax number. But we don't know whether we don't know the fax number because the company might not have a fax number at all. It's an unknown unknown. In these cases, we would also use a null value, a blank.

That's enough to get us started on null values and zero-length strings. You'll learn more about them in Chapter 5.

Conclusion

This chapter defined a few key database terms, exposed you to the various data types, and introduced the concepts of primary keys and null values. Let's move on to the crucial topics of database theory and design, the focus of the next three chapters.

CHAPTER 2

DATABASE DESIGN

The history of relational databases is short. It's been only about 35 years since Edgar Frank Codd (almost always E. F. Codd) first discussed relational databases in IBM Research report RJ599, dated August 16, 1969.

Among the general public, RJ599 might not command the respect or have the cachet of other seminal works, such as *The Wealth of Nations,* by Adam Smith, or *The Origin of Species,* by Charles Darwin. But in an age that emphasizes information above all else, Codd's RJ599 and his other ground-breaking writings have had as much impact on our lives as the works of these more famous authors. In the few decades since Codd's early articles, the relational database has become the most widely used database model.

Learning About Database Design

You will not become a professional database designer by reading the next three chapters. Instead, you will gain an overall understanding of how relational databases work, which you can call upon when faced with database design issues. The chapters should help you use Access more effectively, enable you to ask the right questions of database professionals, and allow you to design some simple databases on your own.

I take you through the steps of creating a relational database that has data on classic television series such as *I Love Lucy* and *All in the Family*. I chose a somewhat frivolous topic for two reasons. Unlike most areas in this book, database design is not a subject that lends itself as much to hands-on, now-*you*-try-it examples where I can keep you engaged and have you learn by doing. I know that my own My Eyes Glaze Over threshold for the sort of concepts you will soon confront is about four pages. I hope to have a better chance of keeping you going through much essential but often less than scintillating material if the database topic is at least fun.

Second, and more important, relational database design is as much art as science. Although there are standard solutions to some database problems, there is no one way to design a database, either from a procedural or a theoretical standpoint. Two database pros can look at the same database and resolve its issues in distinctly different ways.

Many books use well-established relational database models such as order entry (for example, Access's sample database Northwind Traders) to illustrate key concepts. I also make extensive use of the traditional order-entry model. But if you learned how to use Access using Northwind or a database like it, you might already have the order-entry model etched in your mind. In that case, I fear you'll simply glide through the discussion (been there, done that) without gaining a fresh perspective. There also didn't seem much point to simply reworking the material of other database authors.

So although I give examples from the traditional order-entry model to reinforce database concepts you might already have an inkling of, I also offer an artificial database such as classic TV shows for an original, more-art-than-science approach. I think the positives of injecting some fun into a dry technical subject and applying database principles to an untraditional area offset the negatives of using a mock database that might have little practical application.

The following list shows the overall plan for creating the Classic TV database. Tasks 1–10 are covered in this chapter; tasks 11–13 are discussed in Chapter 3, "Understanding Relationships"; and tasks 14–16 are covered in Chapter 4, "Establishing Relationships."

1. Prepare a mission statement
2. Develop mission objectives
3. Determine data needs
4. Create a preliminary list of columns
5. Create a list of tables
6. Refine the lists of fields assigned to tables
7. Eliminate calculated fields
8. Eliminate multipart fields
9. Designate primary keys
10. Eliminate multivalue fields
11. Identify one-to-many relationships
12. Identify many-to-many relationships
13. Refine field names
14. Create relationships in the Relationships window
15. Enforce referential integrity
16. Modify referential integrity through "cascade" options

Legacy Databases

The database design procedure I describe is primarily intended to be instructive. It has major "real-world" limitations; it is a learning tool and should be treated as such.

Among its drawbacks is that it assumes that the new database will be created entirely from scratch. That's rarely the case. Both individuals and organizations usually have some type of existing database in place that must be considered when creating a new database. The old database, in the broadest sense of the term, could be hard copy, such as a stack of reports or a bunch of file cards. It could be an "Ask Joe" system, as in "Whenever we need to know something like that, we ask Joe in Accounting." Most commonly, it is a *legacy database*, a computer-based system that's been around for a few years.

Whenever you create a new database, you want to start with a clean slate, a fresh approach that is not restricted by earlier incarnations of the data. Predecessor databases often have major problems. In fact, the failings of the existing database could be why you're creating a new one.

But legacy and other preceding databases are still valuable: They help you examine the organization's current information requirements. They inform you of the shortcomings in the current information system. And they provide insight into what the organization's future needs might be.

Moreover, legacy databases often command user loyalty even (perhaps especially) when they're about to be replaced. End users do not always embrace change. Inevitably, a new database system will do some things differently than an old one, which long-time employees can find unsettling. The requirements, needs, and attitudes of a database's various audiences are key factors in database design, and it's important to know their likes and dislikes concerning the legacy database.

Putting People First

That brings me to a mundane, squishy, but essential point: Databases are ultimately about helping people. This means that when you create a database for a group of users, especially in a business environment, you have to spend a lot of time talking to them about it. In this important respect, the profession of database design resembles financial auditing. The popular perception is that auditors spend most of their time alone in their offices fidgeting with their calculators among stacks of documents. But auditors will tell you that a 5-minute interview, even (perhaps especially) with an ill-paid clerk, is often more valuable than an hour's worth of vouching receipts. The work of the database designer is similarly people oriented, and strong interviewing skills are crucial.

Creating a database in a corporate setting is beyond my scope. The importance of extensive employee involvement, as well as all the nuts and bolts of creating a database inside and outside the workplace, is described clearly in Michael J. Hernandez's book *Database Design for Mere Mortals (Addison-Wesley, 2003)*. His book is accessible to any reader, and I have relied significantly on his work in preparing this chapter.

Getting Started

Let's say you're one of those people whose favorite TV channels are *TV Land* and *Nick at Nite*. You comb the Internet for histories of shows such as *Gunsmoke* and *The Twilight Zone*, you read biographies of TV actors such as Lucille Ball and Desi Arnaz, and you're curious about when programs such as *Bewitched* and *Happy Days* aired. You decide you want to store all this data somehow so you can retrieve and manipulate it quickly and efficiently.

Mission Statements

Your first step is to prepare a mission statement, which describes the purpose of the database. You could well be wary of mission statements. In the business world, they are often forgotten and ignored in the tumult of running a day-to-day business or meeting a quarterly earnings target. That's true even when the statements are carefully and thoughtfully prepared.

But for databases, mission statements are useful, even mandatory. They help you determine database objectives, and they provide a framework for data collection. For most databases, the more taxing problem is not a dearth of data, but a glut. The mission statement puts constraints on the data to be collected. More important, it provides a central focus and direction for your work.

Examples of Mission Statements

Mission statements obviously vary by the type of organization. For a law firm, a typical mission statement might be "The mission of the Walker and

Goodman database is to maintain the data we use to provide legal services for our clients." For an international charitable organization, it might be "The purpose of the Good Hands database is to safeguard the data we use to alleviate poverty and illness in underdeveloped nations." For a paint business, it might be "The aim of the Rainbow Paint Corporation is to maintain data that helps us provide fine paint products to our customers." Although they're seemingly mundane, these mission statements make it plain that they do not comprehend extraneous objectives, such as tracking the investment portfolios of senior executives (no sly dig intended).

Even a home-grown, nonbusiness database such as one on classic TV shows can benefit from a mission statement. The topic offers many possibilities and can veer in many directions. Is the purpose of the database to record your daily viewing habits and critical remarks? Will it catalogue the DVDs you record or rent? Do you want it to tell you who you were with when you saw Rachel have her baby on *Friends*, or on which TV set you saw the last episode of *M*A*S*H**?

Your Classic TV database could, instead, focus on the programs themselves. What is the program's genre? In other words, is it a rural comedy such as *Green Acres*, a western such as *Maverick*, or a variety show such as *Ed Sullivan*? When did the show air and on what station? Who were the lead actors? What characters did they play?

Writing the Mission Statement

The mission statement should not be used to describe the types of information you want to collect, the tasks you want to accomplish, or the reports you want to create. Instead, it should be a general statement of database purpose—and no more than a sentence or two.

Suppose you decide that you're interested in collecting data about the shows themselves (such as who played the character of Rhoda Morgenstern on *The Mary Tyler Moore Show*), and you are uninterested in any personal experiences associated with them (for example, who you were dating when you saw the last episode of *Northern Exposure*). Some day you plan to write a best-selling book on the best programs in TV history. Here's a possible mission statement for this database:

> "The purpose of the Classic TV database is to maintain data on popular prime-time programs for the pleasure of all television buffs."

Mission Objectives

After you create your mission statement, you must define mission objectives. These are the tasks that the database should accomplish. In a business organization, they would include statements such as "We need to track fixed asset purchases." In nonprofits, they might include "We need to provide donors with information on their contributions for their tax returns." For a police department, one might be "We need to track the location of all detainees in custody."

A mission objective should not be as specific as "We need to create a report each month that shows the breakdown of fixed assets by asset type, the accumulated depreciation of each item, the method of depreciation for each asset class, and any gains or losses recorded on asset sales." Instead, you want to reduce each objective to a single task and eliminate all unnecessary details.

To develop your mission objectives for the TV database, you consider your own interests as well as the ease with which you can acquire data on various shows. Let's assume that you develop the following mission objectives:

"I need to know the show's broadcast history."

"I need to know the main story line of each show."

"I need to know which lead actors appeared on the show."

"I need to know the roles the lead actors of each show played."

Now let's look at the role of mission objectives in deciding what data you need to assemble.

Two Approaches to Database Design

Two basic approaches to database design exist. To oversimplify, one line of attack is to use the mission objectives you've developed to determine which data to collect. The data can then be assigned to fields, and the fields can be organized into tables. (A little later, I'll suggest why you should first determine the fields and then decide which tables will hold them.) This is a top-down approach.

Under the alternative approach, you still prepare mission objectives. But first you determine the data that you want to collect and the fields that will hold the data. You organize the fields into tables and compare the tables and their contents against your mission objectives. You then modify the fields accordingly. This is a bottom-up approach.

Top-down might seem much more logical than bottom-up: How can you decide what data you need if you don't know why you're collecting it? But as a practical matter, you might find it more efficient to determine all the data that currently is being used and that might be needed in the future, and then make sure that this data satisfies all your objectives.

Neither the top-down nor the bottom-up approach is cast in stone. Many database professionals develop their own methods that combine aspects of both approaches.

One key element to consider is cost. Each piece of data collected has a price tag, even if it's very low, and the cost of data varies. You might decide that the added benefit of some data simply isn't worth the cost of collecting it. Similarly, easy availability and low cost might make it attractive to collect and use data that you might otherwise forgo.

In the case of the Classic TV database, let's use a top-down approach to make a preliminary list of the data you might want to include (see Table 2.1).

Table 2.1 Objectives and Data Needs

Objectives	Data Needs
Program broadcast history	Program names, network names, years on air
Story line	Location, synopsis, genre
Lead actors	Actor names, actor gender, actor biographies
Main roles	Character names, character occupations

Begin to Define Columns

As you look over your data needs, the number and nature of the fields begins to take shape.

For example, consider each item in the first two mission objectives "I need to know the show's broadcast history" and "I need to know the main story line of each show." Here is an imaginary thought process you might go through:

- ***Program names***—This would be the official name of the program. You consider whether you need an extra column for the popular name or nickname (for example, Babewatch for *Baywatch*). You ultimately decide that this data is relatively unimportant and infrequent. But you do decide to add a Notes column for this and other assorted data.

- ***Network names***—As you consider network names, you realize that the official name (for example, National Broadcasting Company) and the popular name (NBC) are two types of data that require two columns. You wonder if the official name is really needed, but you eventually decide to include it because neither the official name nor the popular name alone seems adequate.
- ***Network history***—Thinking about network names has made you realize that you also have a strong interest in the networks themselves. You decide to include data on who started them and other historical information. This addition causes some reflection because you wonder if it's within the mission's scope. You briefly consider starting a separate database for network data, but you decide that the database's mission statement is sufficiently broad to include it. You do decide to add a mission objective to your list: "I need to know the history of television networks."
- ***Years on air***—What does "years on air" mean? Does it mean longevity (just the number of years the show ran), or do you also want to know the years the program started and finished? You decide that you need all three columns: Year Started, Year Ended, and Years on Air.
- ***Location***—As you think about what other program data you'd like to include, you realize that you'd like to have a column for the venue, whether real (Queens, New York, for *All in the Family*) or imaginary (Mayfield for *Leave It to Beaver*).
- ***Synopsis***—You want a column that includes in a brief sentence or two the plot of the series. (For example, for *Friends,* it could be "Six attractive New York singles, half guys and half gals, grow into early middle age together.")
- ***Genre***—You want to classify shows by type, such as rural comedy, police drama, and so on.

NOTE Remember, this is just a preliminary list of possible columns. You'll continue to refine the fields as you create the database.

Create a Preliminary List of Columns

After you evaluate the columns required for each of the other three mission objectives, you come up with a preliminary list of columns (see

Table 2.2) and column descriptions. You have checked to make sure that the data is available to you at minimal cost from your own knowledge, the Internet, library resources, and other available sources.

Table 2.2 Preliminary List of Columns

Column	Column Description
Program Name	Official title of show
Network Official Name	Official name of network
Network Popular Name	Abbreviation of official name or commonly used name
Network Notes	History, name changes, other facts of interest
Network Founder	Leading influence behind start of network
Year Started	First year program aired
Year Ended	Last year program aired
Years on Air	Total years on air
Program Location	Primary real or imaginary setting where action occurs
Synopsis	Main story line of program
Program Notes	Any additional facts about program
Program Genre	Type of program
Program Genre Description	Definition of program type with examples
Actor Name #1	Full name of first lead actor
Actor Gender #1	Sex of actor #1
Actor Biography #1	Additional facts about first lead actor
Character Name/ Occupation #1	First lead character name and occupation
Actor Name #2	Full name of second lead actor
Actor Gender #2	Sex of actor #2
Actor Biography #2	Additional facts about second lead actor
Character Name/ Occupation #2	Second lead character name and occupation
Actor Name #3	Full name of third lead actor
Actor Gender #3	Sex of actor #3
Actor Biography #3	Additional facts about third lead actor
Character Name/ Occupation #3	Third lead character name and occupation

The One Big Table Solution

With your initial list of columns drawn up, you're now faced with the decision of how to organize them into one or more grids. Your first instinct is to put them all in one big table, commonly known as a flat file. That way, all your data will be in one place whenever you need it. After all, there doesn't seem to be *that* many columns.

But as you set about adding the first few rows of data to your table, you realize that the one-table-fits-all strategy isn't going to work.

Most of the programs in your table were likely aired on one of four networks: CBS, NBC, ABC, or FOX. Each time you add a new program, you find you're entering the same network data—official name, popular name, and history—again and again (see Table 2.3). You're wasting lots of time making the same keystrokes. Moreover, what will happen when you want to edit a single value in one of the network columns? You have many duplicate entries, so you'll have to find and edit each occurrence of the same value to make sure your data is current. That might be easy to do with a column that has values with few characters, such as the network's popular name. It's a lot harder to do for the `Network Notes` field, which might have many sentences and thousands of characters.

Table 2.3 The One Big Table Solution

Program Name	Network Official Name	Network Popular Name	Network Notes	<<other fields>>
The Andy Griffith Show	Columbia Broadcasting System	CBS	CBS is one of the largest...	
The Bob Newhart Show	Columbia Broadcasting System	CBS	CBS is one of the largest...	
I Love Lucy	Columbia Broadcasting System	CBS	CBS is one of the largest...	

As you begin entering data for actors and their roles, you also find some rows require many more columns than others. Take *The Odd Couple*, a show about two middle-aged guys, one a slob and the other a fussbudget, living in a New York apartment. It has two lead actors, Jack Klugman as Oscar Madison, the sportswriter; and Tony Randall as Felix Unger, the photographer. Because you want to include columns for the actor's name, gender, and biography, as well as his character name and occupation, eight columns are required (4 columns × 2 actors) for all the actor and character values.

Eight columns is not an overwhelming number. But suppose you decide to include the program *Friends* as well. That means you'll have to enter data for *six* lead actors. Four columns are needed for each actor and character, so you'll need 24 columns for all the data. In the list of fields in Table 2.2, you created columns for just three actors, at most. Where can you find room for three other actors?

For some shows, you might pick the top actors and leave it at that. But what true *Friends* fan could possibly decide to leave out even one of the six-member cast? And the problem could get much worse. What are you going to do if you want to enter a record for *Eight Is Enough*? What if they decide to make a TV series of the book *Cheaper By the Dozen*?

Let's try an alternative. Table 2.4 uses two rows to record the values for shows with several lead actors, such as *Friends*. This attempt has the advantage of tables with fewer columns. But this solution won't work, either; you're compounding the problem of duplicate data. Because you have two rows for one program, you'll have to enter the numerous other fields (`Location`, `Network Official Name`, `Network Name`, `Network Notes`) twice.

Table 2.5 shows another option. You put two actors in the first two columns and then stuff the remaining four into the third Actors column. This scheme is perhaps the worse. First, it misrepresents the data because each actor in *Friends* is (in our opinion) equally important. Second, as you'll see a little later, cramming several values of the same type in a single column is a bad idea because it makes it difficult to retrieve, sort, edit, and delete individual values.

Table 2.4 The One Big Table Solution

Two Rows for One Program

Program Name	Actor I	Actor II	Actor III	<<other actor fields>>	<<Network Official Name>>	<<other fields>>
The Odd Couple	Jack Klugman	Tony Randall			American Broadcasting Company	
Friends	Jennifer Aniston	Lisa Kudrow	Courteney Cox Arquette		National Broadcasting Company	
Friends	Matt Perry	David Schwimmer	Matthew LeBlanc		National Broadcasting Company	

Table 2.5 The One Big Table Solution

One Row Per Program

Program Name	<<other fields>>	Actor I	<other actor fields>	Actor II	<<other actor fields>>	Other Actors	<<other actor fields>>	<<other fields>>
The Odd Couple		Jack Klugman		Tony Randall				
Friends		Jennifer Aniston		Lisa Kudrow		David Schwimmer, Matt Perry, Courteney Cox Arquette, Matt LeBlanc		

Midchapter Review

We'll look at the problems of table creation in much more depth in a little while. Right now, let's quickly review what you've done. You first created a mission statement for the Classic TV database. You followed up by developing mission objectives—what you want the database to accomplish. You used those mission objectives to come up with a list of data needs. From those data needs, you developed a preliminary list of columns you could use to store data.

None of these steps is peculiar to relational databases. Creating a mission statement and defining mission objectives aren't bad ideas for any information project—indeed, for achieving any goal. Even when you use a simple spreadsheet to store data, you still have to decide what columns you need and what data to put in them. And my diagnosis of the problems of "one table fits all" could just as easily be used to launch a discussion of the benefits of database models besides relational databases.

I'm going to forgo an extended discussion of earlier alternatives to relational databases, including various spreadsheet designs and hierarchical databases. Suffice it to say that each of these choices has serious structural flaws that a well-designed relational database overcomes. Instead of setting them up as straw men only to knock them down (as I've done with the "one table fits all" flat file), let's move specifically to the task of creating a relational database for classic TV shows.

Relational Database Principles

When you begin creating relational databases for whatever mission, some of the procedures will seem counterintuitive and needlessly complex. Indeed, at times the whole enterprise might seem dubious, at best.

So before going any further, let's flesh out a few broad principles of relational database design. This will give you a better idea of the playing field you'll be working in, and perhaps make some of the methods you'll be using seem less perplexing.

An Indifference to Where Values Are Stored

Let's say you're a fan of the Boston Red Sox. You turn to your hometown newspaper to find out how many games they are in or out of first place. You know that the sports news is always in, say, section D, and Major League Baseball standings are always printed about halfway into the section. You open Section D to the middle and find the baseball stats. You find first the American League standings and then those for its Eastern Division. Your eye moves from left to right as you find the name of the team, its won/lost record and percentage, and the number of games it's in or out of first place. You're delighted to discover that the Sox are leading their division with a .663 percentage, 12 games ahead of the Yankees.

The way you find information in a newspaper is through location. The newspaper positions information consistently in a certain order—sports news, baseball news, American League standings, Eastern Division standings, team name, won/lost percentage, games in/out of first place—so you can easily find what you need.

A relational database is also consistent and logical, but it is organized quite differently. In a newspaper, the first section (or, at least, the first page) always contains headline news, not sports news (unless, of course, sports news *is* headline news). In a relational database, there is no first table—or second, or third, or fourth. No table comes before or after any other table. In other words, tables are not placed in any particular sequence.

Moreover, within a table, it doesn't matter which column comes before or after any other column. For example, a customer address can come before or after the customer name. Nor does it matter which row comes before or after any other row. In a field of last names, the G's can come before the A's, and the C's can come after both. The physical storage of the data does not depend on location.

Of course, when you view your data, you might want to make sure that the last names are alphabetized. Of course, a Red Sox fan will want to see his club listed first if it has the best won/loss percentage. But these are matters of user preference, not database design. Access makes it easy to move columns left and right, and to sort records in any field in either ascending or descending order. Regardless of how you move data, the tables themselves are in no particular hierarchy, nor is any column or row in a specific position.

Thus, be careful how you use phrases such as "the fifth row of the table" or "the table's third column." They might describe a row or column's position in the current display, but there really is no fifth row or third column, as such.

One Field, One Kind of Data

A single field has only one data type. In other words, a column to which you have assigned the `Number` data type will hold only numbers, a column that has a `Date/Time` data type will hold only dates/times, and so on.

This rule seems to be simple common sense and hardly worth mentioning. Yet in actual practice, there is an inclination to break it. For example, at times it might seem to make good sense to enter the value *`between 5/18/2005 and 5/19/2005`* in a `Date/Time` field, or *`64 to 69`* in a `Number` field. But a `Date/Time` field cannot contain words such as *between* and *and*. And `Number` fields can hold only numbers; they cannot describe a range. Access is very strict about allowing values of the wrong data type into columns.

Only One Value in One Row of One Field

In each column of each row, there should be only one value (where allowed, a null value is considered one value). This rule sharply contradicts what you saw in the one-table-fits-all design, where there was a strong inclination to put two, three, or even more values in a single column of a single row.

Much of database design involves ensuring that there is only one value in each field of each row. Staying true to this principle will prompt much head-scratching and perhaps a headache or two as well. But it's a cardinal rule of good database design. You'll be reminded constantly of this principle as you design the Classic TV database.

Break Data into Its Smallest Components

A difficulty in implementing the "one value in each field of each row" rule is defining just what a value is.

For dates and numbers, that usually isn't a problem because they are discrete entities (such as `5/10/2004` and `3,468.7`). But what about text? Is an address, such as 1600 Pennsylvania Avenue, Washington, DC 20500, one value, two values, or more?

The answer is that you want to break data into its smallest components. For example, an address usually includes separate fields for the city, state, and ZIP code. You'll see many examples of this principle at work as you move through the database design process.

Q&A

Q: Hold on a second. I'm not sure what you mean by "smallest component." How small is small?

A: I should say the "smallest meaningful component for the purposes of the database." I don't want you to pulverize data. For example, a city such as New York could theoretically be divided into two values, `New` and `York`, or even seven values, for each of its seven letters. But you wouldn't want to divide the text string `New York` into two values, let alone seven, because in the context of city names, `New` and `York` are not meaningful as separate entities.

To make an attempt at a contrasting case, I can (with some effort) imagine a table in a database for grammarians that stores data about U.S. cities whose names are of Spanish origin. Values such as `El Segundo`, `Las Vegas`, `Los Angeles`, and `Los Alamos` could be meaningfully divided into two fields, one for the article (*las*, *los*, *el*) and the other for the noun that follows.

Keep Redundant Data to a Minimum

Redundant data is like cholesterol: There's "bad" redundant data and "good" redundant data. And like cholesterol, the idea that redundant data can be either good or bad for you is difficult to digest (bad pun fully intended).

As I've already argued, repeating the same data in more than one field can threaten the consistency and integrity of your data. This "bad" redundant data arises from poor database design that forces you to enter the same values in two or more fields unnecessarily.

At the same time, there are duplicate fields with "matching data" that are required for creating a relational database. They enable you to establish relationships, which are essential for bringing together the data in the various tables of your database.

Unless otherwise indicated, when I discuss redundant data, I'm talking about the bad kind.

What Does Data Integrity Mean?

Often when discussing databases you will hear the term *data integrity*. That undoubtedly sounds like a very good thing, but what actually does it mean?

On one level, it means that the data is consistent, accurate, and correct. But there are actually four specific types of data integrity:

- *Entity integrity* means that each row in a table is uniquely identified by a primary key that is never a null value. The table thus has no duplicate records. This concept is discussed in this chapter.
- *Domain integrity* ensures the validity and consistency of data by defining the range of values that are permissible within a specific field. It includes restrictions imposed by the data type, the format, and the field size. This concept is discussed in Chapter 5, "Building Tables."
- *Referential integrity* keeps the relationships between tables synchronized. It is usually enforced by including the primary key of one table as the foreign key of another table. Enforcing referential integrity guarantees that records in the two tables remain in sync whenever data is entered, edited, or deleted. This concept is discussed in Chapter 4.
- *User-defined integrity* encompasses business rules outside the scope of other integrity categories. These are rules imposed by the nature of the organization and the way it conducts business. A typical business rule might be that you sell only to customers whose credit rating meets certain standards. This concept is discussed in Chapters 5, "Building Tables," and 6, "Entering, Editing, and Displaying Data."

Organizing Fields into Tables

Let's get back to developing the Classic TV database. Table 2.6 shows the current list of fields. The list has been modified from that in Table 2.2 to reflect our bad experience with multiple actor fields in the "one-table-fits-all" solution. Thus, instead of fields for `Actor Name #1`, `Actor Name #2`, and so on there is just one `Actor Name` field. The same is true for `Actor Gender`, `Actor Biography`, and `Character Name/Occupation`.

With the decision to use a relational database instead of the discredited one-table-fits-all solution, you now need to create a list of tables and decide which fields go in which tables. Let's accomplish those objectives.

Table 2.6 Classic TV Database

Revised Field List

Field	Field Description	Sample Value
Program Name	Official title of show	Bewitched
Network Official Name	Official name of network	American Broadcasting Company
Network Popular Name	Abbreviation of official name	ABC
Network Founder	Leading organizer	Leonard Goldenson
Network Notes	Chronicle of events	In the 1950s, ABC was the…
Year Started	First year aired	1964
Year Ended	Last year aired	1972
Years on Air	Total broadcast years	8
Program Location	Setting where main action occurs	Westport, Connecticut
Synopsis	Main story line of program	A lovely witch meets a hapless ad exec
Program Notes	Other facts	The show was based on a …
Program Genre	Type	General comedy
Program Genre Description	Definition of program type	All-purpose category for comedies…
Actor Name	Full name	Elizabeth Montgomery
Actor Gender	Sex	Female
Actor Biography	Background	Elizabeth Montgomery first became…
Character Name/ Occupation	Name and livelihood or role	Samantha Stevens/Witch

Mission Objectives and Table Creation

It might seem that the most logical approach would be to structure your tables around your mission objectives, dedicating one table to each objective. This method would apparently ensure that the database meets all of your goals.

But this is exactly the approach you should *not* take.

Consider the following mission objective from the business world, which applies to most companies: "We need to ensure timely receipt of the funds customers owe us." For most firms, the primary means of accomplishing this objective is the customer invoice.

Take a look at the invoice Northwind Traders has prepared for its Save-A-Lot customer (see Figure 2.1). Viewed from top to bottom, you can roughly say that the customer's address comes first, order information (`OrderID`, salesperson, and so on) comes second, order details (products, quantities, prices, and so on) come third, and summary and freight information comes last.

Imagine the breadth and complexity of a table that in every record had data that was as disparate as the address of a customer and the order date of an order. Table 2.7 shows just a few of the fields that table would require. Order #11064 to Save-A-Lot has five products, so you need to repeat the customer contact info five times for that order alone. Imagine if you had a hundred orders with a hundred products in each; you'd have to repeat customer contact info 10,000 times.

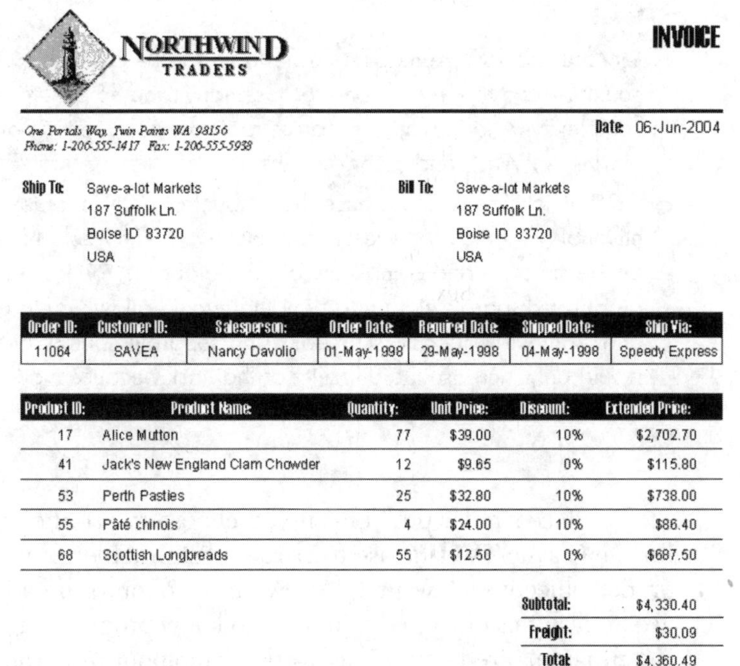

NORTHWIND TRADERS

INVOICE

One Portals Way, Twin Points WA 98156
Phone: 1-206-555-1417 Fax: 1-206-555-5938

Date: 06-Jun-2004

Ship To: Save-a-lot Markets
187 Suffolk Ln.
Boise ID 83720
USA

Bill To: Save-a-lot Markets
187 Suffolk Ln.
Boise ID 83720
USA

Order ID:	Customer ID:	Salesperson:	Order Date:	Required Date:	Shipped Date:	Ship Via:
11064	SAVEA	Nancy Davolio	01-May-1998	29-May-1998	04-May-1998	Speedy Express

Product ID:	Product Name:	Quantity:	Unit Price:	Discount:	Extended Price:
17	Alice Mutton	77	$39.00	10%	$2,702.70
41	Jack's New England Clam Chowder	12	$9.65	0%	$115.80
53	Perth Pasties	25	$32.80	10%	$738.00
55	Pâté chinois	4	$24.00	10%	$86.40
68	Scottish Longbreads	55	$12.50	0%	$687.50

Subtotal:	$4,330.40
Freight:	$30.09
Total:	$4,360.49

Figure 2.1 A customer invoice requires data with several different subjects.

Table 2.7 Customer Invoices

Company	Address	City	OrderID	Order Date	Product	Unit Price	<<other fields>>
Save-A-Lot	187 Suffolk Lane	Boise	11064	01-May-1998	Alice Mutton	$39.00	
Save-A-Lot	187 Suffolk Lane	Boise	11064	01-May-1998	N.E. Clam Chowder	$ 9.65	
Save-A-Lot	187 Suffolk Lane	Boise	11064	01-May-1998	Perth Pasties	$32.80	
Save-A-Lot	187 Suffolk Lane	Boise	11064	01-May-1998	Pate Chinois	$24.00	
Save-A-Lot	187 Suffolk Lane	Boise	11064	01-May-1998	Scottish Longbreads	$12.50	

Q&A

Q: Couldn't you create a separate table for the customers of each country—one for France, one for Germany, and so on—to reduce the complexity. And maybe a separate table for each section of the U.S.—Northeast, West, and so on—as well?

A: That solution would reduce the amount of data in tables. It also might eliminate the need for one or two columns. But it would have little impact on the structure and complexity of the database. You would still need to organize disparate data in a way that would allow you to edit, retrieve, and manipulate it easily. Indeed, using separate country or regional tables would only increase the difficulty of that task because many additional tables would be required.

You face similar problems if you choose to use the mission objectives for the Classic TV database to create a list of tables. For example, consider the objective "I want to know the program's broadcast history." To accomplish this objective, you need to know program names and the years the program aired—in other words, data about *programs*. You also need data about the *networks* on which the programs aired. Table 2.8 shows just a few of the fields in the table, but you can see that you would have to repeat the Network Notes for each program.

Don't get me wrong: Mission objectives do play an important role in ensuring that you have included all the data you need to fulfill the organization's mission. You'll want to compare your final list of fields and tables against your mission objectives to make sure you can accomplish them. But you do not want to use mission objectives as a launch point for creating a list of tables.

Table 2.8 Broadcast History

Program Name	Network Popular Name	Network Notes	Year Started	Year Ended	<<other fields>>
The Andy Griffith Show	CBS	CBS is one of the…	1960	1968	
The Bob Newhart Show	CBS	CBS is one of the…	1972	1978	
I Love Lucy	CBS	CBS is one of the…	1951	1957	

One Subject, One Table

You've seen that mission objectives and the media they require (such as invoices and order forms) are inadequate guides for organizing data into tables. But if you're not going to use these as guideposts, then what *do* you use?

Here's what you need to remember: The key, essential requirement of a table is not that it represent a single *objective*, but that it define a single *subject*.

That's exactly the problem with using mission objectives: They require you to bring together data about several subjects. The invoice is a good example. Customer contact info (names, address, ZIP codes, and the like) is one subject, order data (order dates, shipped dates) is another, product data (product names, suppliers) is a third, and so on. The data for an invoice will, therefore, not come from a single Invoices table. Instead, it will be drawn from several tables—Customers, Orders, Products, and so on—each of which has a single subject.

Use the Fields to Develop Tables

Now the question becomes "How do you develop this list of tables, each of which is dedicated to a single subject?" One of the best ways is to use the fields themselves.

That's really not odd or paradoxical. Think about the way you store items in boxes or organize a to-do list or arrange your kitchen drawers. Most likely, you first look at all the stuff you've got. Most things naturally go with related items, and you organize them accordingly into several groups. There are usually a few items you're not sure what to do with. You stick these in the least objectionable place and make a mental note that you might want to move them later.

I've forgotten nearly all of my high school chemistry. But one thing I do remember is my chemistry teacher standing over a Bunsen burner telling us to "waft gently" the fumes from whatever experiment we had just conducted.

I'd like to ask you to "waft gently" the fields to decide which tables they belong to. In other words, don't extensively analyze the fields, but rather smell them out and get a general sense of which tables they belong in. Later, you'll refine your lists of both tables and fields.

With some gentle wafting, you can place most of the fields in the revised field list of Table 2.6 into appropriate tables. The Networks table contains only data about the networks, the Actors table contains only data about the actors, and so on.

Assigning Ambiguous Fields

A few fields you're not sure where to put. `Year Started` and `Year Ended` seem like they belong with the program, but they also seem somehow connected with the network that broadcast the show. Character roles are also difficult to place. They certainly apply to a specific program, but they are also played by specific actors.

You have to make some decisions, but remember that you're making them on only a temporary basis. You'll continue to refine tables and fields as you move through the design process.

You come up with the preliminary breakdown of tables and fields shown in Table 2.9.

Table 2.9 Classic TV Database

Preliminary Breakdown of Tables and Fields

Programs	Genres	Networks	Actors
Official Name	Name	Official Name	Name
Year Started	Description	Popular Name	Gender
Year Ended		Founder	Biography
Years on Air		Network Notes	
Location			
Synopsis			
Program Notes			
Character Names/Occupations			

I think most of the tables and the choice of fields initially assigned to them are fairly straightforward. You might wonder why Networks and Programs are separate tables. If the database was about, say, various types of entertainment—live theater, horse racing, rock concerts—it's possible that a single table named Television might encompass both the programs and networks tables. But in a database about television itself, programs and networks are distinct subjects. The history of a specific network is separate from a particular show that might have been broadcast on it. Later I describe how programs and networks relate to one another, which should reinforce your sense that they are indeed separate subjects.

The Genres table, which classifies the program into different categories, also might stand a word of explanation. There were alternatives. You could use just the `Synopsis` field to provide a description of the program that told you the genre. "*Green Acres* is a series about a New York lawyer who uproots his wife from their Park Avenue apartment to a pea-size town in the boonies where they routinely get snookered by the locals."

That gives you a general synopsis of the show, and you could enter similar descriptions for other programs in the `Program Notes` field. But this depiction is not helpful if you want to find other shows in your database of the same type. What would you search for? `Boonies`? `Snookered`? On the other hand, suppose you assign a specific genre to the show, such as *`Rural comedy`*. You could then assign that value to similar programs, such as *The Andy Griffith Show* and *Petticoat Junction*, to retrieve comparable shows easily.

As you'll see a little later, you can limit the genres used to describe programs to a specific set of values. Limiting the values you can enter might initially seem to make your database less flexible and more restricted. But by controlling the values you enter in a field, you can increase your ability to classify data into specific groups and, ultimately, increase the value of the information your database provides.

How to Name Tables

I don't think finding suitable table names poses a major challenge. Most of the table names I have used for the Classic TV database—Programs, Networks, and so on—are likely those you would have chosen yourself. Nonetheless, it's worthwhile to state a few guidelines, some of them obvious, for this task. Table names should:

- Describe the subject meaningfully and completely
- Be short and to the point
- Use the plural form
- Be limited to a single subject (including in the table title words such as *and* and *or*, or signs such as the slash [/] and ampersand [&],is a sign of trouble)
- Be actual words instead of acronyms and abbreviations (the use of an abbreviation such as *HIV*, which is unambiguous and universally understandable, would be an exception).

Chapter 5 has more to say about naming tables in an Access database using the Leszynski convention.

Q&A

Q: I understand why the initial one-size-fits-all table was a big problem. But the table setup you suggest seems even more unwise. For example, the Programs table includes character names and occupations. But what good is that if you don't include the actor in the table? I'll remember that Lucille Ball was Lucy Ricardo on *I Love Lucy*, but I can't remember the actor for every character I include.

A: As you'll see, the aim of a relational database system is precisely to make sure you don't have to remember things like that. By breaking your data into its smallest possible components, a relational database gives you maximum flexibility to combine and massage this data to meet all your information needs. Eventually, you can bind the tables in a way that lets you bring together actor data and character data whenever you want.

Refine the Fields

After you make a first stab at putting fields in tables, the next step is to refine your fields. A few classic slip-ups in creating fields are easily noticed. I prefer "slip-ups" instead of "mistakes" or "blunders" because they initially appear to be perfectly logical solutions to the database problems you face. But they violate database principles and will vastly reduce the effectiveness of your database.

Calculated Fields

No value in a table should depend on any other value in the table for its own value. This basic principle of database design might seem to offer more confusion than enlightenment. Perhaps this restatement will make things a little clearer: You must be able to change the value of any field without affecting any other field.

An example should make it plainer still. Your company offers certain discounts on orders for fast payment, closeout sales, volume sales, and so on. The discounts can vary product by product within a single order (see Figure 2.2). The unit price for the same product can vary from order to order as well.

Order ID	Product	Unit Price	Quantity	Discount
10260	Jack's New England Clam Chowder	$7.70	16	25%
10260	Ravioli Angelo	$15.60	50	0%
10260	Tarte au sucre	$39.40	15	25%
10260	Outback Lager	$12.00	21	25%
10261	Sir Rodney's Scones	$8.00	20	0%
10261	Steeleye Stout	$14.40	20	0%
10262	Chef Anton's Gumbo Mix	$17.00	12	20%
10262	Uncle Bob's Organic Dried Pears	$24.00	15	0%
10262	Gnocchi di nonna Alice	$30.40	2	0%

Figure 2.2 This selection of records from the Order Details table of the Northwind database shows that the company offers various discounts on its products, and the discounts can vary within a single order. Although it is not indicated in the figure, the same product can have various discounts, depending on the order.

Assume that the unit price for Product A in Order #101 is $1,000. Assume that the discount for Product A in Order #101 is 10%. Both of these values would be entered and stored in your database. But you would *not* store the actual amount of the discount—that is, 10% of $1,000, or $100. The $100 amount depends on its value *entirely* from other fields, Unit Price and Discount. Access makes it easy to perform such calculations in other objects, so there is no need to store such *calculated values* in tables.

Are there any calculated values in the fields listed in Table 2.9? *`Years on Air`* arouses suspicion. If you know the values for `Year Started` and `Year Ended`, you can calculate the `Years on Air`. The *`Years on Air`* field is unnecessary and should thus be eliminated from the database.

Multipart Fields

A field should contain one distinct item within any value. A *multipart field* contains two or more kinds of values. Recall the following from the section on database principles:

- Each row of each column should have only one value.
- Data should be broken into its smallest components.
- A field should contain values of only one data type, such as `Date`, `Number`, and so on.

A multipart field breaks the first two of these rules and often breaks the third rule as well. Look at the table in Figure 2. 2. Suppose that, instead of three separate fields, the quantity, the unit price, and the discount were all included in a single field. This field would contain three distinct items. It would be difficult to sort, edit, and delete; it would also be impossible to perform calculations on the quantities.

Multipart fields are sometimes a lot harder to recognize than this example would indicate. For example, consider product codes. They often appear as one long string of alphanumeric characters. But they can comprise several distinct items, including product category, product subcategory, manufacturing location, and so on. Whether or not you decide to break up the product code into its constituent elements depends on your database needs. Nonetheless, you should be aware that you are dealing with a multipart field.

Consider the fields of the Classic TV database (see Table 2.9). Do any of the columns appear to be multipart fields? Some of the fields that provide extensive descriptions—such as `Network Notes` in the Networks table and `Synopsis` in the Programs table—might seem to be multipart fields. But just as a sentence isn't a run-on simply because it's long, a field isn't a multipart field simply because there's a lot of information in it. The data in the `Network Notes`, `Synopsis`, and similar columns are perfectly acceptable as fields with the `Memo` data type—in other words, a field with the potential to store lots of text in each row, yet in sum containing only one value.

The Classic TV database has, in fact, two multipart fields. The less egregious error is in the Actors table. Currently, only one column is provided for the actor's name. An actor's name comprises at least two separate items, first name and last name.

The way to resolve a multipart field is to break the value into its components parts and assign each part its own field. Thus, you'll have both `First Name` and `Last Name` fields for actor names.

Q&A

Q: Must a person's name *always* be two or more fields?

A: I admit, the decision isn't always clear cut. Note that the Classic TV database also contains a `Network Founder` field (see Table 2.6). I don't suggest that you divide that field into two. In a table of just a few networks, it seems unlikely that you'll need to manipulate the founders' first and last names discretely.

The `Contact Name` field in the Customers table in Access's Northwind sample database also uses a single field for both first and last names. But here I think the table design is unfortunate because you can enter only one contact name for each customer. If you had several contacts for one customer, which is not at all unlikely, you could find separate first name and last name fields useful for sorting and easier data manipulation.

I'm not arguing that you always need to put first and last names into separate fields, but you'll want to be cautious about this violation of the "one field, one value" principle.

Besides `Actor Name`, one other field violates the multipart field rule—and much more egregiously. In the Programs table, the `Character Names/Occupations` field clearly contains two types of data: the name of the character and the role (see Table 2.10). This multipart field presents definite problems for finding and retrieving data.

Table 2.10 Programs

Program Name	Character Names/Occupations	<<other fields>>
The Andy Griffith Show	Andy Taylor/Sheriff; Barney Fife/Deputy Sheriff	
Bewitched	Samantha Stevens/Witch; Darrin Stevens/Ad executive	
The Lucy Show	Lucy Carmichael/Widow; Vivian Bagley/Divorcee	
Married with Children	Al Bundy/Shoe Salesman; Peg Bundy/Housewife	

For example, suppose you wanted to find all the characters who had the occupation of `baker`. If character names and occupations were in the same field, accomplishing this task would be extremely inefficient. Moreover, what if there were characters named Richard Baker or Sarah Baker? Sure, that's a contrived example. But I think you can see the threat that multipart fields would pose to data integrity in a database of any size and complexity. Clearly, character names and character occupations should be separated into two fields.

To renew the now-tiresome question of people's names, it can be debated whether `Character Names` should be further divided between the character's first name and last name. It could be helpful for finding all the names of the Cartwright boys on *Bonanza*, or the first name of Bob Hartley's wife on *The Bob Newhart Show*. On the other hand, character names such as Aunt Bea on *The Andy Griffith Show* or Uncle Fester on *The Addams Family* feel like single values. For now, let's keep `Character Names` as one field; we'll make two fields out of it a little later.

There's another big problem with the `Character Names/Occupations` field. Even after segregating character names and occupations, you're left with only one field for all the character names and only one field for occupations. If there are several lead characters in a show, as there almost always are, you'll have a bunch of names in one field and several occupations in the other. (You might want to sneak a peak at Table 2.15 to see this table, and then return here.)

To resolve this problem, though, you'll need to understand how *keys* work, so let me first talk about this essential database topic.

NOTE The changes to the tables made in the "Calculated Fields" and "Multipart Fields" sections are incorporated in Table 2.11.

Keys

Each table in your database represents one subject only. But as you've seen, to accomplish your mission objectives, you need data from two, three, or even more of these tables. For example, the invoice you looked at earlier requires values from the Customers, Orders, and Order Details tables, and perhaps other tables as well. Having segregated your data by subject, how do you now tie together these tables so you can combine their values and accomplish your mission objectives?

Keys are a vital part of the answer. Keys are essential for ensuring that each record in a table is uniquely identified. You'll soon see that achieving that objective is crucial if you hope to bring together data from several tables while maintaining data integrity.

Keys as Representative Fields

All social organizations at times need to unite with their peers to achieve common group objectives. High school clubs meet to allocate the use of school facilities equitably. Aluminum makers organize to lobby legislators and influence industrial policy. Toastmaster clubs work together to arrange public-speaking competitions.

To coordinate these efforts, organizations must choose one or more of their members as representatives to external audiences. Because that member essentially *is* the organization to the outside world, the best organizations adopt careful procedures for finding the right person. First, they determine the qualities needed in such an ambassador. Second, they identify individuals in their organizations who have these qualities. Finally, they choose the best candidate for the job.

Qualities of Keys

This process can be compared to the selection of keys in a database. Each table needs to be represented to other tables and throughout the database.

Therefore, you need to select one of the table's members—one of its fields—as its envoy, so to speak, to other tables.

Specific qualities make a field a good nominee to represent the table in the database as a whole:

- First and foremost, each value in the field must be unique. If the field is to uniquely identify a record, no value can be the same as any other.
- There can be no null or zero-length values.
- The field's values will be modified only in rare cases.

Many fields in a table will lack one or more of these qualities and will be immediately disqualified. A few, one, or no fields will have all these qualities. The keys that do meet the standards are known as *candidate keys*. The key you ultimately select to represent the table is known as the *primary key*. The keys you don't select are known as *alternate keys*. (There are also *foreign keys*, but let's hold off on that discussion for now.)

Searching for Keys in the Classic TV Database

Table 2.11 shows the current list of fields for the tables in the database. Let's review the fields to see which might make good candidate keys in each of the tables.

Table 2.11 Classic TV Database

Current List of Fields

Programs	Genres	Networks	Actors
Name	Name	Official Name	First Name
Year Started	Description	Popular Name	Last Name
Year Ended		Founder	Gender
Location		Network Notes	Biography
Synopsis			
Program Notes			
Character Names			
Character Occupations			

Programs

The `Year Started`, `Year Ended`, and `Location` fields are all poor candidate keys for the Programs table. Any one of those fields could easily contain duplicates. It's also possible that you will have null values in those fields.

The `Name` field is more distinctive, and it won't contain null values. But a program name is still not a good candidate key. *Dragnet*, *The Lone Ranger*, and *The Twilight Zone* have all in recent years been revived as new series with the same name. Thus, none of those names would be unique. The `Character Names` and `Character Occupations` fields would also be poor candidates because they could have several values in the same field (a problem we will deal with shortly). `Synopsis` and `Program Notes` are `Memo` fields that can contain an almost unlimited amount of data and, as such, are unsuited to be primary keys.

Genres

At first glance, the genre name could conceivably make a good candidate key in the Genres table. Because it's descriptive, you can make sure that it is unique. You can always create a new genre name, so it need never be null.

But precisely because the genre names are descriptive (urban comedy, police drama), it's entirely possible that you might want to modify their names (yuppie comedy, crime drama) as you develop the database. Thus, it fails the third requirement that the primary key be modified only in rare or unusual circumstances.

The `Genre Description` field will contain one or more sentences to describe the genre. It will have the `Memo` data type and is thus an unsuitable candidate for a primary key.

Networks

It might seem that the `Official Name` field would be a good candidate key in the Networks table. But in the highly fluctuating world of media, the corporate entity changes often. A Columbia Broadcasting System that has been purchased and absorbed by, say, Rupert Murdoch's Fox might be a sufficiently different entity from the one that produced *The Beverly Hillbillies* in the 1960s; you might want to distinguish between them.

It is also unlikely that a huge network such as ABC or CBS would abandon a popular abbreviation with which it is so closely identified. But could the same be said of smaller networks that you might want to include? Thus, `Popular Name` is probably not the best candidate key.

The `Founder` field could have the same value in two fields; the `Network Notes` field is a `Memo` field and, thus, is disqualified.

Actors

As you saw in Chapter 1, "Getting Started," people's names are poor candidates for primary keys, even when the first name and last name fields are taken together.

Other fields in the Actors table do not qualify as good candidate keys. `Gender` can obviously have duplicates, and `Biography` is a `Memo` field.

Artificial Primary Keys

We certainly didn't seem to have much success finding candidate keys. We found just one field (`Popular Name` in the Networks table) that was a possible candidate key, and even then we weren't fully satisfied using it.

If a database were a business, we'd make some compromises and choose less-than-perfect candidates as our representatives. Fortunately, in databases, you have an excellent alternative. You can create a field (called an *artificial key*) and use that as your primary key. In the Customers table see Table 2.12), `CustomerID` serves as a primary key. As you saw in Chapter 1, a field with an `AutoNumber` data type—a field that, by default, starts at 1 and simply adds 1 to each succeeding record—is highly serviceable as a primary key. Let's consider its qualities:

- The value will always be one above that for the previously entered record, so you can be sure that it is unique.
- The `AutoNumber` data type cannot contain null values or zero-length fields.
- You cannot change the value of an `AutoNumber` key.

Table 2.12 Customers

Customer ID Is Primary Key

CustomerID	Company Name	Street Address	City	State	ZIP	<<other fields>
1	Outdoor Emporium	1165 C Street	Arkadelphia	AK	71998	
2	Mountain Mart	14098 Hopyard	Mayfield	MI	49666	
3	Travelers Aid	2 West 19 St.	Sullivan	NH	03445	

Customer ID Is Primary Key

CustomerID	Company Name	Street Address	City	State	ZIP	<<other fields>
4	The Hiker	673 Ignatius Way	Vanderbilt	MI	49795	
5	Gleason's Store	82-17 Francisco	Fargo	ND	58109	

In Table 2.13, ID fields using an `AutoNumber` data type have been added to each table.

Table 2.13 Classic TV Database

Primary Keys Added

Programs	Genres	Networks	Actors
ProgramID PK*	GenreID PK	NetworkID PK	ActorID PK
Name	Genre	Official Name	First Name
Year Started	Description	Popular Name	Last Name
Year Ended		Founder	Gender
Synopsis		Notes	Biography
Location			
Notes			
Character Names			
Character Occupations			

*PK=Primary key

Artificial Versus Natural Keys

The superiority of artificial keys over natural keys (fields that already exist in a table because they define specific traits) is by no means universally accepted. As with Macintosh versus PC users, both artificial and natural keys have their supporters. Of course, some take a middle stance and believe that natural keys work well in some instances and artificial keys work well in others.

On the downside, natural keys can be long and complex, you might need to edit them, and they might turn out to be less unique than originally thought. But artificial keys (and in Access, that usually means keys with the `AutoNumber` data type) have their drawbacks as well. They can mystify users who are unfamiliar with them, especially when records are deleted and there are gaps in the sequence of autonumbers (as described in Chapter 1).

You will usually find it better and easier to use an artificial `AutoNumber` field as your primary key. When you get over the initial hump of learning how they work, they offer the simplicity, uniqueness, and consistency that are desirable in primary keys.

Multivalue Fields

Suppose you're a company that sells food items, like Northwind. You have a Products table with all the items you sell, with one row for each item: ice cream, yogurt, nondairy creamer, and so on. Among the columns, you include a field to store all the flavors for that item: vanilla, blueberry, Irish crème (see Table 2.14).

Or consider a table of Russian authors. Each row is dedicated to one author. You have fields for first name, last name, and birthday. You also have a column for the author's major works (see Table 2.14).

The `Flavors` field in the Products table and the `Major Works` field in the Authors table are known as multivalue fields. These are fields that store more than one value in each row. They're usually easy to identify because, as in the examples, they use commas to separate the various values. The fields are also usually named in the plural—flavors, characters, works, and so on.

I think multivalue fields are among the most difficult database problems to handle, both conceptually and practically. At first glance, the `Flavors` field in the Products table and the `Major Works` field in the Authors table both seem like fine, even elegant, solutions to a common problem. If you know that the number of values for a single characteristic—product flavors, authors' major works, and so on—will vary among records, why try to predict the number of columns you need? Instead of using three—or six, or eight, or who knows how many—columns to store values, wouldn't the best solution be to store all values in a single field and separate them by commas?

Table 2.14 Tables That Include Multivalue Fields

Products

Product	Supplier	Flavors	<<other fields>>
Ice cream	Frozen Delights	Vanilla, Chocolate, Strawberry	
Yogurt	Heavenly Cultures	Vanilla, Blueberry, Asparagus, Strawberry	
Nondairy Creamer	Foodstuffs Inc.	Vanilla, Asparagus, Hazelnut	

Authors

Last Name	First Name	Major Works	<<other fields>>
Dostoevsky	Fyodor	The Brothers Karamazov, Crime and Punishment, The Idiot, The Gambler	
Turgenev	Ivan	Fathers and Sons	
Tolstoy	Leo	War and Peace, Anna Karenina	

But you are designing your database so you can quickly and efficiently retrieve the data you need. Suppose you decide to discontinue an experimental flavor—say, asparagus—from all your products. If `Asparagus` is always a discrete record, it's easy to delete all occurrences of `Asparagus` from your database. If `Asparagus` is but one value in a multivalue field, however, you need to edit each of those records. That task is more difficult and, equally important, more likely to result in error. The threat to data integrity is substantial.

Or suppose you want to retrieve all records on Dostoevsky's *Crime and Punishment*. Surrounded as it is between *The Brothers Karamazov* and *The Idiot*, it will be inefficient to find information on that one book. Or say you want to sort all the books by title. A multivalue field will make it difficult to put all the books in alphabetical order.

Put simply, multivalue fields are difficult to edit, sort, and delete. They violate the essence of good relational database design. You need to get rid of them.

Multivalue Fields in the Classic TV Database

Earlier you saw that the Programs table had a multipart field, `Character Names/Character Occupations`. To resolve this multipart field, you created separate `Character Names` and `Character Occupations` fields (see Table 2.15).

Splitting the field into two columns resolved the problem of having two different types of data in the same field. But the `Character Names` and `Character Occupations` remain multivalue fields. To repeat, they have the two telltale signs of multivalue fields: The values are separated by commas, and the field name is plural.

Table 2.15 Programs

Multivalue Fields

Program Name	Character Names	Character Occupations	<<other fields>>
The Andy Griffith Show	Andy Taylor, Barney Fife, Gomer Pyle	Sheriff, Deputy Sheriff, Gas Station Attendant	
Happy Days	Richie Cunningham, Arthur Fonzarelli	Student, Motorcyclist	
Bewitched	Samantha Stevens, Darrin Stevens	Witch, Ad Executive	
The Lucy Show	Lucy Carmichael, Vivian Bagley	Widow, Divorcee	
Married with Children	Al Bundy, Peg Bundy	Shoe Salesman, Homemaker	

Resolving Multivalue Fields

So how do you fix these multivalue fields?

First, take both the `Character Names` and `Character Occupations` fields out of the Programs table and put them in a new table called Roles. Second, take the primary key from the Programs table and put it in the Roles table as well. Finally, let's split the new `Character`

Name (now singular) field into Last Name and First Name fields to eliminate the multipart field. A separate field is assigned to the character occupation (see Table 2.16).

NOTE Next to the ProgramID, I've included in italics the name of the TV show the ID refers to. *These names are not part of the table*. I've (reluctantly) included them only so you can see the program the ID refers to.

This solution seems counterintuitive; it provides a complex, even convoluted, solution to what seems to be a simple problem.

But using keys to resolve multivalue fields gives you a small taste of how you are going to integrate data in your database. As you'll see, putting the primary key of the original table into the new table enables you to establish a relationship between the original and new tables. By using primary keys to represent the values in each record, you make it possible to bring together values from different tables and integrate the information in your database.

Table 2.16 Roles

Multivalue Fields Resolved

ProgramID	Last Name	First Name	Occupation
1 *(Andy Griffith Show)*	Taylor	Andy	Sheriff
1 *(Andy Griffith Show)*	Fife	Barney	Deputy Sheriff
1 *(Andy Griffith Show)*	Pyle	Gomer	Filling station attendant
2 *(Happy Days)*	Cunningham	Richie	Student
2 *(Happy Days)*	Fonzarelli	Arthur	Motorcyclist

Q&A

Q: Wait a minute: The ProgramID field has a lot of duplicates. Didn't you tell us that a primary key can't have duplicate values?

A: ProgramID is the primary key of the Programs table; it's not the primary key in the Roles table. You haven't assigned a primary key to the Roles table yet; you do so in the next chapter.

Conclusion

It's time again to look back and see what you've done. Here's what you've accomplished since the first review:

1. Drew up a preliminary list of columns and created a list of tables in which to put them.
   You ignored mission objectives and made tables that represented one and only one subject.
2. Took a first stab at putting those columns into tables.
3. Evaluated the columns to see if any were calculated or multivalue fields.
   You dealt with these by creating or deleting new fields.
4. Reviewed the tables for candidate keys and selected a primary key for each table.
5. Reviewed the columns for multivalue fields.
   You did a preliminary fix by creating new tables that included the multivalue field and the primary key of the original table.

At this point, you've no doubt begun to wonder, "Isn't this an awful lot of work to create a database? Isn't there a much simpler method that would do the trick?"

Let me try a mundane but perhaps useful analogy. Remember when you went out trick-or-treating on Halloween? When you got home, you had a ton of candy in your bag. Your dad might have taken all that candy and dumped it quickly into one big jar.

That quickly solved the immediate problem of where to store the candy. But what happened when you wanted to find and eat the miniature Milky Way you remember getting? It was probably hidden in the middle or stuck away at the bottom. You usually wound up dumping out the whole jar to get at it.

On the other hand, if your mom was a database designer, she probably had you carefully sort and arrange the contents, allotting different goodies to different compartments in different containers. Initially, that took a lot longer than stuffing everything in a jar, but afterward you quickly and easily found the Milky Ways when you needed them. In the long run, the time spent organizing your plunder was well worth the effort.

In the next chapter, you'll see how keys are used to create relationships between tables, which enables you to combine data on various subjects and create the objects you need.

CHAPTER 3

UNDERSTANDING RELATIONSHIPS

In this chapter, you will learn about the various types of relationships and how they integrate your data. Three main kinds of relationships exist: one-to-one, one-to-many, and many-to-many. One-to-one relationships are by far the least important and interesting of the three, and I postpone discussion of them until the end of the chapter.

The other two relationships are central to creating powerful and effective relational databases. If you haven't had much exposure to them, you might find them difficult to understand and implement at first. I've tried to provide numerous examples of each type of relationship, in the hope that repetition will enable you to recognize them with ease and use them with confidence. At the end of the chapter, I also spend a little time talking about the formal rules of normalization, which you might come across in your Access work.

Because this chapter builds on the database design skills you learned in Chapter 2, "Database Design," I strongly encourage you to read it before proceeding.

The Primacy of Primary Keys

I previously compared primary keys to employees who represent their companies at industry gatherings. The analogy was okay, as far as it went. But I don't want you to think of primary keys as carousing revelers at a widget-makers' convention. These are powerful, integrating forces that enable you to tightly connect tables.

In that sense, a more appropriate analogy can be found in tribal societies or even any community of extended families where blood relationships are strong. Imagine that one of the up-and-coming members of Family A marries into Family B. This young thing now has an important position in both families. As a product of Family A, he or she represents all of its interests in Family B. At the same time, he or she remains a full-fledged member of Family A.

You'll see a similar process at work in relational databases. You place a copy of the prince of Table A, its primary key, in Table B. The primary key represents all of the fields in Table A and, at the same time, is a full-fledged member of Table B. By placing copies of primary keys in the various tables of your database, you can integrate your data through relationships.

When I say "copy," I don't mean an exact replica, any more than brides and grooms assume the same role in their new families that they had in their old ones. I mean that the field will have the same data type and that the fields will contain "matching data"—in other words, that they will have values that are the same data type and of the same kind.

This analogy will make more sense as you read through the many examples of primary keys presented in this chapter.

One-to-Many Relationships

The one-to-many relationship is by far the most common and most important relationship type. Almost any relational database offers numerous examples of one-to-many relationships. In this section, I provide two examples of one-to-many relationships using the order-entry model, and two using the Classic TV database you worked with in Chapter 2. This way, you'll have plenty of opportunity to see one-to-many relationships at work.

An Order-Entry Model

Let's start with two examples from a typical order-entry model, such as the Northwind sample database. As a wholesaler of camping equipment, you have a table for customer contact information (Table 3.1); it has data about the subject customers. You also have a table for orders (Table 3.2); it has data about the subject orders. Each row in the Customers table represents one customer; each row in the Orders table represents a single order.

Table 3.1 Table of Customer Contact Information

CustomerID (PK)	Company Name	Street Address	City	State	ZIP	<<other fields>
001	Outdoor Emporium	1165 C Street	Arkadelphia	AK	71998	
002	Mountain Mart	14098 Hopyard	Mayfield	MI	49666	

CustomerID (PK)	Company Name	Street Address	City	State	ZIP	<<other fields>
003	Travelers Aid	2 West 19 Street	Sullivan	NH	03445	
004	The Hiker	673 Ignatius Way	Vanderbilt	MI	49795	
005	Gleason's Store	82-17 Francisco	Fargo	ND	58109	

PK=Primary key

Table 3.2 Table of Order Data

OrderID (PK)	CustomerID (FK)	Order Date	Ship Date	Shipper	<<other fields>>
10075	002	10/16/2004	10/18/2004	Acme	
10076	003	10/19/2004	10/21/2004	Empire	
10077	002	10/21/2004	10/23/2004	USPS	
10078	001	10/21/2004	10/24/2004	USPS	
10079	002	10/22/2004	10/27/2004	Acme	

PK=Primary key; FK=Foreign key

Each customer is uniquely identified by the `CustomerID`, which is the primary key of the Customers table. Each customer can appear only once in the Customers table.

The Orders table also has a field called `CustomerID` that tells you which customer placed the order. Any `CustomerID` in the Orders table must also be a `CustomerID` in the Customers table. In the Orders table, `CustomerID` is the foreign key. Database designers use various naming conventions, but the foreign key usually has the same name or a similar name as the primary key from which it was copied.

Any particular `CustomerID` can appear only once in the Customers table, but any `CustomerID` can appear many times in the Orders table. That makes sense because the same customer can have many orders. Put another way, a single customer can have many orders, but no order can have more than one customer.

You can establish a one-to-many relationship between the Customers table and the Orders table through the `CustomerID` field, the field with matching data. `CustomerID` is the primary key in the primary table, the table on the "one" side of the relationship. `CustomerID` is the foreign key in the related table, the table on the "many" side of the relationship.

Let's do one more example before heading to the Classic TV database. Consider the Categories and Products tables in Tables 3.3 and 3.4.

The Categories table contains data about a subject—in this case, categories. Each row in the Categories table represents a single category. The `CategoryID` is the primary key of the Categories table and uniquely identifies each category.

The Products table contains data about the subject products. Each row represents a single product. Each product is uniquely identified by the `ProductID`. The Products table also has a `CategoryID` field, which contains only categories that are included in the Categories table. Each category can appear only once in the Categories table, but the same category can appear many times in the Products table. The two tables have matching data in the `CategoryID` fields.

You can establish a one-to-many relationship between the Categories and Products tables. The Categories table is on the "one" side of the relationship, where the `CategoryID` is the primary key in the primary table. The Products table is on the "many" side of the relationship, where `CategoryID` is the foreign key in the related table.

Table 3.3 The Categories Table Contains Data About Product Categories

CategoryID (PK)	Category	Description
1	Men's Apparel	Outerwear worn by men, such as shirts, sweaters, slacks
2	Women's Apparel	Outerwear worn by women, such as blouses, dresses, pants
3	Home Furnishings	Household items, such as bedding, kitchen appliances, rugs
4	Accessories	Items such as watches, luggage, toiletries
5	Footwear	Outerwear for feet, such as sneakers, slippers, hiking boots

PK=Primary key

Table 3.4 The Products Table Contains Data About Products.

ProductID (PK)	Product Name	CategoryID (FK)	Supplier	<<other fields>>
00123	Hiking Socks	5	Mountain Footwear	
00124	Duffle Bag	4	In The Bag, Inc.	
00125	Garment Bag	4	Luggage 'n More	
00126	Shoulder Tote	4	Successful Accessories	
00127	Hiking shorts	2	Garmendi Garments	

PK=Primary key; FK=Foreign key

Q&A

Q: You said that each value in the foreign key of the related table must appear in the primary key of the primary table. But how do you make sure that values that aren't in the primary table aren't entered into the related table?

A: You'll see how that's done in the next chapter, where you will formally establish the relationship between the two tables. I admit that it's a little confusing: Although I've written "the table on the 'many' side of the relationship," you haven't yet formally created the relationship in the Relationships window. Don't get hung up on this—the important thing is to learn to recognize the various relationship types and how they work.

Classic TV Database

Let's turn to the Classic TV database, whose current state of development is shown in Table 3.5.

Think about how the Networks and Programs tables relate to one another. Each program ran on only a single television network. (I'm talking about the original airing of the show in prime time, not the many channels that might now carry its reruns.) On the other hand, a single network can air many programs.

The Networks and Programs tables have a one-to-many relationship. One of your mission objectives is to know the broadcast history of a program, so you certainly want to be able to combine data from the two tables.

But how can you do that? You need to associate the Networks table with the Programs table so you can integrate the data from both tables when needed. If you look at the current field lists, however, no field in the Programs table has anything to do with the Networks table.

Table 3.5 The Current Status of the Classic TV Database

Current Field Lists

Programs	Genres	Networks	Actors	Roles
ProgramID PK	GenreID PK	NetworkID PK	ActorID PK	ProgramID
Name	Genre	Official Name	First Name	First Name
Year Started	Description	Popular Name	Last Name	Last Name
Year Ended		Founder	Gender	Occupation
Synopsis		Notes	Biography	
Location				
Notes				

PK=Primary key

You need to add a field to the Programs table from the Networks table (see Table 3.6) that will enable you to combine data from both tables. That field must uniquely identify and represent each row of data in the Networks table. That field, as you know by now, is `NetworkID`, the primary key of the Networks table.

By adding the primary key of the Networks table to the Programs table, you have the potential of bringing any of the values from the Networks table (Popular Name, Official Name, Founder, Notes) together with any values from the Programs table.

`NetworkID` is the primary key in the primary table Networks, the table on the "one" side of the relationship. `NetworkID` is also the foreign key in the related table Programs, the table on the "many" side of the relationship (see Table 3.7). The two keys have matching data through which you can establish a one-to-many relationship.

Q&A

Q: You're wrong about a program airing on only one TV station during its run in prime time. I distinctly remember that at some point the courtroom drama *Matlock* with Andy Griffith stopped running on NBC and moved to ABC.

A: You're right. Occasionally a program will air on one network and move to another network. I should have written that no program can run on the same network more than once at the same time.

For now, let's keep things simple by including only the network that originated the show. That's only half a cop-out: The originating network developed the show, and a later move to another network might be of only minor interest. In the section on many-to-many relationships a few pages ahead, I'll give you a detailed explanation of how to include the full broadcast history.

Table 3.6 The Networks Table Is on the "One" Side of the One-to-Many Relationship with Programs

NetworkID (PK)	Official Name	Popular Name	Founder	Notes	<<other fields>
1	Columbia Broadcasting System	CBS	William Paley	CBS was the…	
2	National Broadcasting Company	NBC	David Sarnoff	NBC started as…	
3	American Broadcasting Company	ABC	Leonard Goldenson	In the early days…	
4	Fox Television	FOX	Rupert Murdoch	Barry Diller, along with…	

PK=Primary key

Table 3.7 The `NetworkID` Field from the Networks Table Is Included in the Programs Table as a Foreign Key. Because the Two Tables Now Have Matching Data, You Can Establish a One-to-Many Relationship Between Them.

ProgramID (PK)	Program	NetworkID (FK)	Year Started	Year Ended	<<other fields>>
1	The Andy Griffith Show	1	1960	1968	
2	Happy Days	3	1974	1984	
3	The Bob Newhart Show	1	1972	1978	
4	Newhart	1	1982	1990	
5	Sanford & Son	2	1972	1977	

PK=Primary key; FK=Foreign key

Let's look at another one-to-many relationship in the Classic TV database.

Earlier I described a relationship between the Categories and Products tables, where each product was assigned a single category. Look at the tables and fields in Table 3.5. Do any tables in the Classic TV database have a relationship similar to that of Categories and Products?

Consider the relationship between Genres and Programs. Each row in the Genres table represents one category, or genre, of show; each show in the Programs table is described by a single genre. A single genre can be used to describe many programs, but each program can have only one genre. (You might argue that some TV shows overlap genres, but let's assume just one genre per show.)

Potentially, the Genres and Programs tables have a one-to-many relationship. But how do you record the genre of each program? Currently, there is no field in the Programs table you can use to assign a genre.

Again, you need to add a field to the Programs table from the Genres table that will enable you to combine data from both tables when you need it. That field will uniquely identify and represent each row of data in the Genres table. The field you want is `GenreID`, the primary key of the Genres table.

By adding the primary key of the Genres table to the Programs table, you can join any of the values in the Genres table with any values from the Programs table. `GenreID` is the primary key in the primary table of Genres, which is on the "one" side of the relationship, and `GenreID` is also the foreign key in the related table of Programs on the "many" side of the relationship (see Table 3.8).

Table 3.8 The `GenreID` Field from the Genres Tables Has Been Added to the Programs Table as a Foreign Key. Note That, Although I Placed the `GenreID` Column Next to the `Program` Field, This Is Simply for Presentation. The Field Could Be in Any Position; It Does Not Necessarily Follow `Program`.

Genres

GenreID (PK)	Genre	Description
1	Rural Comedy	Primarily rural setting and characters, such as The Andy Griffith Show
2	General Drama	General category for drama; excludes police and hospital dramas
3	Urban Comedy	Primarily urban setting, themes, and characters, such as The Bob Newhart Show
4	General Comedy	General category for all other comedies
5	Police Drama	Primary characters and themes center on police work, such as Hill Street Blues

Programs

ProgramID (PK)	Program	GenreID (FK)	NetworkID (FK)	<<other fields>
1	The Andy Griffith Show	1	1	
2	Happy Days	4	3	
3	The Bob Newhart Show	3	1	
4	Newhart	1	1	
5	Sanford & Son	4	2	

PK=Primary key; FK=Foreign key

Table 3.9 shows the current status of the Classic TV database.

Table 3.9 The Current Field List for the Classic TV Database After Adding Foreign Keys to the Programs Table

Programs	Genres	Networks	Actors	Roles
ProgramID PK	GenreID PK	NetworkID PK	ActorID PK	ProgramID
GenreID FK	Genre	Official Name	First Name	First Name
NetworkID FK	Description	Popular Name	Last Name	Last Name
Name		Founder	Gender	Occupation
Year Started		Notes	Biography	
Year Ended				
Synopsis				
Location				
Notes				

PK=Primary key; FK=Foreign key

Many-to-Many Relationships

Many-to-many relationships are both more difficult to understand and more difficult to resolve than one-to-many relationships. Don't be frustrated if you need to reread this section a couple times before you understand how they work.

Again, I introduce the relationship type by using an example from the order-entry system. (I've slightly edited two tables you saw earlier in the chapter.) I then give you two detailed examples from the Classic TV database.

Order-Entry System

Let's say that you have an Orders table (see Table 3.10) and a Products table (see Table 3.11). Each row in the Orders table represents a single order; each row in the Products table represents a single product. (If you want a better idea of what these tables might look like, choose Help, Samples, Northwind Sample Database, and view the Orders and Products tables they contain.)

Table 3.10 This Orders Table Contains Data About Orders

OrderID (PK)	CustomerID (FK)	Order Date	Ship Date	<<other fields>>
10075	002	10/16/2004	10/18/2004	
10076	003	10/19/2004	10/21/2004	
10077	002	10/21/2004	10/23/2004	
10078	007	10/22/2004	10/24/2004	
10079	008	10/22/2004	10/25/2004	

PK=Primary key; FK=Foreign key

Table 3.11 This Products Table Contains Data About Products

ProductID (PK)	Product Name	CategoryID (FK)	Supplier	<<other fields>>
00122	Travel Clock	4	High Noon Timepieces	
00123	Hiking Socks	5	Mountain Footwear	
00124	Duffle Bag	4	In The Bag, Inc.	
00125	Garment Bag	4	Luggage 'n More	
00126	Toiletries Kit	4	Hi Jean Products	

PK=Primary key; FK=Foreign key

Consider how products and orders relate to each other. Any single order can be made up of many products. If this were a one-to-many relationship, I'd have finished the last sentence with "and any product can be in only one order." But that, of course, is not true. Any single product can also be included in many orders.

You can say that the tables have a many-to-many relationship.

This is very different from the relationship between Customers and Orders, where every order had only one customer, or Categories and Products, where every product had just one category. In those cases, you resolved the relationship by adding the primary key of the table on the "one" side of the relationship to the table on the "many" side of the relationship as a foreign key.

But that solution won't work for Orders and Products. Suppose you add the primary key `ProductID` to the Orders table as a foreign key. If an order included three products, as it does for `OrderID 10075` in Table 3.12, you would need three separate records in the Orders table for the three products. So you would have to repeat all the data, such as `CustomerID`, order date, and ship date, for all three records. If an order included 10 products, you would need 10 rows for a single order.

Now let's try it the other way around. Suppose you added the primary key `OrderID` to the Products table (see Table 3.13). If a product was included in three orders, as it is for `ProductID 00123`, you would need a separate record in the Products table for each order in which the product was included. Each time a product was ordered, you'd have to repeat data such as product name, `CategoryID`, and supplier in the Products table. If a product was included in 10 orders, you would need 10 rows for just that product.

Table 3.12 This Orders Table Includes the Individual Products in the Order. It Is an Example of Bad Database Design.

OrderID (PK)	ProductID (FK)	CustomerID (FK)	Order Date	Ship Date	<<other fields>>
10075	00123	002	10/16/2004	10/18/2004	
10075	00124	002	10/16/2004	10/18/2004	
10075	00125	002	10/16/2004	10/18/2004	
10076	00124	003	10/19/2004	10/21/2004	
10077	00126	002	10/21/2004	10/23/2004	

PK=Primary key; FK=Foreign key

Table 3.13 This Products Table Contains Data About the Orders in Which the Product Is Included. It Is an Example of Bad Database Design.

ProductID (PK)	OrderID (FK)	Product Name	CategoryID (FK)	Supplier	<<other fields>>
00123	10075	Hiking Socks	5	Mountain Footwear	
00123	10076	Hiking Socks	5	Mountain Footwear	

ProductID (PK)	OrderID (FK)	Product Name	CategoryID (FK)	Supplier	<<other fields>>
00123	10077	Hiking Socks	5	Mountain Footwear	
00124	10077	Duffle Bag	4	In The Bag, Inc.	
00125	10078	Garment Bag	4	Luggage 'n More	

PK=Primary key; FK=Foreign key

Create a Linking Table

You can see that merely putting the primary key of the "one" table as a foreign key in the "many" table is not a solution because the two tables are on both the "one" and the "many" sides. So what is the solution?

You create an entirely new table called a linking table (or a join table) that includes both the primary key from the Products table and the primary key from the Orders table. As in the Northwind database, let's call the table Order Details. In the Order Details table, the two foreign keys `OrdersID` and the `ProductsID` together are the primary key. In other words, this composite primary key has two fields.

Note that this linking table includes two one-to-many relationships. As shown in Table 3.14, the `OrderID` field can appear many times in the Order Details table but, as you've seen, only once in the Orders table. Similarly, a `ProductID` can appear many times in the Order Details table but only once in the Products table.

Table 3.14 The Order Details Table Includes the Primary Keys from Both the Orders and Products Tables. Both Fields Are on the "Many" Side of One-to-Many Relationships.

OrderID CPK/FK	ProductID CPK/FK
10075	00123
10075	00124
10075	00125
10076	00124
10077	00126

CPK=Composite primary key; FK=Foreign key

Is the primary key of the Order Details table unique? Let's review the three key requirements of a primary key:

- Does it uniquely identify each record? Yes, it does. Individually, you'll find the same `OrderID` more than once in the OrderID column, and the same `ProductID` included more than once in the `ProductID` column. But each combination of `OrderID` and `ProductID` in a single row is unique.
- Can it contain null values? No. For every product, there has to be at least one order, and for every order, there has to be at least one product.
- Will the primary key change only rarely? After an `OrderID` has been assigned to an order and a `Product ID` has been assigned to a product, there should be little reason to change them.

The linking table that resolves a many-to-many relationship might or might not have additional fields besides the primary key. Look at Table 3.15. It includes two fields that are exclusively identified by `OrderID` and `ProductID`. The value in the `Quantity` field can be determined only by knowing both the order and the product. Simply knowing either one is not sufficient to determine the quantity. The `Price` field is also exclusively identified by the composite primary key. Prices for any individual product might vary, so it's necessary to know the order in addition to the product to determine the price.

Table 3.15 A Linking Table Can Have Additional Fields That Are Uniquely Described by the Composite Primary Key

Order Details, Including Fields Besides the Composite Primary Key

OrderID CPK/FK	ProductID CPK/FK	Quantity	Price
10075	00123	12	$ 2.99
10075	00124	3	$14.95
10075	00125	2	$19.73
10076	00124	3	$14.95
10077	00126	2	$ 4.95

CPK=Composite primary key; FK=Foreign key

This might not seem an elegant solution; it might seem that tables are proliferating across your database, to little advantage. But the overall objective of associating tables and bringing together the data each contains is achieved.

Classic TV Database

Earlier we considered the relationship between TV shows and networks. Initially, it appeared to be a simple one-to-many relationship. CBS aired such classics as *The Lucy Show*, *Twilight Zone*, *Northern Exposure*, and more. But *The Lucy Show* and the rest didn't appear on CBS one week, NBC the next, and ABC in week 3. So it would seem that many TV shows could appear on one network, but a single TV show was seen on only one network.

But that isn't wholly true. As noted earlier, a few shows started on one network and then moved to another. For example, *Leave It To Beaver* began on CBS in 1957 but soon moved to ABC, where it ran for 6 years. So although one network can broadcast many TV shows, one TV show can appear on two or more networks. The number of TV shows certainly exceeds the number of networks, but it's nonetheless true that Programs and Networks actually have a many-to-many relationship.

You already know one alternative: Choose one network as the primary network (such as the station on which the show originated, the network on which it aired longest, and so on) and simply ignore the second network. In other words, you might decide that the extra data provided by recording subsequent networks simply isn't worth the trouble or expense. The one-to-many design solution remains intact.

But that's not a solution if you want to record the entire broadcast history of programs, which would include the start year and end year for the show on each network that it aired.

If you included the primary key of the Networks table as a foreign key in the Programs table, you'd have duplicate values in fields such as `Location` (see Table 3.16). And if you used the `ProgramID` as a foreign key in the Networks table, you'd have duplicate values for fields such as `Founder` (see Table 3.17). (To develop a better example, I've used imaginary programs and air dates in both tables.)

Table 3.16 This Programs Table Includes `NetworkID` as a Foreign Key. Because Programs Such As `ProgramID 102` Aired First on One Station and Then on Another, You Need to Repeat Data Such As the Program's Location (Kansas City). This Is Not Good Database Design.

ProgramID (PK)	Program	NetworkID (FK)	Location	Year Started	Year Ended	<other fields>
101	That's My Millie	1	Milwaukee	1960	1968	
102	Stanley and Son	1	Kansas City	1959	1961	
102	Stanley and Son	2	Kansas City	1962	1964	
103	Dean's Place	3	Los Angeles	1986	1991	
104	The Zoo	3	San Diego Zoo	1988	1995	

PK=Primary key; FK=Foreign key

Table 3.17 The Networks Table with `ProgramID` Included as a Foreign Key. Because Many Programs Appeared on Each Station, You Have a Great Deal of Repeating Data in the Network Fields (Only `Popular Name` and `Founder` Are Shown Here).

NetworkID (PK)	ProgramID (FK)	Popular Name	Founder	Year Started	Year Ended	<<other fields>>
1	101	CBS	William Paley	1955	1960	
1	102	CBS	William Paley	1959	1961	
2	102	NBC	David Sarnoff	1962	1964	
3	103	ABC	Leonard Goldenson	1986	1991	
3	104	ABC	Leonard Goldenson	1988	1995	

PK=Primary key; FK=Foreign key

Again, the solution is to create a linking table (say, Broadcasts) that includes keys from both tables. The primary key of the Broadcasts table is a composite key. It comprises the primary keys of both the Programs and Networks tables, which in the Broadcasts table become foreign keys. Table 3.18 shows the new table, Broadcasts, with the composite primary key. (The names of the programs and networks are not part of the table; I've included them only to make the table easier to understand.)

Let me put that another way: The Programs table has a one-to-many relationship with the Broadcasts table through the `ProgramID` field. The primary key of the Programs table is `ProgramID`; in the Broadcasts table, `ProgramID` is a foreign key.

The Networks table also has a one-to-many relationship with the Broadcasts table. The primary key of the Networks table is `NetworkID`; in the Broadcasts table, `NetworkID` is a foreign key. The composite primary key of `ProgramID` and `NetworkID` would be unique because no program can run on the same network more than once at the same time.

Table 3.18 The Broadcasts Table Is a Linking Table That Includes the Primary Keys of Both the Programs and Network Tables

ProgramID CPK/FK	NetworkID CPK/FK
101 (*That's My Millie*)	1 (*CBS*)
102 (*Stanley&Son*)	1 (*CBS*)
102 (*Stanley&Son*)	2 (*NBC*)
103 (*Dean's Place*)	3 (*ABC*)
104 (*The Zoo*)	3 (*ABC*)

CPK=Composite primary key; FK=Foreign key

As with the Order Details table, you would want to include in the Broadcasts table any fields that are exclusively described by the composite primary key. In this case, those would be the `Year Started` and `Year Ended` fields (see Table 3.19—again, the program and network names in parentheses are included only to make the table easier to understand). Because a program can move to a different network, only a primary key that comprises both primary keys can exclusively identify the `Year Started` and `Year Ended` fields.

Table 3.19 The Broadcasts Table with Fields That Are Exclusively Identified by the Primary Key

ProgramID CPK/FK	NetworkID CPK/FK	Year Started	Year Ended
101 (*That's My Millie*)	1 (*CBS*)	1960	1968
102 (*Stanley&Son*)	1 (*CBS*)	1959	1961
102 (*Stanley&Son*)	2 (*NBC*)	1962	1964
103 (*Dean's Place*)	3 (*ABC*)	1986	1991
104 (*The Zoo*)	3 (*ABC*)	1988	1995

CPK=Composite primary key; FK=Foreign key

A Three-Field Primary Key

Consider this possibility: Suppose that a program aired on one network, then aired on another network, and then returned to its original network. I don't know if this has ever occurred (probably not), but it is conceivable. What consequences would this have for your table design?

The Broadcasts table in Table 3.20 is the same as that in Table 3.19, with one difference: It includes one extra record for Stanley & Son. Instead of ending its run in 1964, it returned to its original network, CBS, for its final year.

Table 3.20 The Composite Primary Key of `ProgramID` and `NetworkID` Is Insufficient to Uniquely Identify Each Record If a Program Returns to Its Original Network

Broadcasts: Stanley & Son

ProgramID CPK/FK	NetworkID CPK/FK	Year Started	Year Ended
101 (*That's My Millie*)	1 (*CBS*)	1960	1968
102 (*Stanley&Son*)	1 (*CBS*)	1959	1961
102 (*Stanley&Son*)	2 (*NBC*)	1962	1964
102 (*Stanley&Son*)	1 (*CBS*)	1965	1966
103 (*Dean's Place*)	3 (*ABC*)	1986	1991
104 (*The Zoo*)	3 (*ABC*)	1988	1995

CPK=Composite primary key; FK=Foreign key

In that case, the composite primary key would no longer be unique because the same program aired on the same network twice. In other words, the `ProgramID` and `NetworkID` would be identical for two records: the original broadcast of the program (1959–1961), and the broadcast when it returned to its original network (1965–1966). Even a primary key with two fields wouldn't be sufficient to identify every record uniquely.

One good solution is to include `Year Started` as an additional field in what would be a three-field composite primary key. Together, the `ProgramID`, `NetworkID`, and `Year Started` fields would uniquely identify the broadcasts.

Another possible solution would be to add a field showing the sequence of broadcasts (see Table 3.21). The first broadcast of a program would be `1`, the next airing would be `2`, and so on. The three fields of `ProgramID`, `NetworkID`, and `Sequence Number` together would be the primary key and would uniquely identify each record. The advantage of this scheme is that you could use the sequence number to search for only first-run or second-run broadcasts. Other database designers would disagree, however, and note that this design needlessly introduces additional complexity into the database.

In the Classic TV database, I'll assume that TV shows never return for a run on their earlier networks.

Table 3.21 The Sequence Number Column Lets You Uniquely Identify Each Record but Makes the Database More Complex

Broadcasts with Sequence Numbers

ProgramID CPK/FK	NetworkID CPK/FK	Sequence Number CPK	Year Started	Year Ended
101 (*That's My Millie*)	1 (*CBS*)	1	1960	1968
102 (*Stanley&Son*)	1 (*CBS*)	1	1959	1961
102 (*Stanley&Son*)	2 (*NBC*)	2	1962	1964
102 (*Stanley&Son*)	1 (*CBS*)	3	1965	1966
103 (*Dean's Place*)	3 (*ABC*)	1	1986	1991
104 (*The Zoo*)	3 (*ABC*)	1	1988	1995

CPK=Composite primary key; FK=Foreign key

Q&A

Q: I think I know the answer to this question, but please remind me one more time. If relational databases are so great, why do you have to add data in parentheses, which isn't actually included in the tables, to show us what's going on? In other words, why don't any of these tables contain data I can actually use as is, rather than be filled with ID numbers that mean nothing to me?

A: A good table isn't one that meets a specific information need. It is a table that helps the database as a whole satisfy all your information needs. It's irrelevant whether any single table by itself can be used to meet any of your information requirements because you use tables to store data, not to manipulate or display it. Those tasks are the work of the queries, forms, and reports you will create in later chapters.

One More Many-to-Many Relationship

Another many-to-many relationship in the Classic TV database needs to be resolved. Consider the Actors table and the Programs table. Obviously, any one program can have several actors. It's almost as obvious that any one actor can be on several TV shows. For example, Bob Newhart has been the star of the eponymous *The Bob Newhart Show*, *Newhart*, and *Bob*. (He once joked that his next show would be called simply *B*.)

Because one program can have several actors and one actor can be on several TV programs, the Actors and Programs tables have a many-to-many relationship. Again, you can resolve the many-to-many relationship by using a linking table. (I think by now you understand that simply placing the primary key of the Actors table into the Programs table as a foreign key, or vice versa, is not a solution.)

Table 3.22 shows the current status of the database. Reconsider the Roles table, which you created to resolve the `Character Name/Character Occupation` field (if you need to refresh your memory, take a look back at the "Resolving Multivalue Fields" section in Chapter 2). You can use this table as a linking table for Actors and Programs. Here are the fields we have so far:

- `ActorID`—We can add the primary key from the Actors table as a foreign key in the Roles table.

- `ProgramID`—The table already includes `ProgramID` from the Programs table as a foreign key, but you haven't yet assigned a primary key to the table.

  As with the Broadcasts linking table, the primary key of the Roles table will be a composite primary key that includes the primary keys of the two linked tables as foreign keys. In other words, the primary key of the Roles table will be a composite primary key comprising `ActorID` and `ProgramID`, the two foreign keys from the linked tables.
- `First Name` and `Last Name`—You need to know both the program and the actor to determine the character's name. The character's first name and last name are exclusively identified by the primary key of `ProgramID` and `ActorID`.
- `Occupation`—You need to know both the program and the actor to determine the character's occupation. The character's occupation is exclusively identified by the primary key of `ProgramID` and `ActorID`.

Now add three more fields to the Roles table:

- `Year Started` and `Year Ended`—The years the actor made his or her appearance and exited the show are pieces of information you'd like to know.
- `Notes`—You might want to put in additional comments about the nature of the actor's role, as you will see shortly.

Table 3.22 Current Status of the Classic TV Database

Current Field Lists

Programs	Genres	Broadcasts	Networks	Actors	Roles
ProgramID PK	GenreID PK	ProgramID CPK/FK	NetworkID PK	ActorID PK	ProgramID FK
GenreID FK	Genre	NetworkID CPK/FK	Official Name	First Name	First Name
Name	Description	Year Started	Popular Name	Last Name	Last Name
Location		Year Ended	Founder	Gender	Occupation
Synopsis			Notes	Biography	

PK=Primary key; CPK=Composite primary key; FK=Foreign key

Table 3.23 shows a few records from the revised Roles table, which now includes the `ActorID` field. Again, I emphasize that the names in parentheses are not part of the table.

Table 3.23 A Sample of the Roles Table

ActorID CPK/FK	ProgramID CPK/FK	Last Name	First Name	Occupation	<<other fields>>
1 (*Andy Griffith*)	1 (*TAGS*)	Taylor	Andy	Sheriff	
1 (*Andy Griffith*)	9 (*Matlock*)	Matlock	Benjamin	Defense attorney	
2 (*Don Knotts*)	1 (*TAGS*)	Fife	Barney	Sheriff's deputy	
2 (*Don Knotts*)	9 (*Matlock*)	Calhoun	Les	Matlock's neighbor	
3 (*Ron Howard*)	1 (*TAGS*)	Taylor	Opie	Schoolboy	
3 (*Ron Howard*)	2 (*Happy Days*)	Cunningham	Richie	Student	
4 (*Jim Nabors*)	1 (*TAGS*)	Pyle	Gomer	Filling station attendant	
5 (*Henry Winkler*)	2 (*Happy Days*)	Fonzarelli	Arthur	Motorcyclist	

TAGS=The Andy Griffith Show; CPK=Composite primary key; FK=Foreign key

An Alternative Solution

I think the Classic TV database suggested would fill the needs of most couch potatoes. But it's a less-than-perfect solution.

For example, fans of *The Patty Duke Show* will remember that the actor Patty Duke played both Cathy (who has lived almost everywhere, from Zanzibar to Barclay Square) and her identical cousin, Patty (who has seen only the sights a girl can see from Brooklyn Heights). In that case, the `ProgramID` and the `ActorID` would be the same for both characters, and thus the primary key would be inadequate.

More frequently, the same actor on a program plays both a main character and one or two other characters that appear infrequently. For example, on the show *Bewitched*, Elizabeth Montgomery played both the lovely witch Samantha, the main character, and her irritating cousin Serena, who made brief, intermittent appearances.

It's also possible for the same character to migrate to other television shows. For example, Frasier Crane is a character on both *Cheers* and *Frasier*. You might want to include fields that were exclusive to the character (say, personality) that didn't vary by program or actor.

One solution would be to set up a separate Characters table, with fields describing the character alone—first and last name, personality, and so on (see Table 3.24). The table would have a `CharacterID` field as a primary key. You could then place the primary key of the Characters table in the Roles table as a foreign key (see Table 3.25, where again the text in parentheses is not part of the table). The primary key for the Roles tables would then comprise three keys: `ProgramID`, `ActorID`, and `CharacterID`. The Programs, Actors, and Characters tables would all have one-to-many relationships with the Roles table through their respective primary keys.

Let's keep things simple, however, by assuming that the program and the actor together is sufficient for identifying roles.

Table 3.24 A Characters Table That Stores Values About the Subject Characters

CharacterID (PK)	Last Name	First Name	Personality	<<other fields>>
141	Bunker	Archie	Bigoted but lovable	
142	Crane	Frasier	Pretentious yet warm-hearted	
143	Lane	Patty	Happy, fun-loving	
144	Lane	Cathy	Proper, thoughtful	
145	Pyle	Gomer	Simple, goofy	

Table 3.25 The `ProgramID`, `ActorID`, and `CharacterID` Are All Necessary to Distinguish the Role of Patty Lane from Cathy Lane on *The Patty Duke Show*

Roles with Character IDs

ProgramID (CPK/FK)	ActorID (CPK/FK)	CharacterID (CPK/FK)	<<other fields>>
32 (*Cheers*)	39 (*Kelsey Grammer*)	142 (*Frasier Crane*)	
33 (*Frasier*)	39 (*Kelsey Grammer*)	142 (*Frasier Crane*)	
34 (*The Patty Duke Show*)	40 (*Patty Duke*)	143 (*Patty Lane*)	
34 (*The Patty Duke Show*)	40 (*Patty Duke*)	144 (*Cathy Lane*)	
35 (*All in the Family*)	41 (*Carroll O'Connor*)	141 (*Archie Bunker*)	

CPK=Composite primary key; FK=Foreign key

Final List of Fields and Relationships

Table 3.26 shows the final list of tables and fields for the Classic TV database. The method I described for developing it took shortcuts and half-measures. In a real-world situation, you would want to take additional measures to ensure that you had collected all the fields you needed and that they were sufficient to accomplish your mission objectives.

This final list does not represent some state of perfection. Certainly, alternative roads could have been taken. But I've given you some idea of the process of developing field lists and tables, as well as determining primary and foreign keys.

Table 3.26 The Final List of Tables and Fields for the Classic TV Database

Programs	Broadcasts	Genres	Networks	Actors	Roles
ProgramID PK	ProgramID CPK/FK	GenreID PK	NetworkID PK	ActorID PK	ProgramID CPK/FK
GenreID FK	NetworkID CPK/FK	Genre	OfficialName	First Name	ActorID CPK/FK
Name	Year Started	Description	PopularName	Last Name	First Name
Location	Year Ended		Founder	Gender	Last Name
Synopsis			Notes	Biography	Occupation
Notes					Year Started
					Year Ended
					Notes

PK=Primary key; CPK=Composite primary key; FK=Foreign key

Table 3.27 shows all the relationships of the Classic TV database at the beginning of the chapter. You can use such a scheme to go through each relationship one by one, resolving those relationships that need to be resolved while considering alternative design solutions.

You'll notice that the scheme contains many-to-many relationships. You resolved these relationships during the chapter by creating linking tables that include foreign keys from the original tables. The current relationships in the database shown in Table 3.28 thus include no many-to-many relationships, even though, for descriptive purposes, they still theoretically exist. In the next chapter, you will formally establish the one-to-many relationships shown in Table 3.28.

In the chart, the horizontal axis represents the table's relationship to the table on the vertical axis. For example, viewing the relationship between the Genres and Programs tables in the first row, you could say that Genres is on the "one" side and Programs is on the "many" side.

I'm not certain whether showing which table is on the "one" side and which is on the "many" side is helpful or confusing. Some authors distinguish one-to-many relationships from many-to-one relationships, but I don't know how to communicate a difference in a way that will be profitable to you. Instead, I've explained that both tables are in a one-to-many relationship and then indicated which is on the "one" side and which is on the "many" side.

In the following tables, however, it was useful to show the various relationships as 1:M (one-to-many) and M:1 (many to one). Many-to-many relationships are shown as M:M.

Table 3.27 The Relationships of the Classic TV Database at the Start of the Chapter

	Programs	Genres	Networks	Actors	Roles
Programs		1:M	M:M	M:M	M:1
Genre	M:1				
Networks	M:M				
Actors	M:M				M:M
Roles	1:M			M:M	

Table 3.28 The Relationships of the Classic TV Database at the End of the Chapter

	Programs	Genres	Networks	Actors	Roles	Broadcasts
Programs		1:M			M:1	M:1
Genre	M:1					
Networks						M:1
Actors					M:1	
Roles	1:M			1:M		
Broadcasts	1:M		1:M			

Exclusive Identification

One principle of database design that I'd like to re-emphasize is that a primary key should exclusively identify the value of each field within a given record. Each field value for any particular record should be unique in the database, except where it's used as matching data for establishing a relationship. If the primary key doesn't exclusively identify the field, either it's unnecessary or it belongs in another table.

This is a difficult concept to comprehend. Let's look at the final list of tables and fields in Table 3.26 to see how it applies. Consider the table Programs, where `ProgramID` is the primary key. Each of the nonkey fields—`Name`, `Location`, `Synopsis`, `Notes`—is uniquely identified by the primary key. `GenreID` is not unique, but because it is the primary key of the Genres table, you need the field to establish the relationship between the two tables.

Let's take an example to see when the primary key would not exclusively identify a field. Consider an actor's biography. Because a given actor could appear on more than one show, simply knowing the `ProgramID` would not uniquely identify the value in the `Biography` field. If an actor appeared on three different programs, there would be three separate records for the actor's biography.

Note that "exclusivity" and "uniqueness" do not imply that the same value cannot appear many times in a table or in other tables in the database. For example, consider the field `Gender` in the Actors table. Obviously, there are only two possible values, male and female. So the value itself will be repeated many times throughout the table. And it's entirely possible to have a field that identifies gender in more than one table (for example, in an order-entry database, a `Gender` field in a Customers table and a `Gender` field in a Suppliers table for a supplier's representative).

But the `ActorID` for a record that describes Jennifer Lopez will uniquely identify her as a woman, and the `ActorID` for Arnold Schwarzenegger will uniquely identify him as man. There should be no other record in the database in which the gender of actors is identified as such.

Refining Field Names

Let's do a little work to improve the field names. As in database design, naming conventions are, to some extent, a matter of personal preference. But you should be aware of some useful rules. A field name should appear only once in each database. In databases in which you have much contact information, you could have several tables—Customers, Suppliers, Shippers, and so on—that have a field named `Address`. In the Classic TV database, this problem is less pronounced. But in Table 3.26, you still have duplicate fields, such as `First Name` and `Last Name` in the `Actors` and `Roles` fields.

A good way to resolve this duplication is to prefix each field with the name of the table. Some database designers like to include a table prefix for every field; others use the prefix only where they deem it necessary to avoid confusion with similar fields in other tables.

When field names get too long, a common practice is to abbreviate elements. Thus, a customer address in a Customers table becomes `CustAddr`, and the address in the Suppliers table is `SuppAddr`. Other Access experts disagree and prefer to use whole words throughout for completeness and clarity.

Here are a few important rules for naming fields:

- Identify the field fully and unambiguously.
- Use a minimal number of words.
- If you decide to use abbreviations, abbreviate consistently.
  If you abbreviate `Address` as `Addr` for one field, try to use `Addr` for `Address` throughout the database.
- Avoid acronyms where you can.
- Use the singular form (as in `CompanyName`, not `CompanyNames`).
  If the plural seems more appropriate, you might have a multivalue field that needs to be resolved.
- Spell field names without including spaces. If you need to use a separator for clarity, use an underscore instead of leaving a space (as in `UNESCO_ID`).

In Table 3.29, I've renamed the fields listed in Table 3.26 so that they more closely conform to good naming practice and convention. The names do not represent some state of perfection; other (perhaps better) choices are possible.

Table 3.29 The Fields in Table 3.26 Have Been Renamed to Follow Field-Naming Conventions

Revised Field Names

Programs	Broadcasts	Genres	Networks	Actors	Roles
ProgramID PK	ProgramID CPK/FK	GenreID PK	NetworkID PK	ActorID PK	ProgramID CPK/FK
ProgName	NetworkID CPK/FK	GenreName	Netw OfficialName	Actor FirstName	ActorID CPK/FK
GenreID FK	BrdYearStart	GenreDescr	Netw PopularName	Actor LastName	Role* FirstName
ProgLocation	BrdYearEnd		NetwFounder	ActorGender	Role LastName
ProgSynopsis			NetwNotes	ActorBio	RoleOccup
ProgNotes					Role YearStart
					Role YearEnd
					RoleNotes

Legend: PK=Primary key; FK=Foreign key; CPK=Composite primary key
*Actual field names contain no spaces (Role FirstName is RoleFirstName).

Table Types

You saw in trying to resolve all the relationships among the tables in the database examples that you had to create another type of table, the join table. Four types of tables exist:

- Data tables are the primary tables where most of your data is stored.
- Join tables, or linking tables, create a connection between two tables in a many-to-many relationship.
- Subset tables are data tables that contain fields that describe a specific subject and, thus, are better suited to having their own tables.

- Validation tables, or lookup tables, are used to validate data entered into other tables.

I've already discussed data tables and join tables at some length. I briefly discuss the other two types of tables so you can recognize them and know what they are.

Subset Tables and One-to-One Relationships

Occasionally, you'll find that you created a table that apparently represents a single subject, but for various reasons a group or subset of the records has several distinct fields.

For example, let's say you had a database of your music CDs. Most of the music genres represented—jazz, country and western, folk rock—conform to the same general table design, including fields such as `Artist`, `Year Produced`, and `Music Label`. But you also want to include your CDs of Broadway musicals. For the Broadway musicals, you might want to include the composer, the lyricist, the theater where the play opened, and so on.

Broadway musicals have composers and lyricists. Frank Sinatra, Miles Davis, and Metallica albums do not. So if you include Broadway CDs among the others, you're going to have a lot of records with several empty columns. A lot of empty fields don't usually cause major problems. But they can raise eyebrows among managers and users, who want to know just why so many records have so many empty fields.

Creating Subset Tables

Table 3.30 is the main table of music CDs. Tables 3.31 and 3.32 are subset tables for popular music and Broadway musical CDs. You create a subset table by taking the fields that are common to it out of the main table. For popular-music albums, this would include the artist and (perhaps) a `Yes/No` field for whether it's a collection of best hits. For Broadway musicals, the fields might include the composer, the lyricist, the theater in which the play originally ran, and so on.

Importantly, the fields that are common to both popular-music CDs and Broadway musicals—`Album Name`, `Date Bought`, `Retailer`, and so on—remain in the original data table, as shown in Table 3.30.

Table 3.30 The Main Table of Music CDs

DiscID	Album Name	Genre	Date Bought	Retailer	Price
1	Moronic	Rock	9/20/2004	Amazonian	$12.99
2	Dino Sings Ella	Swing	10/10/2004	Music Wearhouse	$14.99
3	My Sweet Jean	Country	10/20/2004	Towel Records	$18.99
4	Britney's Best	Pop	10/22/2004	Towel Records	$16.99
5	South Atlantic	Broadway	10/26/2004	Amazonian	$14.99
6	Before Midnight	Jazz	10/29/2004	Protozoa Records	$16.29
7	Rubber Sole	Rock	10/30/2004	Allenby's	$22.49
8	Katz	Broadway	11/17/2004	Martin's	$18.49
9	Automatic People	Rock	11/9/2004	Albright's	$17.49
10	My Fair Lacy	Broadway	11/20/2004	Music Wearhouse	$14.59

Table 3.31 A Subset Table of Popular-Music CDs

DiscID	Artist	Best Of?	<<other fields>>
1	The Moronics	No	
2	Dean Martine	No	
3	Nashville Band	Yes	
4	Britney Spores	Yes	
6	Dexter Gorton	No	
7	The Beetles	No	
9	R.E.N.	No	

Table 3.32 A Subset Table of Broadway Musical CDs

DiscID	Composer	Lyricist	Theater	<<other fields>>
5	Ricardo Roger	Oskar Hammerstone	Monaco	
8	Andrew Lloyds	Tremor Lunn	Summer Garden	
10	Fred Bottoms	Allan Learner	Mark Hollinger	

Identifying One-to-One Relationships

The Music Discs table has a one-to-one relationship with both of the subset tables. In other words, a `DiscID` can appear only once in the Music Discs table and once in a subset table. The `DiscID` is the primary key of the Music Discs table. It is both a primary key and a foreign key in the Popular Music table and the Broadway Musicals table. The `DiscID` must exist in the Music Discs table to be included in a subset table.

Validation Tables

In the sidebar "What Does Data Integrity Mean?", in the previous chapter, I mentioned that business rules put limitations on your database because of the nature of the organization and the way it conducts its operations. For example, you might have a business rule stating that no customer can have an outstanding balance of more than $10,000. There are various ways to implement business rules, most notably by assigning validation rules at the field or table levels. (Chapter 5, "Building Tables," discusses validation rules.)

Sometimes putting a business rule into effect can be assisted by constructing a validation table. For example, say that a business rule limits exports to a defined set of eight countries. You could create a validation table that includes values with just these eight countries. When you need to enter a country in the data table, your choices would be restricted to these eight values.

The values in a validation table usually change infrequently. Often the table has only two fields, a primary key that identifies each record and the value (see Table 3.33). You place the primary key of the validation table into the data table as a foreign key (see Table 3.34). The two tables have a one-to-many relationship: The `CountryID` field in the ShipCountry table can appear many times, but it can appear only once in the Countries table.

Table 3.33 A Validation Table with Two Fields

CountryID	Country
1	United States
2	Germany
3	Japan
4	South Africa

(continues)

Table 3.33 A Validation Table with Two Fields *(continued)*

CountryID	Country
5	Egypt
6	Saudi Arabia
7	India
8	Peru

Table 3.34 The Primary Key of the Validation Table Is Placed in the Related Table as a Foreign Key

OrderID (PK)	ProductID (FK)	CustomerID (FK)	Order Date	CountryID (FK)	<<other fields>>
10075	00123	002	10/16/2004	3	
10075	00124	002	10/16/2004	2	
10075	00125	002	10/16/2004	2	
10076	00124	003	10/19/2004	4	
10077	00126	002	10/21/2004	7	

PK=Primary key; FK=Foreign key

What Is Normalization?

Publisher William F. Buckley Jr. told a wonderful story about a waiter who had a complaint about Buckley's journal, *National Review*. "I love reading the articles," said the waiter. "But why do you have to use so many big words?"

A year later, Buckley met the same waiter, who thanked Buckley for taking his advice and dumbing down the vocabulary. Of course, Buckley had done no such thing. The waiter had learned the "big words" that had given him such trouble, so they were longer "big."

The database term *normalization* reminds me of that story. The word itself sounds peculiarly technical and opaque. The database theory that it defines is difficult and, for many, impenetrable. (This is by no means a put-down: Database theory is absolutely essential and fundamental to what database designers do; it is just hard to understand.)

But if you look beyond the technical language in which the theory is expressed, you'll find a body of principle that makes much sense. In fact, if you've read and understood this chapter, I think you'll be able to understand the most important rules of normalization. This section will actually serve as a review of what you already know.

An exposure to formal database theory and normalization won't necessarily improve your database design skills. But you will come across some of its terms and rules, and you shouldn't feel intimidated by them (well, no more than necessary). Hopefully this short discussion will put you in the mind-set of Mr. Buckley's waiter: *Normalization* just won't seem like a big word anymore.

As you read through the chapter, you probably noted that much of your work involved excluding duplicate values. The elimination of repeating data is the overall purpose of creating a normal form. The process of creating a database involves satisfying various levels of the normal form. You start at the first normal form, make sure your database satisfies its requirements, proceed to the second normal form, satisfy its requirements, and so on. As you satisfy each requirement, you eliminate redundancy and set up your data so that it can be processed more efficiently and so that it also is less likely to become inconsistent.

As I've indicated, each level of the normal form is stated in dense theoretical language. I try to describe them in simple language. Although there are several levels of the normal form, the first three are generally considered the most important.

First Normal Form

To meet the requirements of the first normal form, you move repeating and multivalue fields to another table. You've done that throughout the chapter. For example, consider a `Books` field (or fields) in an Authors table; the field(s) contain the authors' major works. Each author has written several books.

There are two commonsense approaches to resolving this issue. Table 3.35 shows the "repeated field" approach: You create as many additional columns as you need, one for each book. (The author names are ***not*** part of the table and are included for information purposes only.) Table 3.36 shows the "multivalue" approach: You stuff all the values (books) into one field.

Table 3.35 The "Repeated Fields" Approach to Storing Values

AuthorID	Book 1	Book 2	Book 3	<<other fields>>
1 (*Dostoevsky*)	The Brothers Karamazov	The Gambler	Crime and Punishment	
2 (*Turgenev*)	Fathers and Sons			
3 (*Tolstoy*)	War and Peace	Anna Karenina		

Table 3.36 The "Multivalue" Approach to Storing Values

AuthorID	Books	<<other fields>>
1 (*Dostoevsky*)	The Brothers Karamazov, The Gambler, Crime and Punishment	
2 (*Turgenev*)	Fathers and Sons	
3 (*Tolstoy*)	War and Peace, Anna Karenina	

Neither approach is used in relational databases. As you've seen, a solution is to create an entirely new table (see Table 3.37). You copy the primary key from the original table and include it as a foreign key. Each book is now a separate value. Each record comprises the value of the primary key of the original table and the book name.

Table 3.37 A Resolved Multivalue Field

AuthorID	Book
1 (*Dostoevsky*)	The Brothers Karamazov
1 (*Dostoevsky*)	The Gambler
1 (*Dostoevsky*)	Crime and Punishment
2 (*Turgenev*)	Fathers and Sons
3 (*Tolstoy*)	War and Peace
3 (*Tolstoy*)	Anna Karenina

This is just what you did much earlier in the chapter when we removed TV characters from the Programs table and placed them in a separate table. You placed the primary key of the Programs table, along with the character names, in an entirely new table. This new table is the child table, and the original table is the parent table.

Your work is by no means finished: You still have to decide on a primary key for the new table, identify what other fields will be included (if any), and determine how the table fits into the web of relationships that bind the database together. But you've made an important start.

Second Normal Form

To comply with the second normal form, you need to remove fields that do not depend on the entire primary key. In other words, each column should be kept with the table it describes.

Table 3.38 is similar to the Roles table you've seen, but with one addition and one assumption. The addition is that I've added a `Network` field. The assumption is that there is no separate Networks table. (Again, solely for illustrative purposes, I've included the program and actor names for each ID in parentheses.)

Recall that the table has a composite primary key—that is, the primary key comprises both the `ProgramID` and the `ActorID`. Take a look at the values in the Network column. The values are repeated for the same program. For example, there is one value of `ABC` for each value of `14` (*Bewitched*), so the table tells you twice that ABC is the network of *Bewitched*.

The reason for the redundant data is that the `Network` field depends on only one part of the primary key of the Roles table: `ProgramID`. The network has nothing to do with the other component of the primary key: `ActorID`. Thus, the `Network` field is in the wrong table; it belongs in the Programs table (see Table 3.39) because only the program identifies the network, not the actor.

Table 3.38 The Values in the `Network` Field Are Repeated Unnecessarily Because the `Network` Field Depends on Only One Component of the Composite Primary Key

Roles with `Network` Field

ProgramID (CPK/FK)	ActorID (CPK/FK)	Network	RoleFirstName	<<other fields>>
14 (*Bewitched*)	20 (*Elizabeth Montgomery*)	ABC	Samantha	
14 (*Bewitched*)	22 (*Dick York*)	ABC	Darrin	
18 (_M*A*S*H*_)	27 (*Alan Alda*)	CBS	Hawkeye	

(continues)

Table 3.38 The Values in the `Network` Field Are Repeated Unnecessarily Because the `Network` Field Depends on Only One Component of the Composite Primary Key *(continued)*

Roles with `Network` Field

ProgramID (CPK/FK)	ActorID (CPK/FK)	Network	RoleFirstName	<<other fields>>
18 (*M*A*S*H*)	28 (*McLean Stevenson*)	CBS	Henry	
18 (*M*A*S*H*)	30 (*Gary Burghoff*)	CBS	Radar	

Table 3.39 The `Network` Field Belongs in the Programs Table Because Only the Program Describes the Network

ProgramID	Program	Network	<other fields>
14	Bewitched	ABC	
15	The Odd Couple	ABC	
16	The Twilight Zone	CBS	
17	Northern Exposure	CBS	
18	M*A*S*H	CBS	

Third Normal Form

The third normal form should be mostly familiar to you. To meet its requirements, you need to remove any field that depends on other, nonkey fields.

You tackled this problem in the Classic TV database when you found a calculated field—specifically, `Years on Air`. The number in that field can be derived by subtracting the start date from the end date. In this case, the value in the calculated field depends on the values in one or more fields in the table. Thus, the field is unnecessary.

In Table 3.40, the `Total Discount` field is calculated by multiplying the discount by the unit price. This field should be eliminated because it totally depends on the `Unit Price` and `Discount` fields for its own value.

Table 3.40 The `Total Discount` Field Is a Calculated Field That Violates the Third Normal Form

Order Details with Calculated Field

OrderID	ProductID	UnitPrice	Discount	Total Discount
11600	Clam Chowder	$10.00	5%	$0.50
11600	Dried Apples	$15.00	10%	$1.50
11601	Tartar Sauce	$12.00	15%	$1.80
11601	Mozzarella	$12.00	5%	$ .60
11601	Ravioli Angelo	$15.00	5%	$ .75

Conclusion

In this chapter, you learned about the various types of relationships in a relational database. You discovered how to recognize one-to-many, many-to-many, and one-to-one relationships. You also learned how to resolve many-to-many relationships. The chapter introduced you to the various types of tables, as well as the rules of normalization. In the next chapter, you'll focus on formally creating the relationships you learned about here.

CHAPTER 4

Establishing Relationships

Although I discussed relationships at length in Chapter 3, "Understanding Relationships," I didn't show you how to formally create them in an Access database. In this chapter, you will learn how to establish relationships in the Relationships window. I also explain the three key options that are available in the Edit Relationships dialog box: most notably Enforce Referential Integrity, but also Cascade Update Related Fields and Cascade Delete Related Records.

In affairs of the heart, you'll often hear someone say, "I'm currently in a relationship." Whether the happy couple is in a state of "significant othership" or whether they are merely "erfriends" (as in "Mom and Dad, I'd like you to meet my, er, friend) remains unclear and ambiguous.

In stark contrast, relationships in Access tables are always defined with clarity, and there is no ambiguity about the rights and responsibilities of each partner. There is a plain old vanilla relationship, respectful and generous, but which still leaves both parties with plenty of independence. A relationship can be strengthened immeasurably by enforcing referential integrity, which binds the tables closely together, as if in marriage. Finally, the matrimonial vows can be transformed by enforcing cascading deletes and updates between the tables.

Viewing and Creating Relationships

In Chapter 2, "Database Design," you developed tables and fields for the Classic TV database. In Chapter 3, you identified the existing relationships between tables and developed the final field list shown in Table 4.1. (If you haven't read these two chapters, I strongly encourage you to do so before proceeding.)

Table 4.1 Classic TV Database Final Field List

Programs	Broadcasts	Genres	Networks	Actors	Roles
ProgramID PK	ProgramID CPK/FK	GenreID PK	NetworkID PK	ActorID PK	ProgramID CPK/FK
ProgName	NetworkID CPK/FK	GenreName	NetwOfficial Name	ActorFirst Name	ActorID CPK/FK
GenreID FK	BrdYearStart	GenreDescr	NetwPopular Name	ActorLast Name	RoleFirst Name
ProgLocation	BrdYearEnd		NetwFounder	ActorGender	RoleLast Name
ProgSynopsis			NetwNotes	ActorBio	RoleYear Start
ProgNotes					RoleYearEnd
					RoleNotes
					RoleOccup

Note: Actual field names contain no spaces (e.g. RoleYear Start is RoleYearStart).

When you identified all the relationships in the database, you found that some tables had many-to-many relationships. Recognizing the problems many-to-many relationships pose, you resolved them by creating linking tables. The new tables comprised two one-to-many relationships.

No tables in the Classic TV database have one-to-one relationships. Thus, all the tables are on either side of one-to-many relationships. Using the Relationships window, you can formally establish these one-to-many relationships.

Table 4.2 is a chart of the one-to-many relationships in the Classic TV database. The matrix shows the relationships the tables on the x-axis have with the tables on the y-axis. For example, viewing the relationship between the Genres and Programs tables in the first row, you can say Genres is on the one side and Programs is on the many. (Don't worry much about understanding this table—you will soon see a figure that will make these relationships much clearer.)

Table 4.2 Classic TV Database Relationships Matrix

	Programs	Genres	Networks	Actors	Roles	Broadcasts
Programs		1:M			M:1	M:1
Genres	M:1					
Networks						M:1
Actors					M:1	
Roles	1:M			1:M		
Broadcasts	1:M		1:M			

Viewing Relationships in the Relationships Window

A tour of all the features of the Relationships window will be much more meaningful to you after you create some relationships. But an overview of a typical relationships scheme should be useful now, just so you can see what you're trying to accomplish.

The Relationships window contains field lists of the various tables in the database (see Figure 4.1). All the relationships of the Classic TV database have been established with referential integrity enforced (I'll explain what that is soon) and are currently displayed. The primary keys of the tables are in bold. The table on the "one" side of the relationship has a `1` next to its primary key. An infinity sign next to the foreign key in the related table indicates that it's on the "many" side.

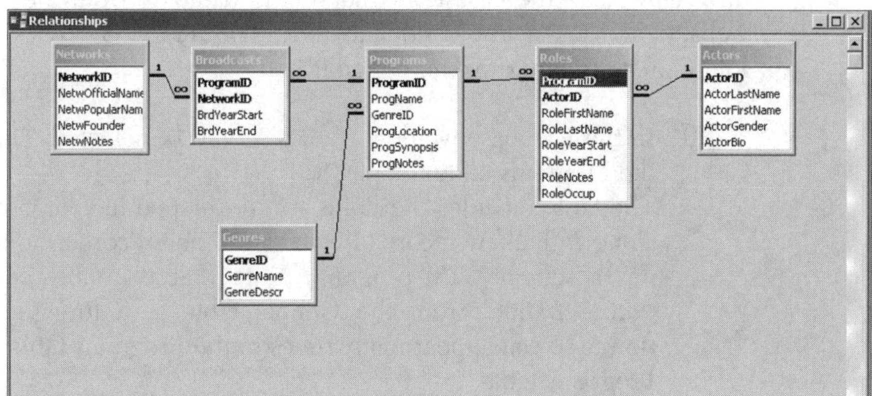

Figure 4.1 The Relationships window, with all the relationships of the Classic TV database displayed.

As one example, Genres and Programs have a one-to-many relationship. There is a `1` next to GenreID, the primary key of the primary table. In the related table of Programs, there is an infinity sign next to the foreign key `GenreID`.

All the tables have at least one relationship with one other table in the database. Thus, you can combine values from any of the tables through the nexus of relationships that exists among them. As you will see in succeeding chapters, this capability to bring values together is central to manipulating and massaging data in an Access database.

Q&A

Q: You say the primary keys are all in bold. In the Broadcasts table, both `ProgramID` and `NetworkID` are bold, yet they both have infinity signs next to them. Doesn't that mean they are foreign keys?

A: The primary key of the Broadcasts table is a composite of both the `ProgramID` and `NetworkID` fields. So although the two fields individually are foreign keys, together they are the primary key of the Broadcasts table. In other words, a field can be a foreign key and part of a primary key at the same time. These topics were discussed in Chapter 3.

Creating a Relationship in the Relationships Window

Let's start by creating a plain vanilla relationship in the Relationships window. Download the ClassicTVChap4.mdb database from the companion website at www.awprofessional.com/title/0321245458 to a convenient folder on your hard drive and open it.

1. In the Database window, Tables should be selected. Double-click the Programs table to open it.
   The table includes the fields you developed in Chapters 2 and 3, along with a few records I've added. Each record uniquely identifies a separate TV program. Note that the table contains the `GenreID` field from the Genres table as a foreign key. Each `GenreID` can appear many times in the Programs table. Close the Programs table.

2. Open the Genres table.
   The table has data about genres. Each record uniquely identifies a different genre. Each `GenreID` can appear only once in the Genres table. There are a total of eight records; there is a `GenreID 8`, but no `GenreID 9`. Close the Genres table.
   Let's formally create the relationship between the Programs and Genres tables.
3. Choose Tools, Relationships.
   I have eliminated all the relationships you saw in Figure 4.1, so you start from a clean slate.
4. In the Relationships window, select `GenreID` in the Genres field list (if it is not already selected). Drag and drop this field *directly* on the `GenreID` in the Programs field list. The Edit Relationships dialog box opens (see Figure 4.2).

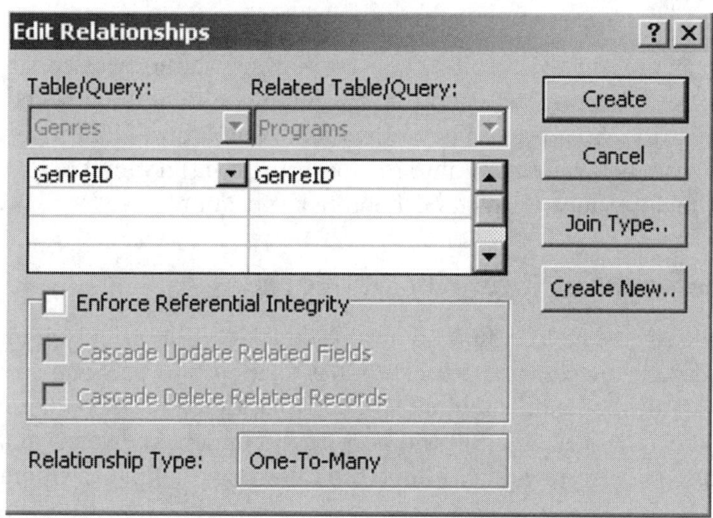

Figure 4.2 You create relationships in the Edit Relationships dialog box.

In the Edit Relationships dialog box, the `GenreID` from the Genres table is on the left (the Table/Query column) and the `GenreID` from the Programs table is on the right (Related Table/Query). `GenreID` is the primary key in the Genre table and is on the "one" side of the relationship. The `GenreID` in the Programs table is a foreign key on the many side of the relationship.

Below the small grid at the top are extremely important options I'll discuss a little later. For now, I also ask you to ignore the Join Type button, which opens the Join Properties dialog box. Joins are discussed at length in the section on multitable queries in Chapter 8, "Queries." Finally, note that at the bottom, the relationship type is One-to-Many.

5. Click Create. There's now a line between the two `GenreID` fields, showing that a relationship has been created. Close the Relationships window.

Now let's see how one of the available options, referential integrity, affects this relationship.

Referential Integrity

In an ancient Microsoft Access book whose author was apparently addicted to TV, there is a listing in the index for something called "residential integrity." So it might be worthwhile to emphasize that the term I'm about to discuss is *referential* integrity and that it has nothing to do with property maintenance or neighborhood beautification.

Referential Integrity at Work

The Access Help definition of referential integrity is "a system of rules that Microsoft Access uses to ensure that relationships between records in related tables are valid, and that you don't accidentally delete or change related data." That's a start. But the best way to understand referential integrity is to see it at work, which I hope the following example accomplishes.

1. In the Database window, click the Forms tab and open the Programs form.
   Why am I asking you to look at a form based on the Programs table instead of the Programs table itself? Although tables are the foundation of your database, you usually use forms to enter, edit, and delete data. (These issues are further developed in Chapter 6, "Enter, Edit, and Display Data.") Because forms are more versatile, I've used a form to help you understand how referential integrity works.

2. Maximize the Programs form. Right-click in any empty area of the form and choose Datasheet View from the shortcut menu (you can also choose View, Datasheet View).
   The form is now in Datasheet view, so it appears as a grid. It has the same columns, the same rows, and the same values as the underlying Programs table. For now, you can consider the Programs form to be the equivalent of the Programs table.
3. In the first record, click in the `GenreID` column. Click the drop-down arrow to see the available values (see Figure 4.3).

ProgramID	Program	GenreID	Location	
1	The Andy Griffith Show	1	Mayberry, NC	Sheriff Andy Taylor, a widower,
2	Happy Days			
3	The Bob Newhart Show			Psychiatrist Bob Hartley tends
4	Newhart		nt	
5	Sanford & Son			Fred Sanford and his son Lamc
6	I Love Lucy			Wacky but lovable Lucy Ricard
7	The Lucy Show		n Francisco, CA	Lucy
9	Matlock			
10	Mister Ed			Ed the talking horse always ha
11	The Mary Tyler Moore Show	5	Minneapolis	Single, turning 30, Mary Richar
12	Rhoda	5	New York	Rhoda is happily married, then
13	The Dick Van Dyke Show	5	New Rochelle, NY	Rob Petrie, head comedy write
14	Bewitched	7	Westport, CT	There's toil and trouble, but lots

1	Rural Comedy
2	Social Comedy
3	General Drama
4	Police Drama
5	Urban Comedy
6	Hospital Drama
7	General Comed
8	Miscellaneous

Figure 4.3 You would ordinarily use the combo box for `GenreID` to select and display the actual genre name such as Rural Comedy instead of the meaningless ID number. I have shown ID numbers in the `GenreID` field only for purposes of this example.

   I created this little box of values, known as a combo box, so you can see the names of the genres. I was able to create it because the Genres and Programs tables have matching data through the `GenreID` field. Note that the box contains all the values from the Genres table. The design of this combo box is artificial, and I'm using it only for teaching purposes. (Combo boxes are discussed in Chapter 11, "Forms/Subforms.")
4. Edit the value in `GenreID` for the first record to **`9`**.
   As you saw from the combo box, there is no `GenreID 9` in the Genres table.
5. Click anywhere in the next record. Access has saved your change. Even though in the previous section you established a relationship between the Programs and Genres tables, Access allowed you to change the `GenreID` to a value that is not in the Genres table.
6. Edit the `GenreID` in the first row back to **`1`**. Close the form.

7. Choose Tools, Relationships to open the Relationships window.
8. Double-click the line between Genres and Programs to open the Edit Relationships dialog box.
   You can also right-click the line and choose Edit, Relationships.
9. Select Enforce Referential Integrity.
   For future reference, note that the Cascade Update Related Fields and Cascade Delete Related Records options, which had been previously grayed out, are now available because referential integrity is enforced.
10. Click OK.
    Look at the line that connects the field lists of Programs and Genres in the Relationships window. As in Figure 4.1, there is now a `1` near the primary key on the "one" side of the relationship. There is also an infinity sign on the "many" side.
11. Close the Relationships window.
12. From the Database window, open the Programs form. Right-click the form and choose Datasheet View from the shortcut menu.
13. Edit the `GenreID` in the first record (for `The Andy Griffith Show`) to `9`. Click in the next record.
    Figure 4.4 shows you the error message you get. Because referential integrity is now enforced, Access won't let you edit the value because there is no record with the `GenreID 9` in the Genres table.
14. Click OK. Press Esc, or edit the `GenreID` back to `1` and close the form.

Figure 4.4 Because referential integrity is enforced, Access allows you to enter only values in the foreign key of the Programs table that are in the primary key of the Genres table.

The Rules of Referential Integrity

I think you can see that enforcing referential integrity has enormous consequences for data integrity. It can ensure that no customer is entered in an order that isn't on an approved customer list. It can make certain no product can be bought whose supplier isn't included on a list of approved suppliers. It can make sure no product can be offered for sale that isn't in a table of available products.

Let me state the rules of referential integrity more formally.

The Necessary Conditions

The following conditions must be in place to enforce referential integrity:

- The matching key from the primary table (in the case you just saw, `GenreID`) must be a primary key or a unique index.
  Let's not worry about indexes right now, but rather focus on the fact that `GenreID` is indeed the primary key of the primary table.
- The related fields must have the same data type.
  There is one extremely important proviso to this rule: A field with an `AutoNumber` data type can be related to a field that has the `Number` data type and a `FieldSize` property setting of `Long Integer`.
  It is this qualification that you just saw at work. The `GenreID` field in the primary table of Genre has the `AutoNumber` data type. The `GenreID` field in the related table Programs has the `Number` data type and the field size of `Long Integer`. I introduced data types in Chapter 1, "Getting Started." A discussion of the `FieldSize` property awaits you in Chapter 5, "Building Tables." But I think you'll recall from high school math that an integer is a whole number and doesn't contain a fraction. Thus, values of `1`, `2`, `3`, and so on in the primary key of the primary table match values of `1`, `2`, `3`, and so on in the foreign key of the related table if the data type is `Number` and the field size is `Long Integer`. Thus, referential integrity can be enforced.
- Both tables are in the same Microsoft Access database.

The Consequent Outcomes

When referential integrity is in force, the following applies:

- You can't enter a value in the foreign key of the related table that doesn't exist in the primary key of the primary table.
  You just saw an example of this: The `GenreID` of `9` wasn't in the primary table, so you couldn't enter it in the related table.

There's one more bit to this rule: You *can* enter a `Null` value in the foreign key, unless the `Required` property for the field is `Yes` (see Chapter 5 for more on the `Required` property).

- You can't change a primary key value in the primary table if that record has related records in the foreign table.
  If you stick with artificial primary keys that have an `AutoNumber` data type and cannot be edited, this rule will not be an issue for you.
- You can't delete a record on the "one" side of the relationship when there are related records in the "many" side of the relationship.

Related Records Can't Be Deleted

Let's look at an example of how related records on the "many" side of the relationship prevent you from deleting a record on the one side when referential integrity is enforced.

1. In the Database window, open the Programs form. Right-click in the form and select Datasheet View.
2. Select the `GenreID` column.
3. Click the A-Z button for an ascending sort.
   The `GenreIDs` are in ascending order. Note that at least two records have the value of `1`.
4. In the Database window, open the Genres table.
5. Minimize the Database window. Choose Window, Tile Horizontally.
6. Select the `ID#1 (Rural Comedy)` record in the Genres table. Press Delete.
   The warning message (see Figure 4.5) tells you that you cannot delete the record because there are related records in the Programs table. The Genres tables is on the "one" side of the relationship, and several records in the Programs table on the "many" side are rural comedies.
7. Click OK.
8. Close the Programs form; if asked, do not save the design changes. Close the Genres table.

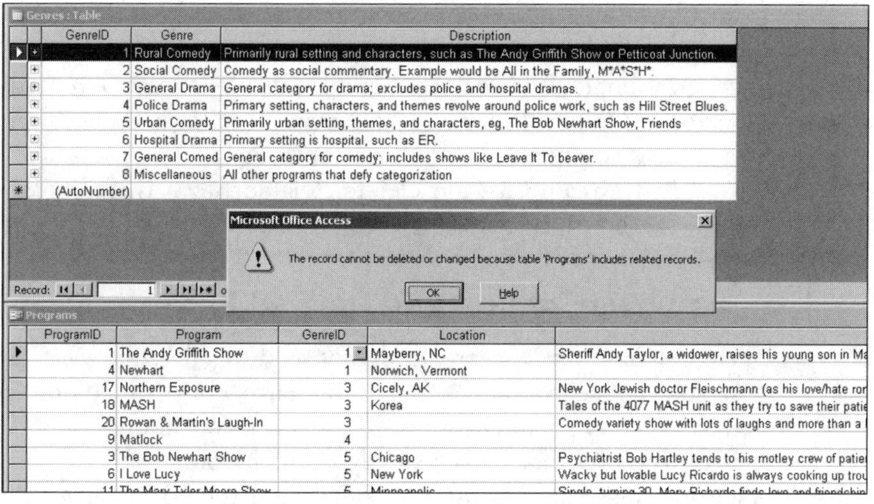

Figure 4.5 Genre `ID#1` cannot be deleted in the Genres table because there are related records in the Programs table. (It doesn't matter whether the Programs table is positioned above the Genres table or vice versa.)

Overriding Referential Integrity

As you can see, the rules of referential integrity are extremely strict. Although they do help ensure the maintenance of data integrity, they can make it difficult to manage your database. For example, as the exercise you just did illustrates, you cannot delete a record in a primary table that has related records in a foreign table. But what if you *want* to delete such a record? Under what circumstances can it be deleted, and what are the consequences of taking this action?

Two options mitigate the strict rules of referential integrity: Cascade Update Related Fields and Cascade Delete Related Records. These choices are available from the Edit Relationships dialog box, and I describe them shortly. But let me emphasize at this point that it is by no means certain that you will want or need to implement either option.

Cascade Update Related Fields is relatively noncontroversial. Furthermore, if you exclusively use `AutoNumber` (that is, artificial) primary keys, it is irrelevant.

Cascade Delete Related Records, however, can be applied whether you use artificial or natural primary keys. It can help to maintain data integrity, but it also has the potential to delete a swath of records from your database. Opinions vary on whether its advantages outweigh its disadvantages, and you might decide not to apply it.

I first explain Cascade Delete Related Records simply because I can show you how it works using the currently open Classic TV database.

The Power of Cascade Deleted Records

The relationships you create tightly bind together the various tables of a database. Thus two tables that do not have a direct relationship can affect each other in profound ways: An action taken in one table can set off a chain reaction that moves swiftly through your database via these interlocking links. As I've implied, deleting a record in one table when the Cascade Delete Related Records option is in force can have major repercussions throughout the many tables of your database.

Cascading Deletes in Two Tables

Before I show you the devastating potential of Cascade Delete, let me start with a simple example of cascading deletes in two tables.

1. Choose Tools, Relationships to open the Relationships window.
2. Double-click the line between Genres and Programs to open the Edit Relationships dialog box.
3. Select Cascade Delete Related Records by clicking the check box. Click OK.
4. Close the Relationships window.
5. If necessary, maximize the Database window. Open the Programs table and then open the Genres tables. Minimize the Database window.
6. Choose Window, Tile Horizontally.
   It doesn't matter whether the Programs table is above the Genres table or vice versa.

7. Select `ID#1 (Rural Comedy)` record in the Genres table. Press Delete.
   This time you get a message telling you that you are about to delete one record in the table, as well as records in related tables (see Figure 4.6). Note also that the `GenreID 1` in the Genres table has been deleted.

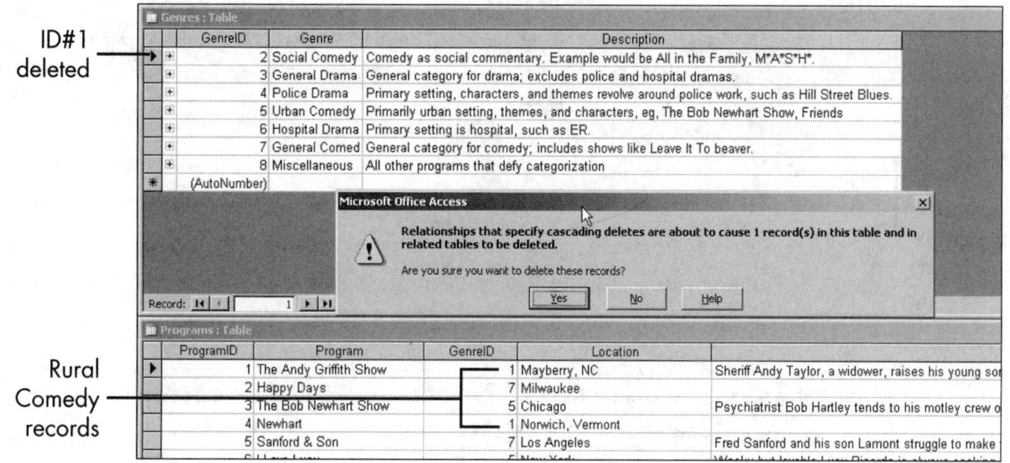

Figure 4.6 A warning message tells you that you are about to delete records in the current table and in related tables. Program IDs `1` and `4` are related records in the Programs table with values of `1` (for rural comedy) in the `GenreID` field.

8. Click Yes to confirm the delete.
   The record is deleted in the Genres table, which is on the "one" side of the relationship. In the related Programs table, the two rural comedy records in Figure 4.6 are now also shown as having been deleted (see Figure 4.7). These records will not be there the next time you open the Programs table.
9. Close both tables and close the database.

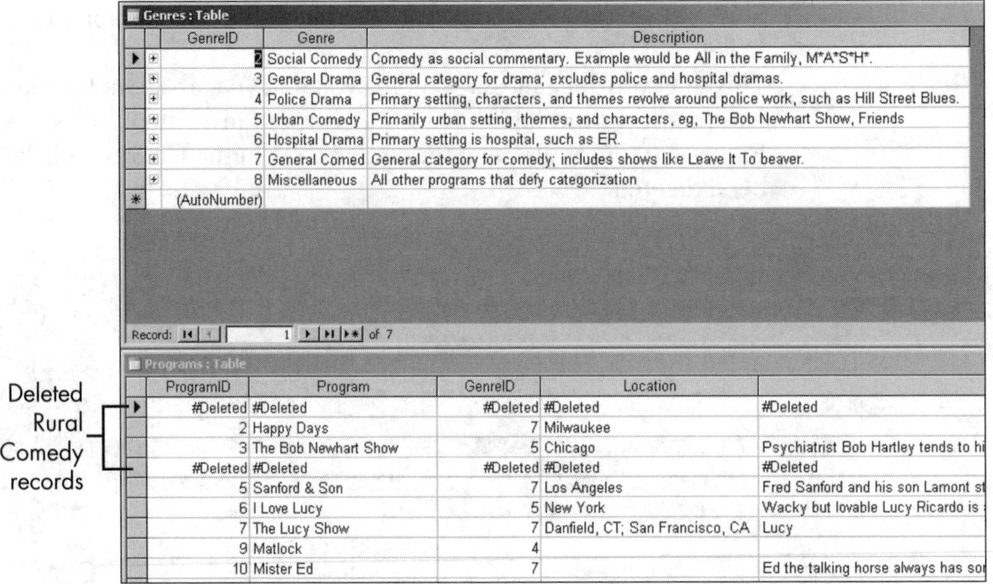

Genres : Table

GenreID	Genre	Description
2	Social Comedy	Comedy as social commentary. Example would be All in the Family, M*A*S*H*.
3	General Drama	General category for drama; excludes police and hospital dramas.
4	Police Drama	Primary setting, characters, and themes revolve around police work, such as Hill Street Blues.
5	Urban Comedy	Primarily urban setting, themes, and characters, eg, The Bob Newhart Show, Friends
6	Hospital Drama	Primary setting is hospital, such as ER.
7	General Comed	General category for comedy; includes shows like Leave It To beaver.
8	Miscellaneous	All other programs that defy categorization
(AutoNumber)		

Record: 1 of 7

Programs : Table

ProgramID	Program	GenreID	Location	
#Deleted	#Deleted	#Deleted	#Deleted	#Deleted
2	Happy Days	7	Milwaukee	
3	The Bob Newhart Show	5	Chicago	Psychiatrist Bob Hartley tends to hi
#Deleted	#Deleted	#Deleted	#Deleted	#Deleted
5	Sanford & Son	7	Los Angeles	Fred Sanford and his son Lamont st
6	I Love Lucy	5	New York	Wacky but lovable Lucy Ricardo is
7	The Lucy Show	7	Danfield, CT; San Francisco, CA	Lucy
9	Matlock	4		
10	Mister Ed	7		Ed the talking horse always has so

Figure 4.7 Cascade Delete Related Records is selected, so when you delete a record on the "one" side of the relationship, records in the related table are deleted as well.

Cascading Deletes in Multiple Tables

This next example demonstrates the enormous force of Cascade Delete Related Records in a database bound together by a nexus of one-to-many relationships. I much prefer examples that have you do the work over those that give you a complicated narrative. But a comprehensive example of the power of the Cascade Deleted Related Records option involves numerous steps, as well as much tiling and scrolling, so I describe the process with figures. I also use the Northwind sample database instead of the Classic TV database because it gives you a better sense of the impact this option can have.

Consider the following example from the order-entry model of the Northwind database. You have Suppliers and Products tables. The Suppliers and Products tables have matching data in the `SupplierID` field. `SupplierID` is the primary key in the primary table of Suppliers; `SupplierID` is also a foreign key in the Products table. The two tables have a one-to-many relationship: A single supplier can supply many products, but any one product can have only one supplier (see Figure 4.8). Importantly, referential integrity has been enforced.

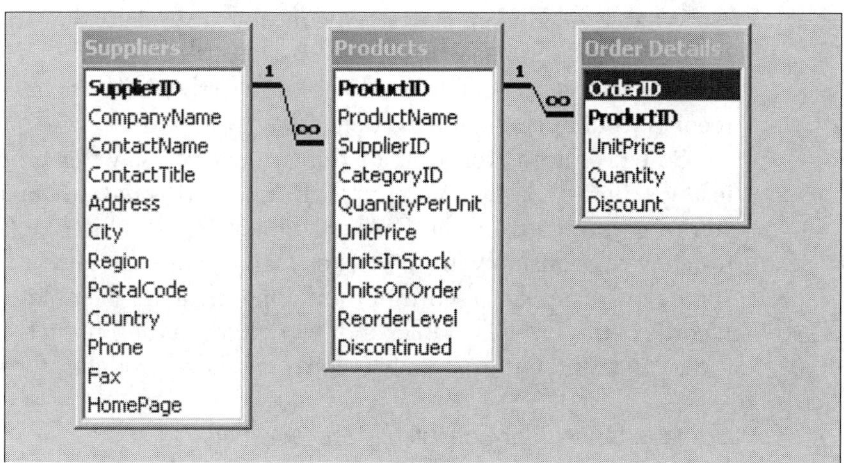

Figure 4.8 Three related tables of the Northwind database in the Relationships window.

One of your important suppliers, Tokyo Traders, goes out of business. You open the Suppliers table (or, more likely, the Suppliers form—again, let's leave that discussion for Chapter 6) and try to delete the record.

But Access won't let you. This supplier sold you several products, so there are several records with this supplier in the Products field (see Figure 4.9). Because a one-to-many relationship exists between the two tables and referential integrity has been enforced, Access won't let you delete a record on the "one" side of the relationship when there are related records on the "many" side.

Suppliers : Table

Supplier ID	Company Name	Contact Name	Contact Title	Address	City
17	Svensk Sjöföda AB	Michael Björn	Sales Representative	Brovallavägen 231	Stockholm
4	Tokyo Traders	Yoshi Nagase	Marketing Manager	9-8 Sekimai	Tokyo
22	Zaanse Snoepfabriek	Dirk Luchte	Accounting Manager	Verkoop	Zaandam

Record: 1 of 29

Tokyo Traders record

Products : Table

Product ID	Product Name	Supplier	Category	Quantity Per Unit	Unit Price	Units In Stock
37	Gravad lax	Svensk Sjöföda AB	Seafood	12 - 500 g pkgs.	$26.00	[illegible]
73	Röd Kaviar	Svensk Sjöföda AB	Seafood	24 - 150 g jars	$15.00	[illegible]
74	Longlife Tofu	Tokyo Traders	Produce	5 kg pkg.	$10.00	[illegible]
10	Ikura	Tokyo Traders	Seafood	12 - 200 ml jars	$31.00	[illegible]
9	Mishi Kobe Niku	Tokyo Traders	Meat/Poultry	18 - 500 g pkgs.	$97.00	[illegible]
48	Chocolade	Zaanse Snoepfabriek	Confections	10 pkgs.	$12.75	[illegible]
47	Zaanse koeken	Zaanse Snoepfabriek	Confections	10 - 4 oz boxes	$9.50	[illegible]

Record: 1 of 77

Tokyo Traders products

Figure 4.9 The supplier Tokyo Traders (`ID#4`) has three related records in the Products table.

What would happen if you were able to delete the Tokyo Traders record in the Suppliers table? If you chose the Cascade Delete Related Records option, the delete would cascade to the Products table, and those records would presumably be deleted as well.

So far, I haven't told you anything new—you saw this process at work just now in the Classic TV example. But in Northwind, what will happen if you remove records in the Products table? The Products table has a one-to-many relationship with the Order Details table (refer to Figure 4.8). If you delete a supplier record in the Suppliers table, the delete cascades to records in the Products table, and the deletes in the Products table will, in turn, delete the Order Details records for those products. Or will they?

Cascade Delete Not Consistently Implemented

Let's see how these phenomena play out under various circumstances. Let's assume that the relationships between Products and Suppliers, and Suppliers and Order Details are as shown in Table 4.3.

Table 4.3 Relationships and Options Selected in Northwind Database

	Suppliers-Products	Products-Order Details
Relationship*	Yes	Yes
Enforce Referential Integrity	Yes	Yes
Cascade Delete Related Records	Yes	No

*I've included Relationship in the table just for clarity. As you know, you can't enforce referential integrity unless a relationship has already been established.

Now let's assume that you try to delete a record in the Suppliers table. At first, it would seem that there would be no problem in deleting it because Cascade Delete Related Records is in force between Suppliers and Products (refer to Table 4.3). But note that Cascade Delete Related Records is *not* in force for the Products-Order Details relationship. So if you try to delete the Tokyo Traders record in the Suppliers table, you won't be able to.

Why? Because records in the Order Details table are related to records in the Products table, which, in turn, are related to the Tokyo Traders record. The records in the Products table *cannot* be deleted because referential integrity is enforced between Products and Order Details, but Cascade Delete is not chosen.

Because the products records cannot be deleted, the Tokyo Traders record in the Suppliers table cannot be deleted, either. As you can see, it's entirely possible that you'll be unsuccessful at deleting a record in a table because of a relationship that seems far removed from it. But that's part of the beauty of a relational database: This interconnectedness enhances data integrity.

Cascade Delete Consistently Implemented

Suppose you change the relationship between Products and Order Details so that Cascade Delete Related Records is now in force between these two tables as well. In that case, if you delete Tokyo Traders in the Suppliers table, its products are also deleted in the Products table, and the order details in which those products were included are also deleted (see Figure 4.10).

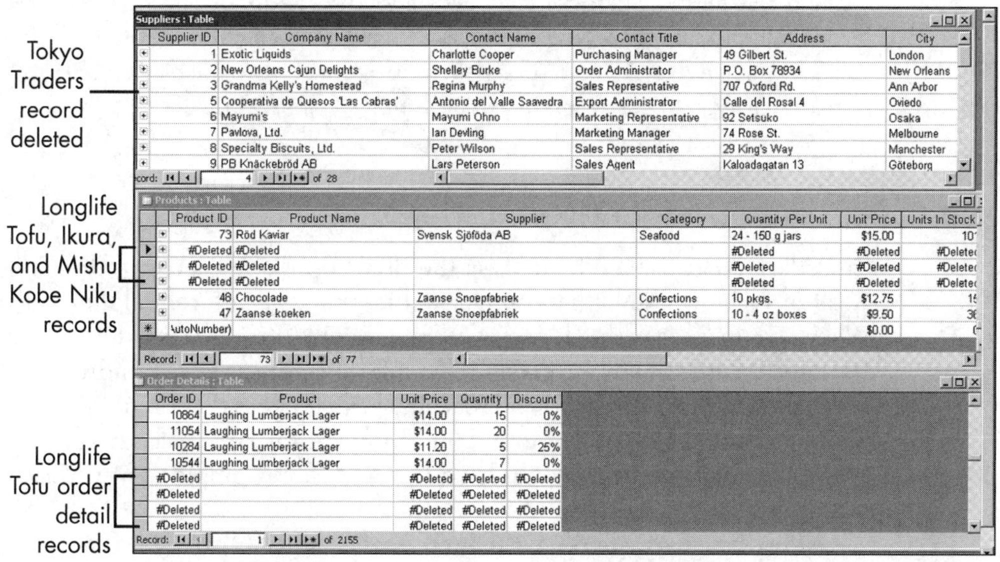

Figure 4.10 This example assumes that Cascade Delete Related Records is implemented between both Suppliers/Products and Products/Order Details. The delete of the Tokyo Traders record (`ID#4`) in the Suppliers table cascades to the Products table, deleting three product records. Among them is Longlife Tofu, whose records are deleted from the Order Details table.

Q & A

Q: Wait a minute. Some of those order details records you just deleted might be for orders that haven't yet been paid for—or even shipped. And I might still have some unsold Tokyo Traders products hanging around in my warehouse. Just because a supplier goes out of business doesn't mean I haven't already sold some of its products, or might not do so in the future. So why am I deleting these records in the Products and Order Details tables? Don't I still want those records for discontinued products to be in my database?

A: You're making the mistake of trying to be thoughtful and realistic when I'm trying to teach you database principles in a vacuum.

Seriously, all kinds of database design issues must be considered in creating a fully functioning order entry system, and these go far beyond this brief introduction to database design. It might well turn out that your solutions demand that Cascade Delete Related Records not be implemented. But I want you to understand how the various options work.

Cascade Update Related Fields

Cascade Update Related Fields is the other option available in the Edit Relationships window that mitigates the rules of referential integrity. When compared with the potent and controversial Cascade Delete Related Records, it will probably seem a little colorless and humdrum. As I indicated earlier, this option affects only primary keys that do not have an `AutoNumber` data type. If you find the argument for `AutoNumber` primary keys convincing, you might not have much reason to implement Cascade Update Related Fields.

Nevertheless, if you do use natural (that is, non-`AutoNumber`) primary keys, this selection could prove useful. Here's an example that shows the option at work.

1. Make a copy of the sample `Northwind.mdb` database. (It's in a folder named something like `Program Files\Microsoft Office\OFFICE11\SAMPLES`, or use Windows Search to find the file.)

It is always a good idea to make a copy of the Northwind sample database to work with. In this case, it is especially important because you will be slightly modifying one of the tables.

2. Open the database. In the Main Switchboard, click Display Database Window.
3. Choose Tools, Relationships to view the Relationships window.
4. Double-click the line between Customers and Orders.
5. In the Edit Relationships dialog box, note that Cascade Update Related Fields is enforced. Click Cancel.
6. Close the Relationships window.
7. In the Database window, open the Customers table. Note that the `CustomerID` is the primary key; it is a `Text` field that consists of five letters.
8. In the Database window, open the Orders table in Design view. Click in the `CustomerID` row. In the lower pane, click the Lookup tab and click in Display Control. Open the drop-down menu and choose Text Box. Save your changes.

   I had you modify the display for the `CustomerID` field so that the `CustomerID` itself is shown instead of the Customer name. (Don't worry if you have no idea why or what you just did. In the next chapter, you'll learn about lookup fields, and you'll understand that I merely asked you to change the display of the field so you can see the actual values that are stored.)
9. Click View to switch to Datasheet view. Select the Customer field. Choose an Ascending (A-Z) sort so that the customer IDs are in alphabetical order.
10. Minimize the Database window.
11. Choose Window, Tile Horizontally.

    Your screen should look like Figure 4.11. (If your Customers table is below the Orders table, that's fine—the table order doesn't make any difference.)

    Note that the first record in the Customers table has the primary key `ALFKI`. Note that the first six orders in the Orders table were made to this customer.
12. In the first record of the *Customers* table, edit the value to **`ALFZZ`**.

Customers : Table

Customer ID	Company Name	Contact Name	Contact Title	Address	
ALFKI	Alfreds Futterkiste	Maria Anders	Sales Representative	Obere Str. 57	Be
ANATR	Ana Trujillo Emparedados y helados	Ana Trujillo	Owner	Avda. de la Constitución 2222	Mé
ANTON	Antonio Moreno Taquería	Antonio Moreno	Owner	Mataderos 2312	Mé
AROUT	Around the Horn	Thomas Hardy	Sales Representative	120 Hanover Sq.	Lor
BERGS	Berglunds snabbköp	Christina Berglund	Order Administrator	Berguvsvägen 8	Lul
BLAUS	Blauer See Delikatessen	Hanna Moos	Sales Representative	Forsterstr. 57	Ma
BLONP	Blondel père et fils	Frédérique Citeaux	Marketing Manager	24, place Kléber	Str
BOLID	Bólido Comidas preparadas	Martín Sommer	Owner	C/ Araquil, 67	Ma
BONAP	Bon app'	Laurence Lebihan	Owner	12, rue des Bouchers	Ma
BOTTM	Bottom-Dollar Markets	Elizabeth Lincoln	Accounting Manager	23 Tsawassen Blvd.	Tsa
BSBEV	B's Beverages	Victoria Ashworth	Sales Representative	Fauntleroy Circus	Lor
CACTU	Cactus Comidas para llevar	Patricio Simpson	Sales Agent	Cerrito 333	Bu
CENTC	Centro comercial Moctezuma	Francisco Chang	Marketing Manager	Sierras de Granada 9993	Mé
CHOPS	Chop-suey Chinese	Yang Wang	Owner	Hauptstr. 29	Be

Record: 1 of 91

Orders : Table

Order ID	Customer	Employee	Order Date	Required Date	Shipped Date	Ship Via	Freight	Ship N
10643	ALFKI	Suyama, Michael	25-Aug-1997	22-Sep-1997	02-Sep-1997	Speedy Express	$29.46	Alfreds Futterkiste
10692	ALFKI	Peacock, Margaret	03-Oct-1997	31-Oct-1997	13-Oct-1997	United Package	$61.02	Alfreds Futterkiste
10702	ALFKI	Peacock, Margaret	13-Oct-1997	24-Nov-1997	21-Oct-1997	Speedy Express	$23.94	Alfreds Futterkiste
10835	ALFKI	Davolio, Nancy	15-Jan-1998	12-Feb-1998	21-Jan-1998	Federal Shipping	$69.53	Alfreds Futterkiste
10952	ALFKI	Davolio, Nancy	16-Mar-1998	27-Apr-1998	24-Mar-1998	Speedy Express	$40.42	Alfreds Futterkiste
11011	ALFKI	Leverling, Janet	09-Apr-1998	07-May-1998	13-Apr-1998	Speedy Express	$1.21	Alfreds Futterkiste
10308	ANATR	King, Robert	18-Sep-1996	16-Oct-1996	24-Sep-1996	Federal Shipping	$1.61	Ana Trujillo Empa
10625	ANATR	Leverling, Janet	08-Aug-1997	05-Sep-1997	14-Aug-1997	Speedy Express	$43.90	Ana Trujillo Empa
10759	ANATR	Leverling, Janet	28-Nov-1997	26-Dec-1997	12-Dec-1997	Federal Shipping	$11.99	Ana Trujillo Empa
10926	ANATR	Peacock, Margaret	04-Mar-1998	01-Apr-1998	11-Mar-1998	Federal Shipping	$39.92	Ana Trujillo Empa
10365	ANTON	Leverling, Janet	27-Nov-1996	25-Dec-1996	02-Dec-1996	United Package	$22.00	Antonio Moreno T
10507	ANTON	King, Robert	15-Apr-1997	13-May-1997	22-Apr-1997	Speedy Express	$47.45	Antonio Moreno T
10535	ANTON	Peacock, Margaret	13-May-1997	10-Jun-1997	21-May-1997	Speedy Express	$15.64	Antonio Moreno T
10573	ANTON	King, Robert	19-Jun-1997	17-Jul-1997	20-Jun-1997	Federal Shipping	$84.84	Antonio Moreno T

Record: 1 of 830

Figure 4.11 The `CustomerID` identifies the customer in both tables.

13. Click anywhere in the next row. In the Orders table, the `CustomerID` has been updated to `ALFZZ` (see Figure 4.12).
14 Close the Customers and Orders tables. If you're asked to save design changes, click No.

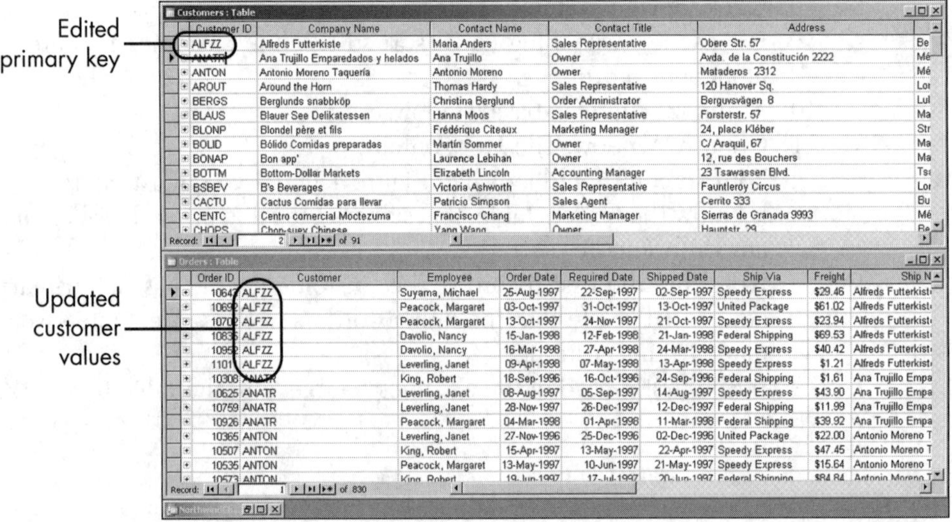

Customers : Table

Customer ID	Company Name	Contact Name	Contact Title	Address	
ALFZZ	Alfreds Futterkiste	Maria Anders	Sales Representative	Obere Str. 57	Be
ANATR	Ana Trujillo Emparedados y helados	Ana Trujillo	Owner	Avda. de la Constitución 2222	Mé
ANTON	Antonio Moreno Taquería	Antonio Moreno	Owner	Mataderos 2312	Mé
AROUT	Around the Horn	Thomas Hardy	Sales Representative	120 Hanover Sq.	Lor
BERGS	Berglunds snabbköp	Christina Berglund	Order Administrator	Berguvsvägen 8	Lul
BLAUS	Blauer See Delikatessen	Hanna Moos	Sales Representative	Forsterstr. 57	Ma
BLONP	Blondel père et fils	Frédérique Citeaux	Marketing Manager	24, place Kléber	Str
BOLID	Bólido Comidas preparadas	Martín Sommer	Owner	C/ Araquil, 67	Ma
BONAP	Bon app'	Laurence Lebihan	Owner	12, rue des Bouchers	Ma
BOTTM	Bottom-Dollar Markets	Elizabeth Lincoln	Accounting Manager	23 Tsawassen Blvd.	Tsa
BSBEV	B's Beverages	Victoria Ashworth	Sales Representative	Fauntleroy Circus	Lor
CACTU	Cactus Comidas para llevar	Patricio Simpson	Sales Agent	Cerrito 333	Bu
CENTC	Centro comercial Moctezuma	Francisco Chang	Marketing Manager	Sierras de Granada 9993	Mé
CHOPS	Chop-suey Chinese	Yang Wang	Owner	Hauptstr. 29	Be

Record: 2 of 91

Orders : Table

Order ID	Customer	Employee	Order Date	Required Date	Shipped Date	Ship Via	Freight	Ship N
10643	ALFZZ	Suyama, Michael	25-Aug-1997	22-Sep-1997	02-Sep-1997	Speedy Express	$29.46	Alfreds Futterkiste
10692	ALFZZ	Peacock, Margaret	03-Oct-1997	31-Oct-1997	13-Oct-1997	United Package	$61.02	Alfreds Futterkiste
10702	ALFZZ	Peacock, Margaret	13-Oct-1997	24-Nov-1997	21-Oct-1997	Speedy Express	$23.94	Alfreds Futterkiste
10835	ALFZZ	Davolio, Nancy	15-Jan-1998	12-Feb-1998	21-Jan-1998	Federal Shipping	$69.53	Alfreds Futterkiste
10952	ALFZZ	Davolio, Nancy	16-Mar-1998	27-Apr-1998	24-Mar-1998	Speedy Express	$40.42	Alfreds Futterkiste
11011	ALFZZ	Leverling, Janet	09-Apr-1998	07-May-1998	13-Apr-1998	Speedy Express	$1.21	Alfreds Futterkiste
10308	ANATR	King, Robert	18-Sep-1996	16-Oct-1996	24-Sep-1996	Federal Shipping	$1.61	Ana Trujillo Empa
10625	ANATR	Leverling, Janet	08-Aug-1997	05-Sep-1997	14-Aug-1997	Speedy Express	$43.90	Ana Trujillo Empa
10759	ANATR	Leverling, Janet	28-Nov-1997	26-Dec-1997	12-Dec-1997	Federal Shipping	$11.99	Ana Trujillo Empa
10926	ANATR	Peacock, Margaret	04-Mar-1998	01-Apr-1998	11-Mar-1998	Federal Shipping	$39.92	Ana Trujillo Empa
10365	ANTON	Leverling, Janet	27-Nov-1996	25-Dec-1996	02-Dec-1996	United Package	$22.00	Antonio Moreno T
10507	ANTON	King, Robert	15-Apr-1997	13-May-1997	22-Apr-1997	Speedy Express	$47.45	Antonio Moreno T
10535	ANTON	Peacock, Margaret	13-May-1997	10-Jun-1997	21-May-1997	Speedy Express	$15.64	Antonio Moreno T
10573	ANTON	King, Robert	19-Jun-1997	17-Jul-1997	20-Jun-1997	Federal Shipping	$84.84	Antonio Moreno T

Record: 1 of 830

Figure 4.12 Because Cascade Update Related Fields is in force, you can edit a primary key with related records. The related records are updated with the change.

The Mechanics of the Relationship Window

A few techniques and tools are worth mentioning when using the Relationships window. I'll get to those in a moment. But let me first emphasize that this window can generate what could be the most misinterpreted message in Access.

When you close the Relationships window after making changes, Access asks if you want to save them (see Figure 4.13). This question applies *only* to the layout changes you've made—the field lists you have added, deleted, or moved around. It has no effect whatsoever on the relationships you created and the edits you made on them. These were saved as you opened and used the various dialog boxes.

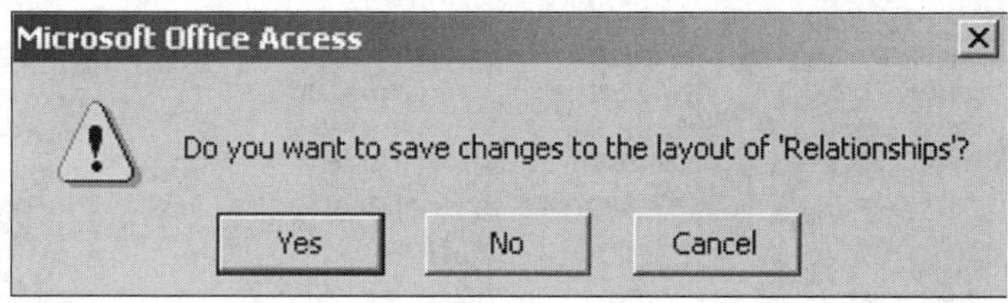

Figure 4.13 This message applies only to the layout of the Relationships window, not to any of the relationships or relationship options you have set.

Now let's move on and discuss various features of the Relationships window that might prove useful.

Show Buttons

The Relationships window has three important Show buttons:

- ***Show Table***—You can use this button to add field lists to the Relationships window. The Show Table dialog box will appear, from which you can select field lists to add them to the window.
- ***Show Direct Relationships***—Let's say you add a single table to the window. If you click this button, all the tables that have relationships with it are added to the window and displayed. If there are other tables in the window and you want to show the direct relationships for only one, select it and then click the button (see Figure 4.14). If you're already showing all relationships, clicking the button has no effect.

Note that choosing this option does not hide any field lists already added to the window. It reveals hidden field lists that are related, but tables that are already visible stay visible.

- ***Show All Relationships***—This button means what it says: It shows all the relationships in the database.

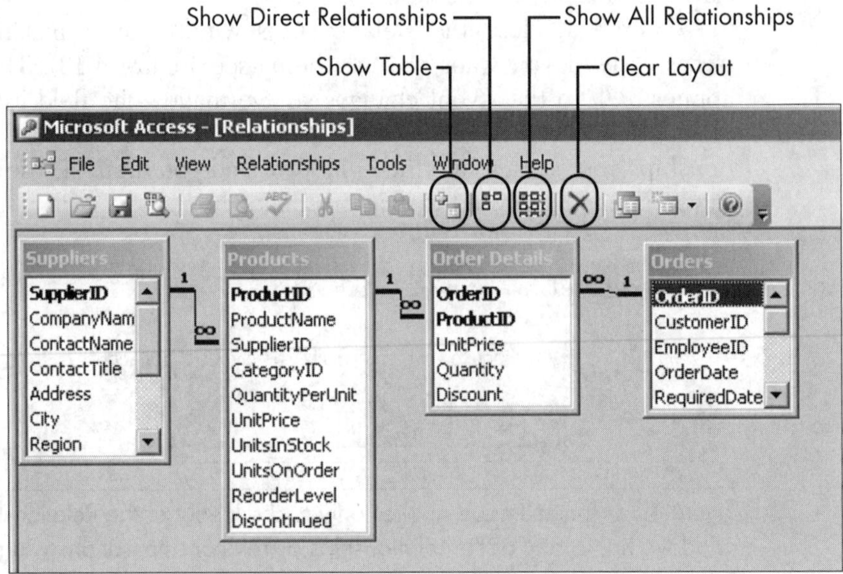

Figure 4.14 Beginning with the layout shown in Figure 4.8, the Orders field list was added by selecting Order Details and clicking the Show Direct Relationships button.

Print the Relationships Window

In early versions of Access, users struggled to print the Relationships window. This shortcoming has now been rectified. In the Relationships window, choose File-Print Relationships. Access creates a report that displays the Relationships window, which you can print and save like any other report. The report is not updated, however, for any changes you make in the Relationships windows afterward; you must create another report.

TIP If you have more than a few field lists, you'll want a landscape orientation. In Print Preview, click Setup on the toolbar, click the Page tab, and choose Landscape Orientation.

Test Data and Conclusion

In Chapters 2, 3, and this chapter, you learned some of the principles of database design. The purpose was to teach you basic relational database principles and give you an overall sense of database design. But please remember that, in my attempt to make a coherent presentation of reasonable length, I've left out important steps in creating a real-world database.

For example, I've mentioned nothing about testing your database. You will want to use *test data* to be sure your database can generate the required queries, forms, and reports that meet your mission objectives. You will want to use both "good" test data and "bad" test data. Good test data—data that is accurate and meets data integrity standards—will show you whether you can enter the data you need and output it in the form of reports. Bad test data is data that violates the rules. You will want to make sure you cannot enter bad data into your database.

Testing your data makes little sense until you designate field specifications, another topic I have barely mentioned. For each field you create, you will determine various characteristics. Do you want the field to be required—that is, must you enter a value in every record? Do you want to include a default value for the field, for easy data entry? Do you want to limit the field to a certain size—say, two characters for a `State` field in a table of contact info? Should there be a validation rule that implements business rules—say, a limit on the number of units you can keep in stock of any item?

These questions can be answered only with a knowledge of field properties, the most important topic in the next chapter on table creation. Note that `ClassicTVChap4End.mdb` shows the `ClassicTVChap4.mdb` database as of the end of the chapter. `ClassicTVChap4AllRelationships.mdb` has the database with all relationships created, as shown in Figure 4.1. These databases can be downloaded from the companion website.

CASE EXAMPLE

This chapter contained an example of Cascade Delete Related Records using three tables in the Northwind database. The example was complicated, so instead of having you perform the steps, I gave you a narrative. Now that you understand how Cascade Delete Related Records works, you might like some hands-on experience in this area:

1. In the copy of the Northwind database you made in the "Cascade Update Related Fields" section, choose Tools, Relationships to display the Relationships window. (If you haven't done that exercise, follow the instructions in step 1 to make a copy of `Northwind.mdb`.)
   Note that there is a one-to-many relationship between Categories and Products, as well as a one-to-many relationship between Products and Order Details.
2. Double-click the line between Categories and Products.
3. Select Cascade Delete Related Records. Click OK.
4. Double-click the line between Products and Order Details.
   In the Edit Relationships dialog box, note that referential integrity is enforced, but the Cascade Delete Related Records is not selected.
5. Click Cancel. Minimize the Relationships window.
6. If necessary, maximize the Database window. Open the Products table.
7. Select the `Category` column. Click the A-Z button for an Ascending Sort. Note that several products are beverages.
8. Close the Products table. Click Yes to save your design changes.
9. In the Database window, open the Categories table.
10. Attempt to delete the `Beverages` record.
    Access won't let you delete the record because there are related records in the Order Details table. Categories and Order Details do not have a direct relationship. But Products and Order Details do, and Cascade Delete Related Records is not implemented. Thus, you cannot delete a record in the Categories table that has related records in the Products table because the Products table has related records in the Order Details table and referential integrity is enforced.
11. Press Escape and close the Categories table.
12. Maximize the Relationships window.
13. Right-click the line between Products and Order Details, and select Edit Relationship.
    This is another way of opening the Edit Relationships dialog box.
14. Select Cascade Delete Related Records and click OK.

15. Close the Relationships window. If you're asked to save the layout of the Relationships window, click Yes.
16. Open the Order Details table. Select the `Product` field. Click the A-Z button for an ascending sort.
17. Scroll down to note that many orders are for `Chai`, a beverage.
18. Close the Order Details table. Click Yes to save your design changes.
19. Open the Categories table.
20. Delete the `Beverages` record.
    Access warns you that you are about to delete one record as well as records in related tables.
21. Click Yes to confirm the delete.
22. Close the Categories table and open the Products table.
    Note that all the products with the category `Beverages` have been deleted.
23. Close the Products table and open the Order Details table.
    Scroll down to note that all the records with `Chai` have been deleted. Close the Order Details table and close the database.

CHAPTER 5

BUILDING TABLES

Chapters 1, "Getting Started," 2, "Database Design," and 3, "Understanding Relationships," explained in general terms how to conceive and construct tables in a relational database, as well as how to develop relationships among them. Chapter 4, "Establishing Relationships," pivoted the discussion toward Access explicitly and described how to formally establish relationships in the program.

Building on these basics, Chapter 5 focuses on the specifics of creating tables in Access. The process includes topics I have mentioned in a general context, such as designating primary keys, assigning data types, and naming fields. But much of the discussion is on new subjects, notably field properties such as `Field Size` and `Validation Rule`.

Tables are the foundation of your database, and they can be compared to other essential cornerstones. The United States of America has existed for more than 200 years; yet its Constitution, upon which its entire political apparatus rests, has changed remarkably little. Other nations have had constitutions the size of books that are routinely discarded as their governments collapse. But the U.S. Constitution, with just 5,000 words or so, continues to serve America well. This is because it was designed well in the first place.

As the Constitution is the foundation of American political life, so are Access tables the bedrock of your database. They will constantly expand as values are continually added—just as Federal regulations multiply, underpinned by the Constitution. And as with the U.S. Constitution, every so often you will want to amend a table by adding new fields or editing its field properties. But if the basic structure of your tables is initially well designed and remains as elegant, spare, and permanent as the U.S. Constitution, your database will thrive.

Understanding Lookup Fields

Let's begin discussing tables by introducing lookup fields. This might seem an odd, even perverse, place to start. Lookup fields are simply one Access feature—a minor one, at that, and certainly not crucial to table creation. Indeed, my own bias is against using them.

But just as the diaries of obscure priests can illuminate profound religious controversies, an understanding of lookup fields is a superb way to introduce table creation in an Access database. Equally important, the topic is an excellent vehicle to review and reinforce the database principles you have learned thus far. The explanation might at first seem just a rehash of Chapters 2 and 3, but ultimately you will find it worthwhile. Nevertheless, if you feel at this point that you've seen one too many one-to-many relationships, and if you feel you have the material in the first four chapters down cold, feel free to jump to the next major section, titled "Creating Access Tables."

The Northwind sample database in Access makes significant use of lookup fields. I start by examining two tables there and comparing them to similar ones in another database that doesn't use lookup fields.

When Is It Okay to Repeat Values?

It will be faster and more effective if I describe an example that shows how lookup fields work instead of asking you to do the exercise yourself (which I usually prefer to do). Feel free to follow along by opening and using the `Northwind.mdb` database. I strongly suggest that you make and use a copy of the Northwind file, which can likely be found in your `Program Files/Microsoft Office/..../Samples` folder, rather than the original file, which is available by selecting Help, Sample Databases, Northwind Sample Database. (I give you an exercise to do in Northwind in a few pages, so you might as well make a copy of the file right now.)

The Northwind database contains the Products table (see Figure 5.1). It has data about the subject products—product names, the supplier, the category, and so on. The table has only one field that has anything to do with the supplier; it contains the supplier name. There is no contact information for the supplier; the contact name, e-mail address, and telephone number are all absent.

Products : Table

Product ID	Product Name	Supplier	Category	Quantit
1	Chai	Exotic Liquids	Beverages	10 boxes
2	Chang	Exotic Liquids	Beverages	24 - 12 oz
3	Aniseed Syrup	Exotic Liquids	Condiments	12 - 550 n
4	Chef Anton's Cajun Seasoning	New Orleans Cajun Delights	Condiments	48 - 6 oz j
5	Chef Anton's Gumbo Mix	New Orleans Cajun Delights	Condiments	36 boxes
6	Grandma's Boysenberry Spread	Grandma Kelly's Homestead	Condiments	12 - 8 oz j
7	Uncle Bob's Organic Dried Pears	Grandma Kelly's Homestead	Produce	12 - 1 lb p
8	Northwoods Cranberry Sauce	Grandma Kelly's Homestead	Condiments	12 - 12 oz
9	Mishi Kobe Niku	Tokyo Traders	Meat/Poultry	18 - 500 g
10	Ikura	Tokyo Traders	Seafood	12 - 200 n
11	Queso Cabrales	Cooperativa de Quesos 'Las Cabras'	Dairy Products	1 kg pkg.
12	Queso Manchego La Pastora	Cooperativa de Quesos 'Las Cabras'	Dairy Products	10 - 500 g
13	Konbu	Mayumi's	Seafood	2 kg box

Figure 5.1 The Products table in Datasheet view.

I've stated that each table in a relational database should have only one subject, and that all the fields in the table should contain data only about that subject. It's easy to assert such abstract principles definitively, but it's far more difficult to put them into practice. How does the "one subject" rule apply in this example? Shouldn't supplier contact info be in a products table? What could be more basic, more critical, more "part of" product data than values that tell you how to get in touch with the people who supply them?

But the issue is not whether a supplier's telephone number lies somewhere within the universe of product data. It certainly does. It's whether the phone number is much more closely associated with another subject, and thus much better included in another table—namely, Suppliers.

Let's take a closer look at the consequences of including supplier contact info in the Products table. Northwind contains a separate Suppliers table (see Figure 5.2), which contains contact information such as address, phone number, and home page. The first record is for Exotic Liquids; the contact is Charlotte Cooper. In the Products table, `ProductIDs` 1, 2, and 3—chai, chang, and aniseed syrup—are all provided by this same supplier, Exotic Liquids. Imagine if you had to store contact info about this supplier for each product. You'd have to enter the telephone number—as well as the contact name, contact title, street address, and so on—again and again for Exotic Liquids. And that would be true for all other suppliers as well.

Suppliers : Table

Supplier ID	Company Name	Contact Name	Contact Title	
1	Exotic Liquids	Charlotte Cooper	Purchasing Manager	49 Gilb
2	New Orleans Cajun Delights	Shelley Burke	Order Administrator	P.O. B
3	Grandma Kelly's Homestead	Regina Murphy	Sales Representative	707 Ox
4	Tokyo Traders	Yoshi Nagase	Marketing Manager	9-8 Se
5	Cooperativa de Quesos 'Las Cabras'	Antonio del Valle Saavedra	Export Administrator	Calle d
6	Mayumi's	Mayumi Ohno	Marketing Representative	92 Set
7	Pavlova, Ltd.	Ian Devling	Marketing Manager	74 Ros
8	Specialty Biscuits, Ltd.	Peter Wilson	Sales Representative	29 Kin
9	PB Knäckebröd AB	Lars Peterson	Sales Agent	Kaload
10	Refrescos Americanas LTDA	Carlos Diaz	Marketing Manager	Av. das
11	Heli Süßwaren GmbH & Co. KG	Petra Winkler	Sales Manager	Tiergar
12	Plutzer Lebensmittelgroßmärkte AG	Martin Bein	International Marketing Mgr.	Bogen
13	Nord-Ost-Fisch Handelsgesellschaft mbH	Sven Petersen	Coordinator Foreign Markets	Frahm
14	Formaggi Fortini s.r.l.	Elio Rossi	Sales Representative	Viale D
15	Norske Meierier	Beate Vileid	Marketing Manager	Hatleve
16	Bigfoot Breweries	Cheryl Saylor	Regional Account Rep.	3400 -

Figure 5.2 The Suppliers table in Datasheet view.

Q&A

Q: I *still* don't understand what the problem is with repeating data in a table, or when it's okay to repeat it and when it isn't. As you point out, the company Exotic Liquids is repeated at least three times in the Products table. So why is *that* repetition okay? In the same table, categories are repeated, unit prices are repeated, and reorder levels are repeated. What's the big deal about repeating stuff?

A: Each record of the Products table uniquely identifies the supplier for that product. When you enter Exotic Liquids as the supplier for the products chai, chang, and aniseed syrup, in each case you've told Access which company supplies the product. Nowhere else in the database is that data entered, and nowhere else is it required. In other words, the data is entered only once.

But to also include Northwind's contact at Exotic Liquids (namely, Charlotte Cooper) for each record would be redundant. Because you have the contact name for Exotic Liquids in its supplier record, you know that if you need to call the company, you want to speak to Charlotte Cooper. It doesn't matter whether the product you want to talk about is chai, chang, aniseed syrup, or any other product Exotic Liquids supplies. (The same company could conceivably have different salespeople for different products, but let's keep it simple.) The contact name Charlotte Cooper is already in the Suppliers table, so there's no need to repeat it ad infinitum—indeed, no need to include it at all—in the Products table.

The key is establishing a relationship between the Products and Suppliers tables, as I'll discuss next.

Why Is There Text in a Number Field?

Now, finally, let's look at a facet of the problem you haven't seen in your previous work. In Design view of the Suppliers table, the first row is `SupplierID` (see Figure 5.3). It has the `AutoNumber` data type. This field is the table's primary key and uniquely identifies each supplier in the Suppliers table. Each supplier in the Suppliers table has a different `SupplierID`, and each supplier has one and only one `SupplierID`.

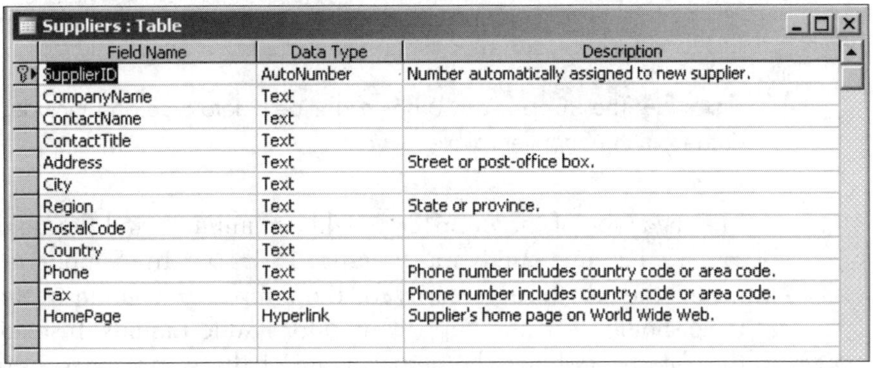

Suppliers : Table

Field Name	Data Type	Description
SupplierID	AutoNumber	Number automatically assigned to new supplier.
CompanyName	Text	
ContactName	Text	
ContactTitle	Text	
Address	Text	Street or post-office box.
City	Text	
Region	Text	State or province.
PostalCode	Text	
Country	Text	
Phone	Text	Phone number includes country code or area code.
Fax	Text	Phone number includes country code or area code.
HomePage	Hyperlink	Supplier's home page on World Wide Web.

Figure 5.3 The Suppliers table in Design view.

In Design view of the Products table, the top pane includes the `SupplierID` field. (As I'll explain a little later, the field's `Caption` property is *`Supplier`*; so in the table's Datasheet view, the column heading is not `SupplierID`, but `Supplier`, as shown in Figure 5.1. Don't let this bother you: This is purely for cosmetics and does not affect any of the following discussion.) The `SupplierID` field in the Products table has the `Number` data type (see Figure 5.4), which means that only numbers can be entered in the field. The `Description` tells you that the value for this field should be the same entry as it exists in the Suppliers table.

In fact, a one-to-many relationship has been established between the Products and Suppliers tables through the `SupplierID` field. (You can verify this by viewing the Relationships window, which is available by selecting Tools, Relationships.) In the Products table, `SupplierID` is a foreign key. Whereas a supplier can appear only once in the Suppliers table (for example, there is only one record for Exotic Liquids), it can appear many times in the Products table (you've already seen three instances of Exotic Liquids).

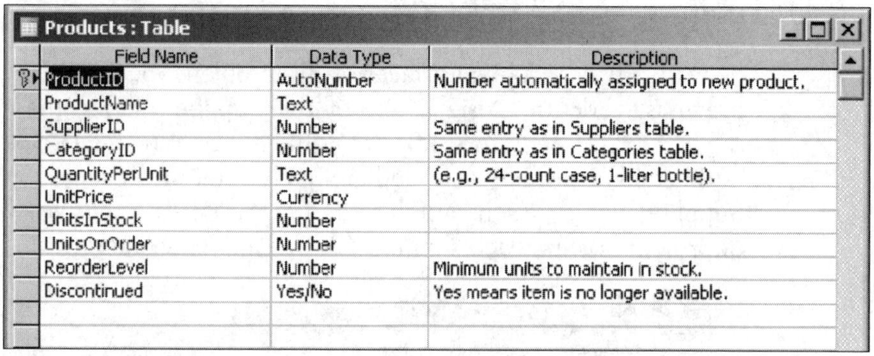

Products : Table

Field Name	Data Type	Description
ProductID	AutoNumber	Number automatically assigned to new product.
ProductName	Text	
SupplierID	Number	Same entry as in Suppliers table.
CategoryID	Number	Same entry as in Categories table.
QuantityPerUnit	Text	(e.g., 24-count case, 1-liter bottle).
UnitPrice	Currency	
UnitsInStock	Number	
UnitsOnOrder	Number	
ReorderLevel	Number	Minimum units to maintain in stock.
Discontinued	Yes/No	Yes means item is no longer available.

Figure 5.4 The `SupplierID` has a `Number` data type and includes matching data from the Suppliers table.

The data type of the `Supplier` field is a number, and the `Description` says it's the same number as the `SupplierID` in the Suppliers table. That means the first three records for the `Supplier` column in the Products table should be `1`, the `SupplierID` for Exotic Liquids. Instead, however, the datasheet shows the actual name of the company (see Figure 5.5). Why? And how can a field have a `Number` data type if it displays text?

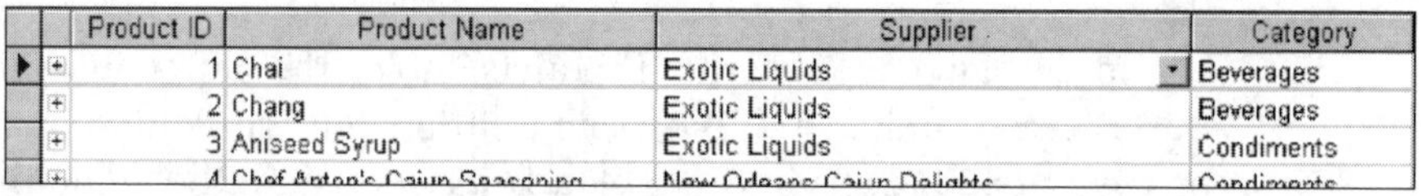

Product ID	Product Name	Supplier	Category
1	Chai	Exotic Liquids	Beverages
2	Chang	Exotic Liquids	Beverages
3	Aniseed Syrup	Exotic Liquids	Condiments
4	Chef Anton's Cajun Seasoning	New Orleans Cajun Delights	Condiments

Figure 5.5 A small section of the Products table in Figure 5.1. The `SupplierID` field, which has the column heading `Supplier`, displays the name of the supplier (Exotic Liquids), not its ID number (`1`).

The Advantage of Lookup Fields

The answer is that `SupplierID` in the Products table is a lookup field. Using the matching `SupplierID`, the field "looks up" the company name in the Suppliers table and replaces the ID with the actual name. The field still stores the `SupplierID` in the Suppliers table, but it now displays the supplier name.

This would seem to present the best of all possible worlds. The field contains that unique ID that enables you to combine all the data from the Suppliers table with that of the Products table in forms, queries, and reports. But instead of a meaningless ID, it displays a value that has meaning that the user can understand.

Let's take a look at what happens when you don't use a lookup field. Download the `NiftyLionsChap5.mdb` database from the companion web site (www.awprofessional.com/title/0321245458) to a convenient folder and open it. This imaginary database is for Nifty Lions, a small mail-order firm that sells various products with lion motifs to the general public. It has many (but not all) of the same tables that are in Northwind, along with similar table structures. It has far fewer records and shorter names, however, so I hope it will be easier to work with.

NOTE I've used the Leszynski naming convention to name the main Access objects. Thus, a Customers table is titled tblCustomers, and a Merchandise table is called tblMerchandise, instead of simply Customers and Merchandise. The Leszynski system is described a little later in a sidebar. It's not a big deal: I've used it mainly because you're likely to see it in other contexts.

NiftyLions has a Suppliers table. As in Northwind, you have a `SupplierID` in the first column and the supplier company name in the second. NiftyLions also has a Merchandise table. As in Northwind's Products table, you have `Product Name` and `Supplier` fields (see Figure 5.6). Unlike Northwind, however, the `Supplier` field shows the actual `SupplierID`, not the supplier name. Thus, the foreign key in the Merchandise table both stores and displays the supplier's `AutoNumber` primary key, which makes all the values for that supplier in the suppliers table available to the Merchandise table.

tblMerchandise : Table

	Item ID	Product Name	Item Description	Supplier	Category
▶	3	Door knocker	All brass; weighs 7.6 lbs	6	1
	4	Bronze vase	Two males, one female, cub	6	1
	5	Doll pair	Daddy and baby, 7" and 4" tall	1	4
	6	Marble statue	Lions of St. Andronico; white; 6" X 3" x5"	6	1
	8	Antique-finish desk clock	Classic lion motif with antique finish; measure	2	1
	9	Kenya paper money	Issued 1978; 20 shillings; reverse shows pride	3	3
	10	Rio Muni stamp set	Vermillion 10+5 cts male and gray 80+20 cts.	3	3

Figure 5.6 The `Supplier` field in the Merchandise table is a number.

Figure 5.7 shows the Merchandise table in Design view, with the cursor in the `SupplierID` field. In the `Field Properties` section below, the `Caption` property is `Supplier`. `SupplierID` and `Supplier` are the exact same field; in the datasheet, however, a caption has been used to make it easier to read.

In the `Description`, a note has been added that the `SupplierID` field is the same as that in the Suppliers table. In the Merchandise table, `SupplierID` is a foreign key. Many products can have the same supplier, while in the Suppliers table the supplier's record can appear only once. But no lookup field has been created. Thus, the actual ID of the supplier is displayed in the Merchandise table.

That's going to be pretty confusing unless you happen to remember the actual name of `SupplierID 1`—and `ID 2`, and `ID 3`, and every other ID. It might not be a problem with seven suppliers, but suppose you had 190 shippers (or 1,000 products, or 10,000 names—the same principle applies for other fields). Thus, you can see the advantages the lookup field offers.

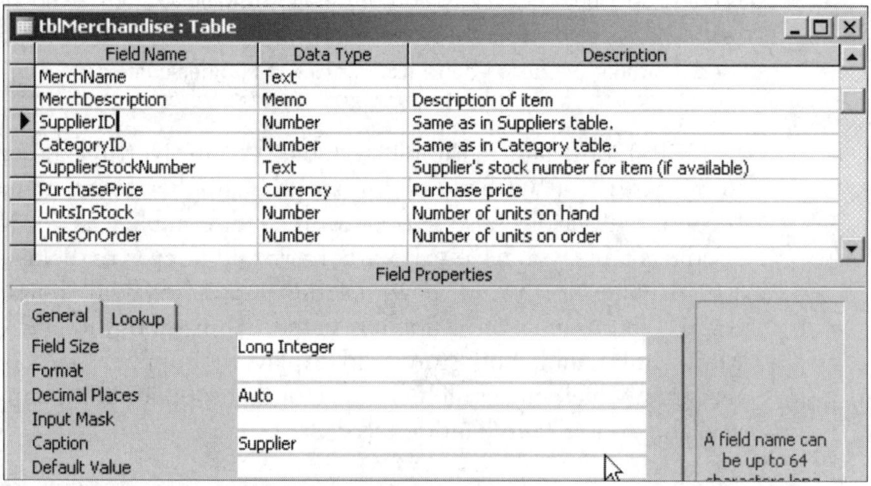

tblMerchandise : Table

Field Name	Data Type	Description
MerchName	Text	
MerchDescription	Memo	Description of item
SupplierID	Number	Same as in Suppliers table.
CategoryID	Number	Same as in Category table.
SupplierStockNumber	Text	Supplier's stock number for item (if available)
PurchasePrice	Currency	Purchase price
UnitsInStock	Number	Number of units on hand
UnitsOnOrder	Number	Number of units on order

Field Properties

General | Lookup

Field Size	Long Integer
Format	
Decimal Places	Auto
Input Mask	
Caption	Supplier
Default Value	

A field name can be up to 64

Figure 5.7 In Design view of the NiftyLions Merchandise table, the `SupplierID` is a number. But no lookup field has been created, so in Datasheet view, you see the actual `SupplierID`, not the supplier name.

The Downside of Lookup Fields

You can readily see the problem with lookup fields by creating a query using the Products table of the Northwind database. Let's create a query that will include only products supplied by Exotic Liquids. (If you need a refresher on simple queries, take a look at Chapter 8, "Queries," before proceeding.) If you haven't already done so, find the `Northwind.mdb` database on your hard drive in the `Program Files/Microsoft Office/..../Samples` folder; make a copy of the file and open it.

1. In the Northwind database window, click the Products table and choose Insert, Query; then click OK.
2. Double-click the field list title to select all the fields.
3. Drag and drop all the fields on the design grid.
4. In the `Criteria` row of the `SupplierID` field, type **exotic liquids**.
   You usually don't need to capitalize *criteria*.
5. Click the View button in the upper-left corner to see your records. You have an error message stating that you have a data type mismatch in the criteria expression (see Figure 5.8). You entered the expression `exotic liquids`. But remember, `SupplierID` in the Products table doesn't have a `Text` data type; it has a `Number` data type. You have to enter the number of the supplier to see your records.

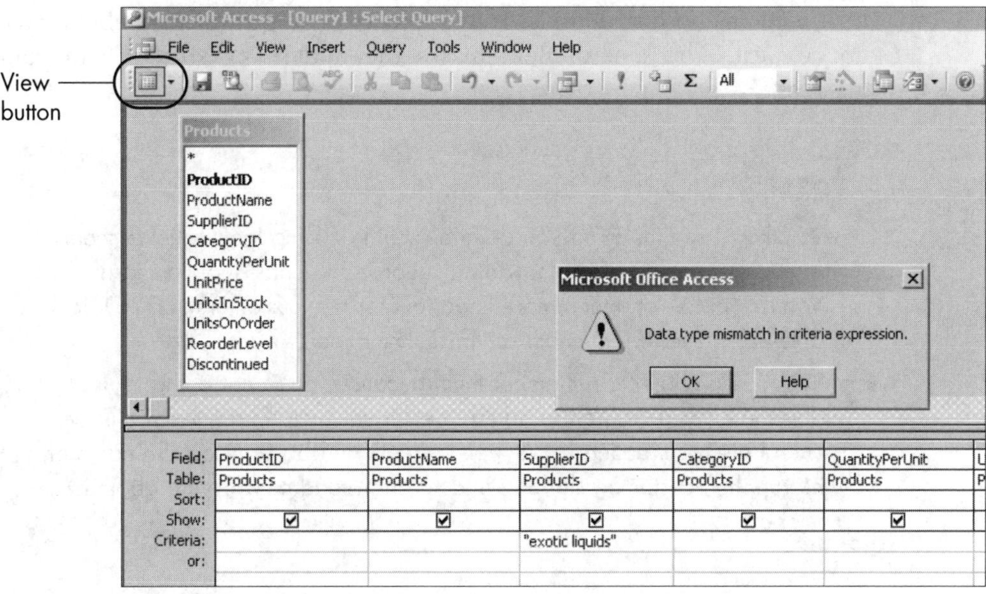

Figure 5.8 When you run the query, you get a data type mismatch error message.

6. Click OK in the error message.
7. In the `SupplierID` column, edit the criteria to **1**.
   The `SupplierID` of Exotic Liquids is 1.
8. Click View to see your records.
   The Supplier `field` shows all the records with Exotic Liquids as supplier.
9. Close the query.
   You can save the query, if you want, or discard it.

In almost every way that actually matters—structure, capability to integrate data, the actual value stored in the field—the `Supplier` field in the Northwind products table and the `Supplier` field in NiftyLions's Merchandise table have the same qualities. Notably, they are both foreign keys on the "many" side of a one-to-many relationship. In only one aspect, the value displayed, do the two fields differ. To the untrained eye, however, the two fields seem quite distinct.

Are there ways to construct this query so you can use supplier names instead of ID numbers as criteria? Certainly. But here's the problem with lookup fields: Based on the datasheet in the underlying table, you had every reason to believe that you could use supplier names as criteria in the `SupplierID` field. When you try that, however, you get an error message that contains no instructions. You're left scratching your head about what to do next. The lookup field masks the underlying structure of your database.

Q&A

Q: Okay, I see the issue you describe, but *not* using lookup fields seems an even bigger problem. How am I supposed to enter suppliers in a Products table—or, much more important for me, customers in an Orders table—if I have to remember all those ID numbers?

A: You don't have to remember them because you're not going to use tables to enter data. You're going to enter values in forms. As you'll see when I discuss creating forms, you'll simply be able to select the name of the supplier, customer, shipper, and so on instead of worrying about ID numbers.

Creating Lookup Fields

Because I'm not enthusiastic about lookup fields, I'm not going to go through an example on how to create them. Suffice it to say that, in Table Design view, you begin by choosing the Lookup Wizard from the Data Type drop-down list for the field.

Q&A

Q: Even if I don't use lookup fields, maybe someone in my office likes them. How can I tell if a lookup field has been created in an Access table?

A: When you click in a field row in Design view, there is both a General tab and a Lookup tab in the lower pane (see Figure 5.7). If a lookup field has been created and is being used, the `Display Control` property on the Lookup tab will be `Combo Box`, and there will be a host of associated properties. If no lookup field has been created, the `Display Control` property will simply read `Text Box`.

What Lookup Fields Can Teach You

Although lookup fields themselves might be suspect, the importance of the principle on which they are based cannot be overstated. The lookup field—and the display of the supplier name instead of the `SupplierID`—was possible only because a one-to-many relationship existed between the two tables. Again and again in Access, you will find yourself bringing together data from different tables by establishing relationships. You will be able to do that because the tables are related to one another. As you have seen, those associations are made possible because the tables have matching data in one field. Whether you're designing multitable queries, adding combo boxes to forms, or including fields from different tables in the Report Wizard, your work rests on this same bedrock rule. That might not be apparent now, but it will be increasingly obvious as you proceed through this book and learn more about Access.

Concluding Lookup Fields

Years ago, I worked with a group of writers in Japan where we often "polished" (read: did a complete rewrite of) Japanese-to-English translations. Translating is more art than science, and translators have much latitude in their work. Many translators (mostly American, but Japanese as well) spent a lot of effort making their English sound as good as possible. But for those of us who had to rewrite the translations anyway, we wanted them to be as pure and "Japanesey" as possible—even if they were ungrammatical. It wasn't that we writers were afraid of being made redundant. It was that we wanted to get a true feel of what the Japanese said.

Perhaps that's not the best analogy, but that gives you a sense of how I feel about Access tables. I don't want little devices in them, such as lookup fields, that supposedly make my life easier. I want to see the values that have actually, truly been stored. If my tables are sound, I can create the queries, forms, and reports I need—and be confident that they are supported in the underlying tables.

Meaningful Primary Keys

A serious charge could be made against my presentation on lookup fields, which runs something like this: Hey, the *real* problem is those `AutoNumber` primary keys you and Northwind are using. Why use a primary key with no meaning whatsoever? If you used a key that truly identifies the field—if you could take one look at the key and know who the supplier is—your problem would be solved. The primary key itself tells you who the supplier is, and there's no need for lookup fields.

I've discussed natural and artificial keys at some length in previous chapters, so I won't debate the issue here again. You might decide to develop and use meaningful primary keys in some or all of your tables, but I still demur. Creating meaningful but unique primary keys is not easy. Few things in life are both meaningful and singular. Even seemingly unique situations can turn out to be not so singular.

Let me just reiterate: The most important thing is that your table organization and structure are solid. If it is, whether you use meaningful prime keys or not, you can create the queries, forms, and reports you need that show the information you want.

Creating Access Tables

Let's turn now to the specifics of creating Access tables for storing your data. Basically five ways exist for creating a new Access table:

- Use the Table Wizard
- Enter data directly into a datasheet
- Import data or link to an external source
- Use a Make Table query
- Build the table in Design view

I will focus on the last choice of starting from scratch in Design view, which is usually preferred. Importing and linking are discussed in Chapter 13, "Importing and Exporting," and make-table queries are described in Chapter 9, "Queries, Part II." That leaves using the Table Wizard and entering data into a datasheet, both of which I quickly dispose of now.

Table Wizard

The Table Wizard is of some use, but not for its intended purpose of creating a table. In the Database window of any database, click Tables and double-click *Create Table by Using Wizard*. The first dialog box of the wizard includes sample fields for both business and personal tables. As you move from table to table in the Sample Tables pane, you can see the possible fields for each. This is one check for making sure you've included all the fields you need.

The Table Wizard gives you some ideas for fields and field names. But unlike some other wizards that truly make object creation simpler and more efficient, I think the Table Wizard offers relatively few benefits. Tables are the foundation of your database, so you should spend the time to build them from scratch rather than use shortcuts.

Direct Entry

To use the direct-entry method, you double-click *Create Table by Entering Data* in the Tables section of the Database window. In the direct-entry method, you enter column names (which become the field names) and a few rows of sample data into a datasheet. For example, let's say you want to create a table for investments. You might enter the following column headings and data for the first few fields:

Security Name	Security Symbol	Shares Owned
Boeing	BA	700
DuPont	DD	550
Ford Motor	F	1,600

If you have entered the values with some consistency, Access will make a reasonable stab at creating a table with fields of the appropriate data type (in this case, `Text` in the first two columns and `Number` in the third) and display format.

There seems little to gain by this process because Access can easily suggest the wrong data types. In addition, by using column headings to name fields, the direct-entry method mingles field names and captions in a way that is disconcerting. I mention this issue again in the "Captions" section.

Table Design Procedure

Table creation is such a vital component of making an Access database, so you usually want to create fields and specify field properties one by one in the Design view of a table. Part of this process is reviewing all field property settings entered by default, to make certain they are the best choices for your fields.

At this point, you have already designed your database; you know the tables you are going to include, the primary and foreign keys in each, and most or all of the fields and their data types. Here is the basic procedure for creating tables:

1. In the Database window, click the Tables button and double-click Create Table in Design View.
2. Enter a field name in the Field Name column.
3. If applicable, designate the field (or fields) as the primary key.
4. Select the data type in the Data Type column.
5. Provide a description.
6. Assign field properties in the Field Properties pane.
7. Save the table with an appropriate name.
   As you've seen, I'm using the Leszynski naming convention, as described in the sidebar. Thus, the tables in the sample databases always have the prefix `tbl`, as in `tblSuppliers`, `tblCountries`, and so on. If you find this baffling and confusing, don't use these prefixes.

8. Enter additional fields as necessary.
9. Designate table properties.

All of the steps except the first are described in detail in the rest of this chapter.

Leszynski Naming Convention

If you've opened the NiftyLions database, you've noticed that the object names are prefixed with an abbreviation that identifies the object. For example a table of suppliers is tblSuppliers, consisting of the prefix `tbl`, which identifies the object as a table, and the subject of the table, suppliers.

This spelling follows the Leszynski naming convention, a system for naming Access objects. The system actually suggests prefixes for a wide range of Access elements, but I have adopted it only for tables (`tbl`), queries (`qry`), forms (`frm`), reports (`rpt`), and macros (`mcr`).

I debated whether to implement the convention to even this small of an extent. Naming a table tblSuppliers instead of Suppliers might seem to be a device to make your life more complicated or needlessly make your database more "techie." But I eventually decided to use it because (a) you'll often see objects named this way, (b) it does identify the object precisely within the Database window and outside it, and (c) when you get used to seeing objects named this way, an object without a prefix seems slightly naked. I think these reasons outweigh the initial confusion you might have already faced by including them. Please note that the use of the Leszynski convention is by no means universal; many firms and users have their own conventions for naming Access elements, including tables.

Creating Fields

Creating fields in tables is among the most important Access tasks. In this section, I discuss naming fields; selecting a data type; if appropriate, designating the field as a primary key; and providing a description.

Naming Fields

I discussed several general rules for naming fields in Chapter 3. Field names should fully describe the field. Like names of other Access objects, a field name cannot include more than 64 characters. Access allows you to include spaces in field names, but because of possible naming conflicts, field names should be spelled solidly: `PurchasePrice`, `SerialNumber`, `PostalCode`, and so on. If you must include a space to avoid confusion, use an underscore instead; for example, in a field of IDs for VIPs, use `VIP_ID`.

NOTE Field names cannot include certain symbols, such as periods and exclamation marks. Microsoft also recommends that certain "reserved words" (such as *Description* and *Report*) not be used for field names. A list of these reserved words and symbols is available online at http://support.microsoft.com/kb/ 286335.

Spelling field names solidly might seem like another instance of simply making life more difficult for yourself. But this rule is usually adhered to. You can easily include a caption (discussed later) so that the public face of the field (the field as it appears in datasheet column headings, in form and report labels, and so on) is, say, `Last Name` (with a space) rather than `LastName`. Actually, after a while, in your own mind's eye, you'll add spaces to solidly spelled field names and recognize `UnitPrice` as `Unit Price`. Nevertheless, for your own ease of use, especially for external users, you'll want to assign captions to make field names more readable.

In the case of common field names that might be required in more than one table (such as `LastName`), prefix the field name with an abbreviation of the table. Naming fields `SuppAddress` (for supplier address) and `CustAddress` (customer address) helps distinguish the address field of the supplier from that of the customer. (Some Access experts argue that there is little point to abbreviating *supplier* and *customer*: Because you can use up to 64 characters, you might as well name the fields `SupplierAddress` and `CustomerAddress`.) In the case of a field that you know you're going to use in only one table (say, a social security number in an Employees table), you might want to dispense with the table prefix.

As crucial as any of these rules are individually, most important is to adopt them consistently in all tables of your database. I can't guarantee that the cost/benefit analysis of naming a field of last names `CustLastName` instead of `Last Name` will necessarily prove positive, but it is good practice.

Assigning Data Types

Data types are selected by opening and selecting the type from the drop-down list in the Data Type column (see Figure 5.9).

The first chapter discussed data types in some detail, and the discussion on lookup fields earlier in this chapter highlights their importance. The topic of changing data types is discussed later in the chapter. The case example at the end of the chapter will reinforce your knowledge of data types. Finally, the complete list of data types and their specifications can be found in the Access Help article "Field Data Types Available in Access (MDB)."

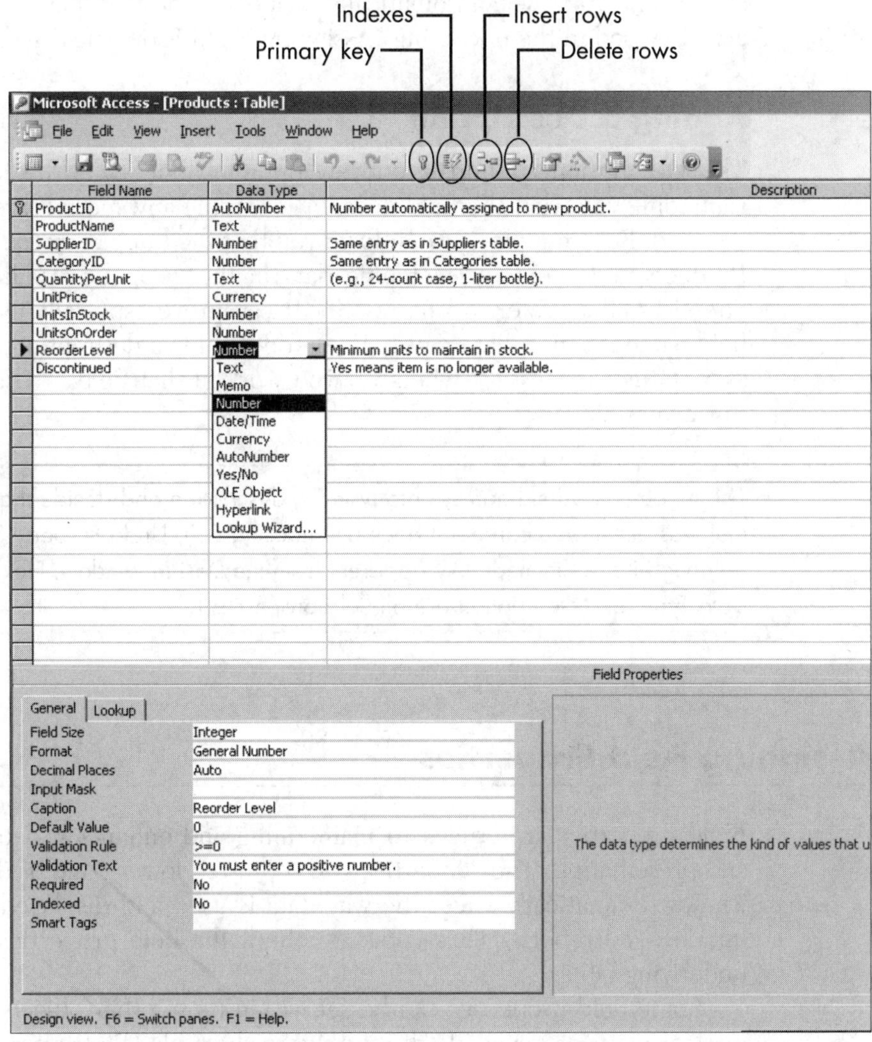

Figure 5.9 A table in design view. As you move from field to field, the field properties in the lower pane change to match the field. The Data Type drop-down list is open to display the data types.

Designating a Primary Key

I don't think more needs to be said at this point about the importance of creating a primary key, a unique identifier, for each table in your database. Nor is there any difficulty in designating a primary key: Select the row (or rows) that makes up the primary key and choose Edit, Primary Key, or click the Primary Key button on the toolbar (refer to Figure 5.9). When you create a primary key, you automatically create an index for that field. Indexes are discussed in the upcoming "Assigning Field Properties" section.

Adding a Description

The Description column is entirely optional, but it can be helpful for reminding you what the field does, or providing any special directions for the field. For example, it can inform you that the `SupplierID` field in the Products table contains matching data in the `SupplierID` field of the Suppliers table (refer to Figure 5.9). It can prove especially useful if the field name is somewhat cryptic. If you do include a description, it appears as a Status bar message whenever you work in that field in Datasheet or Form view.

TIP If you edit a field name, data type, or description and decide that your original was better, you can get it back by choosing Edit, Undo Property Setting. (Although it's not immediately apparent from the Design window, Field Name, Data Type, and Description are all field properties.)

Assigning Field Properties

Field properties are crucial to maintaining and enhancing data integrity and presentation. The properties you set in the lower pane of the Design window dramatically affect the way data is used and displayed in forms, queries, and reports. These objects inherit the field properties from the underlying table.

Some field properties can be set within these other objects, and they may (or may not) override the settings in the table (I'll leave most of that discussion for Chapter 6, "Entering, Editing, and Displaying Data").

Nevertheless, it will simplify your life greatly if, for the most part, you set field properties just once in tables and let them be.

Instead of wasting a lot of paper giving you all the specifications for field properties—particularly `Field Size` and `Format`, which have many details—I've tried to summarize important points and offer observations that might be useful. You can easily access the detailed specs on any field property in Access Help: In the lower pane of Design view, click inside the field property and press F1.

Field Size

You might initially be confused by the `Field Size` property because its settings change dramatically depending on the data type (see Figure 5.10). The property is significant for `Text` and, especially, `Number` data types.

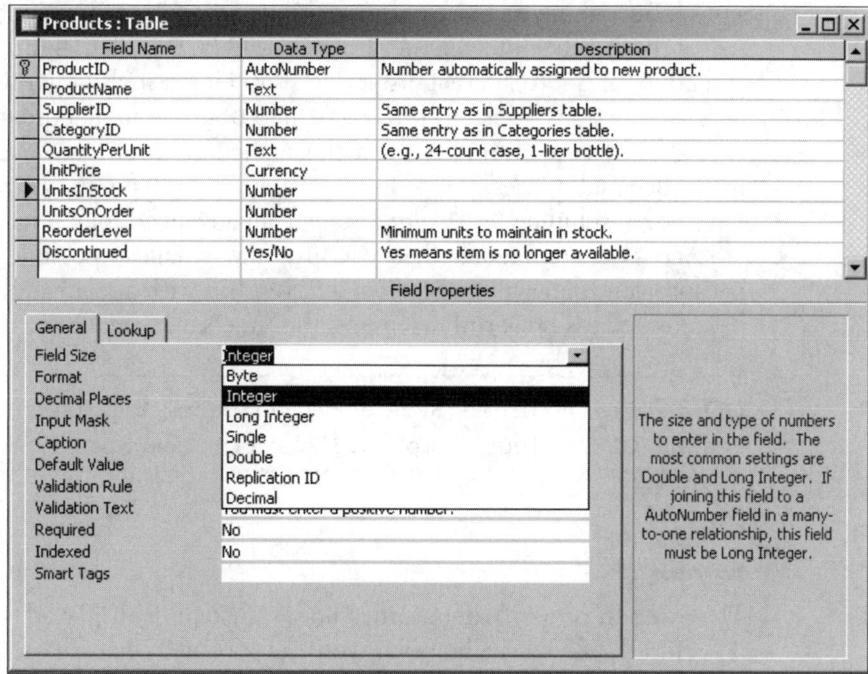

Figure 5.10 The `Field Size` property depends on the data type. The current field is `Units In Stock`, which has the `Number` data type. The selections in the `Field Size` property are for `Number` fields.

Text

For the `Text` data type, the `Field Size` determines the number of alphanumeric characters that can be entered, up to a maximum of 255. The default setting of `50` can be adjusted in the Default Field Sizes section of the Tables/Queries tab of the Options dialog box, available from the Tools menu.

`Field Size` can be extremely useful for maintaining data integrity. In a field reserved for U.S. states, for example, you can make sure that only two-letter abbreviations are entered by setting the field size to `2`. That still won't guarantee that `ME` and not `MA` is entered for Maine; but it will make sure you don't enter `Mer`, `Main`, or `Maine` for Maine.

Numbers

The `Field Size` for numbers determines the number of bytes that can be stored. But I think it's more useful to think of the property as controlling the size of the number and whether fractions can be included. `Byte`, `Integer`, and `Long Integer`, in that order, can store increasingly larger whole numbers (no fractions). `Decimal`, `Single`, and `Double`, in that order, can store increasingly larger numbers with their fractions (`Decimal` can store yet more decimal places). The `AutoNumber` data type is always a `Long Integer` (excluding `Replication ID`, an advanced topic I ignore here).

Access recommends that you use the smallest possible field size because your data will be processed faster. But with a relatively small database, on today's powerful machines, the time saved might not be great.

NOTE There is no `Field Size` property for `Date/Time`, `Currency`, `Yes/No`, `OLE Object`, `Memo`, and `Hyperlink` data types.

Format

The `Format` property determines how your data is displayed, versus how it is stored. Obviously, however, you can't format what isn't stored in the first place, so this property is dramatically affected by what values are actually in your database. For example, suppose you set the `Field Size` for the `Number` data type as `Long Integer`, which allows no fractions. Access still lets you choose a `Fixed` or `Standard` format for the field, both of which show decimal places. But you're going to see just zeroes in those decimal places because there aren't any meaningful places to show.

Your choices in the `Format` property naturally depend greatly on the data type. The selections in the `Format` property of a `Date/Time` field allow you to display a date variously as `9/17/2004`, `17-Sep-2004`, or `September 17, 2004`. These formats are obviously peculiar to this data type. In a `Number` field, your options are much different.

NOTE The `Format` property—particularly for `Date/Time` and `Number` data types—is also substantially affected by Regional Settings in the Windows Control Panel.

You can select predetermined formats by opening the drop-down menu and choosing a format that fits your preferences. If the defined format selections are not to your liking, you can create customized formats. Customized `Date/Time` formats are fairly easy to create; `Text` and `Number` formats of some sophistication are more difficult.

Formats coexist somewhat uneasily with input masks, a property that provides a template for entering data. In Chapter 6, I discuss input masks and their relationship to formats at some length, so I postpone further comment on the `Format` property until then.

Caption

The `Caption` property shouldn't give you any problems. Access field names are often difficult to decipher, at least at first glance. Entering a caption enables you to name the field so that it obeys Access rules and conventions and, at the same time, displays an everyday English label for the column in Datasheet view. Just type in the text string in the `Caption` property that you would like displayed.

NOTE A caption is not an alias, an alternative field name. With a caption, there is still only one field name; you're just using a label to make it more understandable.

Again, the `Caption` property is inherited by objects built on the underlying table. So even if you don't have any trouble distinguishing between `LastName` and `Last Name`, you might want to enter the latter as a caption if you're planning to create any reports for external use.

NOTE You can double-click in the Column Selector of a datasheet and change the column name. I wish this weren't possible. When you edit the name of a column, you're not only editing its caption, but you're editing the actual field name, something you only rarely need or want to do. If you didn't know about this bit of functionality, forget I told you about it. If you did, don't use it.

Decimal Places

Oddly, the harmless-sounding `Decimal Places` property causes much confusion. I've taken a stab at simplification, but I know I haven't covered all possible outcomes. If decimals are crucial to your work, be sure to verify your settings with test data.

The first thing to remember about the `Decimal Places` property is that it has no effect on how many decimals are stored in a `Number` field—only the places displayed. The `Field Size` property determines what's stored. If it's set to `Byte`, `Integer`, or `Long Integer`, Access won't accept or store decimals. The `Single` setting stores up to 7 places, and the `Double` setting stores up to 15.

If you set the `Decimal Places` property to `Auto`, the number of places is determined by the `Format` property. If `Format` is set to `Fixed` or `Standard`, the number of decimal places displayed is two (assuming English United States is your Windows Regional Settings). Thus, a value of `6.7789` entered and stored in a `Number` field with a `Field Size` of `Single`, a `Format` of `Fixed`, and `Decimal Places` of `Auto` is displayed as `6.78`. Access rounds up decimals of 5 and above, and rounds down decimals of 4 and below.

If the `Decimal Places` property is set to a specific number, that number of places is displayed, regardless of the format. In the previous example, if `Decimal Places` was `3`, the number displayed would be `6.779`.

Setting the `Decimal Places` property has no effect if the `Format` is `General Number`. In this case, if you enter `6.7789` and `Decimal Places` is `1`, the display is still `6.7789`.

NOTE For even greater precision in the storage of decimal places, a `Field Size` property called `Decimal` can store up to 28 places.

Validation Rule and Validation Text

Among the most effective devices for maintaining data security is the `Validation Rule` property. You enter an expression in the `Validation Rule` property that restricts the data that can be entered. Validation rules are often used as a means of implementing business rules.

For example, suppose that in a Merchandise table, you have a `PurchasePrice` field for the unit cost of the item. Let's say you don't want any items in your inventory that cost more than $100. You would enter the expression `<=100` in the `Validation Rule` field (no `$` sign is needed).

At the same time, you would enter text in the `Validation Text` property—for example, `Unit price must be $100 or less.` This text will appear in the error message (see Figure 5.11) whenever you enter, say, `$100.50` or `$160`. If you don't enter any validation text, you get a general (and confusing) message stating that one or more values have been entered that are prohibited by the validation rule.

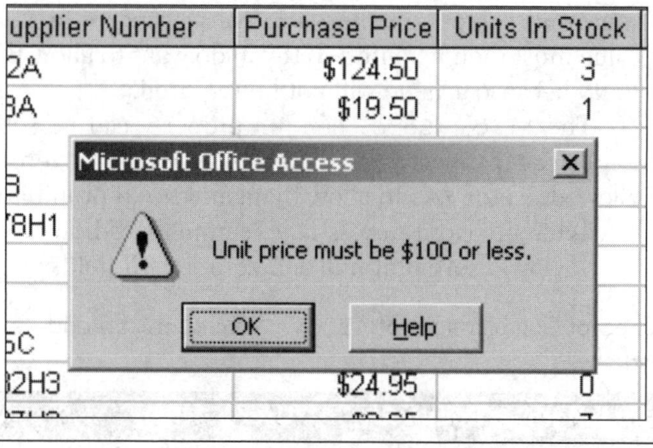

Figure 5.11 The purchase price for the first record has been edited to $124.50. An error message warns that the validation rule for the field has been broken.

If you enter, for example, `$9.7g`, it doesn't matter whether you have entered validation text. Access can't determine whether the validation rule has been broken because the `g` is invalid in a `Currency` field. You would just get a general message that the data is invalid.

The `Validation Text` property is in no way controlled by the `Validation Rule` property. You can enter an expression of `<=100` in `Validation Rule` and `Today is Mary's birthday` in `Validation Text`. Access displays the text you entered whenever the validation rule is violated.

NOTE Expressions and how to create them are important topics in Access. They are discussed more thoroughly in Chapter 7, "Finding and Filtering."

`Required` and `Zero Length`

Both null values and zero-length strings are "no something" entries, so it's worth considering the two properties together. (Both nulls and zero-length strings are discussed in Chapter 1.) Here's the question that the `Required` property answers: Is a null value a valid entry for this field? If you don't want null values, set the `Required` property to `Yes` because an actual value must then be entered. If you do want to allow them, set the property to `No` because a value will not be required.

The `Allow Zero Length` property can be set independent of the `Required` property and determines where a zero-length field will be allowed. Enter `Yes` to allow them and `No` to prohibit them.

Table 5.1 from Access Help summarizes how the two properties variously allow or prohibit null and zero-length fields:

Table 5.1 Effect of Combinations of `Allow Zero Length` and `Required` Properties on Value Stored

Allow Zero Length	Required	User's Action	Value Stored
No	No	Presses Enter Presses spacebar Enters a zero-length string	Null Null (not allowed)
Yes	No	Presses Enter Presses spacebar Enters a zero-length string	Null Null Zero-length string

Allow Zero Length	Required	User's Action	Value Stored
No	Yes	Presses Enter Presses spacebar Enters a zero-length string	(not allowed) (not allowed) (not allowed)
Yes	Yes	Presses Enter Presses spacebar Enters a zero-length string	(not allowed) Zero-length string Zero-length string

Note: To enter a zero-length string, you type double quotation marks ("")

TIP If you create a validation rule, null values aren't allowed. (If you want to allow null values when there is a validation rule, you must add the text string `Or Is Null` to the validation rule.) Using the `Validation Rule` property is a good way to both require a value and set limits on the values that can be entered.

Indexes

As with an index in a book, you can create indexes in Access to help it find values faster. This can be useful for speeding up queries, as well as sorting and grouping. On the downside, creating indexes can slow the updating of field values. When working with small databases, however, creating an index might not make that much of a difference, either positive or negative.

When you set a primary key for a single field, the `Indexed` property automatically becomes `Yes (No Duplicates)`, for an index in which duplicates are not allowed. For fields that are not part of a primary key, you can also set the property to `Yes (Duplicates Allowed)`. If you don't want an index, set this property to `No`.

You can also set multifield indexes. For example, suppose you have a database with thousands of customer records. Many of the records have `Smith` in the `LastName` field. Therefore, you might need to search on two fields—`LastName` and `FirstName`—at the same time. A multiple-field index is helpful in speeding up these searches. Here are the steps:

1. In Table Design view, choose View, Indexes.
2. In the first blank row, type a name for the index in the Index Name column.
3. Click in the Field Name column. Open the drop-down list and choose the first field for the index.
   In the previous example, the `LastName` field would be first.
4. Click in the next row in the Field Name column, open the drop-down list, and choose the next field for the index.
   In the previous example, the `FirstName` field would be selected. You can leave the Index Name column blank.
5. Continue adding fields as necessary, and then close the Indexes dialog box.
   You can add up to 10 fields for any one multiple-field index. If you need to insert a row, right-click in the row above which you want a blank row and choose Insert, Rows.

Figure 5.12 shows a multiple-field index for `LastName` and `FirstName` fields, along with the index for the table's primary key.

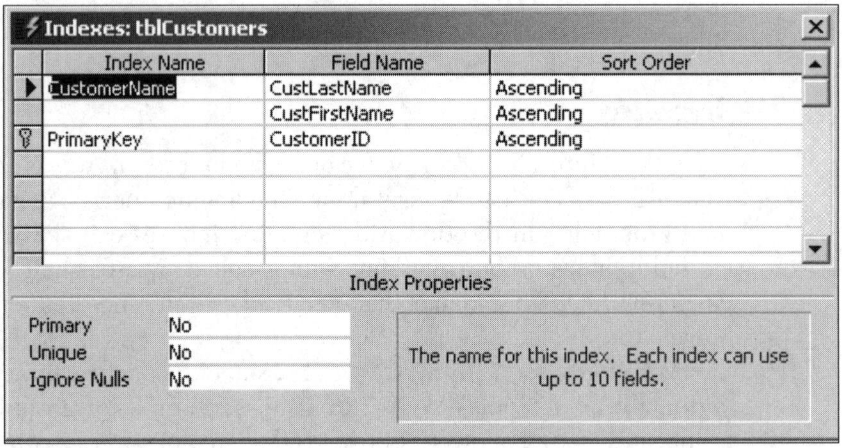

Figure 5.12 You use the Indexes dialog box to create multifield indexes.

Making Changes to Tables and Fields

As with most other things in life, tables sometimes need to change. You might have to modify field names, change data types, adjust field sizes, or add fields. Before you make any significant or extensive changes, be sure to back up your original tables.

TIP Access 2003 makes it easy to back up your database. In the Database window, choose File, Backup Database. In the Save Backup As dialog box, navigate to a convenient folder and save the file.

Modifying Field Names

In earlier versions of Access, the surest way to wreak havoc on your database was to change a field name. For example, you might have edited the name of a field that was in one or more queries. Access would then be baffled about where to retrieve the data for that field because the field as entered in the query no longer existed.

The latest versions of Access adapt somewhat better to field name changes. Beginning in Access 2000, the Name AutoCorrect feature for updating field names has been available from Tools, Options, General tab. In the Name AutoCorrect section, the Track Name AutoCorrect info and Perform Name AutoCorrect options must be checked.

Nevertheless, I still am reluctant to change field names, regardless of whether this option is implemented. (It is turned on by default.) First, the options don't change field names throughout your database in all instances. Second, according to some Access experts, implementing the options could result in reduced performance in certain situations. My personal experience with Name AutoCorrect has been mixed: Sometimes field names I thought would be updated were not.

As stated previously, you can always use the `Caption` property to display a more easily understandable name and leave the field name as it is.

Changing Data Types

Anyone contemplating a change in a field's data type should invoke the entreaty of theologian Reinhold Niebuhr: "God, give us the grace to accept with serenity the things that cannot be changed, courage to change the things which should be changed, and the wisdom to know the difference."

Some changes in data type should cause no unease. For the most part, you can change a field with a `Number` or `Currency` data type to a `Text` data type with little hassle. `Yes/No` and `Date/Time` fields can also easily be changed to `Text`. You can also change from `Text` to `Memo`, and vice versa (although any text in the `Memo` field that exceeds the maximum 255 characters for a `Text` field will be gone).

Conversions from `Text` to `Number`, however, are more ticklish. Values with letters, which are invalid in a `Number` field, will be entirely deleted. Other unpleasant surprises might arise: a value of `786-` in a `Text` field becomes `-786` (a negative number) in a `Number` field.

If you change from `Text` to `Date`, be sure the values are in a valid `Date` format, or they, too, will disappear. The same goes for changing from a `Text` to a `Yes/No` data type. For successful conversion, the values must be entered as either `Yes/No`, `True/False`, `On/Off`, or `-1` for `Yes` and `0` for `No`.

Adjusting Field Sizes

Problems with changing field sizes center on losing data. If you change the `Field Size` of a `Text` field from, say, `20` to `10`, values with more than 10 characters will be truncated—for example, `Indian elephant` becomes `Indian ele`.

With `Number` fields, the major problem is changing from types that enable fractions (say, `Single`) to integer data types (say, `Long Integer`). Also note that the range of the `Integer` field size is from –32,768 to +32,767. If you change to `Integer` and have numbers outside this range, Access changes them to nulls.

Inserting Fields

You might want to insert a field above another field in the table. Click in the row above which you want a field to be inserted and choose Insert, Rows. You can insert multiple rows by highlighting several rows and right-clicking the last row. The number of rows selected is inserted.

Q&A

Q: Wait a minute. Didn't you tell us in Chapter 2 that one of the cornerstones of a relational database was that it didn't matter where a field was located? Didn't you say that no field or record came before or after any other field or record? So why don't you just add the field in the first empty row available?

A: Theoretically, what I wrote was correct. And in Datasheet view, you can move columns and rows with impunity.

But as a practical matter, the default field order is the field order shown in Table Design view. So say you create a form based on the table. The initial order of the controls will be the same as the field order in Table Design view. You can change the field order afterward, but it's easier if it's right the first time. Moreover, if you do need to modify a field property in Table Design view, it's easier to locate a `City` field, for example, when it comes before `State` instead of an unrelated field such as `Middle Name`.

Table Properties

Besides field properties, there are table properties. The table property sheet is available in Table Design view by selecting View, Properties.

Perhaps the two most significant table properties are the `Validation Rule`/`Validation Text` combination. Just as you used a validation rule to limit the range of values in a field, you can use a table property sheet for a rule that applies to two or more fields.

An Orders table presents a typical example. Suppose you have two fields for the number of units in stock, one for the head office (`HeadUnits`) and one for the branch office (`BranchUnits`). The total of the two fields shouldn't exceed 100 units for any one item. The way to ensure that is to enter a validation rule of `[HeadUnits] + [BranchUnits] <=100`. I think that expression is self-explanatory, even if your high school algebra is shaky. Just remember that the fields need to be bracketed and that, in remembering the greater than/less than signs, the piranha (or is it the alligator?) opens its mouth wide to eat the bigger amount. You could also add validation text that would appear in the error message—say, `The total of HeadUnits and BranchUnits cannot exceed 100.`

Another use of `Validation Rule` to maintain data integrity is shown in Figure 5.13. Both `Validation Rule` and `Validation Text` properties have been set for the Merchandise table to ensure that no order should be shipped before it has been recorded. In other words, the date the item is shipped either must be the same or must come after the order date. The expression is `[ShippedDate] >= [OrderDate]`, with `>=` used to mean on or after. The Zoom window, accessed by pressing Shift+F2, is open so that the entire validation text is in view.

5. BUILDING TABLES

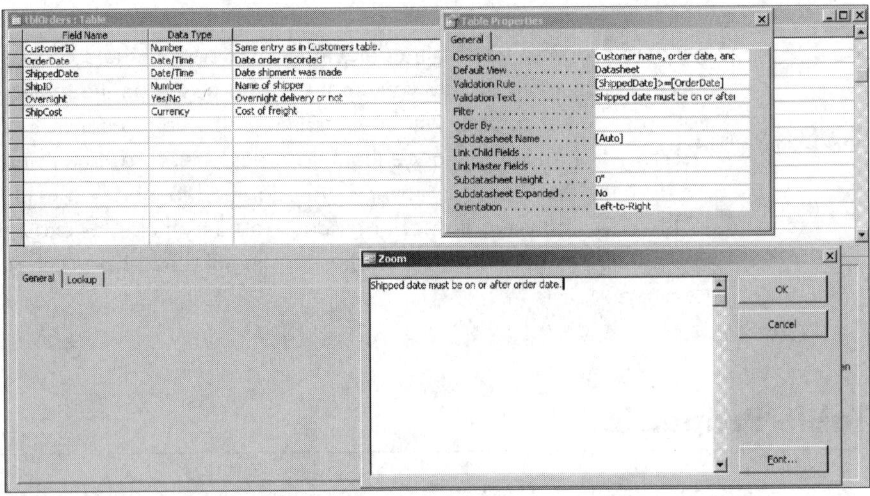

Figure 5.13 The table properties sheet for the Merchandise table, with `Validation Rule` and `Validation Text` entered.

Conclusion

In this chapter, we first examined lookup fields to gain a broader sense of database organization and table structure. We then dug into the specifics of table creation.

We have spent much time on table structure and design. But we haven't actually gotten around to entering and editing data in your database, which is an essential part of your work. The next chapter focuses on these topics.

TIP It's a good idea to get into the habit of compacting your database when you exit, which enables you to use disk space more efficiently. Choose Tools, Database Utilities, Compact and Repair Database.

CASE EXAMPLE

This chapter discussed many of the issues connected with creating tables, but you never actually got around to creating one from start to finish. This case example attempts to remedy that shortcoming. The Nifty Lions database currently has no Employees table. In the following exercise, you create the table using these columns and business rules:

- EmployeeID (primary key)
- Social Security Number
- Employee Last Name
- Employee First Name
- Street Address
- City
- State
- ZIP
- Biography
- Photo
- Date Hired
- Employee Website
- Hourly Wage
- Overtime (i.e., whether the employee is willing to work overtime.)
- Allowed Vacation Days (Must not exceed 10)
- Allowed Sick Days (Must not exceed 10)

Total allowed vacation days and total allowed sick days cannot exceed 20.

Here are the steps for creating the table:

1. In the Database window, double-click Create Table in Design View.
2. In the Field Name column, type **EmployeeID**. Press Tab.
3. Type **a** for an AutoNumber data type. Click in the `Caption` property in the Field Properties pane and type **Employee ID**.
4. In the Description column, type **Unique identifier of employee**. Click the primary key on the toolbar or choose Edit, Primary Key.
5. Click in the Caption property in the Field Properties pane and type **Employee ID**.
6. Choose File, Save As. Save the table as **tblEmployees**. Press OK.
7. Click in the Field Name column of the next empty row. Type **SocSecNum**. Select the Text data type. In the Description column, type **Employee Social Security Number**. Click Save.

   Text was chosen because the field will include dashes between numbers.
8. Click in Input Mask in the Field Properties section. Click the three-dot button. Choose Social Security Number and click Next twice. Click With the Symbols in the Mask, Like This. Click Next and click Finish.

9. Click Caption. Type **SSN**. Set Required to Yes. Set AllowZero Length to No.
10. Click in the next empty Field Name. Type **EmplLastName**. Choose Text. Set Caption to **Last Name**, Required to Yes, and Allow Zero Length to No.
11. In the next empty row, type **EmplFirstName**. Choose Text. Set Caption to **First Name**, Required to Yes, and Allow Zero Length to No.
12. In the next empty row, type **EmplStreetAddress**. Choose Text. Set Caption to **Street Address**, Required to Yes, and Allow Zero Length to No.
13. In the next empty row, type **EmplCity**. Choose Text. Edit the Field Size to **20**. Set Caption to **City**. Enter a Default Value of **Wilmington**. Set Required to Yes and Allow Zero Length to No.
14. In the next empty row, type **EmplState**. Choose Text. Enter a Description of **Use Post Office 2-letter abbreviation**. Edit the Field Size to **2**. Set Format to **>** so the abbreviation will always be displayed as capital letters. Set Caption to **State**. Enter a Default Value of **de**. Set Required to Yes and Allow Zero Length to No.
15. In the next empty row, type **EmplZip**. Choose Text. Enter a Description of **Use USPS 9-digit code**. Save the table. Click Input Mask and click the three-dot button. Choose Zip Code and click Next twice. Click With the Symbols in the Mask, Like This. Click Next and click Finish. Set Caption to **ZIP**, Required to Yes, and Allow Zero Length to No.
16. In the next empty row, type **EmplBio**. Choose a Data Type of Memo. Enter a Description of **Include education and previous employers**. Set Caption to **Biography**, Required to No, and Allow Zero Length to Yes.
17. In the next empty row, type **EmplPhoto**. Choose a Data Type of OLE Object. Enter a Caption of **Photo**. Set Required to No.
18. In the next empty row, type **HireDate** Choose a Data Type of Date. Enter a Description of **First day of work**. Set Format to Long Date, Caption to **Hire Date**, Validation Rule to **>10/1/04**, Validation Text to **Must be after October 1, 2004**, and Required to Yes.
19. In the next empty row, type **EmplWebsite**. Choose a Data Type of Hyperlink. Enter a Description of **Employee's Personal URL**. Enter a Caption of **URL**.
20. In the next empty row, type **HourlyWage**. Choose a Data Type of Currency. Enter a Caption of **Hourly Wage**. Set Required to Yes.
21. In the next empty row, type **Overtime**. Choose **Yes/No**. Enter Description of **Is employee willing to work overtime?** Enter Caption of **Overtime?**.
22. In the next empty row, type **VacationDays**. Choose a Data Type of Number. Enter Description of **Allowed number of vacation days**. Choose Field Size of Integer. Enter a Caption of Vacation Days, a Validation Rule of **<=10**, and Validation Text of **Must not exceed 10**.

23. In the next empty row, type **SickDays**. Choose Number. Enter a Description of **Allowed number of sick days**. Enter a Caption of **Sick Days**. Enter a Validation Rule of **<=10** Enter Validation Text of **Must not exceed 10**.
24. Choose View, Properties. In Table Properties, set Validation Rule to **[VacationDays]+[SickDays]<=20**. Enter Validation Text of **Vacation days plus sick leave days can't exceed 20**. Close the property sheet.
25. Insert a row after HireDate. Type **Birth Date**. Choose a Data Type of Date/Time. Enter a Caption of **Birth Date**, a Validation Rule of **<Date()**, and Validation Text of **Birth date can't be in the future**. Date() is an expression for the current date.
26. Save your work.

Figure 5.14 shows tblEmployees in Design view (I've included the table's property sheet).

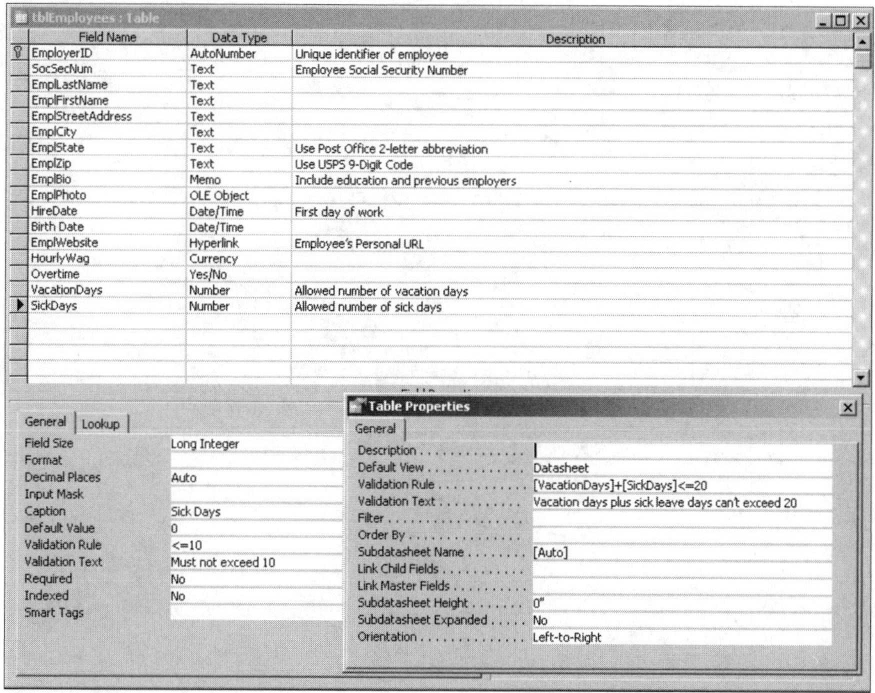

Figure 15.14 The tblEmployees table in Design view.

Figure 5.15 shows in Datasheet view most of the fields of the newly created table, which as yet has no records. You can also compare your work with tblEmployees in the database NiftyLionsEndChap5, which can be downloaded from the companion web site.

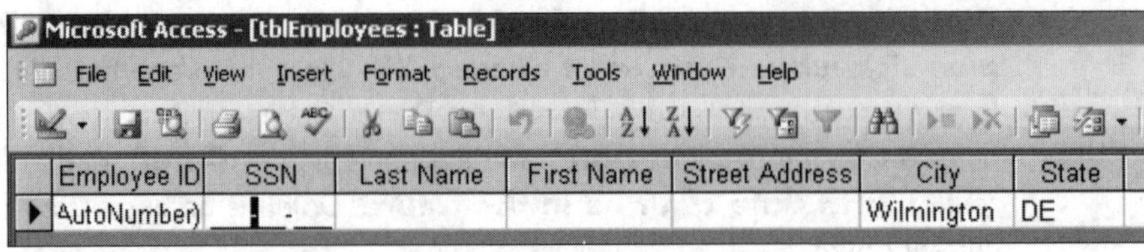

Figure 15.15 The tblEmployees table in Datasheet view.

CHAPTER 6

ENTERING, EDITING, AND DISPLAYING DATA

You can enter data directly into Access tables. That includes unassuming values such as names and dates, as well as more exotic items such as photos, sound files, and PowerPoint presentations.

But most of the time, you'll prefer to enter data in a form—even if it's just a plain old vanilla AutoForm, which you can create in a few seconds. With its powerful graphical features, forms are the best way to enter, edit, and view data on your computer screen.

When you type data into a table, you can easily enter a value in the wrong column or row. Furthermore, if the value is a long text string, much of it will remain out of sight in those tiny datasheet cells. Forms might not offer unlimited real estate, but they do give you a roomier venue for data entry and display. Indeed, values that were partially hidden in the table either are completely visible or can be easily scrolled. And forms do pictures justice: In a table, a photo of the Grand Canyon at dawn is reduced to a two-word description, such as Bitmap Image; in a form, it shines in full glory.

Because forms are often much more elaborate than datasheets and you work in them far more than in tables, there's some tendency to think of forms as the core of your database. But your data is stored in tables; the form is merely a medium to display it. If you recall the story of Cyrano DeBergerac, it was gifted-but-ugly Cyrano who wrote all the beautifully poetic letters that handsome-but-dumb Christian got to read to pretty Roxanne. In database terms, Cyrano is a table, and Christian is a form.

Actually, that hardly does justice to forms. The use of forms isn't simply a matter of aesthetics. Well-designed forms greatly improve the efficiency of data input. You can also combine fields from several tables in a form, which enables you to create documents that are much more comparable to their real-world counterparts than those based on a single table.

In this chapter, we look at data entry and editing, primarily in forms, but also in datasheets. You'll learn about tools and functions that help you display data more effectively. The chapter also lays the groundwork for Chapter 11, "Forms/Subforms," which covers key tools of form creation.

Tables Are the Center of the Access Universe

I want to start by re-emphasizing the primacy of tables, not just relative to forms, but to all other Access objects as well. The Database window does not make the essential role of tables clear; the positioning of the buttons makes it seem that tables are merely first among equals (see Figure 6.1). A graphic representation of Access objects that conveyed their relative significance would look more like the solar system. The tables are at the center of the universe; they are, so to speak, the sun. All other objects are planets that merely revolve around tables.

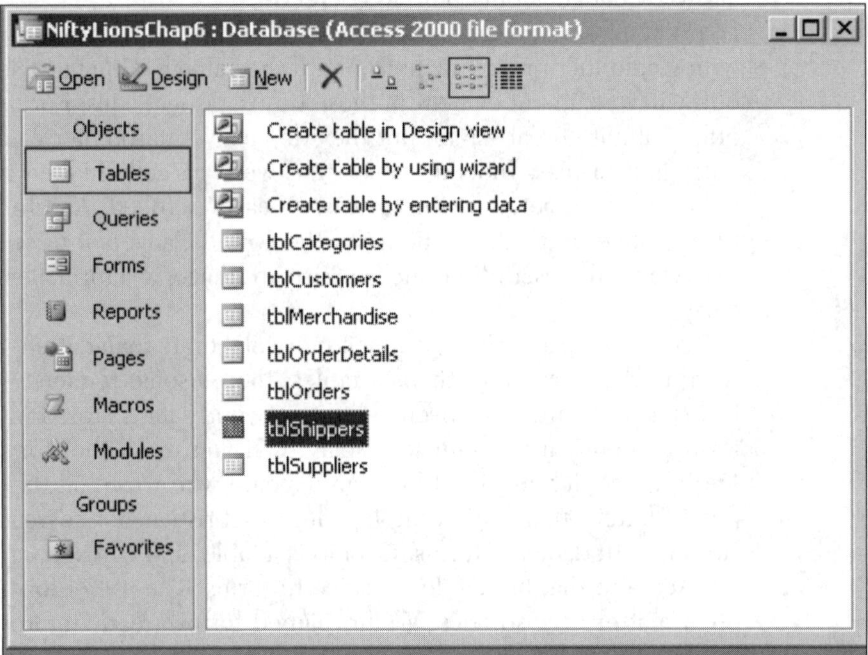

Figure 6.1 In the Database window, tables appear merely as the first of equals rather than as the cornerstones of your database that they truly are.

You can make forms that present your data beautifully onscreen, create exquisite queries that retrieve exactly the information you need, and design reports that powerfully communicate your data to external audiences. But ultimately, all of these are merely manipulations of the data stored in tables. Similarly, you can enter and edit data in tables, forms, or queries (although not in reports). But the ultimate effect of all your work is to delete, add, or alter records stored in the underlying tables.

The upshot is that, if you want to add the value `celery sticks` to your database, or change `celery sticks` to `stuffed olives`, it doesn't matter whether you do it in a table, form, or query. Whatever changes you make to values in these objects are immediately reflected in the table that stores the field where `celery sticks` and `stuffed olives` reside.

Let me reinforce the concept of table primacy with one more example. Let's say you create a form from a table. You immediately add two records and close the form. Later that day, you delete the form. Those records you added to the form remain in the underlying table. And the exact same scenario holds true when you add records to a query.

On the other hand, what happens if you delete the table that is the source for the form or query? The form and query physically remain in your database; but they are essentially empty shells because their underlying foundation has been hacked away. Put more metaphorically, they become like Japanese ronin, Japanese samurai who lost their masters. Without a lord to serve, their lives became purposeless, and the samurai code required that they commit suicide. Although tableless forms are under no such ethical requirement, they are equally doomed.

NOTE Some forms exist independently of any table. These are exceptions, however, and the previous discussion applies to most of the forms you'll work with.

Data Entry in Table, Form, and Query Datasheets

A comparison of menu options in the Datasheet view of a table, a form, and a query, as illustrated in the following example, will demonstrate the similarity of data entry in all three. The `NiftyLionsChap6.mdb` database has a table of customer records, as well as a form and a query that contain all the records from the underlying customers table. To follow along with the example, download `NiftyLionsChap6.mdb` to your hard drive and open the file.

NOTE You used the Nifty Lions database previously, in Chapter 5, "Building Tables." Nifty Lions is a mail-order firm that sells all kinds of items, including figurines, T-shirts, and postage stamps, that have lions on them to retail customers in the United States. The structure of the database is similar to the Northwind sample database, but I've streamlined it by keeping all the business within the United States, using fewer suppliers, and recording fewer orders, for example.

---

1. In the Database window with the Tables button selected, double-click tblCustomers to open it.
2. Click the Queries button and double-click qryCustomers to open it.
3. Click the Forms button and double-click frmCustomers to open it. In the form property sheet, I've set Default View to Datasheet so that it opens in Datasheet view instead of the usual Form view. You can easily change views in a form by clicking the drop-down arrow of the View button and selecting Form View.
4. Minimize the Database window.
5. Choose Window, Tile Vertically.

Your screen should look like Figure 6.2 (don't worry if the objects are in a different order). If you click in each object and open each menu (File, Edit, View, and so on), you'll find that the selections are quite similar (assuming that you've chosen Always Show Full Menus on the Options tab of the Customize dialog box, available from the Tools menu). Indeed, except for a few extra items on the Insert menus of the table and (to a lesser extent) query, all the commands are the same. You can hide and show columns, create filters, use Access tools, and so on.

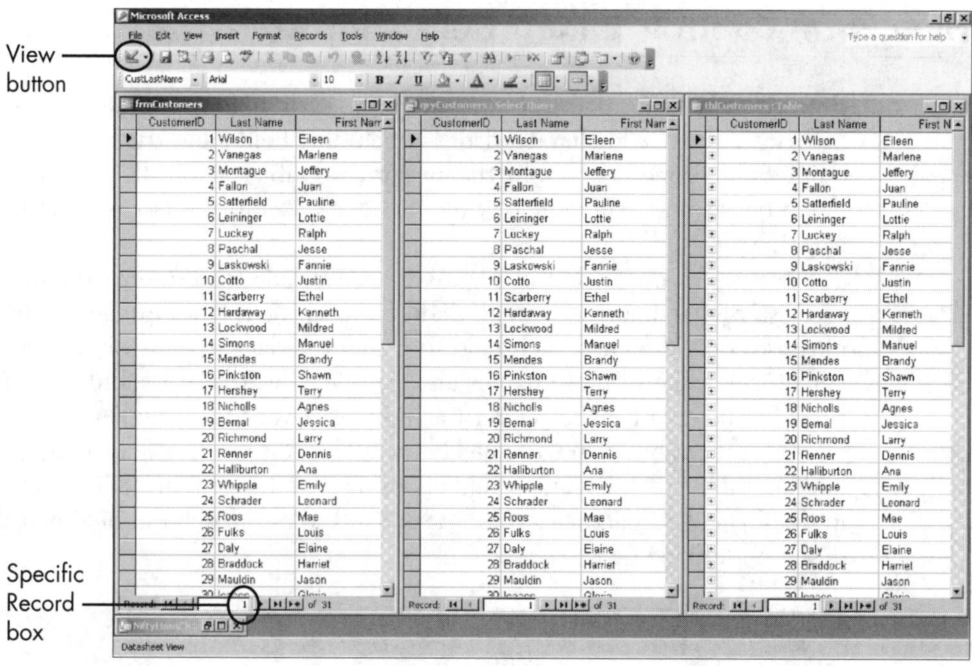

Figure 6.2 Form, query, and table datasheets for Nifty Lions Customers data.

NOTE If you switch from Datasheet view to Form view in the form, the commands stay the same, except for those related to formatting a datasheet. Because the same form in Datasheet view and Form view looks so different, it's easy to think of them as separate objects. They're not. Except for a few commands and properties that specifically affect the selected view, they are the same object, with the same properties. A form in Form view offers better visibility and sometimes enhanced flexibility, but you are still looking at and editing the same group of underlying records.

To restate the key point, you can enter records in any of the three objects, and the tools and procedures remain nearly the same. Any record that you enter and any editing change that you make are stored in the table and, thus, are reflected in all three objects.

NOTE There are some wrinkles to entering and editing records in queries that contain fields from two or more tables. These issues will be easier to understand after you've spent more time with multitable queries. I've therefore postponed a discussion of entering and editing records in queries to Chapter 8, "Queries."

How Form Controls Inherit Field Characteristics

Before I discuss any data-entry techniques, I want to focus on how controls in forms inherit field characteristics—including field name, data type, and other field properties—from the underlying table. This will give you a much better understanding of why the controls in forms look and act the way they do.

The object on the left in Figure 6.3 is a simple (and unrealistic) table in Design view that has a single field for each data type. For illustrative purposes only, I named each field to match the data type (as discussed in Chapter 5, some of these names are "reserved" words that should not be used for fields). The object on the right is a yet-to-be used AutoForm based on the table (you can quickly create an AutoForm by selecting the table in the Database window and choosing Insert, AutoForm). The labels in the form (`AutoNumber`, `Text`, `Memo`, and so on) match the field names in the underlying table.

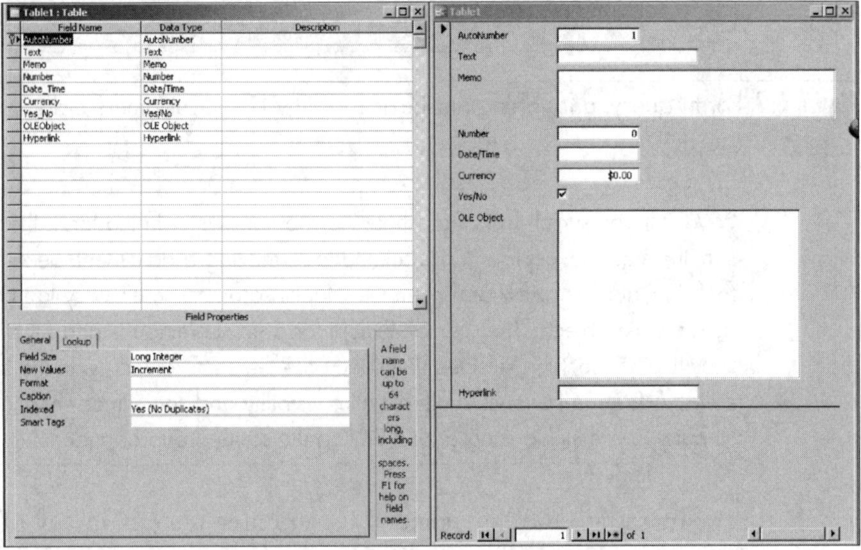

Figure 6.3 A table and form that illustrate different data types.

Notice that the control to the right of each label directly reflects the data type, as follows:

- `AutoNumber`, the primary key that increases automatically by one for each record and cannot be edited, is at its starting position of `1`.
- `Text` is allotted relatively little space (compared with `Memo`) because it holds a maximum of 255 alphanumeric characters.
- `Memo` is awarded a chunk of space because presumably more data will be entered into a field with a data type that can accommodate thousands of characters.
- `Number` has been given a default value of `0` and takes up relatively little space because a very large number can be entered in a small area.
- `Date/Time` is also given little space—you don't need much room for a date.
- `Currency` is formatted as a monetary value.
- `Yes/No` is a check box that you select or deselect because the only two possible values are `true` and `false`.
- `OLE Object` is given the most space of any control because it will likely display some kind of picture or document, for example. To enter an object, you select the box and choose Insert, Object.
- `Hyperlink` is similar to `Text`. But you'll notice that if you start typing in it, the text appears underlined and in blue.

Field Properties in Tables and Forms

As a general rule, the controls in a form inherit the field properties that were set in the underlying table. For example, in the Nifty Lions database, there is a field in the Customers table called `CustLastName` (see Figure 6.4). In Field Properties in Table Design view, the `Caption` property entry is `Last Name`, so the title in the table column is `Last Name`. In the Customers form (which I've shown in Form view), the label for the `CustLastName` field matches that in the `Caption` of the underlying table—that is, it will be `Last Name`.

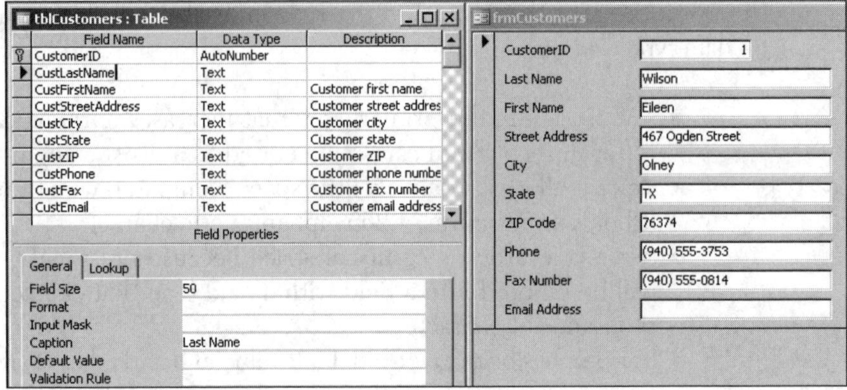

Figure 6.4 The field name is `CustLastName`, but its caption (as shown in the Field Properties pane) is `Last Name`. The label in the form inherits the caption `Last Name`.

But Access also offers you the flexibility of setting control properties in a form for some of the same field properties that were set in a table. Setting the field property in the form has no impact on the field properties in the underlying table. Sometimes that added functionality in the form might be nice to have: For example, you could use a different caption for the field in a form than you used in the table. It also means, however, that field properties in a table and form can be in conflict. Let's see when and where that might be a problem.

Different Property Settings with No Conflict

First, let's take a quick look at setting a property in a form control where there is no potential for conflict.

1. Close tblCustomers and qryCustomers. Maximize frmCustomers (the Customers form).
2. Click View to switch to Design view.
3. Right-click the `Last Name` label and choose Properties, Format tab.
4. Edit the Caption label to **Surname** (see Figure 6.5). Close the property sheet.
5. On the View button, click the down arrow and choose Form View (or choose Form View from the View menu).
   You'll see that the label has the new caption. This is an edit that doesn't cause any conflict with the field properties in the underlying table.

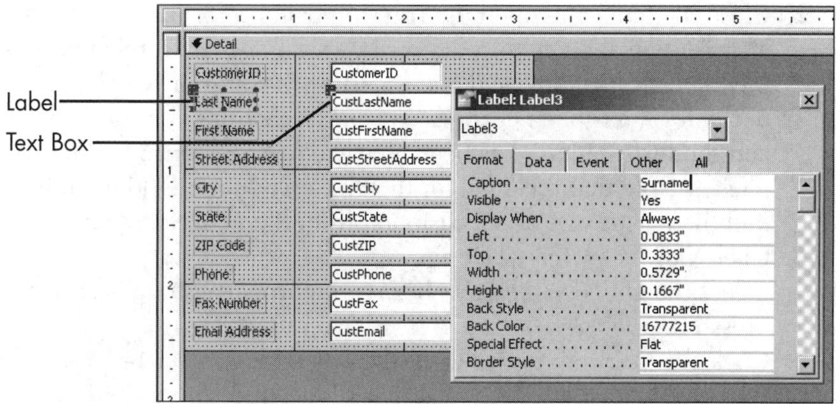

Figure 6.5 The `Last Name` label control is selected and its property sheet is open. The `Caption` property has been edited to `Surname`.

6. Click View to return to Design view.
7. Right-click the CustLastName text box (the control that contains the actual values for the field), and choose Properties, Data tab.
   The Control Source remains `CustLastName`, the actual field name in the underlying table. Merely changing the label in the form has no effect on any of its values.
8. Close the property sheet. Close the form and save your changes.
9. If necessary, maximize the Database window. Open tblCustomers (the Customers table) in Datasheet view.
   The caption for the `CustLastName` field remains `Last Name`, even though you changed the label in the form to `Surname`.
10. Close the table.

Different Property Settings in Conflict

Now we'll take a look at an example in which differences between field properties in the table and control properties in the form raise problems.

1. Open the tblMerchandise table in Design view. Click in the `UnitsInStock` field.
   Note that `Default Value` is set at `1`, and `Validation Rule` is `<=15`. That means each new record will have a value of `1` in this field, and the maximum value for the field is `15`.

2. Close the table and open the frmMerchandise form.
   This is a quick entry form created by selecting tblMerchandise in the Database window and choosing Insert, AutoForm. (The name of the form has been changed to frmMerchandise for consistency, and the form caption has been changed to `Merchandise` for simplicity.) Note that the label for the `UnitsInStock` field has inherited the `Units In Stock` caption from the underlying table.
3. Click View to switch to Design view.
4. Select the UnitsInStock text box. If the property sheet isn't open, press F4.
5. Click the Data tab and click in the `Validation Rule` property. Enter **<20**, an expression that will allow entries of `19` and below. Click in `Validation Text` and type **Units In Stock must be fewer than 20**.
6. Leave the property sheet open, and click View to return to Form view.
7. The current product should be Door Knocker. (If it isn't, right-click in the `Product Name` field, click in Filter For, type **door knocker**, and press Enter.) Move the property sheet if it's blocking your view. Click in the `Units In Stock` column, edit the value to `18`, and press Tab. The text entered for the field in the `Validation Rule` of the table appears in the error message (see Figure 6.6). Click OK.

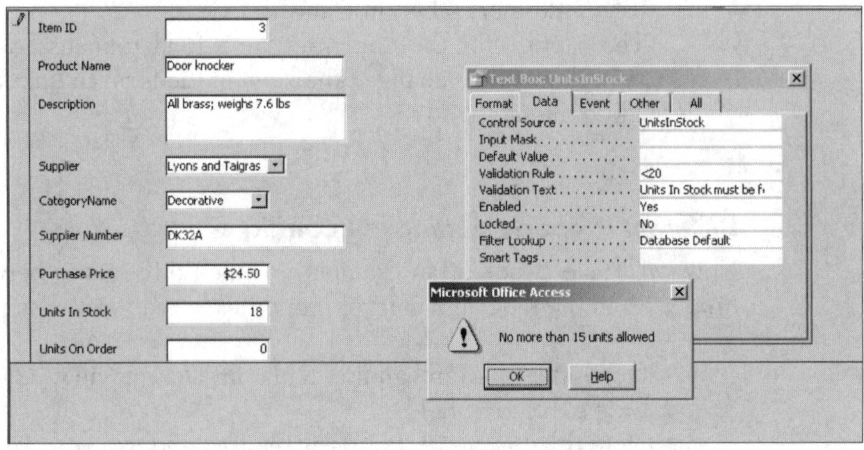

Figure 6.6 The error message is from the field property in the table.

Although your entry satisfied the validation rule in the form (`<20`), it did not satisfy the rule in the table (`<=15`). So it appears that the rule in the table takes precedence over the rule in the form. Or does it?

8. Click OK and edit `Units In Stock` for this record back to `3`.
9. In the property sheet, edit `Validation Rule` to **<8** and edit Validation Text to **Units In Stock must be fewer than 8.**
10. Click in the `Units In Stock` column, edit the entry to **12**, and press Tab.

    Now the error message matches that in the form. Even though the entry satisfies the condition in the table (`<=15`), Access won't let you violate the rule in the form (`<8`).
11. Click OK. Edit `Units In Stock` back to **3**. Close the form and don't save your changes.

Summary of Property Inheritance

Obviously, having different validation rules for different data-entry conduits can cause inconsistencies in your data. Your best bet is to set the validation rule once in the table and then leave matters be. If you do find a need to set separate validation rules in a form, be sure you understand the implications for data integrity.

NOTE The conflicts between field properties in table and form could be further complicated by a validation rule set for the table as a whole. For example, you might have entered a validation rule in the table's property sheet that `Units In Stock` and `Units On Hand` could not exceed 25. Access will separately test each record you enter in the form to make sure this business rule is enforced.

What happens if you change a field property in a table after creating the form? Although the umbilical cord is torn, it is not entirely broken. Access enforces changes in some properties (including `Validation Rule` and `Validation Text`), but not necessarily in others.

The rules of property inheritance are not simple. Here is a summary of the major points:

- A field inherits the `Format`, `Decimal Places`, `Input Mask`, and `Caption` properties from the underlying table. It inherits `Status Bar Text` from the field's `Description`. It also enforces the

`Default Value`, `Validation Rule`, and `Validation Text` properties from the underlying table. The entries for these properties do not, however, appear on the controls' property sheets.

- The settings in control properties in the form do not affect the field properties in the underlying table.
- As a general rule, after a form has been created, control properties are unaffected by changes in field properties in the underlying table. The `Default Value`, `Validation Rule`, and `Validation Text` properties are exceptions to the general rule. Edits to these three properties are implemented in the form as well. This is also true for `Validation Rule` and `Validation Text` properties set for the table as a whole.

NOTE Access 2003 enables you to update certain field properties (such as `Format`) in forms and reports throughout your database when you edit the property in an underlying table. The Show Property Update Options buttons option must first be selected on the Tables/Queries tab of the Options dialog box, available from the Tools menu. When you edit a field property in the table, the Update Properties dialog box appears (you might have to select the option from the smart tag that appears). You can select the objects where you want the update propagated.

- If you set a validation rule for a field in both the table and the form, Access implements both rules. Because both rules apply, whichever one is the more restrictive is the de facto validation rule.
- If you set a default value for a field in a form, it overrides the default value in the table.

Data Entry Methods

Most of us think of data entry as unmitigated drudgery. Like most work, though, data entry has its pleasures and rewards—not least of which is knowing that, when done with care, the information you retrieve from your database will be complete and correct.

Even data-entry enthusiasts welcome any techniques that make the task more efficient. For any individual record, the time saved by any one procedure is minuscule. Incrementally, though, better data-entry methods can save you much time and energy.

Data Entry Mode

One of the primary purposes of forms is to enter data, so it's only fitting that there be a special view dedicated to that purpose. Open any form and choose Records, Data Entry. You're greeted with a blank record. Note that among the navigation buttons at the bottom of the form, the Specific Record box displays `1`, regardless of how many records are in the form. No other records are in view. Each time you add a record, the Specific Record box increases by one; when using the navigation buttons, you have access to only the records you've added during that session. This works nicely when you want to view only those records you just added rather than the entire set. To view all your records again, choose Records, Remove Filter/Sort.

You can set the form to be in Data Entry mode whenever you open it. In Design view, double-click the form selector (see Figure 6.7) to open the Form property sheet. On the Data tab, edit Data Entry to Yes.

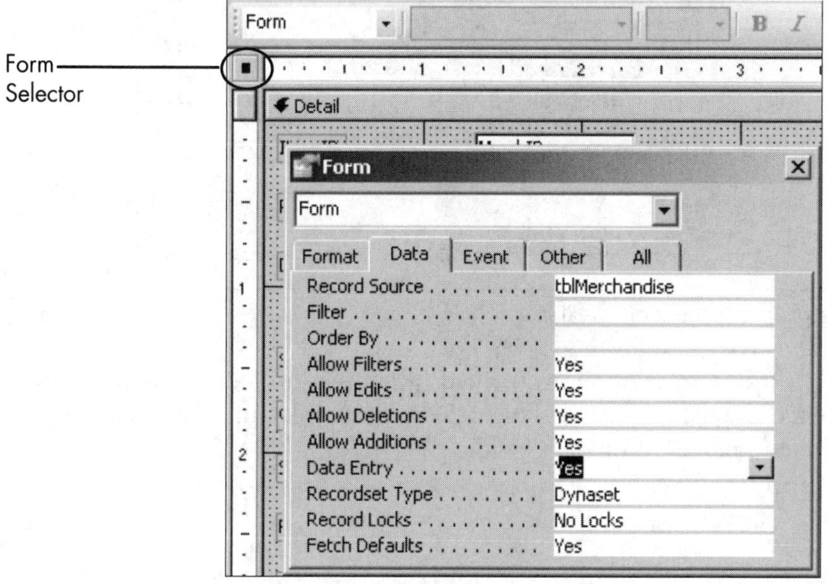

Figure 6.7 The Form Selector opens the Form property sheet.

TIP If there's a form with which you always begin your work, you can have Access open it when you open the database. In the Database window, choose Tools, Startup. In Display Form/Page, choose the form.

Visible Property and Tab Stop

Often when you're entering data, you have values for most fields, but perhaps not for one or two. The vacant fields almost demand to be filled; each time you see them, their emptiness reinforces a sense of failure. More pertinently, you waste time tabbing through empty fields.

You can temporarily hide such a field. Right-click its text box; choose Properties, Format tab; and change the `Visible` property (see Figure 6.8) to `No`. Hiding the text box also hides its label; editing the `Visible` property of the label to `No` hides just the label.

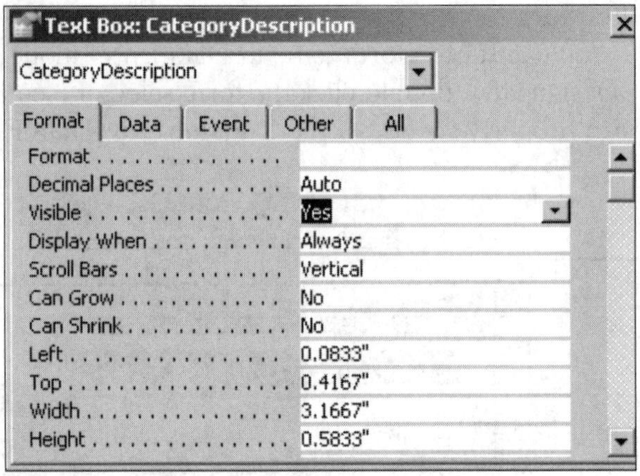

Text Box: CategoryDescription

CategoryDescription

Format | Data | Event | Other | All

Format	
Decimal Places	Auto
Visible	Yes
Display When	Always
Scroll Bars	Vertical
Can Grow	No
Can Shrink	No
Left	0.0833"
Top	0.4167"
Width	3.1667"
Height	0.5833"

Figure 6.8 The property sheet of a text box.

A different solution is provided by setting the `Tab Stop` property on the Other tab of the control to `No`. When you press Tab, Access jumps right by it and moves to the next field.

TIP If you hide the control using the `Visible` property, you don't see it when you print the record. Let's say that you occasionally print records for customers, but you have one or two controls for in-house use only. For that purpose, it's better to hide the field by using the `Display When` property, which is directly below the `Visible` property (see Figure 6.8). You can set it at `Always` (visible), `Print Only`, and `Screen Only`.

Get Special Instructions for a Field

You have two ways to give users special instructions on how to enter data in a particular field. One is to use the `ControlTip Text` property, found on the Other tab of the control's property sheet. The text that you enter for the property is displayed whenever you hover the mouse over the control (see Figure 6.9).

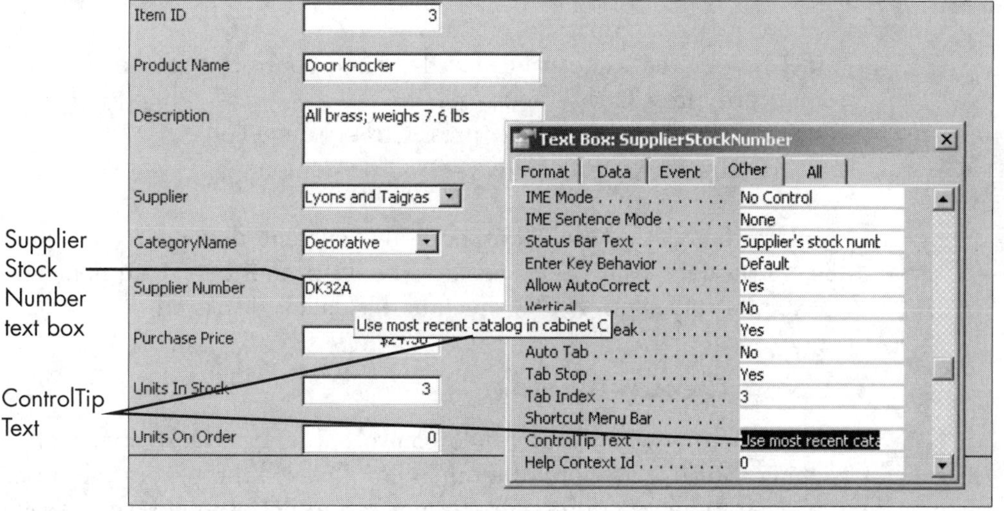

Figure 6.9 When you hover the mouse over the supplier stock number, the text entered in the `ControlTip Text` property is displayed.

As either an alternative or an additive, you could enter instructions in the `Status Bar Text` property on the Other tab. (You might find that the property currently has the field's `Description` from the underlying table. Because the `Description` itself is optional, replacing it shouldn't cause any problems.) The `Status Bar Text` will appear in the status bar whenever the control has the focus.

TIP Even though a Memo text box has exponentially more space than a table cell, you might need more room to read all (or at least more of) what's in there. Use Zoom (Shift+F2) to get the big picture. You might even want to include this hint in `Status Bar Text` as a reminder.

Enter the Same Value

You can take advantage of some useful keyboard shortcuts for inputting values:

- To enter the same value for the same control as in the previous record, press Ctrl+' (apostrophe).
- To enter the current date, press Ctrl+; (semicolon).
- To enter the current time, press Ctrl+: (colon).

Interestingly, you can store both the current date and time in a `Date/Time` field using the second and third shortcuts together. The `Format` property controls how much of this data is displayed.

Tabbing Through Fields

Nothing is wrong with moving field controls around in Design view after designing a form. But more often than not, this will throw your tab order out of sync. When you press Tab to move from field to field, you usually want the focus to travel in an orderly left-to-right, top-to-bottom path. Instead, the focus might dizzily move in every direction.

To reset the tab order, choose View, Tab Order in the Design view of the form (see Figure 6.10). Most of the time, your fields will be in the Detail section. The Custom Order schematic works like the top pane of Table Design view. Move your pointer to the field selector for the field you want to move. (Ignore the Auto Order button because the controls have to be lined up just so for it to work.) When the pointer changes to an arrow, click to select the field. Drag it to its new position on the tab order (see Figure 6.10). Click OK and close the Tab Order dialog box.

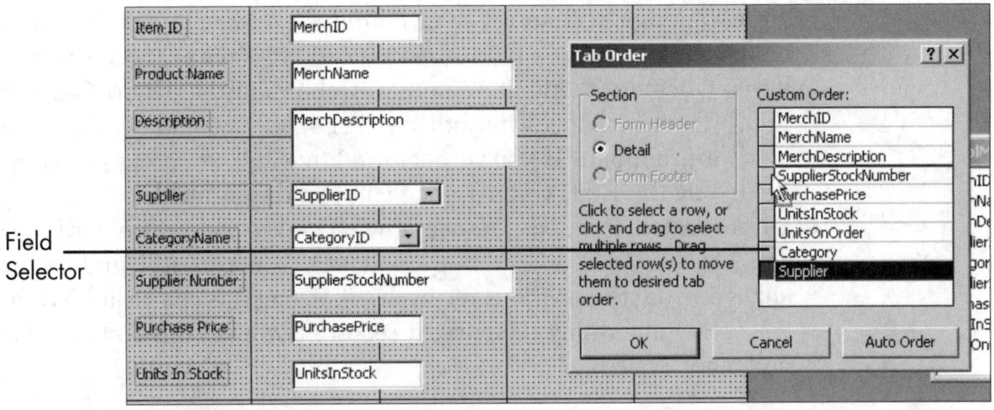

Figure 6.10 The tab order in the Merchandise form is out of sequence. You can have the tab move directly from `MerchDescription` to `Supplier` by moving `Supplier` up in the Tab Order dialog box.

TIP In Design view of a form you work mainly in property sheets, where your changes take effect without clicking an OK button. Thus there is a tendency to just close the Tab Order dialog after you've made a change and assume you're finished. Make sure you click OK or your changes won't take effect.

Understanding the Undo Command

Making a to-do about Undo might seem odd—what is there to say about a command that simply undoes what has been done? Access Undo might not be idiosyncratic or illogical, but it is, well, distinctive. Undo is available in both Form and Design views, but I postpone discussion of the latter until Chapter 11.

If you choose Edit on the menu and look for an Undo command, you'll see three choices (four, if you count the self-explanatory Can't Undo):

- **Undo Typing**—You've just typed, deleted, or edited something in the current field. This command cancels what you've done.

- **Undo Current Field/Record**—Let's say you have a table filled with contact data. You've edited the `First Name` field, pressed Tab, and moved to the `Last Name` field. Now you want to undo whatever you did in the `First Name` field. This command undoes it. Here's another scenario: You've edited the `First Name` field and edited the `Last Name` field. You've moved to `Street Address` but haven't begun to edit it. When you choose Edit, Undo Current Field/Record, changes in both the `First Name` and `Last Name` fields are undone. If you've begun editing the `Street Address` field, only the Edit, Undo Typing command is available.
- **Undo Saved Record**—You've now moved to the next record, but you haven't done any editing on it yet. You can still undo your changes from the previous record by choosing this command. When you've begun editing the current record, however, this command is no longer available.

TIP This tip is almost too obvious to mention, but it's much too important not to. It's the single most important un-doer I know of. When you find yourself in one of those inevitable Access loops in which you are trapped by unceasing error messages, press Esc a couple times, and usually you're set free.

Also note that there is an Undo button on the Form View toolbar. Unlike some other Undo buttons in Microsoft Office, however, you can undo only one action. I prefer to issue Undo from the Edit menu, where I can readily see just which of the Undo commands I am executing.

Using Two-Digit Years for Entering Dates

Access gives you wide latitude in entering dates. Assuming English (United States) as the location in your Windows regional options, the fourth day of the seventh month of 2005 can be entered as `7/4/05` or `July 4, 2005` or `7-4-05`.

One issue, however, is how Access records entries of two-digit years, which is actually determined in the Windows control panel. Under the default settings in Windows 2000 and XP, if you enter dates between `1/1/00` and `12/31/29`, Access assumes it's for 21st-century dates, those between January 1, 2000, and December 31, 2029. If you enter dates between `1/1/30` and `12/31/99`, the assumption is that they are for 20th-century dates between 1930 and 1999. If you are entering dates before

1930 or beyond 2030, enter the full four-digit year to make sure you're entering the correct date.

NOTE Here's how to change these defaults: In the Windows 2000 control panel, choose Regional Options, Date tab and edit the calendar settings. In Windows XP, choose the Regional Options tab in Regional and Language Options. Click Customize, click the Date tab, and edit the calendar settings.

If you want to see four-year dates displayed for time formats that ordinarily have just two years (such as `19-Jul-05`), choose Tools, Options, General tab and set the Use Four-Digit Year formatting option.

Data Entry: Form Versus Substance

As the input of two-digit dates makes apparent, data entry is not necessarily the straightforward activity it appears to be. One reason is that what you enter might not be what you want displayed. For example, a U.S. telephone number has 10 digits (as in `2125551879`), and that's usually all you want to have stored. At the same time, though, you want to see phone numbers displayed in a format such as `(212) 555-1879` or `212-555-1879`.

In the case of a typical phone number, the dashes are just separators for convenience and display. In other cases, though, dashes could be a vital part of the value: An account number of `212-555-1879` might mean something completely different than `212-555-187-9`. In this case, the dash is part of the value, and storing it is essential.

Another factor is that data entry can sometimes be made simpler by using a visual guide. When you enter a phone number in a paper form, for example, you might see three blank spaces enclosed within parentheses for your area code. Some users find such templates helpful for data entry in Access. But their use raises other issues related to data storage and display, as you'll presently see.

Input Masks

An input mask is a template for entering either text or dates. It can be set in the `Input Mask` property for the field in the lower pane of Table Design view. To create the most common masks—for example, for a phone number or a ZIP code—you can use the Input Mask Wizard. The wizard is activated by first clicking in the `Input Mask` property and then clicking the three-dot button at the end of the row (see Figure 6.11). At its best, an input mask offers both easy entry and enhanced data integrity. (The case example at the end of the chapter shows you how to create a custom input mask, which will be available from the Input Mask Wizard whenever you need it.)

General	Lookup
Field Size	50
Format	
Input Mask	...
Caption	First Name
Default Value	
Validation Rule	

Figure 6.11 You must first click in the `Input Mask` property to see the three-dot button that activates the Input Mask Wizard.

NOTE Input masks can also be set in a form. Right-click the text box of the field; choose Properties, Data tab; and enter a mask in the Input Mask property. You can also activate the wizard by clicking the three-dot button at the end of the property. As with other field properties, it's usually preferable to set a mask for a field in a table so that it is inherited when you create any form.

If you open the `frmCustomers` form, you'll find that the `Fax Number` field contains an input mask, which was inherited from the underlying table.

NOTE When you opened the `frmCustomers` form, it was in Datasheet view. You can try the input mask in this view, or you can choose View, Form View (as shown in Figure 6.12). Both views use the same input mask, which shouldn't be surprising because (as I noted earlier) it's the same form.

To see the input mask at its best, click the New Record button, click in the `Phone` field, press Tab, and begin typing **2125556783** in the `Fax Number` field. Immediately a template appears that segregates the area code, exchange, and extension. You can type the 10 numbers of the phone number directly without paying attention to the parentheses and dashes. If you try to type an 11th number, you get a "boing" that tells you additional numbers are not allowed. Press Esc one or more times to delete your entry, and then click in the empty `Phone` field again.

The downside of an input mask can be seen by attempting to supply the fax number for ID 11, Ethel Scarberry. Go to the record and click anywhere in the middle of the `Fax Number` field (as you might ordinarily do when entering data quickly). Instead of seeing the cursor jump to the left, you're stuck in the middle of a template and have to begin navigating left (see Figure 6.12).

CustomerID	11
Surname	Scarberry
First Name	Ethel
Street Address	729 Martin Luther King. Blvd.
City	Mount Olivet
State	KY
ZIP Code	41064
Phone	(606) 555-9277
Fax Number	(___) ___-____
Email Address	

Figure 6.12 The input mask in the `Fax Number` field helps maintain data integrity. Depending on the situation, however, it might make it more difficult to enter or edit the value.

Input Mask Versus Format

Contrast the `Fax Number` field with the `Phone` field. This field has been formatted to display a phone number in the same format as the input mask you just saw without creating a mask (that is, the `Input Mask` property is blank). The `Format` property for `CustPhone` in the underlying table is `(@@@) @@@-@@@@`, with the `@`s standing for required characters. In addition, there's a validation rule of **`Like "##########"`** that requires users to enter 10 numbers.

Go to ID 10 for Justin Cotto and click anywhere in the `Phone` field. The cursor is positioned at the far left. Type **5675554822** and press Tab. Access stores only the 10-digit number but formats it like the fax number. The input mask might ensure that area code and exchange are entered properly, but this alternative method might make data entry simpler.

Let's make one more comparison. Suppose that you want to edit a specific number in the `Fax Number` field. You can click directly on the number that needs editing, and, with a little luck, it is highlighted. In contrast, if you click on a specific number in the maskless `Phone` field, the cursor is positioned between numbers, and you have to erase the number first. Close the frmCustomers form.

TIP If you use both the `Format` and `Input Mask` properties for a single control, the setting in the `Format` property overrides the `Input Mask` property. This could present the best of all possible worlds: You can enter the data in the easiest way possible and display it as you like it. It can also be bewildering if the user doesn't know that both the `Input Mask` and `Format` properties have been set. You might want to include a control tip or status bar text to remind you (and other users) why the format changes when exiting the field.

An Additional Word on Formats

The brief discussions of the `Format` property here and in Chapter 5 do not adequately describe the range of issues this property raises. Most important, I have not discussed customized formats in any depth, nor the many symbols you can use to create them. I haven't provided these charts here, where their text cannot be copied and pasted. Instead, I suggest that, in Design view of any table, you click in the `Format` property for any field. Press F1 to see the symbols and examples of various formats in Access Help.

Q&A

Q: There's a question I've wanted to ask all chapter. Is there any way to print a blank form that can be filled out by hand?

A: The unrealistic answer is, yes. Theoretically, you could open the form in Form view and click New Record. Press the spacebar once in the first field. (Ignore AutoNumber fields.) Choose File, Print. Click Selected Record(s) and click OK.

The realistic answer is, no. The procedure just described probably won't work because you've likely designed your table with required fields, validation rules, input masks, and so on. You'll have to do a good deal of acrobatics to get a completely blank form. Your best bet is to create a new form without any of these impediments that you use especially for printing.

Conclusion

This chapter focused on adding, editing, and displaying records in Access forms. I discussed how forms inherited field characteristics from the underlying table, and I presented specific techniques for better data entry. In the next chapter, I discuss finding and retrieving the records you enter.

Note that you can download the `NiftyLionsChap6End.mdb` file, which shows the objects in the database as they now appear, assuming that you've done the numbered exercises in order. Chapter 6 had relatively few such exercises, however, so `NiftyLionsChap6End.mdb` is not much different from `NiftyLionsChap6.mdb`. It does include the minor changes from the case example that follows.

CASE EXAMPLE

It would certainly be nice if Access offered a wider selection of predefined masks in the Input Mask Wizard. However, you can create customized masks.

Currently, the telephone number in the Shippers table can accommodate only numbers, as in `(212) 555-7685`. You want an input mask in which the last four characters can be either numbers or letters, as in `(212) 555-FAST`. Here's how to add the mask:

NOTE The following example adds a custom input mask that will be available whenever you use Access. You can edit the mask, but I don't know of a way to eliminate all traces of it if you need to delete it. If for some reason you need to keep your copy of Access pristine, don't add this mask.

---

1. Close any open objects.
2. Open the tblShippers table in Design view.
3. Click in the `ShipPhone` field.
4. Click in the `Input Mask` property.
5. Click the triple-dot button in the `Input Mask` property.
6. In the Input Mask Wizard, click Edit List.
7. Click the New Record button at the bottom (see Figure 6.13).

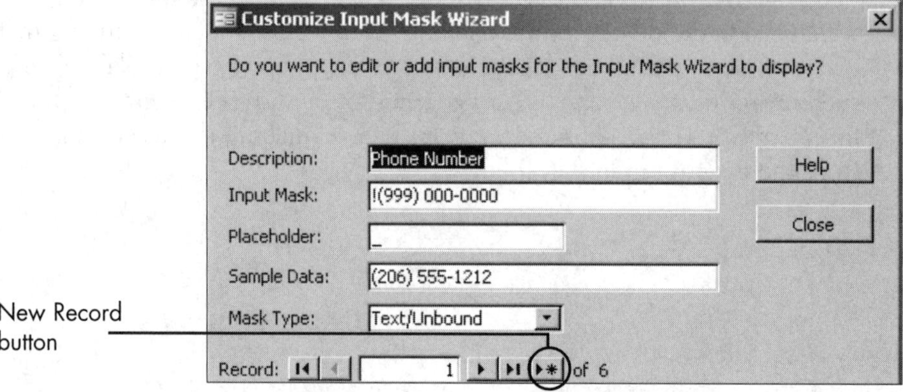

Figure 6.13 The Customize Input Mask Wizard dialog box in the Input Mask Wizard.

8. In Description, enter **Phone Number with Letters**
9. In Input Mask, enter **(000) 000-AAAA**.
   The symbol `0` is a required number; the symbol `A` is a required alphanumeric character. Thus, the last four digits can be either numbers or letters.

10. In Sample Data, enter **(201) 555-FAST**. Leave Placeholder and Mask Type as they are.
11. Click Close.
    Note that the Phone Number with Letters input mask is now among your list (see Figure 6.14). This mask will be available to you in the future in Access.

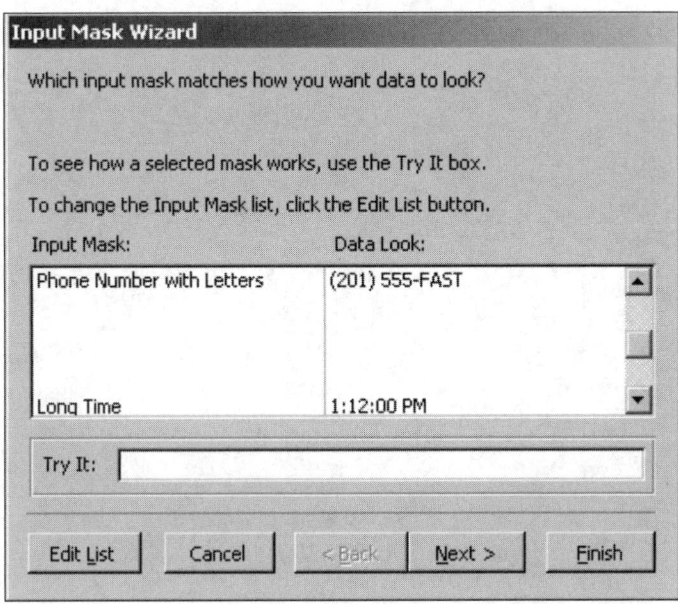

Figure 6.14 The new Phone Number with Letters mask is now among your selections.

12. Select Phone Number with Letters in the Input Mask Wizard.
13. Click Next twice and click Finish.
14. Choose File, Save
15. Click View to switch to Datasheet view.
    Now let's test the new input mask.
16. Click in the `Phone` field for EAN lines. Edit the number to **(305) 555-QUIK** and press Tab.
17. Close the Shippers table.

NOTE This example just scratches the surface when it comes to the possibilities of the masks you can create. As I recommended with the `Format` property, I suggest that you click in the `Input Mask` property in any table and press F1 to see the available symbols and examples of various masks you can use in Access.

CHAPTER 7

FIND AND FILTER

This is the first of three chapters that will help you find, display, and retrieve specific records. It focuses on the Find dialog box and, more important, filters. The chapter also teaches you about wildcards and expressions, which are essential for using Find, filtering records and, more important, creating queries. Although I don't discuss queries until Chapter 8, "Queries," many query basics—AND and OR criteria, the design grid, and operators—are introduced here.

In a well-worn conceit of old TV sitcoms, Ward Cleaver (or Jim Anderson, or Ozzie Nelson) is pillaging the hallway closet. He's looking for his fishing tackle, bowling ball, or soldering iron. Finally he calls out to June (or Margaret, or Harriet) for help, complaining that he can never find anything in this darn house. Mom comes running, takes one look at the shelves, and, with a look that combines tender love and seething exasperation, hands Dad one of his cherished possessions.

If your database is organized with anything like the sparkling economy and ruthless efficiency of June Cleaver's closets, you should have little trouble finding the information you need in Access. Unlike Edison inventing the light bulb, locating the right records in Access should be 1% perspiration and 99% inspiration. Access provides powerful tools for tracking down anything from a few letters in a single value to thousands of records that meet numerous conditions.

There's a progression in the power and scope of Access's "get-it-for-me" tools. At the bottom is the simple Find command, useful for locating and editing a few values. You've used Find often in other Office programs, such as Word. But as a program dedicated to storing and retrieving data, Access has some special features and functions in its Find tool.

The next most robust is the filter, which separates specific records within a datasheet or form. You can quickly segregate records based on certain conditions, or criteria, you set. Users can employ filters for a quick view of customers from a certain state, books of a certain author, or detergents of a certain manufacturer. You can easily remove, reapply, or change the filter to fit your needs.

The creativity and effort you have invested in producing a truly relational database comes to fruition in queries, which, unlike filters, are separate objects in the Database window. Besides retrieving specific records from one table (and often more tables), you can use queries to do calculations, create forms and reports based on the query, make changes to tables, and perform other key functions. Tables might be the foundation of your database, but most of your actual work will be accomplished through queries.

But I'm getting a little ahead of myself. In this chapter, the focus is on Find and filters; let's get to it.

Find and Replace

The best method for locating and editing a few values is often the Find and Replace dialog box, available from the Edit menu in a datasheet or form (see Figure 7.1). On the Find tab, you enter criteria in the Find What box, adjust the other settings in the dialog box, and click Find Next. Access continues to find values that meet the criteria you entered, until you get a message that it couldn't find any matches. The Replace tab works similarly, but it also offers the capability to edit data.

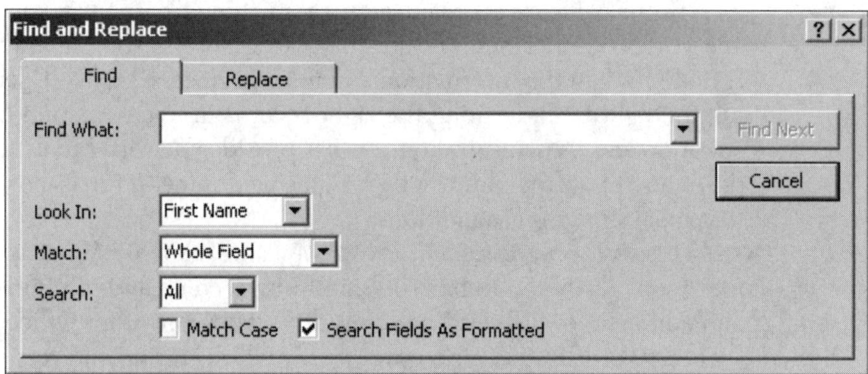

Figure 7.1 The Find and Replace dialog box.

You've probably been using Find dialog boxes in Microsoft Office for years, so I won't belabor its basic functions. Some features are peculiar to Access, however, and are not entirely intuitive. Here are a few tips:

- **Position the cursor correctly**—If you want to find values in a particular field instead of the entire table, make sure the cursor is in that field. Then select the field in *Look In* (instead of the alternative choice, which will be the entire table, form, or query).
- **Take care when choosing directional searches**—Let's say you're working in the middle of a query. You're trying to find a few values you think are at the bottom of the datasheet, so you open the Search list and choose Down. Access searches to the end of the datasheet; if it doesn't find what it's looking for, it calls it quits. Access won't loop back and search the records at the top of the datasheet, nor will it ask you if you'd like that done. The Up selection works the same way, in the reverse direction. Thus, the default selection of All, which searches in all directions, is safest.
- **Avoid the *Search Fields as Formatted* option**—Suppose the field you're searching uses the Long Date format; the value you want is displayed as Monday, November 15, 2004. If you search for 11/15/2004 with this option selected, Access won't find this correct date because the Find format differs from the format in the field. Unless you're specifically searching for values by including the formatting, leave Search Fields as Formatted deselected.

TIP If you're continually finding and replacing data in the same field, consider creating an index on that field to speed up the search. Indexes are discussed in Chapter 5, "Building Tables."

Wildcards

Poker players know well how powerful a wildcard can be. Just like any deuce or one-eyed jack, a wildcard in Access can match things unlike itself. In poker, however, a wildcard can usually match any one of 51 cards. That universality is not true of Access wildcards, each of which is limited to a specific set of values. The correct wildcard positioned strategically can greatly limit the number of accidental hits—that is, records that match the criteria you've chosen but are nevertheless unwanted. Table 7.1 summarizes the wildcards available and how they work. Wildcards are not limited to the Find command; they are extremely useful in filters and queries as well.

Table 7.1 Using Wildcards in Access Find

Name	Symbol	Function	Examples
Asterisk	*	Matches any number of characters	`land*` finds `land`, `landing`, `land-grant`; `*land` finds `gland`, `hinterland`, `never-never land`; `*lan*` finds `land`, `plant`, `clandestine`; `l*n` finds `loan`, `Lyn`, `Lyndon`
Question mark	?	Matches any single alphanumeric character	`c???` finds `call` and `cell` and `c356`, but not `car` (must have four characters)
Square brackets	[ ]	Match any one character between brackets	`l[io]t` finds `lit` and `lot` but not `let`
Exclamation point	!	Does not match the bracketed character	`l[!i]t` finds `let` and `lot` but not `lit`
Hyphen	-	Matches any one character within the prescribed range	`l[e-i]t` finds `let` and `lit` but not `lot`; `l[!e-i]t` finds `lot`, but not `let` or `lit`
Pound sign	#	Matches a numeric character in that position	`m###` finds `m245` but not `mt22` or `mtc2`

To find a symbol that can be used as a wildcard, enclose it in square brackets; for example, `[#]83` finds `#83`.

A Find Example

You likely don't need much help in using Find. But because it is such a useful tool, I've provided a few examples. Assume you're trying to find a customer whose first name you've forgotten, but you know that it begins with j and ends in n.

1. Download the `NiftyLionsChap7.mdb` file to a convenient folder on your hard drive and open it.
2. Click Forms and open the `frmCustomers` form, which is in Datasheet view. Maximize the window.
3. Click in the first row of the First Name column. Choose Edit, Find (or press Ctrl+F).
4. In Find What, type **j*n**.
   Access finds all values that begin with j, end in n, and might or might not have any additional number of characters in between.
5. Your other settings should be as follows:
   - **Look In: First Name**—You took the trouble to move to the `First Name` field, so take advantage of that position by searching on the field rather than the entire datasheet.
   - **Match: Whole Field**—You don't want accidental hits such as `Juanita` or `Jannie`, which would be found for Any Part of Field.
   - **Search: All**—You want to search in all directions.
   - **Match Case: Deselect**—In a small datasheet, Access will find the text quickly, regardless of whether you capitalize the Find What term and select Match Case, or don't capitalize it and leave Match Case deselected. This option is useful when you want to find capitalized text when there are many similar values that are all lowercase.
   - **Search Fields As Formatted: Deselect**—Actually, in this case, it won't make a difference whether you select this option. But it's good habit to get into.
6. Click Find Next. Access finds `Juan`.
7. Click Find Next again. Access finds `Justin`. Click Find Next again, and Access finds `Jason`.
8. Click Find Next again, and Access tells you that the search item can't be found. In other words, there are no more matches.
9. Click OK.

Suppose that, instead of an indeterminate number of letters, you're sure that the first name starts with *j* and ends in *n* and has six letters.

1. Edit Find What to **j????n**.
   Access will find first names that begin with *j*, end in *n*, and have four characters in between.

2. Click Find Next. Access finds `Justin`. Click Find Next again; there are no more matches to be found. Click OK.
   Note that, unlike the previous search using the `*` wildcard, Access didn't find `Juan` or `Jason`. In both of these names, there are only three letters between the *j* and *n*, not four, as required by the four `?` wildcards.

A Find and Replace Example

Now let's find and replace some text. Suppose you need to edit the record of Manuel Simons. You want to change the street name in the street address for this customer from `Carranzo` to `Karanzo`. Because `Carranzo` is probably fairly distinctive, it's better to search directly for that text string and then verify the customer name instead of search for a first or last name that's perhaps not so uncommon.

1. Without closing the Find dialog box, click in the `Street Address` field.
2. Click the Replace tab.
3. Highlight the existing text in Find What and type **carranzo**.
4. Type **Karanzo** in Replace With.
5. Your settings should be as follows:
   - **Look In: Street Address**—As before, you moved here purposely for the added speed afforded by searching one field instead of an entire table, so take advantage of it.
   - **Match: Any Part of Field**—You're not sure where `Carranzo` is in the value, and you're pretty sure it's not the whole value, so have Access look for it in any part.
   - **Search: All**—You want to search in all directions.
   - **Match Case: Deselect**—You can avoid accidental hits by capitalizing the search term and selecting this option. But ignoring capitalization is probably simpler, especially in small tables, and especially for incompetent typists.
   - **Search Fields As Formatted: Deselect**—As noted previously, it's usually best to keep this option deselected.

6. Click Find Next. Verify the address is for Manuel Simons. (If necessary, move the Find and Replace dialog box.) Click Replace to edit the street address.
7. Click Find Next, just to make sure there were no other Manuel Simons on Carranzo. Click OK in the "Search Item Not Found" message.
8. Close Find and Replace. Close the form.

Default Search/Edit Options

To a limited extent, you can change the default selections in the Find dialog box—that is, those that apply when you open it. On the Tools, Options, Edit/Find tab, you have three choices:

- **Fast Search**—This is the default of the defaults. The whole field must be a match, and only the current field is searched.
- **General Search**—This setting provides the widest search. It sets Match to Any Part of Field, and the entire table is searched.
- **Start of Field Search**—The Match setting is set to Start of Field; Look In is set to the current field.

To change this option, click the type of search you want and choose OK. When you close the database, exit Access, and then reopen the database, your new selection will be in effect.

Filters

You filter a table, form, or query by applying criteria to view a selection of data or, more formally, a subset of the records. There are several filtering methods, including Filter by Selection, Filter Excluding Selection, Filter For Input, Filter by Form, and Advanced Filter/Sort. Different filtering tools can be accessed from either the Filter submenu on the Records menu, the (right-click) shortcut menu, or the toolbar. Table 7.2 summarizes these options.

Table 7.2 Filter Selection Methods

Method	Records, Filter Menu	Shortcut Menu	Toolbar Button
By Selection	Yes	Yes	Yes
Excluding Selection	Yes	Yes	No
Filter for Input	No	Yes	No
Filter by Form	Yes	No	Yes
Advanced Filter/Sort	Yes	No	No

Excluding Selection and Advanced Filter/Sort buttons can be added to the toolbar. Right-click it, choose Customize, and follow the directions in the Customize dialog box.

Each method has advantages and disadvantages. Moreover, these methods can be used in combination: You can start out using one method and switch to a second (or yet a third) to refine the filter. The extended exercise in using filters that follows uses the Merchandise form, which has the same fields as the Merchandise table. Spliced among the many steps are a few comments about each method and how it works. Filtering is not a difficult topic, but some aspects are not self-evident, as you'll see presently.

NOTE At this point, it would be ideal to introduce expressions, which are essential for creating filters and queries. But I believe you'll gain a better appreciation of expressions if you work with filters first to see how expressions are used. I think you'll grasp how the operators known as `AND` and `OR` work from my brief descriptions. But if you have problems, see my discussion of these operators later in the chapter.

Filter by Selection

To get a filter by selection example under your belt, follow these steps:

1. Open the `frmMerchandise` form, which is in Datasheet view. Maximize the window. Briefly review the data.

2. In the `Category` field, find any value of Decorative. Right-click the value and choose Filter by Selection.
   You have filtered for records with `Decorative` in the `Category` field (see Figure 7.2). Only those nine records are now displayed.
3. In the Supplier field, right-click any instance of Lyons and Taigras and choose Filter by Selection.
   You have further filtered the nine `Decorative` products records to display only those supplied by Lyons and Taigras.

NOTE The Filter by Selection and Filter by Form buttons are on the middle of the toolbar. To their right is Apply/Remove Filter, a toggle button whose function switches when the filter is applied or removed (see Figure 7.2). The Records menu and the Records, Filter submenu together contain these and all other filter commands.

Filter by Selection Filter by Form Apply/Remove Filter Find

Microsoft Access - [Merchandise]

File Edit View Insert Format Records Tools Window Help Type a question for help

	Item ID	Category	Product Name	Description	Supplier	Supplier Number	Purchase Price	Units In Stock
▶	3	Decorative	Door knocker	All brass; weigh	Lyons and Taigras	DK32A	$24.50	3
	4	Decorative	Bronze vase	Two males, one	Lyons and Taigras	V523A	$19.50	1
	6	Decorative	Marble statue	Lions of St. Anc	Lyons and Taigras	S48B	$72.60	2
	8	Decorative	Antique-finish desk clock	Classic lion mot	Ohio Traders	L4578H1	$17.20	2
	12	Decorative	Garden lion statues	Pair; stone finis	Ohio Traders	L4582H3	$24.95	0
	20	Decorative	Wall calendar	African settings	Ohio Traders	L4522H1	$5.00	8
	22	Decorative	Throw rug	Lioness and twc	Ohio Traders	L4599H8	$22.00	5
	25	Decorative	Cub figurine	Porcelain; 4" X:	Chatchka Choices	LL33A26	$11.00	8
	30	Decorative	Garden ornaments	Pair; stone-finis	Lyons and Taigras	G87A	$67.00	1
*	AutoNumber)						$0.00	5

Figure 7.2 You can use Filter by Selection to quickly filter your records for a single value—in this case, `Decorative`.

Although these examples correctly indicate the ease of using Filter by Selection, this method actually works in quite specific ways:

- If you select the entire contents of a field, Access filters for only that exact match. Thus, a filter for `Ann` displays only records with `Ann`; it does not display records with `Anne`, `Ann Marie`, or `Mary Ann`.
- If you select the first word in a two-word field, Access finds records in which the text is a match at the start of the field. If you select `East` in `East New York`, for example, the filtered records will include `East Huntington` and `Eastern Montana`, but not `Hudson East` or `Heastville`. The criterion for the filter is `east*`.

Similarly, filtering for `East` in `Hudson East` (where the text string `east` is at the end) displays `Hamptons East` and `Orlando Feast` but not `East Kansas` or `Peasterville`. The criterion for the filter is `*east`.

- If you make a selection of any text string at the beginning of the field, Access displays only values that have that text string at the beginning of the field. Thus, if you highlight and filter for `Bake` in `Bakersfield`, Access displays records with `Bakerstown` but not `Andenbake` or `Andenbaker`. Similarly, filtering for `bake` in `Andenbake` finds records with `Littenbake` but not `Bakersfield` or `Andenbaker`.
- If you select a text string in the middle of the field, Access displays any value with that string, regardless of the position in the text string in the value. Thus, if you filter for `land` in `Orlando`, Access displays records with `Lands End`, `Greenland`, and `Netherlands`. The criterion is `*land*`, with wildcards at both the beginning and end of the text string.

Q&A

Q: You said the Merchandise table has the same fields as the Merchandise form. But I just compared the two. In the table, the Category and Supplier columns have numbers, which are the `CategoryID` and `SupplierID`. In the form, the columns display text, the actual category and supplier names. I opened Tools, Relationships to refresh my memory of the database's relationships. I understand that the fields that have data about categories and suppliers are foreign keys in the Merchandise table. I understand that they are on the many side of one-to-many relationships with, respectively, the Categories and Suppliers tables. I understand that, because these relationships have been established, I can combine and integrate the data in these tables. It is certainly convenient and informative to have actual category and supplier names instead of meaningless ID numbers.
But didn't you drag us through that long, tedious example at the beginning of Chapter 5 just to tell us not to use lookup fields? It seems to me that's exactly what you're doing here.

A: You're right, in that the principle is exactly the same: You're looking up values from the table on the "one" side of the relationship and displaying them in the foreign key from the related table. But remember, you're working in a form, not a table. The form's Datasheet view makes table and

form appear as identical objects, but they have different purposes. You use the form to view and enter data, whereas you use tables to store data. For viewing and entering values, you want to look up non-ID values because a category of `toys` is far more meaningful than a CategoryID of `4`.
The tool in the form that enables you to look up values is a combo box. You learn how to create combo boxes in Chapter 11, "Forms/Subforms."

Filter Excluding Selection

Suppose you want to see all records except those containing a certain value. You can use Filter Excluding Selection:

1. Right-click any value of `0` in the `Units On Order` field.
2. Choose Filter Excluding Selection.
   Any records with `0` units on order are removed from the filter.

As you can see, Filter Excluding Selection works the same way as Filter by Selection, except that records with values that match the criteria are not displayed.

Filter by Form

Filter by Form provides a graphical interface for choosing filter criteria. Each field has a drop-down list that contains all its values (assuming that the list is 1,000 entries or less), which makes it easy to select criteria. You can also start typing criteria in the field, and Access will propose the most likely candidate by completing the value for you.

1. Click Remove Filter.
2. Click Filter by Form.
3. Choose Edit, Clear Grid.
   This eliminates any existing criteria in the Filter by Form interface.
4. Click in the `Category` field, open the drop-down list, and select Toys.
5. Click in the `Supplier` field. Type **s** for Stewart Productions. Press Tab.
   Two conditions must now be true at the same time to have a match: The category must be Toys, and the supplier must be Stewart Productions. When two conditions must be present to have a match, you are using `AND` criteria (see Figure 7.3).
6. Click Apply Filter. Stewart Productions supplies two toys.

TIP When you switch to the Filter by Form window, you will often see criteria on the grid. Don't rely on this display to accurately reflect the current filter, whether or not applied. As you'll see presently, you should use Advanced Filter/Sort instead.

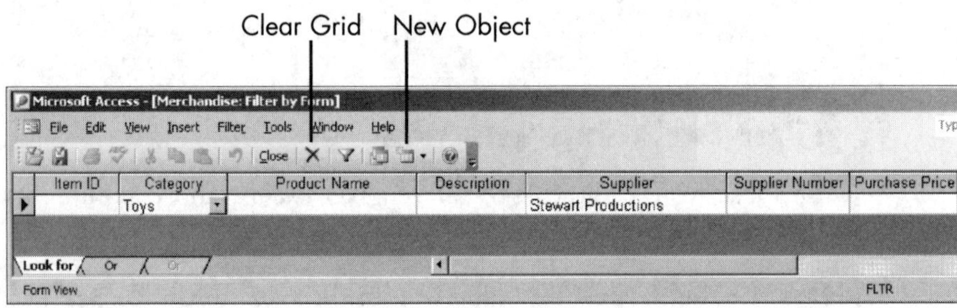

Figure 7.3 The Filter by Form window with `AND` criteria.

Let's try another example with Filter by Form. Suppose you want to view all products made by Stewart Productions and all products made by Feline Fantastics.

1. Click Filter by Form.
2. Delete Toys in the `Category` field.
3. Click the Or tab at the bottom of the screen (see Figure 7.4).
4. Open the drop-down list in the `Supplier` field and choose Feline Fantastics.
5. Click Apply Filter.

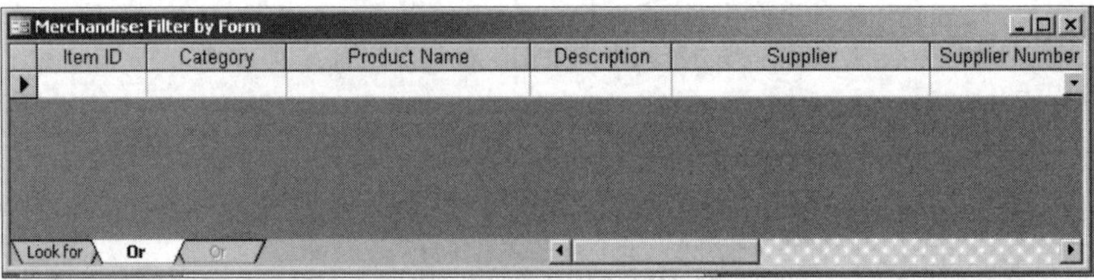

Figure 7.4 Each time you add `OR` criteria in Filter by Form, an additional Or tab appears at the bottom of the screen. To add filters for additional suppliers, click the Or tab that's farthest right.

In this case you've used OR criteria. Products are displayed under two conditions. First, they must be supplied by Stewart Productions. Second, they must be supplied by Feline Fantastics. If either condition is true, the record is shown. A total of 10 products were provided by either Stewart Productions or Feline Fantastics.

Here's a final example:

1. Click Filter by Form.
2. On the Look For tab, open the drop-down list in the Category column and select Toys.
3. Click Apply Filter.
4. Review the records (see Figure 7.5). Note that there are toys from both Stewart Productions and Feline Fantastics, but there are also products from other categories made by Feline Fantastics.

Merchandise

Item ID	Category	Product Name	Description	Supplier	Supplier Number
5	Toys	Doll pair	Daddy and baby	Feline Fantastics	
15	Novelty	King of Jungle T-shirt	Full-maned mal	Feline Fantastics	
21	Novelty	Screen saver	Software with va	Feline Fantastics	
23	Toys	Stuffed small	Sitting lion, plus	Stewart Productions	A457A
24	Toys	Stuffed large	Sitting lion, plus	Stewart Productions	A457B
26	Novelty	Beer mug	Lion shield emb	Feline Fantastics	
32	Toys	Jigsaw puzzle	African pride sc	Feline Fantastics	
(AutoNumber)					

Record: 1 of 7 (Filtered)

Figure 7.5 The record set includes only toys made by Stewart Productions but all products made by Feline Fantastics The Status Bar at the bottom of the screen tells you that the datasheet has been filtered and gives you the number of records in the filter.

In this filter, you've used both AND and OR criteria together. There are two sets of conditions. First, any toy made by Stewart Productions is displayed. The product both must be a toy and must be made by Stewart Productions, so you are using AND criteria.

Second, in addition to toys made by Stewart Productions, all products made by Feline Fantastics are displayed. Here you are using OR criteria. Either set of conditions—that it's a toy made by Stewart Productions, or that it's a product made by Feline Fantastics—can be true to have a match.

Filter for Input

Filter for Input is useful when you can't immediately locate a value to use Filter by Selection, or you want to use an expression (such as >7, as used in the following example). You can also enter expressions in Filter by Form or Advanced Filter/Sort, but Filter for Input is fastest.

1. Right-click anywhere in the Purchase Price field.
2. Click in Filter For and type **>7** (see Figure 7.6). Press Enter. Only products with purchase prices above $7 are displayed.

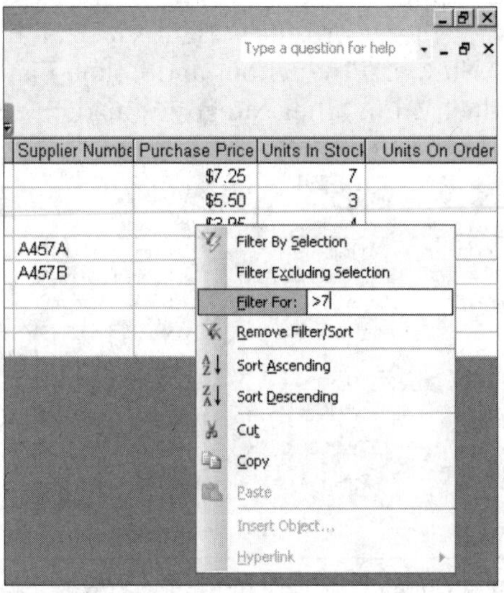

Figure 7.6 You can enter expressions using Filter for Input.

When you enter a string of alphanumeric characters in Filter for Input, Access filters for only an exact match. For example, if you enter **manager**, only Manager will be found, not Accounting Manager, Manager of Operations, or Managerial Operations. You can use wildcards, however, so that shouldn't be a problem. Filtering for ***manager*** will give you all those hits and likely others as well.

Advanced Filter/Sort

Advanced Filter/Sort offers the greatest flexibility for creating filters and sorts. It's also extremely useful for diagnosing a wayward filter.

1. Click Remove Filter.
2. Click Filter by Form.
3. Click Clear Grid (see Figure 7.3 if you can't find this button).
4. Open the Suppliers drop-down list. Choose Lyons and Taigras.
5. Click Apply Filter. No records are displayed.
   Assume that you have no idea why the filter didn't retrieve any records for supplier Lyons and Taigras. You want to see exactly which criteria Access searched for.
6. Choose Records, Filter, Advanced Filter/Sort (see Figure 7.7).
   This grid is similar to the design grid of the query.
   At top, you see the scheme that shows how Access finds supplier company names: It uses `SupplierID`, the field with common data, to "look up" the `SuppCompanyName` in the Suppliers table. But on the Criteria row, note that Access interpreted the criteria you selected as "Lyons" AND "Taigras"—two separate values—because **`and`** is a word reserved for AND criteria. You need to edit the criteria to find the supplier records you want.

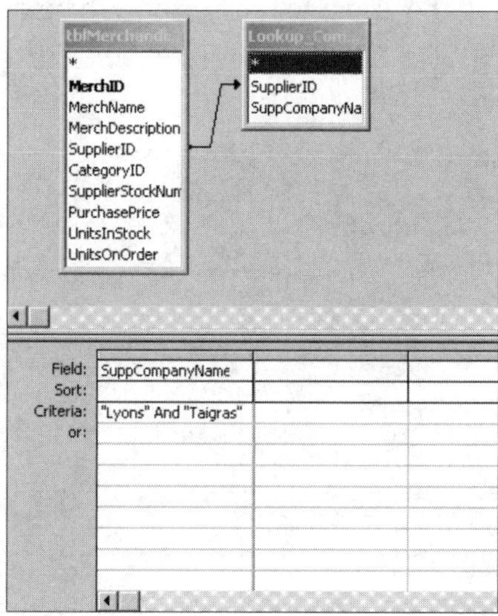

Figure 7.7 The Advanced Filter/Sort window provides a detailed look at the filter.

NOTE Interestingly, if you had selected any occurrence of Lyons and Taigras in the datasheet and filtered by selection, you wouldn't have had any problem. As noted earlier, when you choose the entire value in filter by selection, the match must be exact, and thus the criteria would be "Lyons and Taigras". In this case, Access would have interpreted the entire string as a literal value rather than as an expression. These terms are defined later in the chapter and in the glossary.

7. Click in the Criteria row. Edit the criteria to **"Lyons and Taigras"**.
8. Click Apply Filter. The five records that match Lyons and Taigras are displayed.
   The Advanced Filter/Sort window is also useful for sorting on two fields when the two sorts are in opposite directions.
9. Click Remove Filter.
10. Click the Category column selector to select the field. Click the Ascending (A–Z) button on the toolbar for an Ascending sort.
11. Choose Records, Filter, Advanced Filter/Sort.
    You can see that the CategoryName column now has an ascending sort.
12. Delete the SuppCompanyName column from the Advanced Filter grid.
13. Double-click PurchasePrice from the tblMerchandise field list to add it to the grid. On the Sort row, type **d** in the PurchasePrice column for a descending sort that will sort products by highest price first (see Figure 7.8).

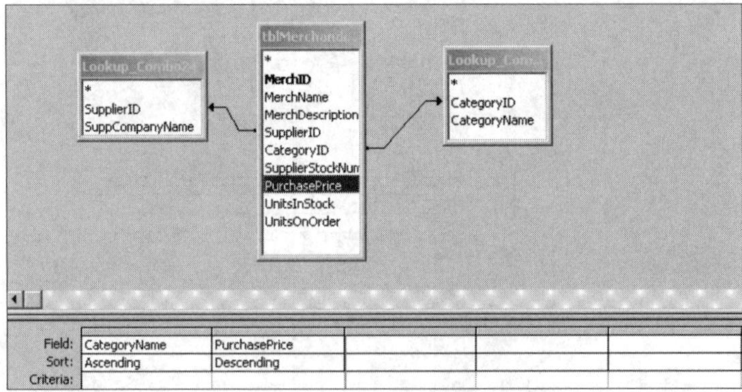

Figure 7.8 In Advanced Filter/Sort, you can use the design grid to set sorts in two fields that go in opposite directions. (The field lists in the top pane have been lengthened and rearranged for a better view.)

14. Click Apply Filter. The products are sorted first by category and then, within each category, by descending product price.
15. Close the form and save your changes.

As the example makes clear, Advanced Filter/Sort offers the most versatility of all filter methods, and it also defines all aspects of the query. It's extremely useful for troubleshooting any filter problems, as well as creating more advanced filters.

NOTE Chapter 8 discusses how you can save a filter as a query.

Filters in Reports

Whether or not a filter is applied in a report created from a table or query depends on how the object was created. Try this exercise:

1. In the Database window, open the tblCustomers table and briefly review the data.
2. In the State column, select any CA value.
3. Right-click and choose Filter by Selection.
4. Close the table and click Yes to save your layout changes.
5. With tblCustomers selected in the Database window, choose Insert, AutoReport.
6. Scroll through the report by using the Next Page navigation button. The report has data from both California and non-California companies.
7. Choose File, Save As; save the report as rptAllCustomers and close it.
8. Open the tblCustomers table.
9. Click Apply Filter.
   Because you saved the filter upon exit, you can reapply it upon opening.
10. On the Table Datasheet toolbar, click the arrow on the New Object drop-down button and choose AutoReport (see Figure 7.3 if you can't find this button).
11. Scroll through the records. Only those from California are included.
12. Save the report as rptCaliforniaCustomers and close it.
13. Click Remove Filter and close the table.

The `Filter On` property on the Data tab of the Report property sheet determines whether the records in a report are filtered. In both reports, the Report Wizard copied the saved filter from the table; however, for rptAllCustomers (created in the Database window), it did not apply it (see Figure 7.9). You can edit the Filter On property to Yes or No to apply or remove a filter when you run the report. The filter itself is displayed in the Filter property. In this case, you won't have any problem reading it, but complex filters are more difficult to decipher.

I won't spend any more time on filters in reports. I think you'll find it better and easier to use queries, including parameter queries, to generate reports with criteria. These topics are dealt with in Chapters 8, "Queries," and 9, "Queries, Part II."

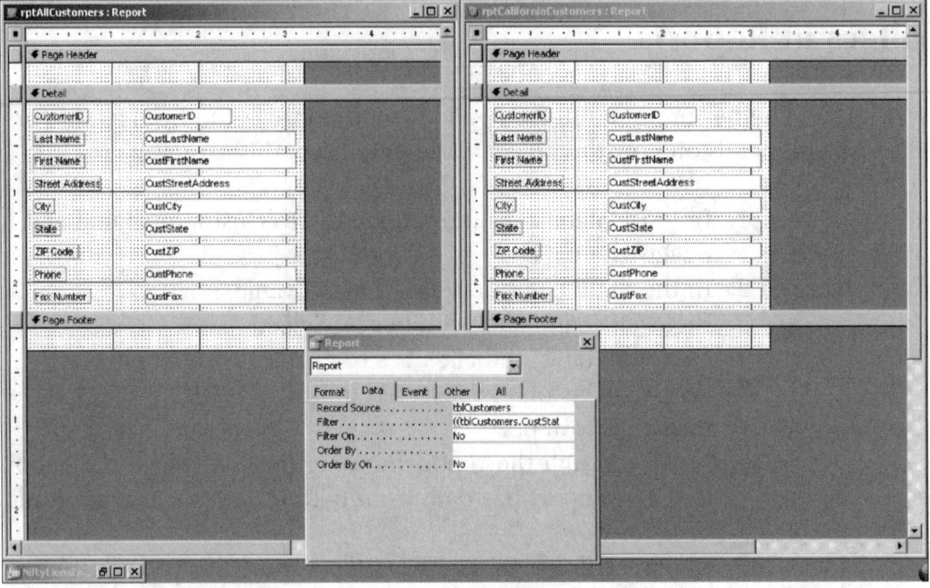

Figure 7.9 In this figure, the two customer reports are tiled and shown in Design view. The rptAllCustomers report currently has the focus, and the report property sheet shows that Filter On is No. If you switch the focus to rptCaliforniaCustomers, Filter On is Yes.

Expressions

In an introductory Access book that I wrote, I named one chapter "It's Only an Expression." The title might or might not have been catchy, but it certainly didn't do expressions justice. They are essential to your work in Access, and they are indispensable for finding and retrieving records in filters and queries. Whether you are using the Find command to locate a `Jane` in a `First Name` field or setting criteria with multiple conditions in advanced queries, you are using expressions to tell Access which records to retrieve.

Unfortunately for the nonmathematical, the dictionary definition of an expression doesn't offer much enlightenment: any combination of mathematical or logical operators, constants, functions, and names of fields, controls, and properties that evaluates to a single value. Half the words in the definition themselves require definition (the sidebar on expression terminology offers some help).

Instead of spending a lot of time on terminology, I think you'll find it more instructive to see some expressions in action. I have categorized them by operator, which tells Access the type of action to perform. Besides the few examples of expressions here, you'll have many more opportunities in the next two chapters to work with expressions in queries.

Expression Terminology

Perhaps the least enjoyable part of using Access is learning abstract terminology that can be cryptic. These terms are important for discussing expressions, however, so here are some definitions:

Operators are symbols that tell you what action will be performed on the expression. Examples include `+`, `-`, `AND`, `OR`, `NOT`, `>`, and `<`.

Constants include `Yes`, `No`, `True`, `False`, and `Null`. These are values that do not change.

Literal values, or *literals*, are actual values (numbers, dates, names) that Access evaluates exactly as written. Examples abound: `pony`, `685`, `Siam`, `3/22/96`.

Functions return a value based on the results of a calculation or some other expression. The `Sum()` function, for example, returns the sum of whatever is in the parentheses. Functions are discussed in the next chapter.

Identifiers are elements in an expression that refer to the value of fields, controls, properties, and so on. The format of an identifier depends on the context. For example, the full identifier for a `UnitsInStock` field in a Products table would be `[Products]![UnitsInStock]`. But in a query based on the Products table, you can refer to the field simply as `[UnitsInStock]`.

LIKE

Let's start with an example using the all-important `LIKE` operator.

1. Open the `frmMerchandise` form.
2. Choose Records, Filter, Advanced Filter/Sort.
3. Click Clear Grid to remove all existing criteria.
4. Double-click MerchName to add it to the grid.
5. Type **bronze vase** on the Criteria row.
6. Click Apply Filter.
   Access finds the bronze vase record.
7. Choose Records, Filter, Advanced Filter/Sort
8. Edit the criteria to **Like "bronze vase"** (see Figure 7.10).
   The quotation marks, which signify that the text string between them is a literal value, will already be in place.

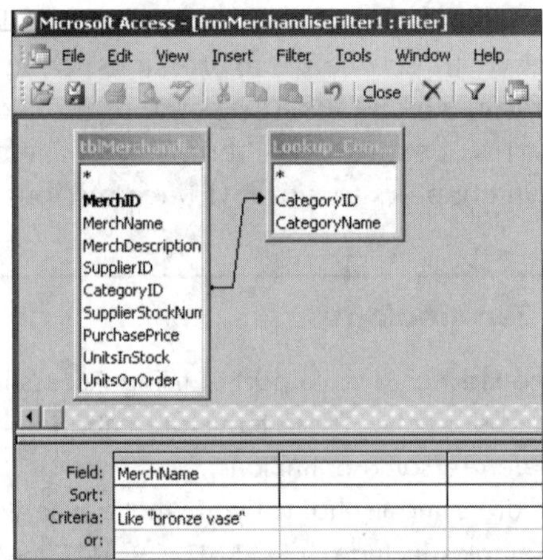

Figure 7.10 The `LIKE` operator finds matches for the text string `bronze vase`.

9. Click Apply Filter. The same record is selected.

As you can see, the `LIKE` operator matches the pattern you specify. You can type the operator as `like` or `LIKE` or `Like` or even `LiKE`; Access displays it as `Like`.

The expression `Like "bronze vase"` includes the `LIKE` operator, which tells Access to perform a specific action. The other element, `"bronze vase"`, is the literal value that Access evaluated. As steps 5–6 of the example demonstrate, if you just want to match a literal value in Access, you do not need to include an operator.

The `Like` operator is usually used with wildcards. The expression `Like "*d"` means "find me values that end in `d` with any number of characters before it." You'll see many more examples of the `Like` operator at work when I discuss queries in Chapters 8 and 9.

AND and OR

You used the AND and OR operators earlier in the chapter. You use AND criteria when two or more conditions must be true at the same time, and OR criteria when any of several conditions is sufficient.

Another View of AND and OR

Because AND and OR operators are so important to your Access work, let's look at them from a simple vantage point, just in case you're having trouble distinguishing the two.

Given their importance in Internet search engines, new Access users are often aware of the AND and OR operators—if not the precise terminology, at least their practical application. Let's use the Advanced Search page at Google for general examples of AND and OR that are not specific to Access.

Say you're looking for information about camping in the Adirondacks. To find that information, you enter **camping Adirondacks** in the With All of the Words box at the top of the page (see Figure 7.11).

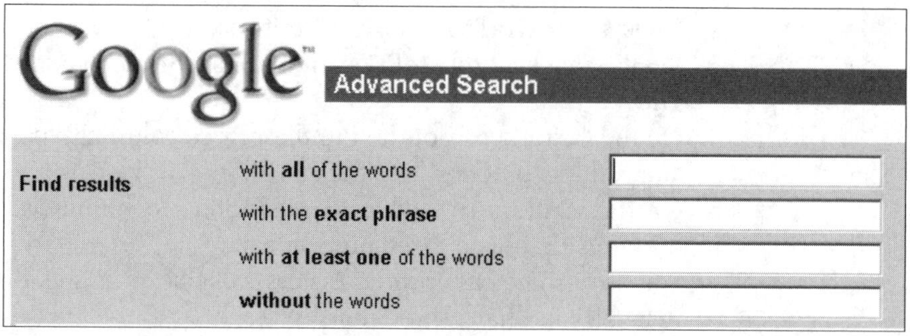

Figure 7.11 Internet surfers have become familiar with the use of AND or OR criteria through search engine forms. When all the words must be found, you're using AND criteria. When any of several words—that is, any of several conditions—will be a match, you're using OR criteria.

Why all of the words? If you entered `camping` alone, you'd get pages on the great outdoors from Timbuktu to Kalamazoo. If you entered just `Adirondacks`, you'd get pages on biking in the Adirondacks, protecting the Adirondacks, and museums in the Adirondacks. Both keywords are needed for your search.

In this case you're using the `AND` operator. Two conditions—the presence of each of the keywords—must apply to have a match.

Now say you're just looking for general information about either the Adirondacks or the Poconos. You use the At Least One of the Words box to enter **Poconos Adirondacks**.

Why at least one of the words? A page on either resort area is a good hit, so a single URL need not include both terms. Nevertheless, when you search for at least one of the words, the engine could return pages that have both keywords on the same page.

In this case, you're using the `OR` operator. Either condition—a match with `Adirondacks` or `Poconos`—will do just fine. If both conditions happen to be met on one page, that's okay, too (you don't know whether that's a more useful match until you view the page).

Examples of AND and OR

On the design grid, `AND` criteria is entered on the same row, and `OR` criteria is entered on different rows. You'll use `AND` and `OR` criteria in the case example at the end of this chapter and in Chapters 8 and 9. But let's do a quick exercise now to make sure you understand the difference.

1. Choose Records, Filter, Advanced Filter/Sort.
2. Click Clear Grid to remove all criteria.
3. Double-click PurchasePrice and UnitsInStock to add them to the grid.
4. On the Criteria row of the PurchasePrice column, type **<10** to find all products that cost less than $10.
5. On the Criteria row of the UnitsInStock column, type **3** to find products that have three units in stock.
   You are using `AND` criteria. Access will find products that cost less than $10 and have three units in stock.
6. Click Apply Filter. Access finds three products with that criteria.
7. Choose Records, Filter, Advanced Filter/Sort.
8. On the Criteria row of the UnitsInStock column, cut **3**. Paste it in the Or row of the same column (see Figure 7.12).

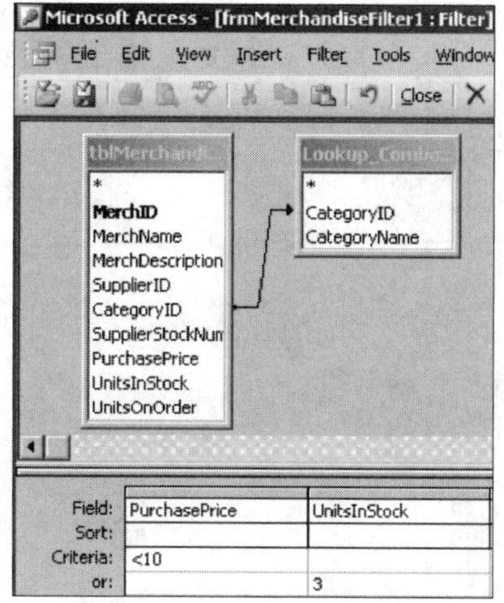

Figure 7.12 The design grid contains `OR` criteria because both the Criteria and Or rows contain criteria.

You are now using `OR` criteria. Access will find all records that are either priced at less than $10 or have three units in stock.

9. Click Apply Filter to see your record set.

   Your record set includes `Item ID #3`, which costs more than $10 but is included because there are three units in stock.

NOT

The `NOT` operator can be used to reverse any operator. For example, placed before the expression `LIKE "laundry"`, the expression becomes `NOT LIKE "laundry"`—that is, it will retrieve records that don't match the text string `laundry`. Here's another use of the `NOT` operator:

1. Choose Records, Filter, Advanced Filter/Sort.
2. Edit the criteria to **not <10**.

   The expression `not <10` is equivalent to `>=10`—that is, greater than or equal to `10`.
3. Click Apply Filter.

   Now Access finds all the products with purchase prices equal to or above $10, as well as those records that cost less than $10 but have three units in stock (see Figure 7.13).

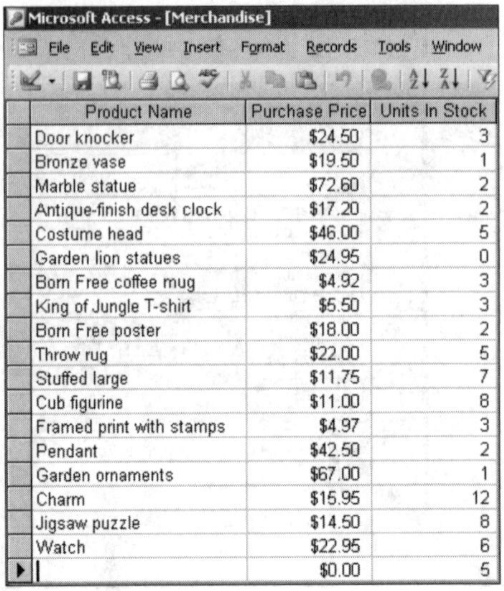

Microsoft Access - [Merchandise]

Product Name	Purchase Price	Units In Stock
Door knocker	$24.50	3
Bronze vase	$19.50	1
Marble statue	$72.60	2
Antique-finish desk clock	$17.20	2
Costume head	$46.00	5
Garden lion statues	$24.95	0
Born Free coffee mug	$4.92	3
King of Jungle T-shirt	$5.50	3
Born Free poster	$18.00	2
Throw rug	$22.00	5
Stuffed large	$11.75	7
Cub figurine	$11.00	8
Framed print with stamps	$4.97	3
Pendant	$42.50	2
Garden ornaments	$67.00	1
Charm	$15.95	12
Jigsaw puzzle	$14.50	8
Watch	$22.95	6
	$0.00	5

Figure 7.13 The datasheet now includes products that meet `OR` criteria , which includes an expression using the `NOT` operator. (For a better view and easier comparisons, I've hidden most of the columns in the data sheet.)

IS

The `IS` operator has very limited use. If you want to look for records with null values, use the expression `Is Null`. If you don't want to include null values, use `Is Not Null`.

In `frmMerchandise`, nine records don't have supplier numbers. Because they are blank, you don't know whether they are null values or zero-length fields.

1. Choose Records, Filter, Advanced Filter/Sort.
2. Click Clear Grid.
3. Double-click SupplierStockNumber to add it to the grid.
4. Type **is null** in the Criteria row.
5. Click Apply Filter. The seven records that have null values are displayed.

NOTE If you want to match zero-length strings instead, don't use the `IS` operator; type "" (double quotation marks) in the Criteria row of the applicable field.

Arithmetic Operators

I don't think the arithmetic operators +, -, *, and / (for addition, subtraction, multiplication, and division) will cause you any concern. The ^ operator might be unfamiliar; it is used for exponents—raising a number to a specific power.

Note that the asterisk (*) is both an operator and a wildcard. It is a wildcard when used with the `LIKE` and `NOT` operators, but it is a multiplication operator when used with calculated expressions such as `[ListPrice]*1.08`. You'll see arithmetic operators more in the next two chapters.

Comparison Operators

You've already used comparison operators such as > and <. If you understand that the operator >= means "greater than or equal to," you won't have a problem with other comparison operators, such as =, <, <=, >, and >=. One operator that you might not be familiar with, however, is <>, which means "not equal to." For example, `<>100` tells Access to search for values that do not equal 100.

Note that the <> operator differs from `NOT`, which means "not true." If you want to exclude records with cities that begin with *m*, enter the expression **`Not "m*"`**; don't use **`<> "m*"`**.

Comparison Operators with Text

As this example indicates, you can use comparison operators with not only numbers and dates, but text as well. Try the following exercise:

1. Choose Records, Filter, Advanced Filter/Sort.
2. Click Clear Grid.
3. Double-click the `MerchName` field.
4. In the Criteria row, type **>=g**.
5. Click Apply Filter.
6. Select the Product Name column and click the Sort Ascending (A–Z) button.

   Only products that begin with g through *z* are displayed in the datasheet (see Figure 7.14).

Item ID	Category	Product Name	Description	Supplier	Sup
12	Decorative	Garden lion statues	Pair; stone finished; 8 1/	Ohio Traders	L45
30	Decorative	Garden ornaments	Pair; stone-finish, alabas	Lyons and Taigras	G87
32	Toys	Jigsaw puzzle	African pride scene; 211	Feline Fantastics	
9	Novelty	Kenya paper money	Issued 1978; 20 shillings	Ronaldo the Lion-He	
15	Novelty	King of Jungle T-shirt	Full-maned male with bla	Feline Fantastics	
28	Novelty	Lioness coffee mug		Ohio Traders	L37
6	Decorative	Marble statue	Lions of St. Andronico; w	Lyons and Taigras	S48
29	Jewelry	Pendant	14K lioness with necklac	Beaumont Jewelry	P16
18	Toys	Playing cards	Deck with various lion ph	Lyons and Taigras	PC
10	Novelty	Rio Muni stamp set	Vermillion 10+5 cts male	Ronaldo the Lion-He	
21	Novelty	Screen saver	Software with various lior	Feline Fantastics	
19	Clothing	Socks	Gray with black line lion	Stewart Productions	S34
24	Toys	Stuffed large	Sitting lion, plus, 26"	Stewart Productions	A45
23	Toys	Stuffed small	Sitting lion, plush, 14"	Stewart Productions	A45
22	Decorative	Throw rug	Lioness and two cubs; 4'	Ohio Traders	L45
20	Decorative	Wall calendar	African settings	Ohio Traders	L45
33	Jewelry	Watch	Round face; male picture	Beaumont Jewelry	W7

Figure 7.14 The use of comparison operators, such as >=, is not limited to numbers and dates. They can also be used with text to find values that begin before or after a letter of the alphabet.

Between...And...

The `Between...And...` operator is often used with dates and numbers. For example, the expression `between 3/1/05 and 3/31/05` in a field with a `Date/Time` data type finds records for all dates in March 2005. You can also use `Between...And...` for finding a range of names, or a range of prices. For example, `between 4 and 22` would find prices between $4 and $22. Note that this expression is the same as `>=4 and <=22`.

NOTE Access uses a pound sign (#) to denote a literal that is a date (as in `#3/1/05#`) or time (as in `#1:00:00#`), as compared with the quotation marks used for text strings.

Try this exercise:

1. Choose Records, Filter, Advanced Filter/Sort.
2. Click Clear Grid.
3. Double-click the `UnitsInStock` field.
4. In the criteria row, enter **between 3 and 7**.
5. Click Apply Filter. Access finds records with three, four, five, six, or seven units in stock.
6. Close the frmMerchandise form.

Conclusion

This chapter introduced you to the Find and Replace dialog box, filters, wildcards, and expressions. This foundation will be extremely useful as you explore queries in the next two chapters.

You can compare your work in this chapter to the `NiftyLionsChap7End.mdb` file, which shows the database objects as they appear at the end of the chapter.

CASE EXAMPLE

The following case example reviews some of the tools and techniques you learned about in this chapter.

1. Open the frmCustomers form.
2. In the `State` field, select any instance of `CA`, right-click, and choose Filter by Selection.
3. Select any instance of `Sacramento`, right-click, and choose Filter by Selection.
4. In the `ZIP Code` field, select 94205, right-click, and choose Filter Excluding Selection.
5. Choose Records, Filter, Advanced Filter/Sort (see Figure 7.15) to see the criteria you've designated.

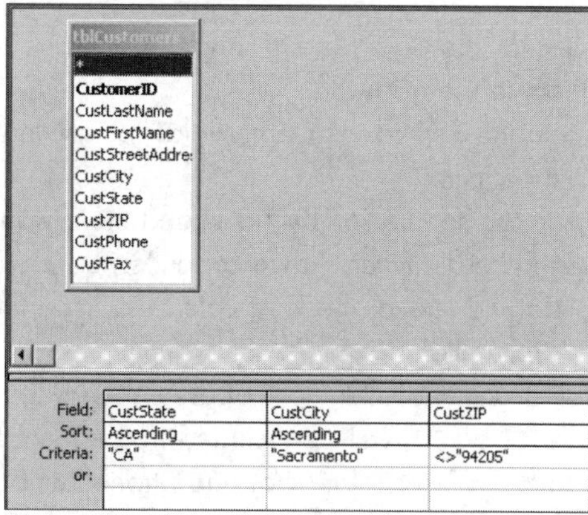

Figure 7.15 The design grid shows that the filter has three conditions, all of which must be true at the same time.

6. Choose Filter, Filter by Form.
7. Click Clear Grid.
8. In the `Phone` field, type **213***.
9. Click in the `ZIP Code` field. Open the drop-down list and select 90096.
10. Click the Or tab at the bottom of the screen. Open the drop-down list in the `Phone` field. Select 2075550847.
11. Click the next Or tab (the one farthest right). Open the drop-down list for the `City` field and select Bakersfield.
12. Click Apply Filter. The datasheet has three records (see Figure 7.16).

	Custome	Last Name	First Name	Street Address	City	State	ZIP Code	Phone	Fax Number
▶	3	Montague	Jeffery	72-63 Cook Avenue	Bakersfield	CA	93311	(661) 555-0248	
	12	Hardaway	Kenneth	1988 Excelsior	Los Angeles	CA	90096	(213) 555-8067	(213) 555-3272
	20	Richmond	Larry	9308 Montcrist	Portland	ME	04112	(207) 555-0847	(207) 555-1233
*	)Number)								

Figure 7.16 The filter uses a combination of `AND` and `OR` criteria.

13. Choose Records, Filter, Advanced Filter/Sort.
14. Delete the `CustZIP` column. Review the criteria on the Design grid.
15. Click Apply Filter. Try to determine why each of the five records was chosen (choose Records-Filter-Advanced Filter/Sort as necessary).
16. Click Remove Filter.
17. Choose Records, Filter, Advanced Filter/Sort.
18. Click Clear Grid.
19. Double-click the `CustState` and `CustCity` fields, in that order, to add them to the grid.
20. Type **a** in the Sort row for both fields for ascending sorts.
21. Click Apply Filter.

The records are sorted first by state, and then, within each state, by city.

22. Choose Records, Filter, Advanced Filter/Sort.
23. In the Criteria row of the CustState field, type **>k**.
24. Click Apply Filter.

    Note that any two-letter state abbreviation beginning with *k* or greater, such as `KY` or `TN`, will be included in the records.
25. Click Remove Filter. Note that one phone number is a null value.
26. Right-click anywhere in the `Phone` field.
27. Type **is null** in Filter For. Press Enter.

    The record with a null value in the `Phone` field is displayed.

28. Click Remove Filter. Click Filter by Form.
29. Edit the expression in the Phone field to **Is Not Null**.
30. Click Apply Filter.
    All the records except the one containing the null in the `Phone` field are displayed.
31. Close the form and any other open windows, and exit Access.

CHAPTER 8

QUERIES

"You use a query to answer questions about your database" is a catchy phrase sometimes used in Access training materials. It's helpful as a starting point for discussing queries—but only as a starting point. As a definition, it leaves out action queries, which don't answer questions but rather change your database. More important, it doesn't embrace the extraordinary breadth of a query's powers, which extend to viewing, integrating, editing, and analyzing data in a multitude of ways. Indeed, it might be more appropriate to ask which Access tasks a query can't do than what it can.

In this chapter, I cover select queries, the most common query and probably what you think of when you hear "query." I begin by discussing some basic but key subjects, such as the various methods for adding all fields of a table to a query, the differences between queries and filters, some simple functions, and similarly useful topics. At about the halfway point, I discuss multitable queries, which is where all the energy you put into designing a relational database begins to pay off. Finally, I introduce Structured Query Language (SQL). The topic is more appropriately the subject of an entire book or series, but you'll get a feel for what it is and see a practical use for it in creating a UNION query.

The Nature of Queries

I suppose it's frivolous to portray one Access object as more pleasant and agreeable to create than the others. You build objects because you need them, not to fill idle hours.

Still, compared with building other Access objects, it's hard not to have some special affection for the query. Tables require toying with those ornery primary keys, as well as pondering settings for long lists of field properties. Forms and reports of any complexity offer a Hobson's choice of tedium through control-by-control construction, or disappointment from cookie-cutter wizards.

In contrast, the query is a veritable playground. The unadorned design grid is simple and entirely straightforward. Fields can be added and deleted with ease. Criteria can quickly be edited again and again to retrieve different record sets.

NOTE You can use parameter queries to quickly apply different criteria in the same query. They eliminate the need to create a new query for each set of criteria. Chapter 9, "Queries, Part II," discusses parameter queries.

Not that queries won't cause you any problems. If you stick to simple queries that can be created with a few strategically placed entries on the design grid, you should have few worries. But building queries with expressions and functions of some sophistication is a different matter: A single misplaced bracket can cause much misery. All in all, though, queries are the most flexible, powerful, and enjoyable objects with which to work.

Queries Versus Tables

One quality of queries that must be emphasized is that they are dynamic. Because the datasheet of a table and a query look alike, it's easy to think that the objects themselves are fundamentally the same. But they are quite different. When you create and save a query, all you are saving is the query's structure—the fields, sorts, criteria, and so on. The records themselves are stored in tables. Each time you run a query, the result is re-created with the current records from the underlying table(s). This dynamism is an essential characteristic of a query's nature.

Queries Versus Filters

The similarities between filters and queries will be readily apparent, so it's useful at this point to discuss how they differ. Queries are permanent objects in your database with their own icon in the Database window. Filters are temporary snapshots of specific records in a table, form, or query.

Longevity might not be their most distinguishing feature, however. Queries can easily be deleted from your database, whereas a filter can be saved in a datasheet or form and be quickly reapplied upon opening. Thus, the seemingly short-term filter can actually outlive the supposedly eternal query.

The most profound distinction lies in their use. You'll usually create a filter to find and view records with specific criteria in a form or table and to solve the task of the moment. You'll use queries in many different ways, most notably as the record source for forms and reports.

Query Design Versus Advanced Filter

Further evidence of how filters and queries differ can be seen from a comparison of the Query Design and Advanced Filter windows. At first glance, they appear similar, with field lists at the top and the design grid below (see Figure 8.1). In both, you create sorts in the Sort row and designate criteria in the Criteria and Or rows.

Important differences emerge in their capacities and functions, however. As you saw in Chapter 7, "Find and Filter," when you filter a datasheet or form, all fields are automatically included in the record set. You use the design grid only to set sorts and designate criteria within that specific object. In a query, you use the design grid to indicate the specific fields you want included. You can add individual fields or entire field lists to the grid from any of the tables or queries in your database.

Thus, in a query there's an additional row called Show. It has a check box that indicates whether the field will be displayed in the results (see Figure 8.1). As you'll see presently, you deselect the box when you want to use a column just to set criteria. In Chapter 9, you'll see that the query design grid has the capability to display additional rows as needed for creating total, crosstab, and action queries.

8. QUERIES

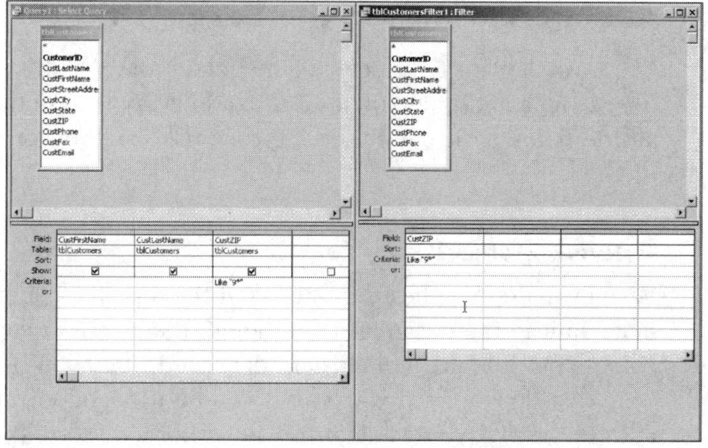

Figure 8.1 The Query Design window is on the left, and the Advanced Filter window is on the right. In the query, the `CustFirstName`, `CustLastName`, and `CustZIP` fields have been added to the grid to display them. The `CustZIP` column is also used to designate criteria. Unlike a query, in which you must include a field on the design grid to display it, on the Advanced Filter grid, you need to include only the fields you want to filter.

TIP For a better look at the contents of the Query Design window, drag the bottom pane down a couple of inches. That will give you plenty of room to display lengthy field lists in the top pane, as Figure 8.1 demonstrates.

Building Queries

Let's say you're building a query from a single field list—that is, one table or one query. The fastest way to get started is to select the table or query that contains the data you want to use in the Database window and choose Insert, Query. In the New Query dialog box, you have several choices for creating a query. The Simple Query Wizard is simple—so simple, in fact, that it doesn't help much in creating queries. The other query wizards—Crosstab (discussed in Chapter 9) and Find Duplicates and Find Unmatched (both described in this chapter)—all have their uses. But they will likely represent a minority of the queries you create. Most of the time, you'll use the default Design View selection.

Adding All Fields to the Design Grid

Often you'll want to select specific fields from a field list to include in the query. But sometimes you'll want to add every field in the list. You can add all the fields by using either the "asterisk" method or the "drag-'em-all" method.

Asterisk Method

When you double-click the asterisk at the top of a field list, you add all the fields in it to the design grid. Although the asterisk occupies only a single column on the grid, all fields are displayed when you run the query.

What do you do if you want to add criteria or sorting? You separately add the field(s) you want to use for criteria or sorts (see Figure 8.2). As indicated earlier, you deselect Show in these columns so the values in the field don't appear twice.

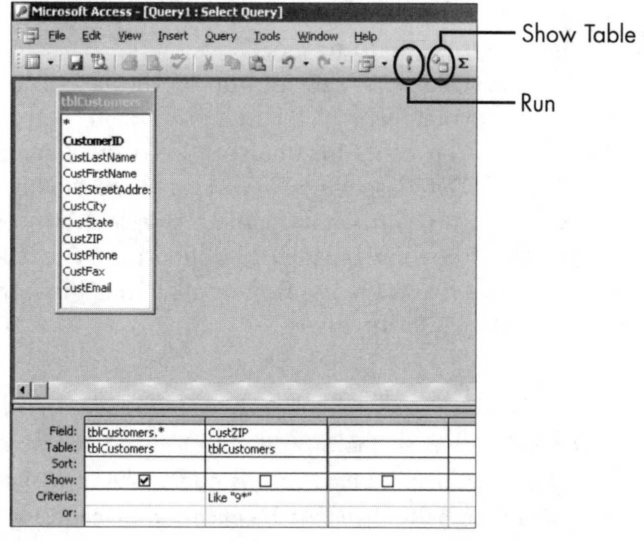

Figure 8.2 The asterisk in the Field row of the first column indicates that all fields in tblCustomers will be included in the query, even though they are not entered individually on the grid. The second column is used just to designate criteria, so the Show box has been deselected.

Let's create a simple query that uses the asterisk to select all fields:

1. Download the `NiftyLionsChap8.mdb` file to your hard drive.
2. In the Database window, select the tblCustomers table.
3. Choose Insert, Query. With Design View selected, click OK.
4. Double-click the asterisk to add all fields to the design grid. Maximize the window.
5. Double-click CustLastName to add the field to the grid.
   You can also add fields to the design grid by drag-and-drop. Within a field list, you can press Ctrl or Shift, respectively, to select fields one by one or select a range of contiguous fields in the list.
6. On the Criteria row of CustLastName, type **>m** for customers to retrieve records of customers whose last names begin with *m* through *z*.
   Access adds quotation marks around the *m* when you click in another row.
7. Type **a** in the Sort row of CustLastName for an ascending sort. Deselect Show in this column.

8. Choose File, Save or File Save As. Save your query as **qryCustomersMZ**.
9. Click the View button on the far left of the toolbar (View) to see your records.
   You can run, or execute, a select query in several ways. In the Database window, you can open the query. Within the query itself, you can switch from Design to Datasheet view, either by clicking the View button or by choosing View, Datasheet View. You can also choose Query, Run or click the Run button (see Figure 8.2).
10. Close the query.

NOTE If you set the `Output All Fields` property to `Yes` in the Query property sheet, it's the same as adding the asterisk to the design grid. (The Query property sheet can be accessed by choosing View, Properties in Design view.) You might prefer the asterisk method, however, because the design grid is always displayed, whereas the property sheet is usually hidden.

"Drag-'Em-All" Method

In the "drag-'em-all" method, each field in the field list occupies a separate column on the grid. You start by double-clicking the title bar of the field list, which selects all the fields. You can then drag and drop the fields as a group onto the grid.

This method has the advantage of making it easy to specify criteria and sorts. But there's a huge difference between the methods. With the asterisk, the query is continuously updated for additions and deletions of fields in the underlying tables. With the drag-'em-all method, the query is not updated for those changes.

Create a Query from a Filter

If you create a filter that you'd like to have as a permanent object, you can easily save it as a query. Because a filter displays all fields, however, the `Output All Fields` property in the filter will be set to `Yes`. Try this exercise:

1. Open the tblCustomers table.
2. Select the `Last Name` field and click the Sort Ascending (A–Z) button.

3. In the `State` field, right-click any instance of `CA` and choose Filter By Selection.
4. Choose Records, Filter, Advance Filter/Sort.
5. Choose File, Save As Query.
6. Name the query **qryGoldenStateCustomers** and click OK.
7. Close the Advanced Filter window and close the table. Don't save your changes.
8. In the Database window, click Queries and then open qryGoldenStateCustomers. All fields are displayed.
9. Click View to switch to Design view.
   Although two columns on the grid have been used to specify a sort and criteria, the Show box is deselected in both. Seemingly, no fields should be displayed.
10. Choose Properties on the View menu.
    The `Output All Fields` property is set to `Yes`. That's the reason all fields are displayed in the datasheet.
11. Close the property sheet and close the query.

TIP You can undo actions that you just performed in the Query Design window. If you just edited an entry on the design grid or added a field to a column, choose Edit, Undo Cell Edit. If you just changed a property setting, the Edit, Undo Property Setting command will be available.

Unique Values

The `Unique Values` property is useful for eliminating duplicate records in a single table. For example, let's say you want a simple list of the states in which you have customers. Follow these steps:

1. Select the tblCustomers table in the Database window.
2. Choose Insert, Query and, with Design View selected, click OK.
3. From the field list, add the `CustState` field to the design grid.
4. In the Sort row, type **a** for an ascending sort.
5. Click View to see your records. You have the list of states, but the values are repeated.
6. Click View to return to Design view. Right-click anywhere in the top pane outside the field list and choose Properties.
7. In the Query property sheet, edit the `Unique Values` property to `Yes`. Close the property sheet.

8. Click View to return to Datasheet view. Each state is now listed just once.
9. Choose File, Save. Save the query as **qryUniqueValues** and close it.

Sorting

The sort is one of the most important query tools. As you saw with advanced filters, one advantage of using the design grid to apply sorts is that you can combine descending and ascending sorts.

Applying sorts is not difficult in Access, but there is an element of uncertainty because you can set sorts both in the Sort row of the design grid in Design View, and in Datasheet/Form views. Confusion arises when you set a sort in Datasheet or Form view that reverses the sort you set in Design view. If you plan to use a query as the basis of a form or report, you'll find it simpler and more efficient to designate sorts on the design grid. When you're reviewing records in datasheet/form views, use the sort buttons as you need them, but don't save the changes.

Q&A

Q: I'm still not sure I understand how sorts work in queries. What happens if I choose an ascending sort for `ProductName` in the design grid and a descending sort for the same field in the datasheet? Which one takes precedence?

A: The one you saved in the datasheet takes precedence. If you're having problems figuring out what's going on with your sorts, here's what to do. In the Query Design window, right-click in any open area of the top pane and choose Properties. Scroll down to the `Order By` property and delete whatever's in there. Review your sorts on the design grid to make sure they're okay, and save your changes.

Adding Calculated Fields

Queries give you the freedom to both retrieve records and manipulate them. Notably, you can add fields that display the results of a calculation on stored values.

Using an Arithmetic Expression

For example, suppose you were anticipating that purchase prices would rise uniformly for all products about 8%. You want to create a field that will show what the new prices will be for each product.

You've used expressions to set criteria; now you'll use one to create a calculated field.

1. Select the tblMerchandise table in the Database window. Choose Insert, Query. With Design View selected, click OK.
2. Add `MerchName`, `MerchDescription`, and `PurchasePrice` to the design grid.
3. Click in the Field row of the fourth column.
4. Enter an expression as follows:
   a. Type **[PurchasePrice]**. You enclose the field name in brackets.
   b. Type *. An asterisk is the operator for multiplication.
   c. Type **1.08**. You want 100% of the original price plus an 8% increment. 108% expressed as a number is 1.08.

   The complete expression is **`[PurchasePrice]*1.08`**.
5. Click View to go to Datasheet view (see Figure 8.3). The numbers seem reasonable, but they are not expressed as currency. Also, the column name of Expr1 is unhelpful.

	Product Name	Item Description	Purchase Price	Expr1
	Door knocker	All brass; weighs 7.6 lbs	$24.50	26.46
	Bronze vase	Two males, one female, cub	$19.50	21.06
	Doll pair	Daddy and baby, 7" and 4" tall	$7.25	7.83
	Marble statue	Lions of St. Andronico; white; 6" X 3" x5"	$72.60	78.408
	Antique-finish desk clock	Classic lion motif with antique finish; measure	$17.20	18.576
	Kenya paper money	Issued 1978; 20 shillings; reverse shows pride	$1.25	1.35
	Rio Muni stamp set	Vermillion 10+5 cts male and gray 80+20 cts.	$1.75	1.89
	Costume head	Lioness; plush fur; fits all adults	$46.00	49.68
	Garden lion statues	Pair; stone finished; 8 1/2" x 11" x 17"	$24.95	26.946
	Born Free T-shirt	Photo of male, "born free" text under lion phot	$9.65	10.422
	Born Free coffee mug	Photo of male in wild with born free caption	$4.92	5.3136
	King of Jungle T-shirt	Full-maned male with black background; 50%	$5.50	5.94
	Child overalls	Lion pride design; 100% cotton; two pockets	$8.00	8.64
	Born Free poster	From 1966 movie	$18.00	19.44
	Playing cards	Deck with various lion photos	$2.50	2.7
	Socks	Gray with black line lion drawing	$3.50	3.78
	Wall calendar	African settings	$5.00	5.4
	Screen saver	Software with various lion photos	$3.95	4.266
	Throw rug	Lioness and two cubs; 4' X 6'	$22.00	23.76
	Stuffed small	Sitting lion, plush, 14"	$7.25	7.83
	Stuffed large	Sitting lion, plus, 26"	$11.75	12.69
	Cub figurine	Porcelain; 4" X 3"	$11.00	11.88
	Beer mug	Lion shield emblem	$6.43	6.9444
	Framed print with stamps	Male photo; 1989 Zambia set	$4.97	5.3676
	Lioness coffee mug		$4.50	4.86
	Pendant	14K lioness with necklace	$42.50	45.9
	Garden ornaments	Pair; stone-finish, alabastrite; 16" x 8 1/2" x 1	$67.00	72.36
	Charm	14K ornament for bracelet	$15.95	17.226
	Jigsaw puzzle	African pride scene; 211 pieces	$14.50	15.66
▶	Watch	Round face; male picture	$22.95	24.786
*			$0.00	

Figure 8.3 The field with recalculated prices has been added, but it needs to be formatted. It lacks an informative caption, and the values should be expressed as currency.

6. Click View to return to Design view. Click in the Field row of the Expr1 column. Press Shift+F2 to open the Zoom window. Edit `Expr1:` to **ExpectedPrice**. Click OK to close the Zoom window.
7. Right-click the column and choose Properties.
   Because this is a new field, there are no properties from an underlying table to inherit, so you need to set properties on your own.
8. Click in Format, open the list, and choose Currency.
9. Click in Caption. Type **Expected Price**. Close the property sheet.
10. Click View. The column heading now shows the caption `Expected Price` and the figures are expressed as currency.
11. Choose File, Save. Save the query as **qryExpectedPrices**. Close the query.

NOTE Formatting the column as currency does not change its values, which sometimes extend beyond two decimal places (see Figure 8.3). In recent versions of Access, you can use the Round function to round to the intended number of decimal places. The Round function is discussed in the Microsoft Knowledge Base article 210564.

Using Expressions with Functions

If you looked at the glossary of expression terms in Chapter 7, you might recall that a function returns a value based on the results of a calculation or some other expression. Aggregate functions are particularly useful for findings sums, averages, and other calculations.

I discuss aggregate functions in Chapter 9, but let's first take a look at a few other functions to see how they work. One useful set of functions is `Left`, `Mid`, and `Right`, which let you extract parts of text values. These can be helpful in extricating, say, the most meaningful part of an account or parts number from a long text string.

Let's use the `Phone` field in the Customers table as an example. Let's say you want to create three columns that will extract the three-number area code, the three-number exchange, and the four-number extension.

1. Select the tblCustomers table in the Database window. Choose Insert, Query and, with Design view selected, click OK. Maximize the window.
2. Add `CustPhone` to the grid.

3. In the first row of the second column, type **AreaCode: Left ([CustPhone], 3),** where:
   - `AreaCode` is the column name.
   - `Left` is the function that tells Access to extract values, beginning from the first character on the left.
   - `[CustPhone]` is the field.
   - `3` is the number of characters to extract.
4. In the first row of the third column, type **Exchange: Mid([CustPhone],4, 3),** where:
   - `Exchange` is the column name.
   - `Mid` is the function.
   - `[CustPhone]` is the field.
   - `4` is the position of the first character as counted from the left.
   - `3` is the number of characters to extract.
5. In the first row of the fourth column, type **Extension: Right ([CustPhone], 4).**

   The Right function works the same as the Left function, except that you start extracting characters from the right. There are four numbers in the extension, compared with three in an area code—hence the different numbers in the expressions.
6. Choose File, Save; name the query **qryExtractFunctions** and click OK.
7. Click View to see your records (see Figure 8.4). Close the query.

Phone	AreaCode	Exchange	Extension
(940) 555-3753	940	555	3753
(227) 555-8237	227	555	8237
(661) 555-0248	661	555	0248
(970) 555-7532	970	555	7532
(252) 555-7531	252	555	7531
(347) 555-9232	347	555	9232
(802) 555-6349	802	555	6349
(303) 555-7668	303	555	7668
(717) 555-1778	717	555	1778
(567) 555-5482	567	555	5482
(606) 555-9277	606	555	9277
(909) 555-8067	909	555	8067
(229) 555-2438	229	555	2438
(304) 555-9650	304	555	9650
(712) 555-1488	712	555	1488

Figure 8.4 A sample of the records extracted from the `Left`, `Mid`, and `Right` functions.

Q&A

Q: Wait a minute. If the `Left` function is supposed to fetch the first three characters starting from the left, why are there three numbers in the Area Code column? Isn't the first character a beginning parenthesis? Wouldn't that make the first column have strings such as `(94`, `(22`, and `(66`?

A: Only the nine digits of the phone number are stored in the underlying table; the parentheses and dashes are not. If these symbols had been stored as well, you'd be exactly right: The expression `Left ([CustPhone], 3)` would have yielded in the first row of the second column `(94` instead of `940`. In this case, you would want to use the `Mid` function to extract the area code. The expression would be `Mid([CustTelephone],2,3)` because `2` is the position of the first character you want as counted from the left (namely, the first number of the area code) and `3` is the number of characters you want to grab.

Back in Algebra Class

Suppose Acme Widget determines its unit selling prices by adding $2 to its unit purchase price and multiplying the amount by 140%, or 1.4. You're Acme's chief accountant. How do you write this expression so that Access understands it?

One reasonable possibility would seem to be `[PurchasePrice]+2*1.4`. But assume that the purchase price is $3. The expression might evaluate to `$7`: `3+2=5` and then `5*1.4=7`. But it might also evaluate to `$5.80: 3+(1.4*2)=5.8`.

Here are two rules that will help you write calculated expressions:

- Access performs any operation within parentheses first.
- Access performs multiplication and division before addition and subtraction.

According to the first rule, if you write the expression as `([PurchasePrice]+2)*1.4`, Access adds the $2 to the purchase price first and then multiplies it by 1.4. This is the expression you want.

According to the second rule, if you write the expression as `[PurchasePrice]+2*1.4`, Access multiplies 2 by 1.4 first and then adds it to the purchase price. This is the expression you don't want.

Suppose that, instead, you want to take 140% of the purchase price first and then add $2 to it. You could write the expression as `[PurchasePrice]*1.4+2`. Access does the multiplication first and adds the $2 afterward. But to be on the safe side and to make things clearer, your best solution is to include parentheses and enter `([PurchasePrice]*1.4)+2`.

Top Values Property

It seems that modern societies care only about the biggest and the best. If a company can't have the best-selling brand in a market, it often doesn't want to be in it at all. The weekly box office totals from the movie industry focus only on the top ten moneymakers. On the PGA tour, scratch golfers who finish 58th on Sunday might as well have stayed in bed.

The `Top Values` property is well suited to the needs of our times. It finds the highest values and the lowest. Access determines the "top" records based on the sorting criteria you specify. It can be set in either absolute or percentage terms, so you can use it to find the top 1% of this or the top five of that. In fact, you can limit the records found to any number or percentage in either direction you choose. In a column of baseball batting averages, for example, you could find the top 75 hitting artists or the 20% at the bottom who can be counted on to strike out with the bases loaded.

Here are three things to remember when using the `Top Values` property:

- The field you sort on is the one that Access uses to find the top or bottom values. If you sort on two fields, make sure the sort you want for top values is the column farthest left in Query Design view.
- The required sort order is sometimes opposite to your initial inclination of what's needed. In a list of prices, for example, use a descending sort to find the highest prices. (That advice is applicable for all sorts, but it has special relevance here.)
- Most important (even if most mundane), remember to reset the `Top Values` property setting to `All` when you're done with it. The `Top Values` setting will be saved along with the query, and it will be in force when you open and run it. You can easily wind up viewing just a small fraction of the records you need.

Find a Top (or Bottom) Number of Records

Let's do a few examples to see how `Top Values` works. Suppose you want to find the five items in Nifty Lions's inventory that have the highest price.

1. Select the tblMerchandise table in the Database window. Choose Insert, Query and, with Design View selected, click OK. Maximize the window.

2. Save the query as **qryTopMerchPrices**.
3. Add the `MerchName`, `MerchDescription`, `PurchasePrice`, and `UnitsInStock` fields to the design grid.
4. Type **d** in the Sort row of the `PurchasePrice` field for a descending sort.
   To show the most expensive products first, use a descending sort to sort the `PurchPrice` field from highest to lowest.
5. Click View, briefly review the fields and records, and return to Design view.
6. On the Query Design toolbar, click the drop-down arrow next to All and select 5 (see Figure 8.5).
7. Click View to go to Datasheet view. The records are sorted by purchase price, with the most expensive products listed first.
8. Click View to return to Design view. Open the drop-down list for the `Top Values` property and change the `Top Values` property to `All`.

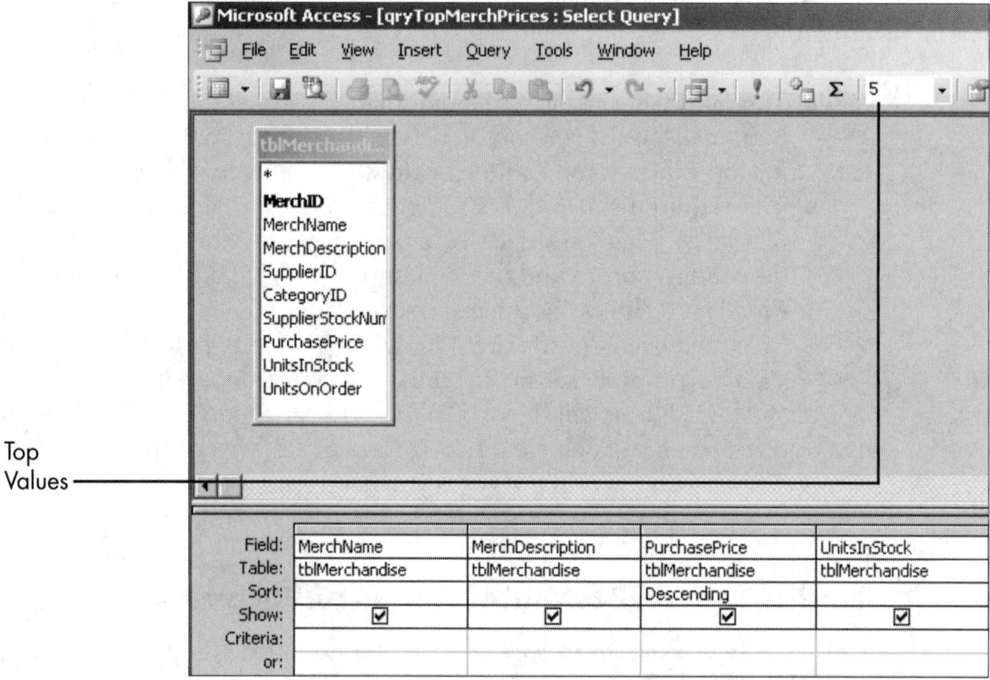

Figure 8.5 The `Top Values` property is used to find numbers at the extreme and not-so-extreme.

NOTE If there are records with duplicate values in the last slot of eligible top values, Access retrieves all those records. Here's an example: Let's say you want to find the five products with the most units in stock. In the `UnitsInStock` field, the products with the most units have values of `12`, `11`, `10`, `9`, `8`, `8`, and `4`. Access retrieves both records with 8 units (that is, the products in the fifth, or last, position from the top), but not the record with 4 units. So Access retrieves six records instead of five. Thus, you might occasionally get more records than you specify.

Find a Top (or Bottom) Percentage of Records

Suppose you want to find the products with the lowest 70% of all prices. In other words, the 30% of products with the highest prices will not be included.

1. In the Sort row of the `PurchasePrice` field of qryTopMerchPrices, open the drop-down list and choose Ascending.
   An ascending sort lists the lowest-priced items first and the highest-priced items last.
2. Highlight All in the Top Values box. Type **70%**.
   Besides the few choices in the drop-down list, you can type numbers and percentages directly into the Top Values box for the specific fraction you want.
3. Click View to switch to Datasheet view. Products in the lowest 70% of all records are displayed.
4. Close the query and save your changes.
5. In the Queries section of the Database window, double-click qryTopMerchPrices to open it.
   The records are still sorted by ascending price, and only the top 70% are displayed.

Let me re-emphasize that, unlike a filter that needs to be applied, a saved `Top Values` property is in force when you open and run the query. Because you just created the query, that's not an issue. But I hope you'll agree that my admonition about resetting the `Top Values` property to `All` before exiting the query is worth considering. You can always set the `Top Values` property anew when you open the query. If you do want to save the `Top Values` property, consider including that fact in the query name (as in `TopFiveSellers`).

NOTE As a query property, `Top Values` is on the Query property sheet and can be specified there as well. To open the Query property sheet, right-click in any open area of the upper pane of the Query Design Window and choose Properties.

Multitable Queries

Until now, all the queries you've done in this book have been based on one table. That's fine for learning some basics and a few features and techniques. But it isn't why you're using Access or why you bought this book. All the hard work of organizing data into tables and creating relationships starts to pay off when you create queries using more than one table.

As I've emphasized often, the way you organize data into tables has little to do with how you actually use that data. You organized your database for maximum efficiency and speed, without worrying about the final purposes to which its data will be put.

Specifically, you don't care that customer names are not in the Orders table, even though they're needed for the order form you want to create. You're indifferent that supplier phone numbers are absent from the Products table, even though they're required for the inventory reports you need to build. You remain serene in the face of an Orders table with no mention of products purchased and in what quantities because you know you can easily bring both orders and order details together in one place when you need them.

That place is a multitable query.

Multitable Queries with Two Tables

Let's first look at a multitable query with two tables. In Chapter 5, I argued that lookup fields in tables were unnecessary. The example I used centered on the `SupplierID` field in the Suppliers and Products (or Merchandise) tables. I'm going to restate the problem the `SupplierID` field presents and then show you how a multitable query solves it.

1. In the Database window, open the tblSuppliers table. Review the data and note that it contains only information about suppliers.
2. Click View to switch to Design view.
   The primary key is `SupplierID`, which uniquely identifies each supplier in the table. Its data type is `AutoNumber`.
3. Close the Suppliers table.
   Open the tblMerchandise table and review its data.
   Look at the Supplier column. The IDs refer to companies in the Suppliers table. Simply as IDs, however, they are cryptic and mystifying. Which companies do these IDs refer to? Close the Merchandise table.
4. Choose Tools, Relationships to open the Relationships window. Locate the Suppliers and Merchandise field lists.
   To refresh your memory, the heavy line between the field lists indicates that the two tables have a one-to-many relationship and that referential integrity has been enforced. The field through which they are related is the `SupplierID` field, which has matching data. The `1` indicates that each supplier can appear only once in the Supplier table; the infinity sign indicates that a single supplier can appear any number of times in the Merchandise table.
5. Close the Relationships window.
   The Suppliers and Merchandise tables have a one-to-many relationship, which ensures that you can create a query that will bring together data from both tables and show the name of the supplier that makes each product.

NOTE Shortly, I'll mention why you don't need to have a relationship to bring together data from two tables. But if you do have one, you're golden.

Let's create a query that shows not only the supplier for each product, but other contact info as well.

1. In the Database window, click Queries and click New. With Design View chosen in the New Query dialog box, click OK.
2. In the Show Table dialog box, select tblSuppliers, press Ctrl, select tblMerchandise, click Add, and click Close. Maximize the Query Design window.

In the query, notice that the line between the two field lists is the same as it was in the Relationships window. Because the two fields have matching names and data, you can create a query using fields from both tables. Access retrieves records where the fields from both tables are equal—that is, where they have matching data.

NOTE It makes no difference that the `Merchandise` field list is on the left and the `Suppliers` field list is on the right. If you want to put the lists "in order," click the Merchandise title and drag it to the right of `Suppliers`.

---

3. In the `Merchandise` field list, double-click `MerchName` to add it to the design grid.
4. From the `Suppliers` field list, double-click `SuppCompanyName`, `SuppContFirstName`, `SuppContLastName`, `SuppContTitle`, and `SuppPhone`.
   Note that there isn't any need to include the `SupplierID` field from either field list; having the relationship in place is all you need.
5. Save the query as **qrySupplierContactInfo**.
6. Click View to see the records.
   Here's all the information you need, but it's not in any meaningful order. Let's sort the data by product name.
7. Click View to return to Design view. In the MerchName column, type **a** in the Sort row for an ascending sort.
8. Click View to see the records. Click View to switch to Design view, which should look like Figure 8.6. Save your changes.

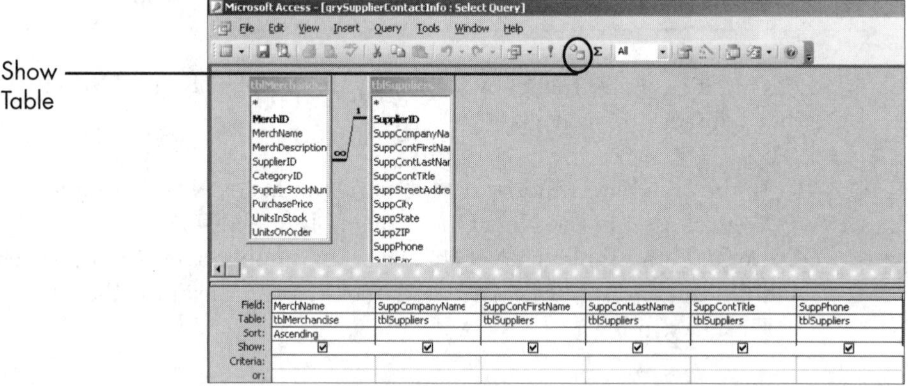

Figure 8.6 The multitable query shows the relationships between field lists.

Multitable Queries Using Three Tables

Suppose you'd like to add category descriptions for each product to the query. That data is not in the Suppliers or Merchandise tables, but it is in the Categories table.

1. In the Database window, open the tblCategories table, review the data, and close the table.
2. Choose Tools, Relationships to open the Relationships window.
   The Categories table has a one-to-many relationship with the Merchandise table through the `CategoryID` field. Because this relationship exists, you can add the Categories table to the query and include its data in your results.
3. Close the Relationships window.
4. In the Query Design window of qrySupplierContactInfo, click the Show Table button (refer to Figure 8.6 for its location) and add the tblCategories table.
   Each category can appear only once in the Categories table, but it can appear any number of times in the Merchandise table.
5. Select `CategoryDescription` in the `Categories` field list and drop it in the SuppCompanyFirstName column (see Figure 8.7).
   The `Description` field is now included in the query, next to the `MerchName` field.

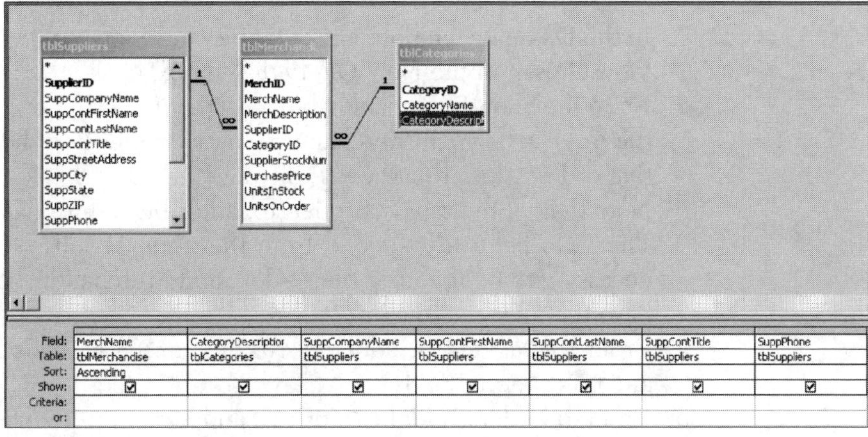

Figure 8.7 A query using three tables.

6. Click View to see the additional field.
7. Save the query as **qrySuppContDesc** and close it.

Q&A

Q: What do I do if there isn't a field of matching data between two tables? Can I still create a multitable query, or am I out of luck?

A: You can use an intermediate table that has fields with matching data in both tables. When you think about it, that's really what you just did. You were able to include data from both the Suppliers and Categories table in the query, even though they don't have a common field, because the Merchandise table contained both the `SupplierID` and `CategoryID`. The next exercise provides a good example.

Multitable Queries with Criteria

Let's look at a slightly more complex example using criteria. Assume that Nifty Lions learns there are safety problems with some merchandise it handles and it has to contact customers who received those products. First, it needs to contact any customer who received items made by Feline Fantastics. Second, it needs to contact any customer who received products made by Ohio Traders in orders shipped before 8/15/04. (That's probably not the most realistic example, but it will provide a nice illustration.) Here's how to create a query that provides you with the information you need:

1. In the Database window, click Queries and click New. With Design View chosen in the New Query dialog box, click OK.
2. From the Show Table dialog box, add the tblCustomers, tblOrders, tblOrderDetails, tblMerchandise, and tblSuppliers field lists, in that order. Close the Show Table dialog box.
   Note that all the tables are tied together by one-to-many relationships. No fields are needed from the OrderDetails table, but it's necessary to tie together the Orders and Merchandise tables.
3. Save the query as **qrySafety**.
4. From tblCustomers, add the `CustFirstName`, `CustLastName`, and `CustPhone` fields.
5. From tblOrders, add the `OrderID` and `ShippedDate` fields. From tblMerchandise, add `MerchName`. From tblSuppliers, add `SuppCompanyName`.
6. On the Criteria row of the `ShippedDate` field, type **<8/15/04**. On the same row in the `SuppCompanyName` field, type **ohio traders**.

As discussed in Chapter 7, both conditions must be true, so you're using AND criteria; this is entered on the same row.

7. On the Or row of the SuppCompanyName, type **feline fantastics**. Only one condition need be true, so you're using OR criteria.
8. Type **a** in the Sort row of the CustLastName field to sort the orders by customer name and click outside the first column. Your design grid should look like Figure 8.8.
9. Click View to see the customers you need to contact and the products you need to inform them about.

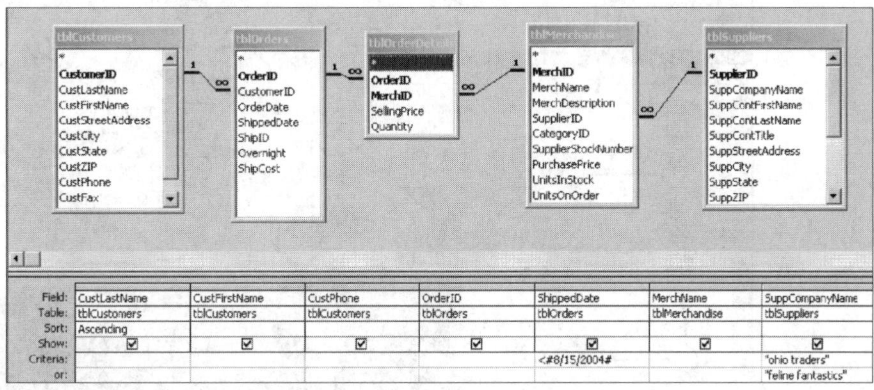

Figure 8.8 The query uses both AND and OR criteria, strategically placed on different rows.

Q&A

Q: I follow the logic of what you're saying about matching data. But to be honest, I don't have a gut feel for how it's used to retrieve these records. So many things are going on at once in this query; the records seem to come from every direction.

A: Maybe Figure 8.9 can help. I've tiled the five tables used in the query. I've also scrolled the records so you can follow how the values for the first record in the query, for Jessica Bernal, are retrieved.

I'll start at the top of the first column: Bernal's customer ID is 19. Below in the Orders table, you can see that customer #19 made order #25. In the Order Details table, you see that order #25 includes item #15.

Moving to the top of the second column, item #15 in the Merchandise table has supplier #1. Finally, in the Suppliers table, note that supplier #1 is Feline Fantastics.

In the query, Feline Fantastics was OR criteria that was unrestricted by shipping date. So even though you can see in the Orders table that the order wasn't shipped until 8/31/04, it is still included in the records.

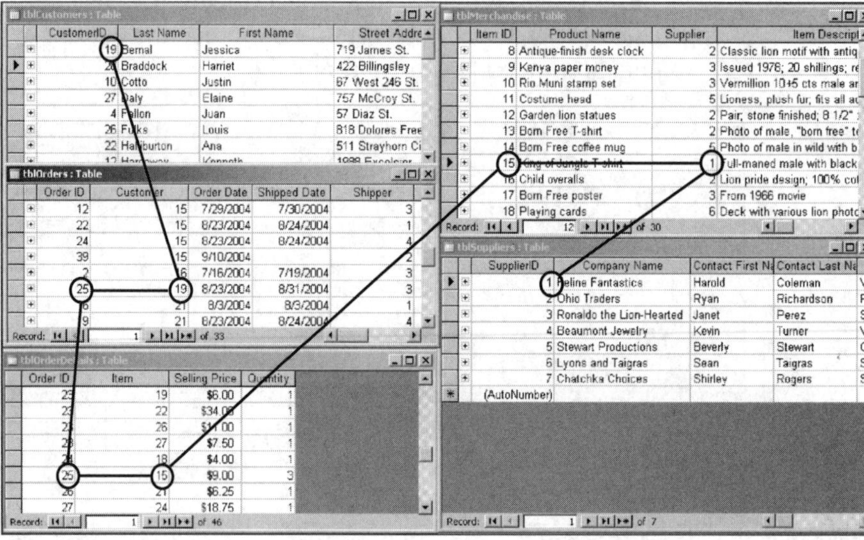

Figure 8.9 The matching data among the tables enables Access to retrieve the records you need.

Relationships Versus Joins

To work with Access queries effectively, it's helpful to distinguish between relationships and joins. It's not a concept that's easily grasped. First I quickly define both terms; then I talk about the difference in a touchy-feely sort of way, and then I tell you "what you need to know."

Definitions

As you've seen, a relationship is an association established between common fields in two tables. A join is also an association between a field in one table and a field in another table, but within the context of a specific query.

The join makes it possible to combine data from different tables and execute a multitable query.

Touchy-Feely Explanation

When you establish a relationship in Access between two tables, you've essentially sold them an engagement ring. When you enforce referential integrity, however, you've pronounced them man and wife. Each table is entering an extended family with which it establishes strong bonds. As you've seen with cascading deletes, an action taken in one table can ripple through the entire database with enormous consequences. In a well-integrated database, relationships are not easily severed.

Let's say it's Saturday night. If you're married, it can be assumed you'll be spending it with your spouse. That's the way Access considers relationships when it comes to multitable queries. When you earlier added the Suppliers and Merchandise tables to the query, Access didn't even bother to ask whether these two tables wanted to be joined together. Because they were in a relationship, it was just assumed that for purposes of the query—for that Saturday night—they would want to be together.

And Access is nearly always right. If you're creating a multitable query, the relationships you've already established will create joins between the tables for that particular query.

But although Access automatically creates join lines for tables that have a relationship, two tables don't need to have a relationship to be joined. They could simply meet up for purposes of the query—that one Saturday night date—and depart.

Consider the example you did using the Suppliers and Merchandise tables. If the two tables didn't have a relationship, you could have simply dragged the `SupplierID` field from one field list to the other to create a join for that particular query. In fact, if the two fields have matching data and one of the join fields is a primary key, Access takes the initiative and creates the join for you (assuming that Enable AutoJoin is implemented, as it is by default; the option is on the Tables/Queries tab of the Options dialog box, available from the Tools menu). Although this join can be saved for a particular query, it does not establish a relationship between the tables.

What You Need to Know

My explanation may or may not have been helpful. But you'll be okay if you remember that:

- If you've crafted a database that is completely integrated through relationships, you'll rarely need to create joins on your own. Access will automatically create the joins you need to perform multitable queries.
- If you do not want to establish a relationship between tables, you can create a join between them for purposes of the query if there are fields in each table with matching data. Simply drag the field with matching data from one field list to the other.

Creating a Join Manually

Let's look at an example in which no relationship exists between two tables but you can use a join to create a query and find the data you need. The example might not be your most likely information requirement, but it's not completely unrealistic, either.

Suppose you want to determine whether there are any customers and suppliers who are in the same state. In Figure 8.10, I have hidden and tiled several columns in the Customers and Suppliers tables. If you compare the two tables carefully, you'll notice that only one customer and supplier are in the same state: Customer Halliburton and supplier Lyons and Taigras are both in Illinois.

The two tables do not have a relationship, but their state fields have matching data. Instead of scrutinizing table lists, let's create a query and use a join between the two state fields to find this record quickly.

1. In the Database window, click Queries and click New. With Design View chosen in the New Query dialog box, click OK.
2. Add tblCustomers and tblSuppliers to the design grid.
   There is no relationship between these tables, and no join has been established.
3. Save the query as `qrySuppliersCustomers_SameState`.
4. In the tblCustomers field list, click `CustState` and drag and drop it on `SuppState` in the tblSuppliers field list.
   You see a line between the two fields, which shows you've created a join.

5. Double-click `CustFirstName` and `CustLastName` from the Customers field list to add them to the grid.
6. Double-click `SuppCompanyName` and `SuppState` from the Suppliers field list to add them to the grid (see Figure 8.11).

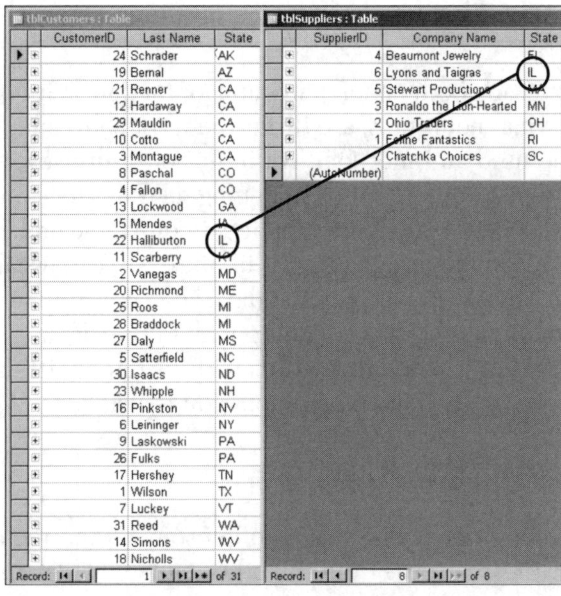

tblCustomers : Table

CustomerID	Last Name	State
24	Schrader	AK
19	Bernal	AZ
21	Renner	CA
12	Hardaway	CA
29	Mauldin	CA
10	Cotto	CA
3	Montague	CA
8	Paschal	CO
4	Fallon	CO
13	Lockwood	GA
15	Mendes	IA
22	Halliburton	IL
11	Scarberry	KY
2	Vanegas	MD
20	Richmond	ME
25	Roos	MI
28	Braddock	MI
27	Daly	MS
5	Satterfield	NC
30	Isaacs	ND
23	Whipple	NH
16	Pinkston	NV
6	Leininger	NY
9	Laskowski	PA
26	Fulks	PA
17	Hershey	TN
1	Wilson	TX
7	Luckey	VT
31	Reed	WA
14	Simons	WV
18	Nicholls	WV

Record: 1 of 31

tblSuppliers : Table

SupplierID	Company Name	State
4	Beaumont Jewelry	FL
6	Lyons and Taigras	IL
5	Stewart Productions	MA
3	Ronaldo the Lion-Hearted	MN
2	Ohio Traders	OH
1	Feline Fantastics	RI
7	Chatchka Choices	SC
(AutoNumber)		

Record: 8 of 8

Figure 8.10 A single customer and supplier are in the same state.

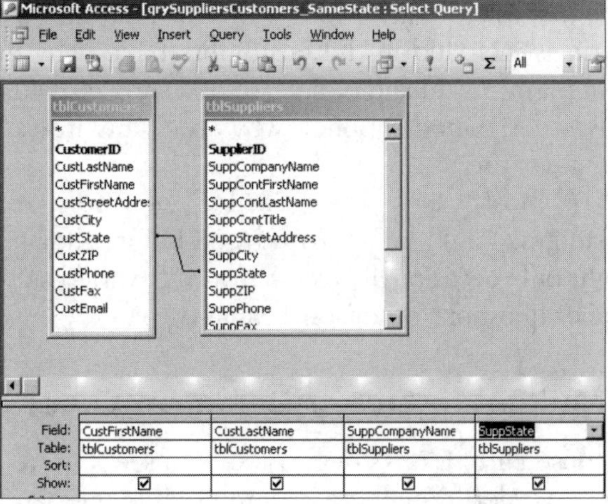

Figure 8.11 In this query, a join could be created manually because the two fields have matching data.

7. Click View to see the one record with matching data.
8. Save your changes and close the query.

Inner Versus Outer Joins

There are both inner joins and outer joins. Inner joins, which are also known as equi-joins, are by far the most common. All the queries you have done used an inner join. An inner join retrieves records only when there are equal values (that is, matching data) in the common field in the tables. As you saw, if you have suppliers in one table and merchandise in another, and a common `SupplierID` in both, you can use an inner join to create a query that matches merchandise data with supplier data. When you create a multitable query, an inner join is the default. If you want to create queries in which only records with matching data are retrieved, you don't have to worry what type of join you're using.

Introducing Outer Joins

What are outer joins? In an outer join, all the records from one table and only those records from the other table in which there's matching data are retrieved. Because all the records are retrieved from one table, you can find which of them don't have matching records in the other table.

Outer joins work nicely in auditing and other exception-to-the-rule tests that ask "What's wrong with this picture?" questions. For example, if a firm is included in the customers table, why don't you see any orders from them? Or imagine the case of a supplier with no products. If a firm is truly a designated supplier, why aren't any items from its product line in your inventory?

In most cases, there will be entirely reasonable explanations: Customers might be approved well before they place any orders; the firm might only occasionally use many of its varied suppliers. But these are the type of questions outer joins can answer.

A Multitable Query Using an Outer Join

Suppose Nifty Lions's owner wants to see if there are any customers without any orders. You'll create a multitable query using an outer join to find these records.

1. Open the tblCustomers table and review the data.
   Note that there is only one record for every customer. The primary key for the Customers table is `CustomerID`.
2. Close the tblCustomers table. Open the tblOrders table and review the data.
3. Select the Customer column. Click Sort Ascending.
   Notice that although each customer could appear only once in the Customers table, it can appear many times in the Orders table.
4. Close the tblOrders table without saving your design changes.
5. Choose Tools, Relationships to open the Relationships window. Find the Customers and Orders tables.
   There is a one-to-many relationship between the two tables through the `CustomerID` field.
6. Close the Relationships window.
7. In the Database window, click Queries and click New. With Design View chosen in the New Query dialog box, click OK.
8. Add the tblCustomers and tblOrders tables. Close the Show Table dialog box.
   Note that you see the same line between the field lists that you saw in the Relationships window. These two tables are joined through the `CustomerID` field, and you can perform a multitable query.
9. Double-click `CustLastName` and `CustFirstName` from the Customers table to add them to the design grid.
10. Double-click `OrderID` from the Orders table to add it as well.
11. Save the query as **qryNoOrderCustomers.**
12. Double-click the join line between the two field lists to open the Join Properties dialog box.
    In the Join Properties dialog box, both tables are included, along with the `CustomerID` through which they are joined.
    The current join is the default inner join. Access will only include records where the joined fields—namely, `CustomerID`—are equal.

Q&A

Q: Why does the dialog box refer to the "left table name" and "right table name"? Do those names get switched as I move the field lists in the query design window?

A: No, they refer to the order in which the tables are named in the Structured Query Language (SQL) statement. You might also see the terms "left outer join" and "right outer join." I discuss SQL shortly.

To compare an inner with an outer join, run the query as you would usually do.

1. Close the Join Properties dialog box. Click View.
   Access has used the `CustomerID` field to match customers with orders. In the Record Selector area, note that there are 33 records in your results.
2. Click View to return to Design view. Right-click the join line between the two field lists. Select Join Properties to open the Join Properties dialog box.
3. Change the selection to **2** (see Figure 8.12).
   You're now using an outer join. Access retrieves all the customer records and only those records from the Orders table in which the `CustomerID` fields are equal.
   Don't be deceived by this "only-ness" of the outer join. *Only* sounds like relatively few records will be matches. In fact, in many companies, most customers are "live" and have orders. So for most of the records, there will be a match, and nearly all your results will include records from both Customers and Orders tables.

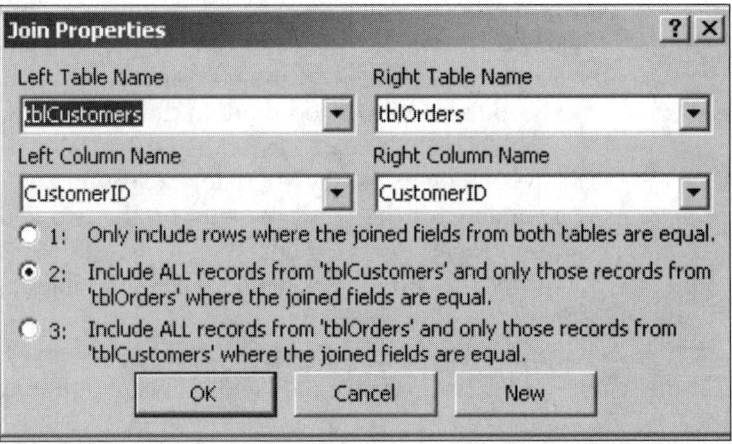

Figure 8.12 In the Join Properties dialog box, you select the join type.

4. Click OK and click View to see the records.
   Note that are now 44 records in the datasheet, 11 more than when you used an inner join. That means that there must be at least 11 customers who have not yet made orders.

5. Select the `OrderID` field and click Ascending Sort. The customers without orders are listed first.
6. Click View to return to Design view.

TIP Do you recall the Is Null operator? You can use it to display only those customers with no orders. In the Criteria row of the `OrderID` column, type `Is Null`. You can then click View to find customers with no matches (no orders).

---

7. Right-click the join line and choose Join Properties.
   Take a look at option 3 in the dialog box. When would you use this type of outer join? In this case, Access retrieves all the Orders records and only those records in the Customers table in which there are matching customers. But as I've noted, don't be misled by the word *only*. There should be matches for all the records—what kind of order doesn't have a customer? In the Nifty Lions database, all orders have customers.
   As you can see, though, this is just the kind of "What's wrong with this picture?" question that an auditor or manager might want to ask. If an order doesn't have an approved customer, that could indicate some type of criminal activity.
8. Close the query and save your changes.

Find Unmatched Query Wizard

If you find all this business about innies and outies confusing, Access provides the easy-to-use Find Unmatched Query Wizard as a substitute for many outer-join queries.

Click Queries in the Database window, click New, and choose Find Unmatched Query Wizard in the New Query window. If you understood the previous example, you'll have no trouble dealing with the wizard. Here's an overview of its five screens:

- Select the table from which you want to retrieve all the records. In the example where you found customers without orders, that is the Customers table.
- Select the table from which you want to find "only" those records with matching data. In the example, that is the Orders table.

- Select the field with matching data. Access usually makes it easy for you. In this example, it selects `CustomerID` for both tables (see Figure 8.13).
- Select which fields you want to see in the query. These are fields from the "all" table. In the example, you used the `CustLastName` and `CustFirstName` fields.
- Name your query and run it.

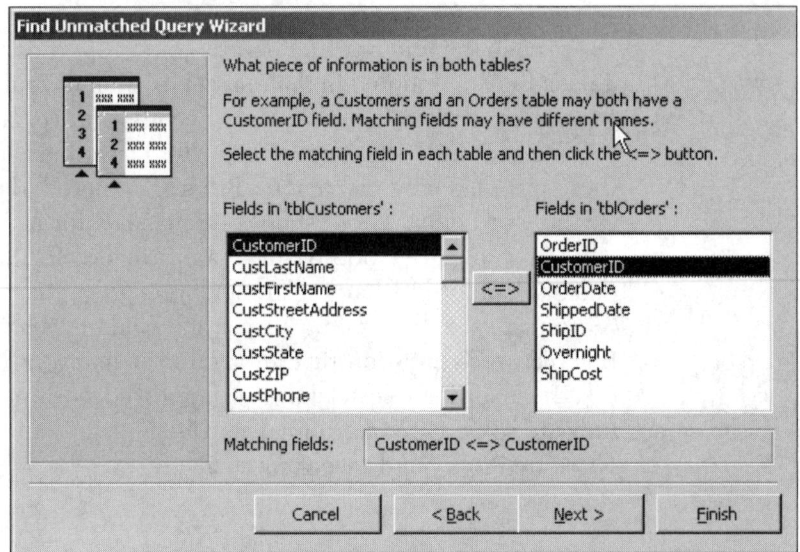

Figure 8.13 This dialog box in the Find Unmatched Query Wizard specifies the field with matching data.

Multitable Queries Conclusion

Just one final word about multitable queries. Although outer joins are indeed useful, there's a reason that inner joins are the default join. Most of the queries you'll do likely will require an inner join. So even if you don't fully understand the difference between inner and outer joins, remember that the type of join you probably want has already been selected for you.

SQL

Let's say your friend is spending the summer in Tokyo. The mailing address he gives you has the text string `chome`, which in Japanese roughly means "division" or "section."

The Japanese post office will have no problem interpreting *chome* on an envelope you address to him. On the other hand, *chome* is not Japanese. It only approximates in English the pronunciation of the actual Japanese word, written as 丁目.

Something similar is at work when you add fields, sorts, criteria, and more on the design grid. In the past several pages, I've been telling you to "create a query in Design view." That's not strictly accurate. What I've really been saying is to "use the graphical interface of the design grid to enter characters and symbols that Access can convert into a statement in Structured Query Language (SQL), a database language that Access understands and uses to run a query."

Do You Need to Know SQL?

If you've opened the drop-down for the View button on the Query Design toolbar, you've likely noticed that one of your choices is SQL. You can view in SQL view any query you create in Design view. It's good to have a little knowledge of SQL to have some appreciation of the language Access understands.

Most of the basic queries you'll likely want to make in Access can be created on the design grid without any understanding of SQL. But some queries, such as a union query, must be written in SQL. More important, SQL is the language of relational databases; if you want to do more advanced work in the field, you'll want to have a knowledge of the area.

Even if you have no real need for SQL, I don't want you to be so terrified of the term that you can't deal with it on any level. As you saw with the equally daunting *normalization* in Chapter 3, "Understanding Relationships," at least some aspects of complex and intimidating database subjects are perfectly accessible to nonprofessionals.

On the other hand, you're probably aware that "a little knowledge is a dangerous thing." Read the following dip-your-toe-in-the-water discussion in that light as well. To gain a solid understanding of SQL, I recommend *SQL Queries for Mere Mortals*, by Michael Hernandez and John Viescas (Addison-Wesley, 2000).

In this section, you'll learn a few SQL keywords to create a simple query. You'll also use SQL to execute a `UNION` query, a query type that can be created only in SQL.

Quick SQL Start

The key clauses in an SQL statement are listed in Table 8.1.

Table 8.1 SQL Statements

Keywords	Description
`SELECT`	Required. Begins the SQL statement and names the fields that will be selected from tables.
`FROM`	Required. Names the tables that contain the fields in `SELECT`.
`ORDER BY`	Not required. Determines the sort.
`WHERE`	Not required. Specifies criteria.

The first key clause is `SELECT`. You use it to start the SQL statement and select the field(s) you want in your query.

The second key clause is `FROM`. You use it to tell Access which table(s) contain the fields you specified in the `SELECT` clause (the `SELECT` part of the statement).

Let's create a very simple query using these two keywords. You'll retrieve records for the first two fields of the Categories table:

1. In the Database window, click Queries and click New. With Design View chosen in the New Query dialog box, click OK. Close the Show Table dialog box without adding any tables.
2. Save the query as **qrySQL_Practice**.
3. Click SQL on the View button. (If SQL is not displayed, click the drop-down arrow of the View button and select SQL View.)
   You see the word `SELECT` followed by a semicolon.
4. Highlight the semicolon and delete it.
   The semicolon closes the statement and tells Access you're done. But Access is usually quite forgiving if you don't include it. So for the purposes of this exercise, I ask you to delete it for now.
5. Click after `SELECT`. Press the spacebar once. Type **CategoryID**
   This tells Access to retrieve the `CategoryID` field.

6. Type a comma after `CategoryID` and press the spacebar once. Type **CategoryName**.
   You use commas to separate the fields you want to retrieve. Your statement thus far is `SELECT CategoryID, CategoryName`.
7. Press Enter.
   You could just press the spacebar, but I think it's clearer to put each clause on separate lines.
8. Type **FROM tblCategories**
9. Click View to run the query and have Access retrieve your records.

Apply a Sort with `ORDER BY`

You can sort the records by using the keyword `ORDER BY`. Let's sort by ascending `CategoryName`:

1. Open the View drop-down list and select SQL View.
2. Click after tblCategories and press Enter.
3. Type **ORDER BY CategoryName**
4. Click View to see your records.
5. Click the View drop-down and select SQL View. Add a space after `CategoryName` and type **DESC**.
   For a descending sort, add **DESC** after the field.
6. Click View to see your records. The records are now sorted by category name in descending order.

Add Criteria with `WHERE`

You use the `WHERE` clause to add criteria to your SQL statement. The `WHERE` clause must follow the `FROM` clause. Suppose you want to select just those categories that begin with the letters *G* through Z:

1. Click the View drop-down button and select SQL View.
2. Click after tblCategories. Press Enter.
3. Type **WHERE tblCategories.CategoryName>"g"**.

Here are the details:

- `WHERE` is the keyword.
- `tblCategories.CategoryName` is the identifier for the field. It includes the table name, followed by a period, followed by the field name.

- > is the greater-than comparison operator.
- `g` is the literal value, which you enclose in quotation marks. Figure 8.14 shows the SQL statement.

```
SELECT CategoryID, CategoryName
FROM tblCategories
WHERE tblCategories.CategoryName>"g"
ORDER BY CategoryName DESC;
```

Figure 8.14 The SQL statement in SQL view.

4. Click View to see your records (see Figure 8.15).
   Only categories beginning with letters after g are included.
5. Save the query and close it.

	Category ID	Category Name
▶	4	Toys
	3	Novelty
	5	Jewelry
*	(AutoNumber)	

Figure 8.15 Access retrieves `CategoryID`s and names for categories that begin with the letters *g* through *z*.

NOTE Don't be surprised or upset if Access modifies your SQL statement when you switch between Design and SQL views.

`UNION` Queries

Usually when you create queries, you want to include various fields from various tables, but you don't want to physically combine them. In a `UNION` query, you can combine fields with compatible data types (such as text with text, numbers with numbers) in a single column. The fields in the underlying tables remain as they are.

For example, imagine that to improve the logistics operations at your firm, you want to do a telephone survey of both suppliers and shippers. The researcher doing the survey asks you for a list of companies and their phone numbers that makes no distinction between suppliers and shippers.

You therefore need a list that combines the `CompanyName` of the Suppliers table with the `CompanyName` of the Shippers table, and the phone fields of the two tables as well. You can use a `UNION` query to obtain this information.

1. In the Database window, click Queries and click New. With Design view chosen in the New Query dialog box, click OK. Close the Show Table dialog box without adding any tables.
2. Choose View, SQL View. Delete the colon after `SELECT`.
3. Press the spacebar once and type **SuppCompanyName AS CompanyName**.
   `SuppCompanyName` is the field that contains supplier company names in the Suppliers table. The `AS` keyword renames the field in the query.
4. Type a comma, press the spacebar once, and type **SuppPhone AS CompanyPhone**.
   Similarly, you rename the phone field so it applies to both suppliers and shippers.
5. Press Enter.
6. Type **FROM tblSuppliers**.
   You use the `FROM` clause to designate the table.
7. Press Enter twice. Type **UNION SELECT**.
   As you can see, the `UNION` query requires two SQL `SELECT` statements. Each has the same number of fields in the same order.
8. Press the spacebar once. Type **ShipCompanyName AS CompanyName, ShipPhone AS CompanyPhone**.
   As with the supplier fields, you rename them so that the field names apply to all values.
9. Press Enter. Type **FROM tblShippers** to specify the table where the fields reside.
10. Press Enter twice. Type **ORDER BY CompanyName;**.
    This clause sorts the values. The semicolon ends the statement.
11. Your window should look like Figure 8.16. Save the query as **qryCompanyPhones**.

```
SELECT SuppCompanyName AS CompanyName, SuppPhone AS CompanyPhone
FROM tblSuppliers

UNION SELECT ShipCompanyName AS CompanyName, ShipPhone AS CompanyPhone
FROM tblShippers

ORDER BY CompanyName;
```

Figure 8.16 A `UNION` query can be designed only in SQL View.

12. Click View to see your records.
    The query includes both shipper and supplier phone numbers, sorted by company name.

> **Q&A**
>
> **Q:** You knew this question was coming: How do I format the phone numbers so they're easier to read? While I'm at it, what about some clearer column headings?
> **A:** Well, you know you can do those things in Design view. Because it's a `UNION` query, however, that view isn't available. But it's not a big problem. Here's what you can do: Choose File, Save As; open the bottom drop-down dialog box; and save the query as either a form (which, remember, has a Datasheet view) or a report. Use the `Caption` property on the `CompanyName` and `CompanyPhone` labels to set column headings. You can format the phone numbers by using the `Format` property (see Chapter 6, "Entering, Editing, and Displaying Data," for help). The solution database `NiftyLionsChap8End.mdb` includes this form as `frmCompanyPhones`.

Updating Records in a Query

Suppose you create a query. You review the records and want to make some changes to the stored records in the underlying table(s). Will your editing be successful?

The dreaded answer is, "It depends." Let's try entering records in a query under different conditions to see what works and what doesn't.

I'm using the Categories and Merchandise tables for this example. In the Database window, choose Tools, Relationships to open the Relationships window. As you've seen previously, the two tables have a one-to-many relationship through the `CategoryID` field. The Categories table is on the "one" side, and the Merchandise table is on the "many" side. Close the Relationships window.

Update Records in One Table

Let's first review updating records in just one table.

1. In the Database window, click the Tables button and select tblCategories. Choose Insert, Query. With Design View selected, click OK.
2. Save the query as `qryCategoriesAndProducts`.
3. In the Categories field list, add the `CategoryName` and `CategoryDescription` fields to the design grid.
4. Click View to see your records.
5. In the Jewelry record, click in the Description column. Add a comma after watch and type **bracelet**.
6. Press Enter.
   Because the query is based on only one table, you had no problem adding the text.

Update Records in Two Tables that Have a One-to-Many Relationship

Things get more complicated when you want to add records to a query based on two tables that have a one-to-many relationship.

1. Click View to return to Design view.
2. Click Show Table. Select the tblMerchandise table and add it to the Design window.
3. Add the `MerchName` and `MerchDescription` fields to the grid.
4. Click View to return to Datasheet view.
5. As an artificial exercise, click in the last row of the `Category Name` field. Type **Jewelry** and press Tab. Type **Pendant, charm, watch, bracelet**. Press Tab and try to type **Bracelet**. Access won't let you. Press Escape once (or twice, if necessary) to erase your entries.

6. Click View to return to Design view. From the **Merchandise** field list, add the `CategoryID` field to the design grid. Drag the CategoryID column so that it's the first column in the grid. Your Query Design window should look similar to Figure 8.17. (I made the panes equal in size and lengthened the field lists for a better view.)
7. Click View to return to Datasheet view. In the `CategoryID` field, type **5**, which is the ID for jewelry, and press Tab. Access automatically enters the values for the `Category Name` and `Description` fields.
8. Press Tab twice. Type **Bracelet** in the `Product Name` field. Access now has no problem accepting an entry in the `Product Name` field.
9. Press Undo Current Field/Record to erase the entry.
   Note that you could have made an additional entry in the `Item Description` field and saved this record like any other.
10. Close the query and click Yes to save your design changes.

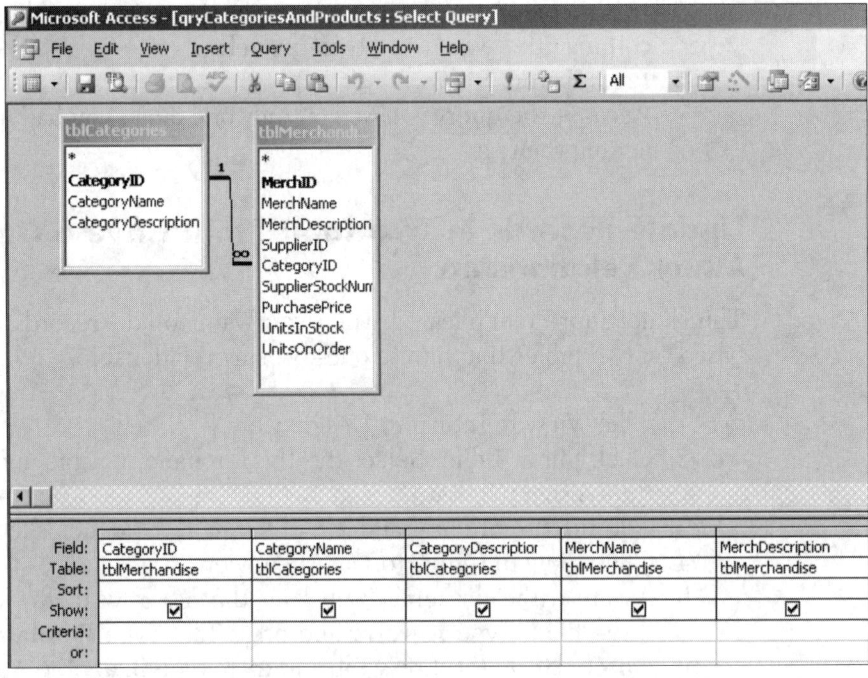

Figure 8.17 A multitable query in Design view. Be sure that the `CategoryID` in the first column is from the Merchandise table.

What just went on here? Access initially didn't allow you to enter new records in the multitable query. Then you added the join field from the "many" side of the relationship (namely, `CategoryID` from the Merchandise table) to the query. When that field was part of the query, Access accepted new records.

Although these two examples are useful, they do not tell the whole story. If you intend to use queries significantly for updating data, you'll want to take a look at the article "When Can I Update Data from a Query?" in the "About Updating Data" section of Access Help.

Find Duplicates Query Wizard

Before closing this chapter, I'd like to mention quickly the easy-to-use Find Duplicates Query Wizard.

Suppose you have a table of contact info for suppliers. You want to check whether you've entered any supplier records twice. The field for supplier names doesn't allow duplicates—that is, its `Indexed` property is set to `Yes (No Duplicates)`. But the field for street addresses allows duplicates—that is, its `Indexed` property is set to `No` or `Yes (Duplicates OK)`.

If you have duplicates in the street address, it's possible that you have entered two records for the same company, using variations of the company name. It's also entirely possible that you have two different suppliers at the same street address.

This is the kind of information the Find Duplicates Query Wizard helps you discover. It can be particularly useful when you've imported data from another source and want to verify that there are no duplicate records.

The Find Duplicates Query Wizard can be selected in the New Query dialog box. The instructions provided in the wizard are straightforward, and I don't think you will have any problems using it.

Conclusion

This chapter covered the basics of query creation and usage, most notably the use of joins to create multitable queries.. You can compare the queries you created with those in the NiftyLionsEndChap8 database. In the next chapter, you will use many of the techniques learned here to create specialized queries that will improve your productivity and your capacity for data analysis.

CHAPTER 9

Queries, Part II

This chapter focuses on several types of queries that can help you review and analyze your data. Parameter queries make it easy to quickly change criteria so you can retrieve the records for, say, Nevada instead of Nebraska. You use total queries to find sums, averages, and other aggregates. Crosstab queries are sophisticated total queries that help you break down data for easier analysis.

A fourth topic, action queries, is also included, although it's a slightly uncomfortable fit. Virginia Woolf told us that "A rose is a rose is a rose." But if she ever met an action query, I doubt she would say "A query is a query is a query." Unlike the select queries that are central to your day-to-day Access work, action queries perform some operation on your data, such as editing values or appending records to a table. Usually they are used on large numbers of records, although they can be applied in smaller databases as well.

With the possible exception of action queries, all the queries in this chapter should be enormously helpful in your work. Let's get to it.

Parameter Queries

The word *parameter* is now often used as a cliché in bloated, pompous corporate speech, so you might come to parameter queries with an attitude of skepticism. Be assured that, despite its name, the parameter query is a model of elegant design—and extremely useful, to boot.

As you saw in Chapter 8, "Queries," in the usual select query, you enter criteria on the design grid to restrict the records retrieved to those that meet certain conditions. For example, suppose you want to retrieve customer orders from a specific country. You include the `ShipCountry` (or similarly named) field in your query and enter the country—say, Canada—in the Criteria row of that column.

However, suppose you want to use the same query again and again, but with slightly different criteria. For example, you might have created a query for customer orders that has all the fields, sorts, and so on just the way you want them. But sometimes you want orders from Canada, other times from Mexico, or Guatemala, or Austria. In each case, you would have to open the query in Design view, go to the `ShipCountry` field, and edit the criteria for the specific country. Do that once a week, and it's no big deal; do it once an hour, and it's a hassle.

The parameter query offers a solution. Instead of editing the criteria each time on the grid, you can have the query prompt you for the country you require. You enter your criteria (that's exactly what it is—criteria) and run your query.

Are Parameter Queries Really Useful?

You might be wondering, "Wouldn't it be better to use a filter than a query for this objective?" I think the advantages of a parameter query over a filter for certain tasks will become apparent as you read through the chapter. Entering criteria in dialog boxes can be easier than creating filters each time. Moreover, remember that a parameter query is a full-fledged query, so you have all the functionality that a query maintains, including greater flexibility for building forms and reports based on the query.

It might still not seem like a parameter query will save you much time over editing the design grid, even if you often need to change the criteria. A simple comparison of a parameter and a nonparameter query should squelch any doubts. You'll first create a "regular" query using criteria, and then you'll create a parameter query. You'll use `NiftyLionsChap9.mdb`, which you can download to your hard drive.

False Parameter Value Dialogs

During the 1992 presidential campaign, Ross Perot's vice presidential candidate, Adm. James Stockdale, famously said, "Who am I? Why am I here?" If you came here to find out why an Enter Parameter Value dialog box suddenly appeared on your screen from out of nowhere, you're probably asking yourself the same questions right now. None of the discussion thus far—and none that follows—has any connection to what you were working on when the dialog box appeared.

Several reasons exist for why you might get an Enter Parameter Value dialog box when no parameter query has been created. Possibly the most likely cause is that there's a mistake in a field name somewhere in the query design grid.

For example, let's say you created a calculated field that shows a 12% increase in purchase prices. In the first row of a column on the design grid, you entered this expression:

```
ExpectedPrice: [Purchase Price]*1.12
```

That looks good, except that the field name is probably spelled as one word—`PurchasePrice`, not `Purchase Price`. The extra space throws Access for a loop and, in a vain cry for help, it offers up the Enter Parameter Value dialog box.

So when this dialog box appears and there's no parameter query in sight, you can usually take that as a sign of trouble. As you check your work, pay special attention to the spelling of field names.

Creating a Nonparameter Query

The Customers table contains contact data for Nifty Lions's customers. Suppose you're the sales manager and you regularly like to review your customer base by individual state. You decide to create a query that includes all the fields from the table, with an additional column to designate state criteria:

1. Click the Tables button and select the tblCustomers table.
2. Choose Insert, Query. With Design View selected, click OK.
3. From the field list, double-click the asterisk (*) to add all the fields to the query.
4. Choose File, Save and save your query as qryCustByState.
5. Double-click `CustState` to add it to the grid. Deselect the check box in the Show row of the design grid.
   `CustState` is already included in the records because you added all fields. You'll use this second column only to set criteria, so you deselect Show so its values won't be displayed twice.
6. Type **ca** in the Criteria row of the CustState column.
7. Click the button at the far left end of the toolbar (View). You see only records from California.
8. Save the query and close it.
   Suppose that two hours later you want to see all your customers from Colorado.
9. In the Database window, select qryCustByState and click Design.
10. Highlight `"ca"` in the Criteria row of the `CustByState` field and type **co**.

11. Click View or Run to see your records. Your datasheet includes only records from Colorado.
12. Close the query and save your changes.

Creating a Parameter Query

After continually opening the query in design view and editing criteria, you decide to try a parameter query to accomplish the same task.

1. In the Database window, click Tables. With tblCustomers selected, choose Insert, Query. With Design View selected, click OK.
2. From the field list, double-click the asterisk (*) to add all the fields to the query. Double-click `CustState` to add it to the grid. Deselect the Show check box in the CustState column.
3. Choose File, Save and save your query as qryCustByStateParameter.
4. Click in the Criteria row of the `State` field. Type **[Enter state abbreviation:]** (see Figure 9.1).

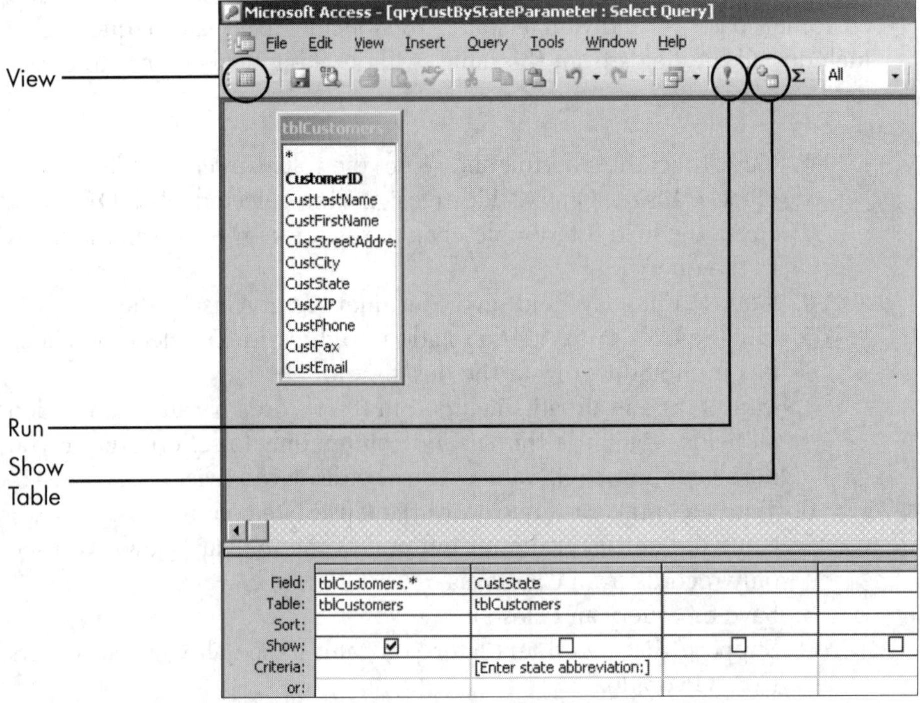

Figure 9.1 In the Criteria row, you type the text you want to appear in the Enter Parameter Value dialog box.

As you'll soon see, the text between the brackets appears in the Enter Parameter Value dialog box as a prompt for you to enter criteria.

5. Save your changes and close the query.
6. In the Database window, click Queries and double-click qryCustByStateParameter.
7. In the Enter Parameter Value dialog box (see Figure 9.2), type **ca** and click OK.
   Customer records from California are retrieved.

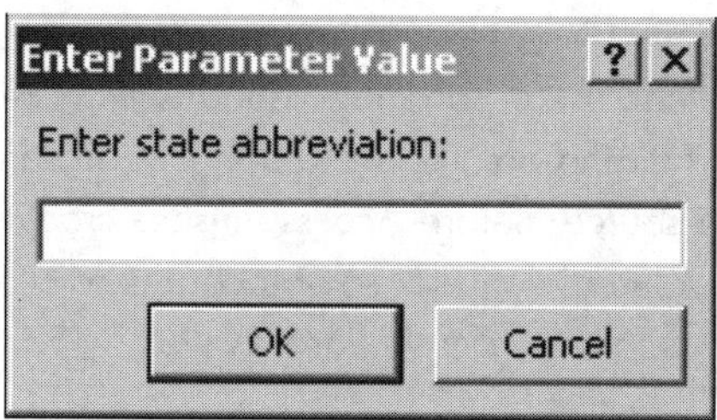

Figure 9.2 You enter the criteria you want in the Enter Parameter Value dialog box.

8. Click View to return to Design view.
   Notice that the design grid is unchanged—the text in the Criteria row of the `CustByState` field is the same as when you saved it.
9. Click View to run the query. Type **mi** in the dialog box. Click OK to see your records. The two customers from Michigan are retrieved. Close the query.

Q&A

Q: All right, I understand the convenience of a parameter query. But one thing I don't get. You showed us in Chapter 7, "Find and Filter," how you can see exactly how records have been filtered in a datasheet—namely, by choosing Record, Filter, Advanced Filter/Sort. I tried that when I was viewing the customer records for California, but the design grid was completely blank. Shouldn't there have been criteria indicating that the records were for California?

A: You didn't do any filtering. When you entered `ca` in the Enter Parameter Value box, it had the same effect as entering `ca` in the Criteria row for the `CustState` field. Instead of creating a filter, you ran a query.

Creating a Report Using a Parameter Query

You can quickly create a report based on your parameter query.

1. With qryCustByStateParameter selected in the Datasheet window, choose Insert, AutoReport.
2. In the query prompt, type **ca**. Access creates a report of California customers.
3. Close the report without saving your changes.

NOTE You can use a parameter query with a Report Wizard as well. In the New Report dialog box, select Report Wizard and use the parameter query as your record source. Before Access finishes creating the object, it issues the Enter Parameter Value dialog box so you can enter criteria. The same general technique applies to the Form Wizard as well.

Parameter Query with a Wildcard

You can also use a parameter query with a wildcard. For example, let's say you want to see records for customers whose last names begin with a certain letter or letters. Create a query as you would normally do. In the Criteria row of the `LastName` field, enter **Like [Enter the first two letters of last name] & "*"**. The expression consists of the following elements:

- The `Like` operator, which tells Access to match the text string
- The prompt text of `Enter the first two letters of last name`, enclosed in brackets
- The `&` operator for concatenation (a topic discussed at length in Chapter 10, "Reports")
- A string literal containing the `*` wildcard, which means any number of characters can follow the first two letters

If you recall studying the `Validation Text` property for fields, you'll remember that Access doesn't compare the validation text with the actual validation rule. Whatever you enter in `Validation Text` is what Access displays as an error message when the validation rule is broken.

The prompt text in a parameter query is similar. The contents are valuable and should tell you or the user exactly what to do. But Access doesn't pass judgment on it. You can type **[Pink, pink elephants; pink, pink elephants]** in the Criteria row of a `State` field, and Access won't protest.

So if you're using a parameter query with a wildcard, you can make the prompt say whatever you want and thereby suit it to your needs. For example, you can type `[Enter the first letter of last name]` or `[Enter the first few letters of last name]`. If you use the first string, you're suggesting to users that they enter `b` to get records for Barton, Boyton, and Buckner. If you use the latter, you're suggesting they enter `bal` to get Baldridge, Ballon, and Balderman, or `bald` to get Baldridge and Balderman.

Parameter Query with Two Values

You can also use parameter queries that require more than one entry. For example, you might have criteria in a single field that requires two entries, such as a `Date` field that uses the operator `Between...And`. You could also have a parameter query using criteria in two fields.

Suppose you want to create a parameter query to find the shipping cost for all orders for various time periods. As you recall from Chapter 7, you use the `Between...And` operator.

1. In the Database window, click Queries and choose New. With Design View selected, click OK.
2. Add the tblOrders table to the Design window and close the Show Table dialog box.
3. Add the `OrderID`, `OrderDate`, and `ShipCost` fields to the grid.
4. In the Criteria row of the `OrderDate` field, enter the expression `Between [Type the beginning date:] And [Type the ending date:]` (see Figure 9.3).
5. Choose File, Save. Save the query as `qryOrderDatesParameter`.
6. Click View.
   Because the criteria uses the `Between...And` operator, you are prompted by two dialog boxes: one for the beginning date and the other for the ending date.
7. Type **8/20/04** and click OK. Type **8/28/04** and click OK.
   Your query shows order IDs, order dates, and shipping costs for the period between 8/20/04 and 8/28/04 (there were no orders between 8/20/04 and 8/22/04). Save your changes and close the query.

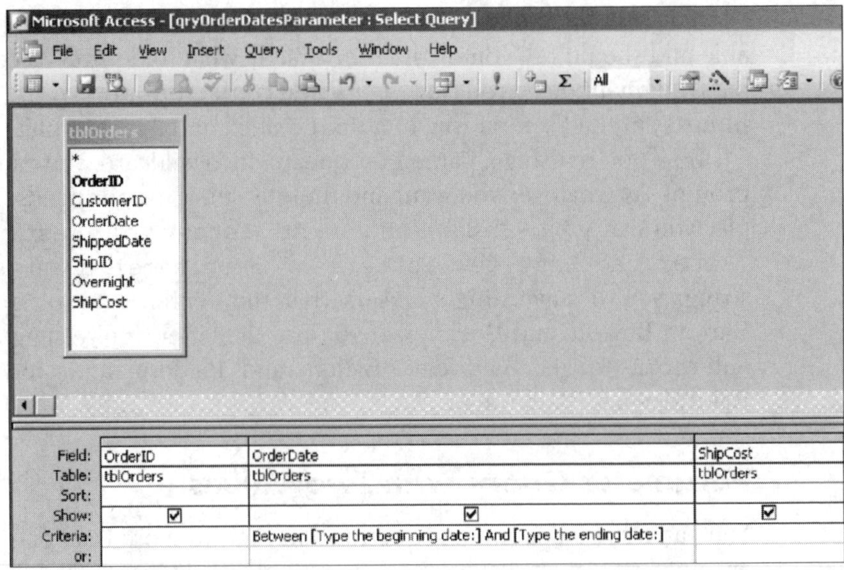

Figure 9.3 You can use a parameter query with the `Between...And` operator.

Now let's try a parameter query using two different fields. We can search for orders on a particular date that had shipping costs between $X and $Y. Here's how to create the query.

1. In the Database window, click Queries. Double-click Create Query in Design View.
2. Add tblOrders to the design grid and close the Show Table dialog box.
3. Add the `OrderID`, `OrderDate`, and `ShipCost` fields to the grid.
4. In the Criteria row of the `OrderDate` field, type **[Enter the date:]**.
5. In the `ShipCost` field, type the expression **Between [Enter the minimum ship cost:] And [Enter the maximum ship cost:]** (see Figure 9.4).
6. Choose File, Save. Save the query as `qryShipCostParameter`.
7. Click Run. In the Enter the Date prompt, type **8/23/04**.
8. In Enter the Minimum Ship Cost, type **4** and click OK. In Enter the Maximum Ship Cost, type **10** and click OK.

   A reminder: When you enter currency amounts, dollar signs are unnecessary.

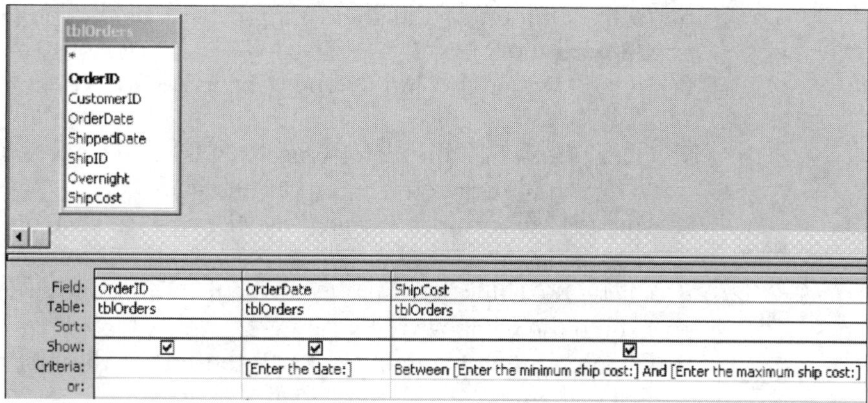

Figure 9.4 You can use a parameter query with criteria in two fields.

9. The query returns orders on 8/23/04 that have shipping costs of between $4 and $10.
10. Close the query and save your changes.

Query Parameters Dialog

The Query Parameters dialog box is available by choosing Query, Parameters. In this grid, you can enter the fields that require criteria and the data type of the field.

For creating parameters in fields of most data types, the Query Parameters dialog box is not necessary. But it does offer certain benefits, as you will see presently. It is also required for certain queries, including crosstab queries and in situations when one of the prompts is for a field from a table in an external database.

A Query That Requires the Query Parameters Dialog Box

The Query Parameters dialog box is required in another instance: when you have parameters in two fields and one of them has the `Yes/No` data type. Try this example:

1. Create a new query in Design view based on the tblOrders table.
2. Add the `OrderID`, `ShippedDate`, `Overnight`, and `ShipCost` fields.
3. Choose File, Save. Save the query as `qryOvernightOrders`.
4. Click View, briefly review the fields and records, and return to Design view.

5. In the Criteria row of the `ShippedDate` field, type **[Enter the shipped date:]**.
6. In the Overnight column, type **[Enter Yes or No]** in the Criteria row.
7. Click View. For the date, type **8/24/04** and click OK. For the `Overnight` parameter, enter **yes** and click OK.
   You get an error message that there is a problem with the expressions.
8. Click OK. Copy `[Enter the date:]` from the `ShippedDate` field to the Clipboard.
9. Choose Query, Parameters. Paste the text in the first row of the first column.
   The Query Parameters dialog box can also be issued by right-clicking in the top pane and choosing Parameters from the shortcut menu.
10. Press Tab. Open the drop-down list and select Date/Time. Click OK.
11. Copy `[Enter Yes or No]` from the Overnight column.
12. Choose Query, Parameters. Paste the text in the second row of the first column.
13. Press Tab. Open the drop-down list and choose Yes/No (see Figure 9.5).
14. Click View. Type **8/24/04** in the first prompt and click OK. Type **yes** in the second prompt and click OK.
    There are three orders that were shipped overnight.
15. Close the query and save your changes.

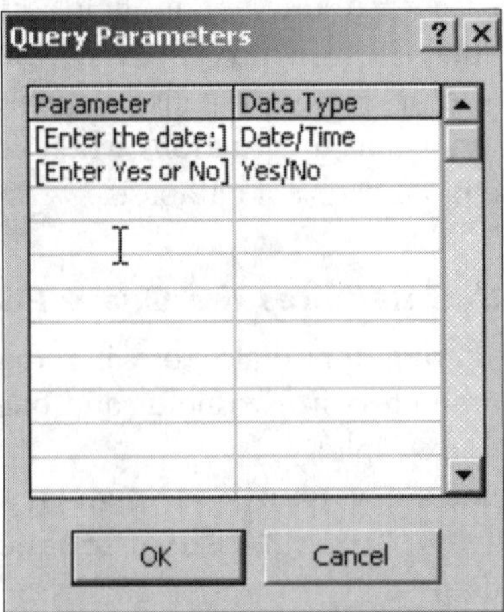

Figure 9.5 The Parameters Query dialog box is required when you have parameters in two fields and one has the `Yes/No` data type.

A Query in Which the Query Parameters Dialog Box Is Helpful

Now let's take a look at a typical parameter query that doesn't require the Query Parameters dialog box but one in which it might be helpful.

1. Create a new query in Design view based on the tblOrders table.
2. Add the `OrderID` and `OrderDate` fields to the design grid.
3. Choose File, Save and save the query as `qryParameterDialog`.
4. Click in the Criteria row of the `OrderDate` field. Type **[Enter date of order:]**.
5. Click View. In the Enter Parameter Value dialog box, type **82304**. This date is obviously missing slashes, but don't correct it.
6. Click View. Access returns no records.

   At this point, you don't know whether there really were no records for 8/23/04 or whether you just made a mistake in entering criteria.
7. Click View to return to Design view. Copy the contents of the Criteria row in the `OrderDate` to the Clipboard.
8. Choose Query, Parameters.
9. Click in the first column of the first row and paste the contents from the Clipboard.
10. Press Tab. Open the drop-down list and type **da** for `Date/Time`. Click OK.
11. Click View. In the Enter Parameter Value dialog box, type **82304** and click OK.

    You see the error message in Figure 9.6.

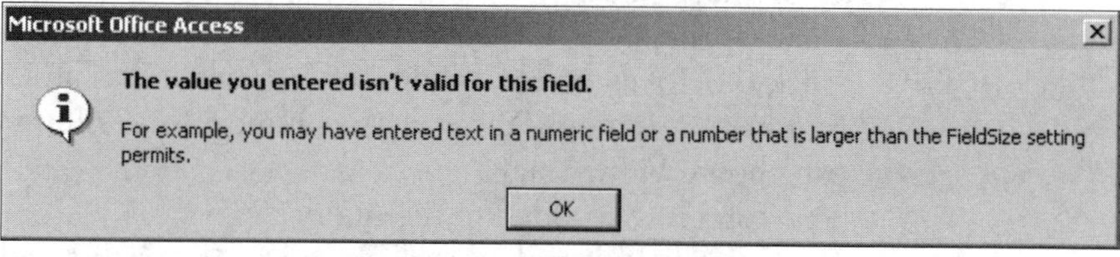

Figure 9.6 The Query Parameter dialog box helps provide an appropriate error message.

12. Click OK. Edit the criteria to **8/23/04** and click OK to see your records.
13. Close the query and save your changes.

I don't want to imply that using the Query Parameters dialog box is a cure-all for the sloppy typist. Even if you have made appropriate entries in the dialog box, you might still retrieve no records or the wrong records because you made some mistake in entering criteria. Nevertheless, using the dialog box gives you a head start in resolving criteria errors.

Totals Queries

Totals queries enable you to find sums of values by using aggregate functions. Their capacities are extremely important and useful. You can count the number of orders in March, find the average freight per order, calculate the total number of units on hand for a product category, and so on.

How is creating a totals query different from creating other queries? In terms of technique alone, the major difference is the addition of the Total row to the design grid. You make selections in the Total drop-down list to designate the aggregate function you want to use, the grouping you want, and which fields are to be used for criteria. Although the utility of each function obviously depends on database and user, I focus on three of the most important aggregates: `Sum`, `Avg`, and `Count`.

Finding a Sum for All Records

Let's first create a simple query that sums a field. The Merchandise table has a field for the units in stock for each product. You can create a totals query that sums the field. Then you'll compare this method with typing an expression using the `Sum` function to find the same number.

1. In the Database window, select the tblMerchandise table. Choose Insert, Query. With Design View selected, click OK in the New Query dialog box.
2. Choose File, Save. Save the query as `qryUnitsInStock`.
3. Click the Totals button on the toolbar, which has an image of the Summation symbol (Σ) on it (see Figure 9.7). Alternatively, you can choose View, Totals.
   The Total row is added to the query.
4. From the field list, double-click `UnitsInStock` to add it to the grid.
5. Open the drop-down list in the Total row and choose Sum (see Figure 9.7).
6. Click View. Access has totaled the field.
   Let's give the field an easier-to-understand caption than `SumOfUnitsInStock`.
7. Click View to return to Design view. Right-click anywhere in the first column and choose Properties.
8. In the `Caption` property, type **Total Units**. Close the property sheet.

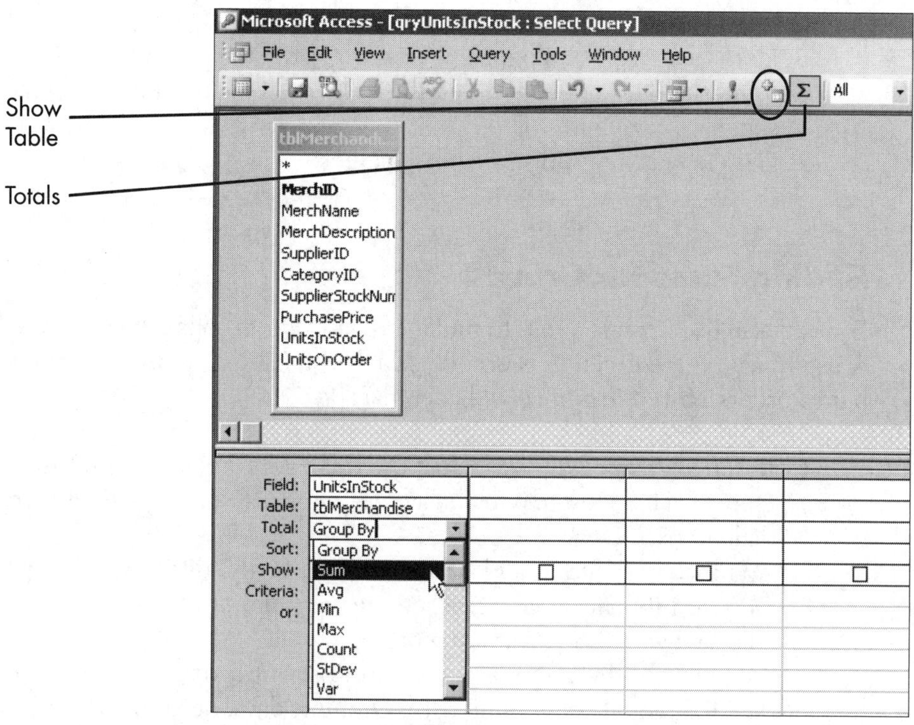

Figure 9.7 You can select the aggregate function from a drop-down list in the Total row.

Now you'll find the same total by creating an expression with the `Sum` function:

1. Click in the first row of the second column.
2. Type **Sum([UnitsInStock])**, which includes these elements:
   - `Sum` is the function that sums the field.
   - `[UnitsInStock]` is the field that's being summed.
   - Parentheses enclose the entity being summed.
3. Click View. The results in both columns are the same.
   You could similarly edit the caption of the second column.

TIP To quickly resize a column so you can see the full title, move your pointer to the right border. When the pointer is a double arrow with a bar, double-click for a "best fit."

---

4. Click View to return to Design view.
   Note that Access recognizes that the expression in the second column is a totals query and that the first and second columns are the same.
5. Close the query and save your changes.

Finding Sums for Groups

You can also use a totals query to find aggregates for groups. One extremely useful aggregate function is `Count`, which you can use to find the number of orders Nifty Lions received each day.

1. In the Database window, select the tblOrders table. Choose Insert, Query. With Design View selected, click OK in the New Query dialog box.
2. Add the `OrderDate` and `OrderID` fields to the design grid.
3. Choose File, Save. Save the query as `qryOrdersByDate`.
4. Click View and review the records.
   As it stands, the query is rather useless, but it does show you the data that you'll be working with. On most days, only one order was made, but on a few days, several orders were made. Notice, for example, that on 8/23/04, eight orders were made. If you add the number of `OrderID`s for each day, you get the number of orders by date. Put more formally, you'll count the `OrderID`s and group them by date.
5. Click View to return to Design view. Click the Totals button on the toolbar. The Total row is added to the grid.
6. In the Total row of the `OrderDate` field, the Total row setting should be `Group By`.
   `GROUP BY` is a keyword in SQL for dividing data into groups.
7. Click in the Total row of the `OrderID` field. Open the drop-down list and select Count (see Figure 9.8).
8. Click View and review the records.
   You have the total orders for each date. Notice, for example, that on 8/23/2004, eight orders were made.
9. Click View to return to Design view.

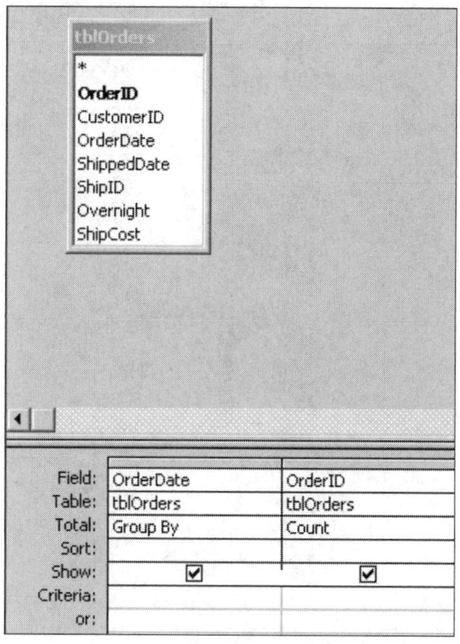

Figure 9.8 The `Count` function can be used to find the number of orders on each day.

Findings Sums with Two Groups

You can easily add a second group to the totals query. For example, the `Overnight` field in the Orders table is a `Yes/No` field that shows whether an order was shipped overnight. Add it to the grid as a second group:

1. Click the `Overnight` field in the field list. Drag and drop it into the OrderID column.
   The Total row setting is `Group By`.
2. Click View and review the records.
   The records are grouped first by the date and then by overnight and nonovernight shipments. For example, take a look at August 23 orders. Of the eight total orders, three were shipped overnight and five were shipped by regular freight.
3. Click View to return to Design view.
4. Move your pointer to the column selector at the top of the Overnight column. When the pointer becomes a down arrow, click to select the column. Click and drag the column to the left of the Order Date column.
5. Click View and review your records (see Figure 9.9).

Overnight?	Order Date	CountOfOrderID
☑	7/19/2004	1
☑	8/2/2004	1
☑	8/23/2004	3
☐	7/16/2004	2
☐	7/19/2004	1
☐	7/20/2004	1
☐	7/21/2004	1
☐	7/23/2004	1
☐	7/26/2004	1
☐	7/27/2004	1
☐	7/28/2004	1
☐	7/29/2004	3
☐	8/2/2004	1
☐	8/3/2004	1
☐	8/5/2004	1
☐	8/23/2004	5
☐	8/25/2004	1
☐	8/27/2004	1
☐	9/1/2004	1
☐	9/3/2004	1
☐	9/7/2004	1
☐	9/8/2004	1
☐	9/9/2004	1
☐	9/10/2004	1

Figure 9.9 The orders are grouped first by whether they were sent overnight and then by date.

TIP You can change the display of the `Yes/No` field from a check box to text that displays `Yes` for positive and `No` for negative. In Design view, right-click in the Overnight? column and select Properties. Click the Lookup tab. Open the drop-down list and select Text Box.

Using `WHERE` to Set Criteria

You can add criteria to totals queries so that only records that meet specific conditions are summed. For example, suppose you want to count only orders for customers who live in California, Colorado, Nevada, or Washington. You can use the `WHERE` clause to set criteria.

In this query, you'll also learn about the `IN` operator, which makes it easy to specify multiple values for a single field. Here's how to modify the query:

1. Choose Tools, Relationships to open the Relationships window. Note that the `Customers` and `Orders` tables have a one-to-many relationship. The `CustState` field designates the customer's state. You can add the `CustState` field and specify criteria to limit the records to those customers for those four states.

2. Close the Relationships window.
3. In the `qryOrdersByDate` query, click View to return to Design view.
4. Click Show Table (see Figure 9.7 if you've forgotten its location). Click tblCustomers and click Add. Close the Show Table dialog box.
5. Double-click `CustState` to add it to the grid.
6. Open the drop-down list in the Total row of the `CustState` field and choose Where.

   You'll remember that `WHERE` is an SQL keyword used for designating criteria. Also note that the Show box is deselected.
7. Click in the Criteria row of the `CustState` field. Type **In(ca,co,nv,wa)**.

   The `IN` operator makes it easy to include all four states in a short expression. You include each of the states you want and separate them by commas, with no spaces between them. Note that you could have typed `ca Or co Or nv Or wa` for the same results. In other words, any one of the states is a match. You could also have typed each state abbreviation in a separate row in the Criteria area of the design grid (see Figure 9.10).
8. Click View to see the order count for these four states, which are grouped first by their overnight status and then by date.
9. Save your work and close the query.

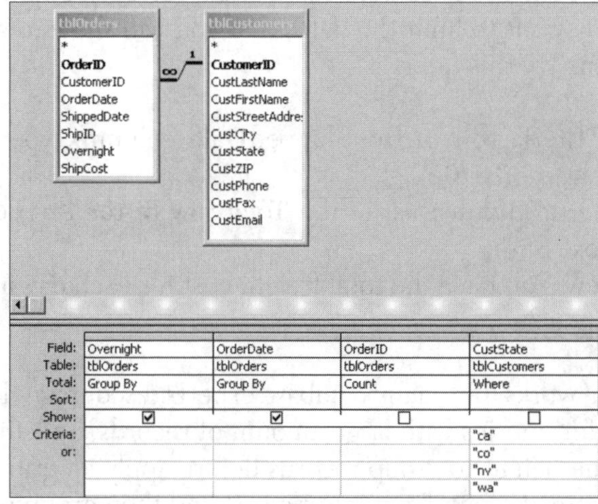

Figure 9.10 The criteria in the `CustState` column is correctly but inefficiently entered as `OR` criteria.

Advanced Examples Using Criteria

Abraham Lincoln famously said, "You can fool all the people some of the time, and some of the people all of the time, but you cannot fool all of the people all of the time."

When you use criteria in total queries, things work a little differently. You can sum all the records and show some of them, sum some of the records and show all of them, or sum some of the records and show some of them.

That's hardly Lincoln-esque speech. Let's try to unravel the mysteries of using criteria in total queries.

Start by creating a new query:

1. In the Database window, select the tblOrders table. Choose Insert, Query. With Design View selected, click OK in the New Query dialog box.
2. Save the query as `qryLateAugustOrders`.
3. Double-click `ShippedDate` and `ShipCost` to add them to the grid.
4. Click the Totals button to add the Total row.

Setting Criteria

You might want to include criteria for a field you're grouping on. For example, you may want to limit the dates that you will show totals for to a certain time-span. Try this query:

1. In the Criteria row of the ShippedDate column, type **Between 8/20/04 and 8/31/04**.
2. Open the drop-down list in the Total row of the `ShipCost` field and choose Sum.
3. Click View. You have the total freight cost for each day in the period you specified.

This example works, but many database experts discourage the method used, especially for queries with large amount of records. Specifically, they argue that it is inefficient to group records before applying criteria (as the example does) instead of applying criteria first and then grouping records. They would therefore recommend that criteria be set in a separate column using `WHERE`, as follows:

1. Click View to return to Design view.
2. Double-click `ShippedDate` to add a second column of this field to the grid.
3. Open the drop-down list in the Total row of this new column and choose Where.
   Note that the Show check box is deselected.
4. Cut `Between 8/20/04 and 8/31/04` from the first `ShippedDate` field and paste it into the Criteria row of the second `ShippedDate` field.
5. Click View. You get the same results as you did in the last example.

Setting Criteria in an Aggregate Field

Let's modify this query a bit to find the average freight cost for each day. In this case, you would likely also want to know just how many orders there were on each day.

1. Click View to return to Design view.
2. Click `OrderID` in the field list. Drag and drop it into the ShipCost column.
3. Open the Total drop-down list in the OrderID column and select Count.
4. Open the Total drop-down list in the ShipCost column and select Avg.
5. Click View to see your records (see Figure 9.11).
   The query shows the average freight grouped by date and also the number of orders on that day.

	Shipped Date	CountOfOrderID	AvgOfShipCost
	8/23/2004	1	$2.57
	8/24/2004	6	$7.89
	8/26/2004	1	$2.95
	8/27/2004	1	$8.95
▶	8/31/2004	1	$7.95

Figure 9.11 Records are limited only by date.

Now suppose you want to see only days when the average freight cost was above $5. Remember, you've included all records between 8/20/04 and 8/31/04 in your calculations. Now you can just show those days when the average freight cost was above $5.

1. Click View to return to Design view.
2. Type **>5** in the Criteria row of the ShipCost column. Click View to see your records.
   The days when the freight cost was below $5 (namely, 8/23/04 and 8/26/04) are no longer included.

Excluding Records Before and After Performing Calculations

Now let's say you'd like to exclude from the calculations any order with a freight cost below $2.75. Now you're excluding records before you do any calculations.

1. Click View to return to Design view.
2. Cut `>5` from the Criteria row of the ShipCost column (you'll soon paste it back).
3. Click View to see your records (because you eliminated the criteria from the last example, these should again match Figure 9.11).
4. Click View to return to Design view.
5. Double-click `ShipCost` to add a second column of the same field to the grid.
6. In the Total row of the second ShipCost column, open the Total drop-down list and choose Where.
7. In the Criteria row, type **>2.75**.
8. Click View to see your records (see Figure 9.12).

	Shipped Date	CountOfOrderID	AvgOfShipCost
▶	8/24/2004	4	$10.95
	8/26/2004	1	$2.95
	8/27/2004	1	$8.95
	8/31/2004	1	$7.95

Figure 9.12 Records are limited by date and freight cost.

9. Click View to return to Design view.
10. Click in the Criteria row of the first `ShipCost` field. Paste `>5`.
11. Click View to see your records (see Figure 9.13).
12. Close the query and save your changes.

	Shipped Date	CountOfOrderID	AvgOfShipCost
▶	8/24/2004	4	$10.95
	8/27/2004	1	$8.95
	8/31/2004	1	$7.95

Figure 9.13 Records are limited by date, freight cost, and $5 threshold for average cost.

Compare the three sets of results in Figures 9.11 through 9.13.

In Figure 9.11, the records were limited only by date. In Figure 9.12, orders with freight costs below $2.75 were not included in the calculation. So the order count on 8/24 was only 4, versus 6 in Figure 9.11. Thus, the average freight cost for 8/24 rose. In addition, freight costs for 8/23 were excluded entirely because they amounted to only $2.57 and did not reach the $2.75 threshold.

Figure 9.13 resembles Figure 9.12, but the 8/26 record of freight costs of $2.95 were eliminated from the record set after calculating the average because they did not exceed the required $5 limit.

Crosstab Queries

Take almost any subject: sports, finance, politics. The professionals who make their money analyzing what goes on are always talking about "breaking down the numbers." Traffic accidents in Pleasantville totaled 72 last month; how many occurred east of Main Street, and how many west of Main Street? The freshman class at Ivy University has 1,784 students; how many come from each country? Total employees at Acme Widget number 3,587; how many are in each of the Production, Marketing, and Financial divisions?

Often you'll want to find and compare breakdowns among different items in a single group. For example, you might want to see the country-by-country totals for the freshman class at each of the Ivy League schools.

This is the kind of information delivered by the crosstab query, a type of totals query that summarizes data by tabulating it across the values of two fields (thus the term *crosstab*, short for "cross tabulation"). As with other totals queries, row headings are actual values. Unlike other totals queries, however, column headings in a crosstab query are also values rather than field names and totals. You'll soon see how this arrangement provides a matrix that generates totals where the two values intersect.

You can create a crosstab query from scratch or by using the Crosstab Query Wizard in the New Query dialog box. But the wizard has its downside: You can use only one table. In any case, as with the Find Unmatched Query Wizard, it pays to understand how the wizard works so you can work with it and modify it when necessary. When you create a crosstab query from scratch, the wizard becomes self-explanatory.

TIP You can use a workaround for the one-table limitation of the Crosstab Query Wizard. You can create a multitable query and then use the query as the basis for the wizard. But in that case, it might be just as easy to create a crosstab query from scratch.

Overview

Let's briefly examine the steps required for creating a crosstab query before you actually make one.

You start a crosstab query like any other: You create a new query in Design view and add the tables that have the data you need to the Design window. When you choose Query, Crosstab Query, you'll see two new rows in the design grid: Total and Crosstab.

A crosstab query has three key elements:

- **Row headings**—You add one or more fields to the grid to use as row headings. In other words, these columns form the values down the "side" of your crosstab result. The Total row should be set to Group By; the Crosstab row is set to Row Heading.
- **Column headings**—The values Access finds in this field form separate columns across the top of your crosstab result. You add only one field to the grid for these column headings. Set the Crosstab row to Column Heading and the Total row to Group By.
- **Value**—This is the calculation displayed in the intersection of the Row Heading values and the Column Heading values. You add the field whose values will be used in your calculation. You set the Crosstab row to Value, and the Total row to the type of summary you want.

You can also add criteria. First add the field that will further define the records retrieved. Set the Total row to Where and keep the Crosstab row empty. Type your expression in the Criteria row.

Creating a Crosstab Query

Suppose you're a Nifty Lions owner. You want to see how many orders each of your shippers is handling, broken down by state. You can use a crosstab query to view this information.

What data do you need? The Orders table has `OrderIDs`. The Shippers table has the names of shippers. And the Customers table has a field for the customer's state. If you count `OrderIDs`, you can find the number of orders each shipper handled by state.

1. Create a new query in Design view.
2. Add the tblCustomers, tblOrders, and tblShippers tables.
   Note that the tables are tied together by one-to-many relationships.
3. Save the query as `qryOrdersByShipper`.
4. Choose Query, Crosstab Query.
5. From the tblCustomers table, double-click `CustState` to add it to the grid. In the Total row, keep Group By. Click in the Crosstab row, open the drop-down list, and choose Row Heading.
6. From the tblShippers table, double-click `ShipCompanyName` to add it to the grid. In the Total row, keep Group By. Open the drop-down list in the Crosstab row and select Column Heading.
7. From the Orders table, double-click `OrderID`. Click in the Total row, highlight Group By, and type **c** for "count." Click in the Crosstab row, open the drop-down list, and select Value (see Figure 9.14).
8. Click View to run the query and see the breakdown of orders by shipper by state.

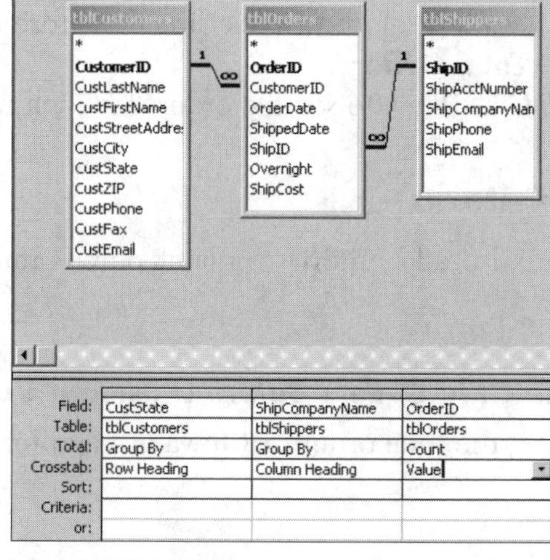

Figure 9.14 In a crosstab query, you specify both column and row headings and a value that will be summed.

Additional Row Headings

You can add more row headings to break down the values further. For example, suppose that for each state you'd like to see a further breakdown between regular and overnight orders. Here's how to add the necessary column:

1. Click View to return to Design view.
2. In the Orders field list, click Overnight. Drag and drop it into the ShipCompanyName column.
   The Overnight column is the second column from the left.
3. In the Crosstab row of the Overnight column, type **r** for "row heading."
4. Click View to see the breakdown.
   You'll notice that orders for some states, such as California and Colorado, are now divided between regular and overnight orders.

Add a Total Column

You might want to add a column that shows the total orders for each state. Let's name this column Total Orders. Here are the steps:

1. Click View to return to Design view.
2. Double-click `OrderID` in the Orders field list to add it to the grid.
3. Set the Total row for this column to Count and the Crosstab row to Row Heading.
4. In the Field row, click directly before the `O` in `OrderID` and type **Total Orders:**.
5. Click View to see the orders for each row.

Add Criteria

You can also add criteria to count only certain records. Here are some examples:

Include Only Orders Before a Certain Date

Note that the total orders for Iowa is 5 and for Pennsylvania is 3.

1. Click View to return to Design view.
2. From the Orders field list, double-click the `ShippedDate` field to add it to grid.
3. Set the Total row to Where.
4. In the Criteria row, type **<8/25/04** to include only orders before August 25.
5. Click View. Note that the state totals are now 4 for Iowa and 1 for Pennsylvania.

Include Only Orders for Certain States

You can also limit orders to those from certain states.

1. Click View to return to Design view.
2. Cut the Criteria text for the `ShippedDate` field (you'll paste it a little later).
3. Double-click the `CustState` field in the Customers field list.
4. Open the drop-down list in the Total row for the new field and set it to Where.
5. In the Criteria row, type **Like c*** to display only states beginning with *c*.
6. Click View. Only records for states beginning with the letter *c* are displayed.
   Note that California's nonovernight orders total 3.

Include Only Orders for Certain States Before a Certain Date

Now you'll include criteria for both the state and date.

1. Click in the Criteria row of the `ShippedDate` field.
2. Paste the text you just cut: `<8/25/04` (see Figure 9.15).
3. Click View to see your records (see Figure 9.16).
4. Because you now exclude orders on or after 8/25/04, California's nonovernight records total only 2.
5. Save the changes and close the query. Close the Nifty Lions database.

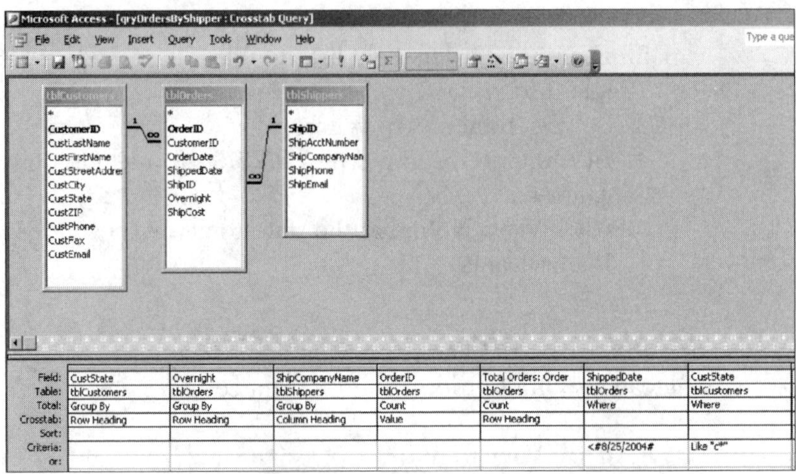

Figure 9.15 In this crosstab query, the record set is restricted by both the state and the date.

qryOrdersByShipper : Crosstab Query

State	Overnight?	Total Orders	Apollo Shipping	Faster Delivery	USPS
CA	☑	1			1
CA	☐	2	1	1	
CO	☑	1		1	
CO	☐	2	1	1	

Figure 9.16 Unlike a select query, a crosstab query has values in both column and row headings.

Action Queries

If a select query were a film, the credits at the end would announce with complete confidence: "No underlying values have been harmed in the making of this query." If it were an action query, however, the People for the Ethical Treatment of Data would want to keep a close eye on the production.

Until now, you've been working with queries that retrieve records from tables. You have manipulated and calculated the records in various ways. But the values stored in the underlying tables remain untouched.

The action query, as its name implies, is a "do something" query. It is indeed a query, and it's created on the design grid. But instead of simply retrieving records, the action query can have a powerful impact on your tables. I next discuss four types of action queries: make table, delete, append, and update.

Warning Label

Before I go any further, let me shout an obvious but necessary warning: Because action queries can change thousands of records at once, they have the power to decimate your database. There is no Undo command for an action query. Don't execute any action queries until you make sure all of your records are safely backed up.

On the other hand, I don't want to scare you off using them, either. Action queries can be helpful when you need to change many records quickly. To take a look at out how they work, I'm going to ask you to make a copy of the sample `Northwind.mdb` database. (It's in a folder named something like `Program Files\Microsoft Office\OFFICE11\SAMPLES`, or use Windows Search to find the file.) The Northwind database has lots of records, so it will work better than the relatively sparse Nifty Lions. The examples will be mostly artificial and pointless, but they will show you how the various action queries work.

Make Table

Occasionally, you'll want to create a new table based on an existing table that you can use in the same or (more often) another database. Often you can just copy the table from the Database window and paste it; you can save just the structure of the table or both the structure and the records (see Chapter 13, "Importing and Exporting," for a discussion of these procedures). But the make table query offers the advantage of setting criteria to limit the records you want.

1. With your copied Northwind database opened, double-click the Orders table to open it.
   The Orders table has data about all of Northwind's orders. Note that there is a `Freight` field with the shipping charge. You'll make a new table that contains just orders with freight charges above $100.
2. Close the Orders table. With the Orders table selected in the Database window, choose Insert, Query. With Design View selected, click OK.

Note that an action query uses the same design grid as other queries.

3. Choose Query, Make Table Query (see Figure 9.17).

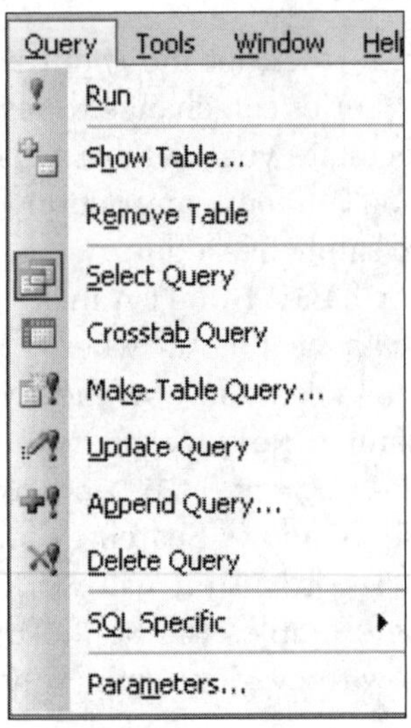

Figure 9.17 The icons for action queries all include an exclamation point.

Note that the Make-Table query has an exclamation point in its icon. All the action queries include this punctuation.

4. In the Make Table dialog box, type **Heavy Freight Orders** for the table name. Create the table in the current database. Click OK. Note that I have used a name that is consistent with the naming convention used for other Northwind objects.
5. Double-click the * in the Orders field list. All the fields from the Orders table will be included in the new table.
6. Double-click `Freight` to add it to the grid. Deselect the check box in the Show row.
7. Type **>100** in the Criteria row of the Freight column (see Figure 9.18).

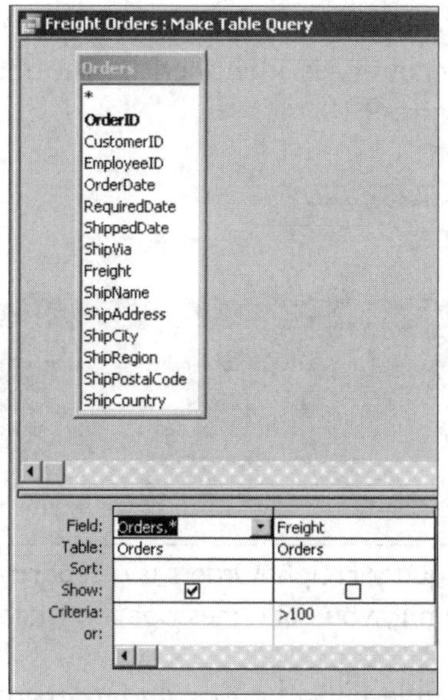

Figure 9.18 A make-table query in Design view.

8. Click View to go to Datasheet view. Note that there are 187 records in the datasheet.
   This step is optional, but it's a good idea to preview the records Access will paste into the new table. You can effectively review the potential impact of an action query before doing any damage and to ensure that it will do what is expected.
9. Click View to return to Design view. Click Run. Access tells you that it will paste 187 records into a new table. Click Yes to confirm. Note that you had to click Run to have the query create the table. In select queries, clicking View had the same effect as running it.
10. Choose File, Close. Click Yes to save the design of the query. Type **Freight Orders** and click OK.
    Often make-table and other action queries are created just for one-time use and are not saved. But you'll save it here to see how a saved action query works.
11. In the Database window, click Tables and open Heavy Freight Orders. It has the 187 records you viewed in the query. Close the table.

12. Click Queries. Find the Freight Orders query.
    The query is identified by the make table query icon, shown in Figure 9.19.

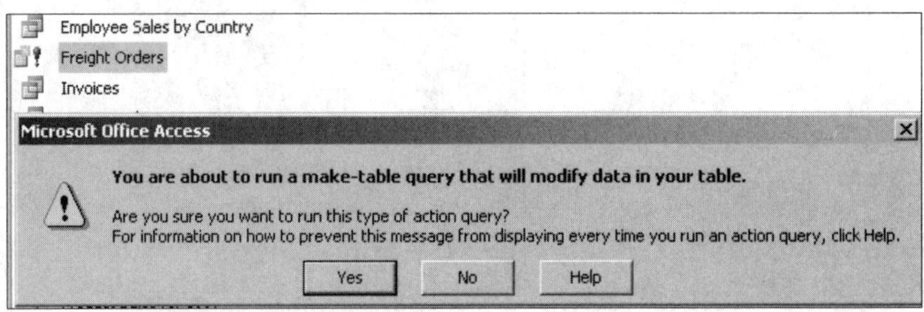

Figure 9.19 The action query Freight Orders is a separate query in the Database window. When you attempt to run it, you get a message that states the impending action.

13. Double-click the Freight Orders query to run it. You get a message that you are about to run a make-table query (refer to Figure 9.19). Access will make you another table using the same criteria. (If it's in the same database, you need to rename the table with the same name, or Access will delete it.)
    Another option would have been to open the query in Design view. You could then modify the criteria and run the query from there.
14. Click No in the message.

Creating a Delete Query

When I warned you that action queries can wreak havoc with your records, I was primarily thinking about the delete query. Besides removing the records in the specific table, the deletions can spread like a southern California wildfire and rip out records throughout your database.

Let's see why. Choose Tools, Relationships. The Orders table has relationships with several tables, but it has a one-to-many relationship with the Order Details table. Double-click the line that connects the two field lists to open the Edit Relationships dialog box. (It's tricky—you have to click in the little bit of open space right in the middle of the line.) Cascade Delete Related Records is in force.

As you saw in Chapter 4, "Establishing Relationships," if you delete a record on the "one" side of the relationship, all the records on the "many" side will be deleted as well. So if you delete, say, `Order ID 10255`, all the order detail records for `10255` will be affected, too.

The effect of a delete query can be much more dramatic. Suppose you delete records in the Customers table. The Customers table has a one-to-many relationship with the Orders table. If Cascade Delete Related Records were in force between Customers and Orders, orders for those customers would be deleted as well. And if you delete Orders records, related records in the Order Details are gone, too.

Of course, that might be exactly what you want to have happen, which is why you selected Cascade Delete Related Records in the first place. But recognize the wave of destruction you might be unleashing. Some database experts recommend that cascading deletes not be implemented precisely because of the devastating impact it might have.

Now let's do the example.

1. Right-click the relationship line between the Orders and Order Details tables.
2. Choose Edit, Delete and confirm your change.
   You're going to add back the Orders records a little later, so leave the order details records as they are. By deleting the relationship, the order details records will remain untouched.
3. Close the Relationships window.
   If for some reason you modified the layout of the Relationships window, you will be asked whether you want to save these changes. As discussed in Chapter 4, this "save your changes" message when you close the Relationships window applies only to modifications to the layout, not to the editing of any relationships.
4. In the Database window, select the Orders table. Choose Insert, Query and, with Design view selected, click OK to create a new query.
5. Choose Query, Delete Query. The Delete row is added to the grid.
6. Choose File, Save. Name the query `Delete Freight Orders` and click OK.
7. Double-click the asterisk in the field list to add all the fields to the grid.
8. Open the drop-down list for the Delete row.
   You have two choices, From and Where. From indicates the field or fields from which you are deleting records. Where denotes that the column contains criteria that in some way will limit the records to be deleted. Leave the selection as From.

9. Double-click `Freight` to add it to the grid. The Delete row displays `Where`.
10. Type **>100** in the Criteria row of the Freight column.
11. Click View. As in the make table query, you see the 187 records that will be deleted.
12. Click View to return to Design view.
13. Click Run and confirm the deletion by clicking Yes.
14. Open the Orders table. There are now only 643 records in it, 187 fewer than the 830 that existed before you ran the query. Close the Orders table.
15. Close the query and save your changes.

Creating an Update Query

As its name implies, you use an update query to change many records at once. Suppose the ruling in a court case required shippers to refund 12% of the freight charges to Northwind for all orders to France or Italy. You could create an update query to reduce freight costs for orders to those countries by 12%.

1. In the Database window, choose the Heavy Freight Orders table. Choose Insert, Query and create a new query in Design view.
2. Save the query as `Update Freight Orders`.
3. Double-click the `Freight` field to add it to the grid.
4. Double-click the `ShipCountry` field to add it to the grid.
5. Save the query as `Freight Discount Update`.
6. Choose Query, Update Query. The Update To row appears on the design grid.
7. In the Update To row of the Freight column, type **[Freight]*0.88**. This expression will reduce the freight cost by 12%.
8. In the Criteria row of the `ShipCountry` field, type **France Or Italy**.
9. Click View to see the records that will be affected.
   First, note that these freight prices are before the update query has been run and the 12% discount has been effected.
   Second, although you did include all the information needed to run an update query, it would be nice to see just which records you will be updating.

10. Click View. Double-click `OrderID` to add it to the grid. In the Update To column, type **[OrderID]**.
    These additions enable you to see the `OrderID`s that will be updated.
11. Double-click `ShipCountry` to add it to the grid. In the UpdateTo Column, type **[ShipCountry]**.
12. Click View to see the 14 records that will be updated.
13. Click View to return to Design view. Delete the OrderID and ShipCountry columns you just added.
14. Click Run. Access tells you that 14 records will be updated. Click Yes to update the records.
    You can't undo an action query after you've run it. But using a little algebra, you can accomplish the same task.
15. As shown in Figure 9.20, edit the Update To row of the Freight field to **[Freight]*(1/0.88)**.
16. Click Run to run the query and confirm. Click View.
    The freight costs are now the same as before you ran any update queries.
17. Close the query and save your changes.

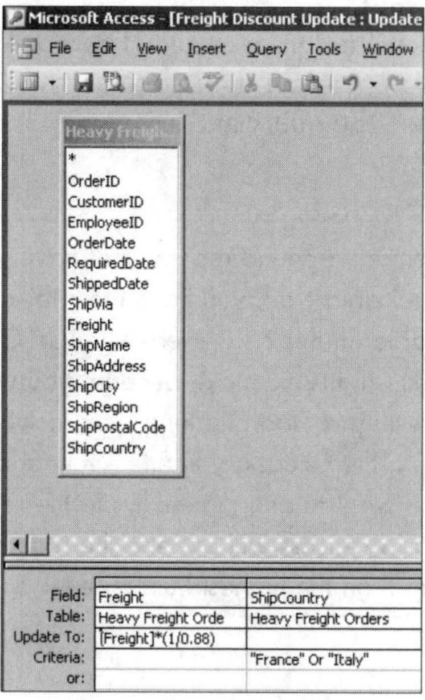

Figure 9.20 In this update query, criteria is entered in the `ShipCountry` field to limit the records that are updated.

Creating an Append Query

Last in the set of action queries is the append query, which is used for adding records to another table. We'll add the records from the Heavy Freight Orders table back to the Orders table.

1. In the Database window, choose the Heavy Freight Orders table. Choose Insert, Query and create a new query in Design view.
2. Save the query as Orders Append.
3. Choose Query, Append Query.
4. In the Append To dialog box, open the Table Name drop-down list and select Orders. The database is the current database. Click OK.
5. Double-click the asterisk in the Heavy Freight Orders field list to add all the fields to the grid.
   Because all the fields in both the source and target tables are the same, you can just double-click the asterisk to include all fields.
6. Click View. These 187 records will be added back to the Orders table.
7. Click View to return to Design view. Click Run and confirm the append.
8. Open the Orders table. There are 830 records, just as there were before you ran the delete query. Close the Orders table.
9. Close the query and save your changes.

NOTE When you append records that have a primary key with an `AutoNumber` data type, you have the choice of including the primary key from the source table (in this case, Heavy Freight Orders) in the target table (in this case, Orders). In this example, because you wanted to append the records with the same IDs they've had all along, you included the primary key on the design grid. (By using the asterisk, you effectively added the `OrderIDs` to the query.)

If you want to assign new IDs to the records, don't include the primary key on the grid. Access will append the records, the first of which will have an ID one larger than the highest number ever entered in this `AutoNumber` field.

Completing Action Queries

Just for completeness, leave the Northwind database exactly as you started it. (Because you made a copy, this section is completely optional.)

1. Choose Tools, Relationships to open the Relationships window.
2. Click `OrderID` in the Orders field list. Drag and drop it on `OrderID` in the Order Details field list.
3. Select Enforce Referential Integrity and Cascade Delete Related Records. Click Create. Close the Relationships window.

In this example, you created five new objects. First, you created the new table Heavy Freight Orders. Second, you created four action queries, all of which can be easily identified on the Queries tab of the Database window by their exclamation marks.

Conclusion

This was the last of three chapters that focused on queries. In this chapter, you learned about parameter, total, crosstab, and action queries. You can download and compare the solution databases NiftyLionsEndChap9.mdb and NorthwindEndChap9.mdb with your own work.

The importance of queries to your Access work will continue to be evident in the next chapter, which centers on report creation.

CASE EXAMPLE

Let's continue using the Northwind database to get some extra practice with crosstab queries.

Assume that the employee who is responsible for taking the order also decides on the shipper. You're Northwind's president, and you're reviewing how the company uses its three shippers. You're curious to see whether different levels of management have a preference for one shipper over another. You'll use a crosstab query to help.

The Crosstab Query

What data do you need? The Employees table has job titles, whereas the Shipper table has shipper names and the Orders table has `OrderID`s. If you count the `OrderID`s, you will get the breakdown of orders by job title for each shipper.

1. Create a new query in Design view and add the Employees, Orders, and Shippers tables.
2. Save the query as `Shippers By Employee`.
3. Choose Query, Crosstab Query. The Total and Crosstab rows are displayed.
4. From the Employees field list, double-click `Title` to add it to the design grid.
5. In the Total row, keep Group By. In the Crosstab row, choose Row Heading.
6. In the Shippers table, double-click `CompanyName` to add it to the grid. In the Total row, keep the Group By setting. In the Crosstab row, choose Column Heading.
7. From the Orders field list, double-click `OrderID` to add it to the grid. If you count the `OrderID`s by each shipper and by job title, that gives you the information you're looking for.
8. In the Total row, select Count. In the Crosstab row, select Value (see Figure 9.21).

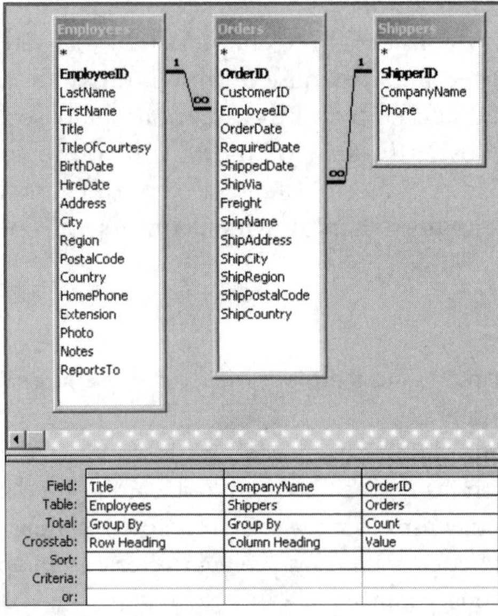

Figure 9.21 The crosstab query has a row heading, a column heading, and a value.

9. Click View. Access provides the breakdown of orders by shippers.

Refine Your Crosstab Query

It would be nice to have a column of total orders for each employee classification.

1. Click View to return to Design view.
2. Double-click `OrderID` from the Orders field list to add it to the grid.
3. Set the Total row to Count and the Crosstab setting to Row Heading.
4. In the Field row of the column, click directly before the `O` in `OrderID` and type **Total Orders:**.
5. Click View. You now have the total orders for each employee classification. After reviewing the data further, you'd also like to see the breakdown by employee for each title.
6. Click View to return to Design view. From the Employees field list, select `LastName` and drop it into the CompanyName column. LastName is now the second column on the grid.
7. Keep the Group By selection in the Total row and select Row Heading for the Crosstab entry.
8. Click View to see your records. You now have the breakdown of employees, along with their title. (You can view the query in the solution database NorthwindEndChap9.mdb.)
9. Close the query and save your changes.

CHAPTER 10

REPORTS

Maybe you can't judge a book by its cover, but appearances do matter. Readers will reject even the most compelling information if they can't easily understand and digest it. In Access, you use reports to create attractive hard copy (usually meaning paper printouts) that can be quickly grasped and absorbed.

Most of the design tools you use in a report you can also use in a form. As graphical media for conveying information, the two have much in common. But whereas reports are usually used to create hard copy, the function of a form is primarily to enter or edit data. In addition, forms tend to center on individual records, whereas reports usually have a wider focus that captures a broader picture.

A report has many advantages over a datasheet. You can include extra blank space for notes and comments. A thoughtful design will organize raw data in ways that will make it far more meaningful. With a report, you can display images such as photos, maps, and diagrams. Notably, report tools make it extremely easy to generate summary statistics such as totals and averages that are of key importance to information users.

Learning How to Create Reports

The Report Wizard reminds me of my mother's old dishwasher. Overall, it was easy to use and the dishes got clean. But occasionally a washed glass had a bit of film on it.

The Report Wizard is similarly effective and inconsistent. Compared with most other Access objects, reports are difficult to create. Unless you're simply displaying a few fields, building them from scratch is a headache. The gloriously efficient Report Wizard is thus a most welcome tool.

But even when the wizard is at its best, its reports are a little, well, scruffy. They require some tinkering—a wider text box here, a larger font there—to get them in shape.

The main problem with the Report Wizard is not these small imperfections, though. As with other wizards, it (mostly) gets the job done. But if you use it exclusively, you don't learn any of the methods and techniques needed to create a report. That's a huge drawback when, inevitably, you want to edit something in it. Take a look at a fairly simple report in Design view (see Figure 10.1). To the uninitiated, it almost screams "Don't even think of changing anything."

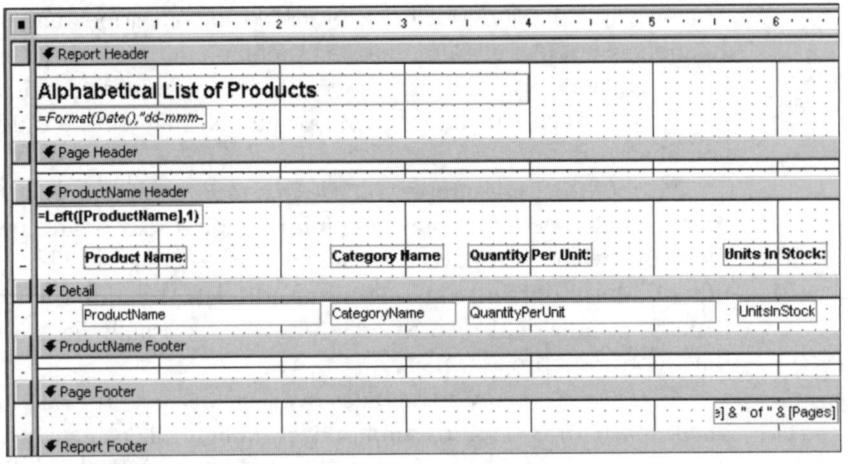

Figure 10.1 Almost any report in Design view looks complex if you don't know its intricate workings.

So here's the game plan for this chapter. First you'll create a report from scratch. You'll delve into its innards to understand how a report works. Along the way, you'll learn or extend your knowledge of key report techniques such as grouping, concatenation, and calculated expressions.

Then you'll create a similar report using the wizard. By that time, you'll have a much better feel for what the Report Wizard is up to when it asks you all those questions. You'll then compare the reports created under both methods. In the case study, you'll learn a few more techniques and tools for creating better reports.

You might find the close detail of this chapter excruciating. But if you've tried to create or modify reports, you know how a single misplaced control can throw your entire report out of whack. Don't let all the minutiae stand in the way of the important goal of getting a handle on the overall construction and design of the report.

The Asia Database

For a change of pace and to give you exposure to another database, in this chapter you'll use the Asia database (`AsiaChap10.mdb`). The database includes "official" statistics on Asian nations, adapted from the renowned *CIA World Factbook* (in the public domain at www.cia.gov/cia/publications/factbook). As with all government stats, they have their limitations. Often they are reliable, but some should be taken with a grain (or megaton) of salt. By their very nature, certain statistics (such as land area) are much more accurate than others (such as GDP per capita).

Let's take a quick look at this database. Copy `AsiaChap10.mdb` to a convenient folder on your hard drive. Open the database and choose Tools, Relationships to open the Relationships window (see Figure 10.2). The Countries table (which, per the Access naming convention we've been using, is titled tblCountries) contains some key data about each nation, including area, population, and fertility rate.

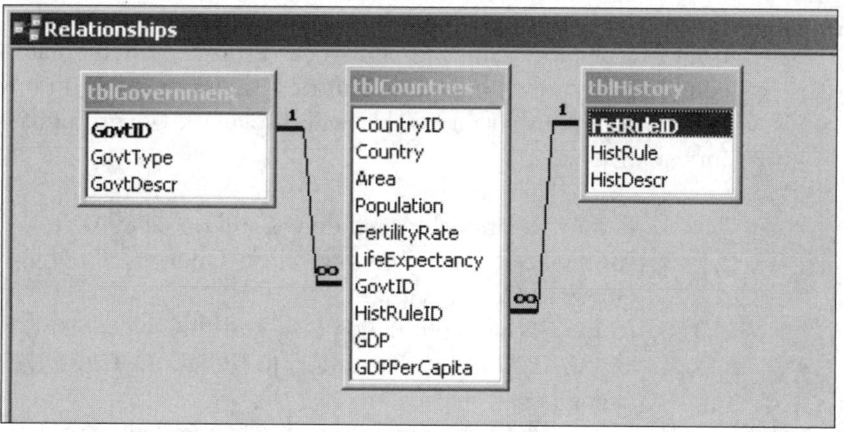

Figure 10.2 The Relationships window for the Asia database.

There are also two validation (or "lookup" tables), tblGovernment and tblHistory; these support data integrity, uniformity, and simplicity. Two foreign ID keys in the Countries table enable one-to-many relationships with the lookup tables.

The Government table assigns types (monarchy, republic, and so on) to the various forms of administration in place on the continent. As you can imagine, a single type encompasses a wide range of governmental forms and situations. But the types can serve as a crude measure of the sort of government that was in place in the year 2002.

The History table has data about the major foreign powers that controlled the country before their independence. Because I've assigned a single type of historical rule to each country, the data is overly general and simplistic. Still, it's fair to say that the Dutch were in Indonesia, the British were in India, and the Japanese remained independent from foreign rule.

TIP To get a better feel for the database, open the tables and view them in both Datasheet and Design view. If you need a refresher on relationships and lookup tables, take a look at Chapter 4, "Establishing Relationships."

Begin the Report by Creating a Query

Usually you'll want to create a report from a query that pulls together data from two or more tables as your record source. You'll create a query that combines key fields from tblCountries, such as area and population, with fields from the other tables that will display the government type and historical legacy.

1. If your Relationships window is still open, close it.
2. In the Database window, click Queries. Double-click Create Query in Design View.
3. In the Show Table dialog box, add tblGovernment, tblCountries, and tblHistory (in that order) to the query. Close the Show Table dialog box.
4. If necessary, maximize the design window. From the Countries field list, double-click the `Country`, `Area`, and `Population` fields to add them to the grid.
5. From the Government field list, add `GovtType` to the grid. From the History list, add `HistRule` (see Figure 10.3).
6. Click the View button at the far left of the toolbar to switch to Print Preview view and view your records.
7. Choose File, Save and save the query as `qryAdministration`.
8. Close the query.

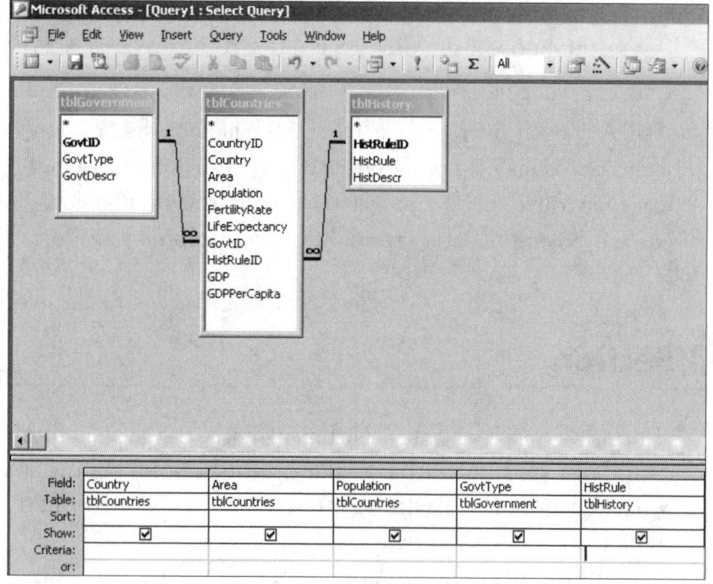

Figure 10.3 The query in Design view.

NOTE The source of a report doesn't have to be a query. For example, you can create an AutoReport, a simple columnar listing of all fields and field values in a table, by selecting the table in the Database window and choosing Insert, AutoReport. In that case, the source for the records is the table itself. But because the power of a relational database is manifest in bringing together data from different tables, queries are a much richer and more pertinent example.

Beginning a Report in Design View

Now you'll use this query as the basis for a new report that you'll design from scratch:

1. In the Database window, select `qryAdministration` and choose Insert-Report.
2. With Design View chosen, click OK.
   The query field list should be in view; if not, choose View, Field List (or peek ahead to Figure 10.1 to locate the Field List button on the toolbar). If a property sheet is open, close it.

3. Choose View, Page Header/Footer to get rid of these two sections.
4. Choose File, Save. Save the report as `rptAdministration`.

TIP Architects have to worry that the buildings they design will look as good in concrete as they do on paper. Access users don't have that problem. You can click the View button again and again to see what effects your work in Design view is having on your report. You can also print a page.

Detail Section

Reports consist of controls that provide the labels, field values, lines, page numbers, and more that make up the report. Where and how often those controls appear on the printed report is determined by the section in which the control appears.

Only the Detail section is currently in view. This section is the main body of the report and is usually used to display actual values. Theoretically, you don't need a Detail section to have a report. But as a practical matter, nearly all reports have one.

1. Double-click the title bar in the field list to select all the fields.
2. Drag and drop them 1.5 inches from the left and two rows of dots from the top.
   There are two sets of boxes for each field. Text boxes are on the right; they contain the actual field names, and they're the controls that display the fields' values. The labels are on the left; they display the captions for each field, as determined by the `Caption` property in the underlying tables. Notice that the `GovtType` and `HistRule` fields use the captions `Government Type` and `Historical Rule`, respectively, which are easier for readers to understand.
3. Click View to see the report in Print Preview.
   When viewing the actual report, two views are available: Print Preview and Layout view. Print Preview gives you the entire report; Layout view shows you just a few sample pages. Long reports can require much formatting, so Layout view saves time if all you need is a quick look. This report is short, so you can use Print Preview.

A few things need fixing in the report (well, more than a few, but let's concentrate on essentials). The fields are a little close together. Some of the `Country` and `Government Type` values are truncated. Also, numbers are currently aligned right; they'd probably look better aligned left. And it would be nice if the `Country` field values were bold.

1. Click View to return to Design view.
2. All text boxes are currently selected (the selector handles are in view on all four sides of each). To increase spacing between fields, choose Format, Vertical Spacing, Increase. Do it again.
   Now you'll widen the text boxes.
3. With all text boxes currently selected, choose View, Properties. Note that the property sheet says `Multiple Selection`, which means that more than one element is selected. The settings you make in this property sheet will apply to all currently selected elements.
4. On the Format tab, edit the Width to `1.35"`, which will apply to all selected text boxes. Close the property sheet.
5. Click anywhere outside the text boxes to deselect them. To left-align the numbers in the report, click the Area text box, press Shift and continue to hold it down, and then click the Population text box. On the Formatting toolbar, click the Align Left button (if you can't find it, take a peek at Figure 10.5).
6. Click the Country text box and click Bold on the Formatting toolbar.
7. Click View to see your work.
   Your records should look like those in Figure 10.4. If they don't, click View to switch to Design view and compare your work to the Detail section in Figure 10.5. (Ignore the Page Footer, which I discuss next.)

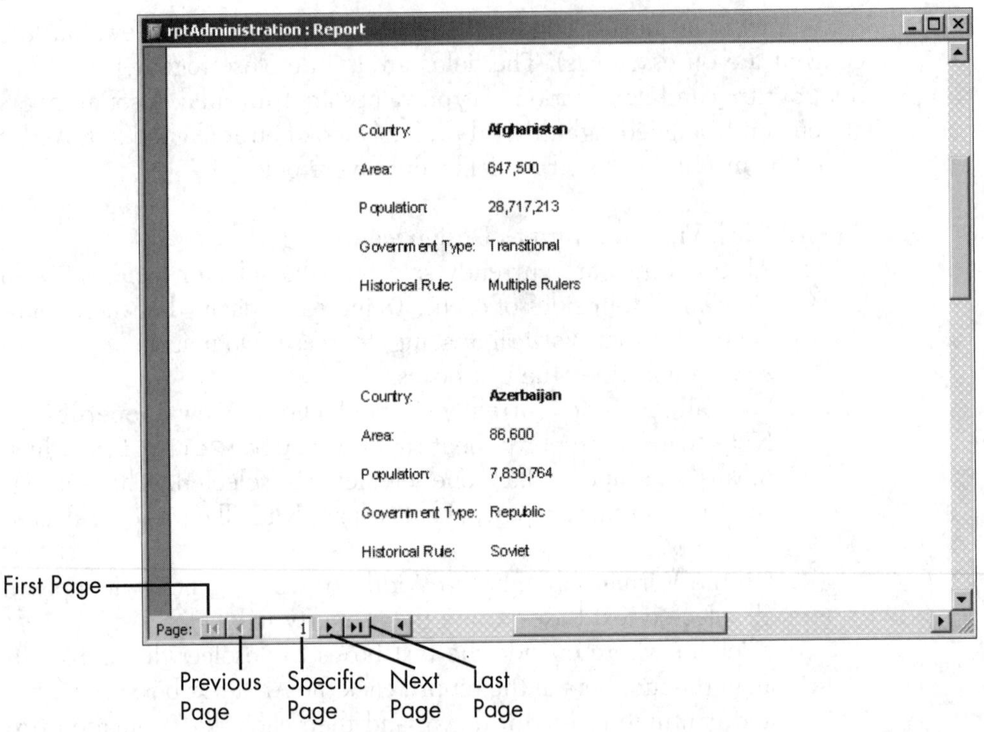

Figure 10.4 The Administration report.

TIP Reports have a lot of different elements; it's easy to choose the wrong one. Keep an eye on the title of the property sheet to make sure you're changing the height of, say, a text box, and not its label, its section, or some other control.

Page Header and Footer

As you saw previously, the Page Header and Footer on the View menu hides and unhides these two sections. The controls you create in the page header and footer print, respectively, at the top and bottom of every page.

If you want to use just the header or the footer, there's an easy way to make the other exist in name only. You'll be using only the Page Footer here, so you'll show both sections and then hide the Page Header:

1. Click View to return to Design view.
2. Choose View, Page Header/Footer.
3. Right-click Page Header and choose Properties. On the Format tab, set Height at `0"` and close the property sheet.
   The Page Header is now simply a bar with no area. Now you'll use the Page Footer to display page numbers, one of its more common uses:
4. Choose Insert, Page Numbers.
5. In the Page Numbers dialog box, select Page N for the format and Bottom of Page for the position. Edit the alignment to `Left`. Show Number on First Page should be selected. Click OK.
   These settings are purely for teaching purposes. You might want different choices for your own report.
6. Click View to see the report. Scroll down to the bottom of the page. The page number appears as Page 1.
7. Click the Next Page button. At the bottom of the page is Page 2.
8. Click View to return to Design view. Find the page number control in the Page Footer. As shown in Figure 10.5, there is an expression inside: `="Page " & [Page]`.

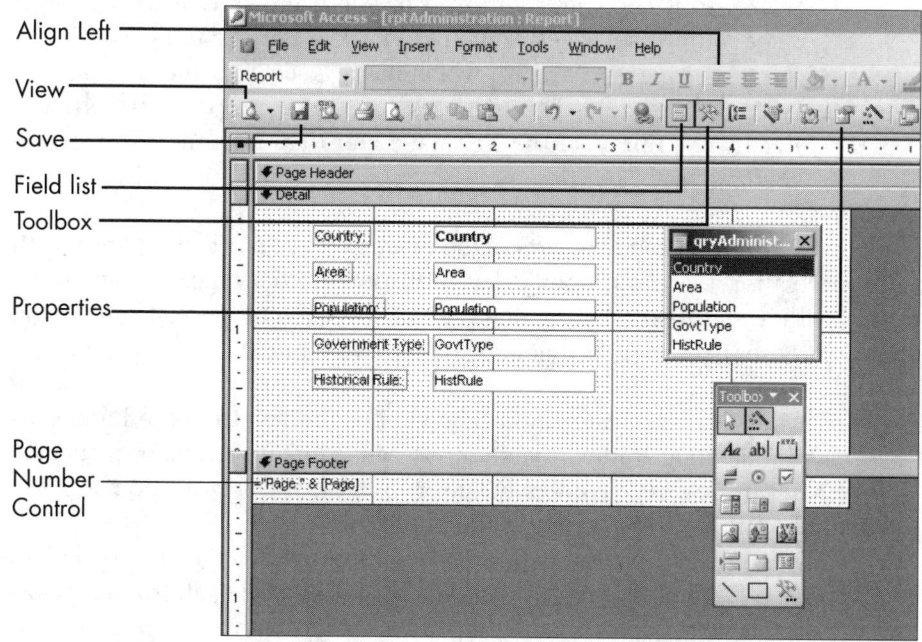

Figure 10.5 The expression in the Page Footer gives you page numbers on each page.

Using Concatenation

Chapter 7, "Find and Filter," introduced expressions and how to construct them. In Chapter 9, "Queries, Part II," you used the `&` operator in a parameter query but without explanation, which I promised to provide in this chapter. So here I review expressions and explain the `&` operator by answering this question: How does `="Page " & [Page]` give you page numbers on every page?

Deconstructing the Expression

Let's look at each part of the expression:

- You start with the = sign. In the text box of a report, you use this to tell Access to get ready for an expression.
- Next is `"Page "`. When you viewed the page numbers in Print Preview (Page 1, Page 2, and so on), each began with `Page`. This is a text string that Access prints exactly as it's written. It's really just a label. When you create expressions, you put text strings in quotation marks, so it becomes `"Page"`. But you want to have a space after `Page`; otherwise, pages would read `Page1`, `Page2`, and so on. So the full text string is `"Page "`, which has a space after the *e*.
- Now for `[Page]`. This denotes the `Page` property, which tells Access to print `1` on the first page and then add one to each succeeding page.

Overall, you have two parts to the expression: the text string `Page` with a space after it, and a property that returns a number on each page, starting with `1` and increasing by one on each succeeding page. How do you bring these two elements together to give you `Page 1`, `Page 2`, `Page 3`, and so on?

The answer is concatenation. The word is derived from the Latin *concatenare*, meaning "to link together." Because linking has its own specific meanings in Access, it's probably better to think of concatenation as a way to bind or tie together certain elements.

The symbol of concatenation is the ampersand (`&`). In the complete expression `="Page " & [Page]`, the `&` tells Access that, after it has printed `Page` and left a space, it should print the page number.

Bringing Fields Together with Concatenation

Perhaps the most important use of concatenation is tying fields together in a single control. I've emphasized that the way you store information has little to do with the way you ultimately want to use it. You therefore break down the data and store it in its smallest and purest form. This gives you maximum flexibility when you want to combine data in queries and reports.

People's names, for example, are usually stored in `FirstName` and `LastName` fields (there are exceptions). That makes sense because you'll often want to use either the first or last names separately (such as sorting people by family name).

But on numerous occasions you want first and last names to appear together in the normal way (as in `Henrietta Maccabee` or `Jake Timberlane`), as in an invoice. You could position the `FirstName` and `LastName` text boxes on the grid so that they are flush. But that's a sloppy and inelegant solution because the spacing between first and last names will inevitably be irregular.

The answer is concatenation, which lets you tie field values together so you can't tell that they are separate fields. Here is how to create the name in a report:

- Type = to signal that's it's an expression.
- Type **[FirstName]**, the first name field.
- Type **&** to tie what comes before to what follows.
- Type " ". This is a single blank space, surrounded by quotation marks to indicate it's a text string.
- Type **&** to tie what comes before to what follows.
- Type **[LastName]** for the last name field.

The complete expression is `=[FirstName] & " " & [LastName]`.

Report Header and Footer

In certain respects, the Report Header/Footer is similar to the Page Header/Footer. Most notably, a single command—Report Header/Footer on the View menu—toggles between hiding and unhiding both header and footer. As with the Page Header/Footer, either section can easily be eliminated by adjusting its height to 0 inches.

Unlike a page footer or header, however, a report header or footer appears only once: at the beginning and end of the report, respectively. The report header can be used for a title, the publishing entity, the date, and (perhaps) an introduction. The footer that closes the report is primarily used for summary information, such as the total of all values of particular fields.

Adding a Title to the Report Header

A Report Header often creates a cover page—that is, a full, standalone page 1. The case example at the end of the chapter builds such a page. Right now, let's just create a short title at the top of page 1.

1. In Design view of rptAdministration, choose View Report Header/Footer.
2. In the toolbox, click the Label button (refer ahead to Figure 10.7 for its location; if your toolbox isn't visible, choose View, Toolbox). Drag the crosshairs pointer to the Report Header section and click anywhere inside it.
3. Type **National Governments** and click outside the box.
4. Click the label to select it and press F4 to open its property sheet.
5. On the Format tab, scroll down to Font Size and edit the setting to `16`. Edit the Font Weight to `Bold` and Text Align to `Center`.
6. Move your mouse to the upper-right handle of the label and click when the pointer becomes a double-arrow (see Figure 10.6). The text of the label is in full view.

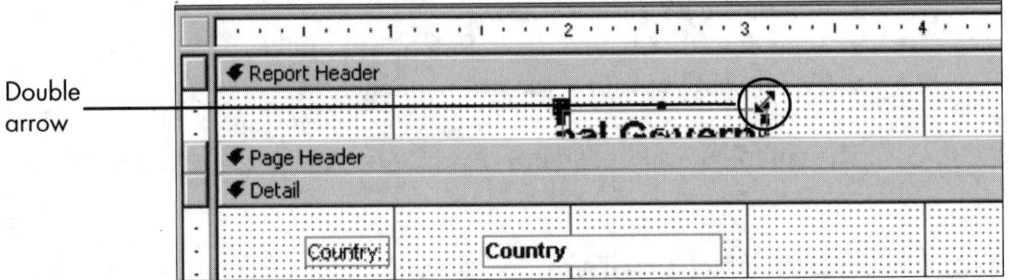

Figure 10.6 When you click the double arrow, the control resizes so the label is in full view.

7. On the Format tab, edit the `Width` slightly to `2.5"`. Edit `Left` to `2"`, `Top` to `0.5"` and `Height` to `0.5"` Your Report Header should look like Figure 10.7.

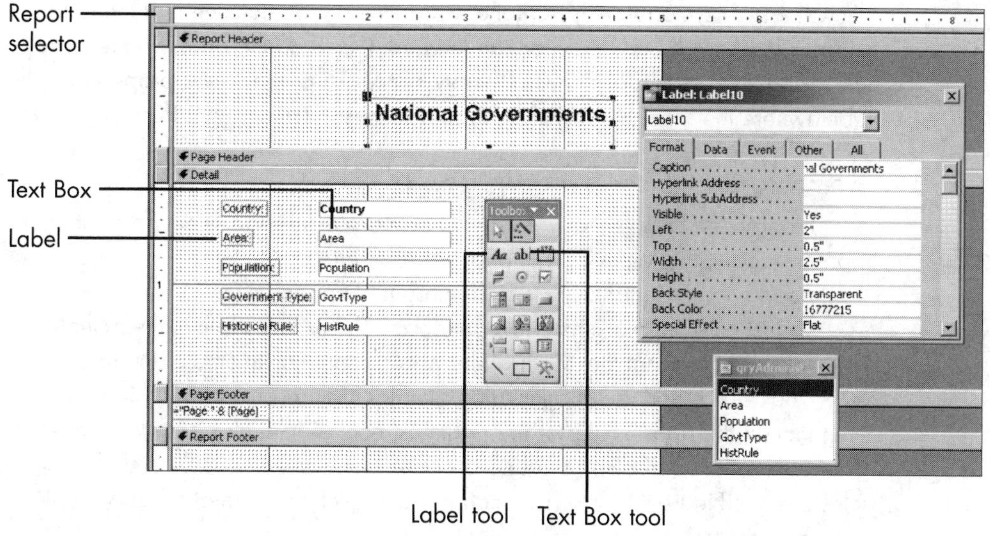

Figure 10.7 The report with a label control for the title.

8. Close the property sheet.
9. Click View to see the report.

Printout Problems

It's little use designing great-looking reports if they don't print on paper correctly. Let me deal with two common problems.

How Do I Center a Title on the Page?

Create the title and make font selections first so you know how wide the label will be. In the example, the label is 2.5 inches wide. (I had you edit the width slightly so it was a round number and, hence, easier to work with.) I'll assume you're working with letter-size paper and Portrait orientation, so the width is 8.5 inches. (Portrait versus Landscape orientation is discussed briefly in the "Layout" subsection of the section "Creating a Report Using the Report Wizard," near the end of the chapter.)

The page is 8.5 inches wide and the label takes up 2.5 inches, so you have 6 inches (8.5 inches – 2.5 inches) of empty space. You want half of 6 inches to be on both the left and right of the label, which is 3 inches on each side.

Choose File, Page Setup. On the Margins tab, you can see that the default margins for Access are 1 inch on the left and 1 inch on the right. So the margin will take 1 inch of that 3 inches of empty space. Thus, the `Left` property for the label (where the label begins) should be 3 inches – 1 inch, or 2 inches.

EVERY SECOND PAGE OUT OF MY PRINTER IS BLANK!

The problem here is that your report or margins are too wide. To print your report correctly, the following equation must be true:

Report width + left margin + right margin <= paper size

I've just covered margins and paper size. The report width is the actual width of the report, not the width of the printed text. For example, in Figure 10.7, look at the horizontal ruler and note that the report width is 5 inches, even though the right border of the rightmost control (the title) is at 4.5 inches. (The report width can also be found on its property sheet. Double-click the report selector—see Figure 10.7 for its location—and click the Format tab to view the `Width` property.)

Assume that the report width is 7 inches and margins are 1 inch on both sides. The equation becomes: 7 inches (report width) + 1 inch (left margin) + 1 inch (right margin) = 9 inches.

That's greater than the paper size of 8.5 inches, so you have a problem. Often the best solution is to reduce the width of the report. If the right border of the rightmost control is at 4.5 inches, the report width need not be 7 inches. If you made the report width 5 inches, your equation becomes a satisfactory 5 inches + 1 inch +1 inch <= 8.5 inches. Similarly, you could make the margins slightly smaller.

NOTE You've been using property sheets to edit the various parts of a report. It's often easier to use your mouse to move, resize, and format sections, controls, and other report elements. You'll get some practice doing that in the following section.

Adding Totals in the Report Footer

Now let's use the Report Footer. Suppose you'd like a grand total for the area of all Asian countries. Here's how to create the control and calculated expression that will give you this number:

1. Move your mouse to the bottom of the Report Footer section. When the pointer becomes a double arrow with a bar, drag it to the 1-inch mark on the vertical ruler.
   You could have also right-clicked the Report Footer bar, chosen Properties, and set the `Height` property on the Format tab at `1"`.
2. In the toolbox, click the Text Box tool (see Figure 10.7).
3. Drag the pointer to the Report Footer section and position the crosshairs 1 inch from the left and 0.5 inch from the top. Click your mouse.
4. Select the label, the box on the left. Move your pointer to the middle selector handle on the right border (see Figure 10.8). When the pointer becomes a double arrow, drag it to the .75-inch mark on the horizontal ruler.

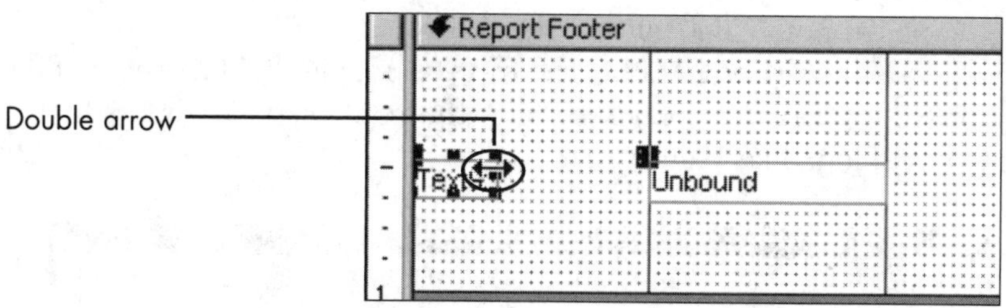

Figure 10.8 The selected label, with sizing handle and double arrow.

5. Click inside the label. Delete the existing text. Type **Total Area** and press Enter. Click the Bold button on the Formatting toolbar.
6. Select the text box and click inside it. Enter an expression as follows:
   a. Type = to tell Access you want an expression.
   b. Type **Sum**, the function that calculates a total.
   c. Type (**[Area]**), the field enclosed in brackets and parentheses.
   d. The entire expression is **=Sum([Area]**). Press Enter.
7. Press F4 to open the property sheet for the text box. On the Format tab, edit the `Format` property to **Standard** and **Decimal Places** to **0**.
8. Close the property sheet. Click View to switch to Print Preview, and click the Last Page button (refer to Figure 10.4 to refresh your memory of its location). The total area is displayed at the bottom of the page.

When you know how to create a control for the total area, it's simple to add one for the population:

1. Click View to return to Design view. The total area control should still be selected.
2. Choose Edit, Duplicate. A copy of the text box and label appears directly below the existing controls.
3. Move your pointer toward the text box. When the pointer becomes an open hand, drag the duplicate text box 0.5 inch from the top and 4 inches from the left.
   If you don't know how to move controls, the section "Manipulating Controls" in Chapter 12, "Forms/Report Design Elements," will help you.
4. Select the label. Click inside it, highlight `Area`, and edit it to `Population`. Click outside the control.
5. Select the text box. Within the expression, highlight `Area` and edit it to `Population`. Click outside the control. Your report footer should look like Figure 10.9.

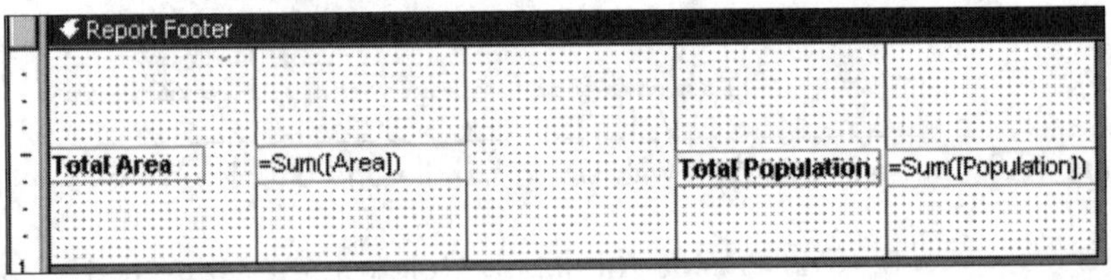

Figure 10.9 Controls for summing population and area in the Design view of the report.

6. Choose File, Save (or click the Save button).
   It's a good idea to save your report periodically if you've done significant work on it.
7. Click View, click the Last Page button, and scroll to the bottom of the page. The `Total Population` control has been added.

Sorting and Grouping

Thus far, you might have found creating a report tedious, but you probably haven't found it difficult. To quickly review, you've used:

- The Detail section, the body of the report, to display your records.
- The Page Footer to print a page number. You could have as easily used the Page Header, which prints the page number at the top of each page.
- The Report Header, which prints once at the top of the report, for the title.
- The Report Footer, which prints once at the end of the report, for aggregate totals.

With the introduction of grouping, you might find that things become a little more difficult. The concept itself is not hard to get, but the nuts and bolts of making grouping work can be confusing. I first want to make sure you understand grouping; then I go step by step through the process of implementing it.

Political Magazine Database

Before adding grouping to the `National Governments` report, it will be easier to see how it works in a database with just a few records. I use the `PoliticalMagazines.mdb` database, which is available from the usual webpage. You do not need to open it to review this section, but it's there if you need it.

The Political Magazines table (see Figure 10.10) has data about several small, imaginary journals of opinion. The `Politics` field shows its political slant: whether it is more likely to be read by wooly-headed internationalists (left) or warmongering unilateralists (right). The `Location` field shows where the editorial staff is headquartered; the estimated circulation is self-explanatory.

tblPoliticalMagazines : Table

	Name	Politics	Location	Circulation
	Human Happenings	Right	Washington	65,000
	Metne Reader	Left	Minneapolis	225,000
	National Appraisal	Right	New York	158,000
	The Country	Left	New York	159,000
	The New Democracy	Left	Washington	61,000
▶	The Weekly Criterion	Right	Washington	55,000
*				0

Figure 10.10 Table of political magazine data.

The records are currently sorted in the datasheet by name. In Figure 10.11, these same records are displayed in a report where they are grouped by their political bent and, within the group, sorted by name. Both the group and the sort are in ascending order (they're alphabetized): Left precedes right, and within the left group, Metne Reader precedes The Country.

Left

Metne Reader	Minneapolis	225,000
The Country	New York	159,000
The New Democracy	Washington	61,000

Right

Human Happenings	Washington	65,000
National Appraisal	New York	158,000
The Weekly Criterion	Washington	55,000

Figure 10.11 Magazine data grouped by political tendency.

As you can see, grouping eliminates the need to repeat the values of `Left` and `Right` for each record. As readers, you can quickly organize and distinguish the magazines that are on the left from those on the right.

Another powerful advantage of grouping is that, just as you created summary statistics for the entire report, you can add summary statistics for each group. Figure 10.12 shows the same report with the average circulation for each group. (I used the Report Wizard to make it look a bit more professional.)

Political Magazines

Left			
Metne Reader	Minneapolis	225,000	
The Country	New York	159,000	
The New Democracy	Washington	61,000	
Avg			**148,333**
Right			
Human Happenings	Washington	65,000	
National Appraisal	New York	158,000	
The Weekly Criterion	Washington	55,000	
Avg			**92,667**

Figure 10.12 Grouped magazine data with aggregate totals.

Sorting and Grouping Dialog Box

Now let's create a group in the `rptAdministration` report. Despite its name, thus far the primacy of government-type data is not obvious in the report. Just as you grouped records by political tendency in the Political Magazines table, you can group records in the report to spotlight the country's form of government.

You create groups in the report's Sorting and Grouping dialog box. First, let's change the current sort of `CountryID` (the sort in the original query) to government type:

1. Choose View, Sorting and Grouping.
   You can also click the Sorting and Grouping icon, which is shown in Figure 10.13.
2. In the Field/Expression column, open the drop-down list and choose GovtType.
3. In the Sort Order column, keep Ascending to sort alphabetically.

4. Close the dialog box. Click View and scroll through your records. The records are now sorted in ascending order (alphabetically) by government type: communist, constitutional monarchy, dictatorship, and so on.

   Now you'll create the group:
5. Click View to return to Design view. Click View, Sorting and Grouping. Click in the first row.
6. In the Group Properties section, edit `Group Header` to `Yes` and press Enter.

   The Sorting and Grouping Indicator now displays the grouping symbol in the first row, next to `GovtType`. You can see that a `GovtType` header has been created above the Detail section.
7. Edit `Group Footer` to `Yes` and press Enter (see Figure 10.13). The `GovtType` footer is now below the Detail section.
8. Close the dialog box. Choose File, Save to save your changes.

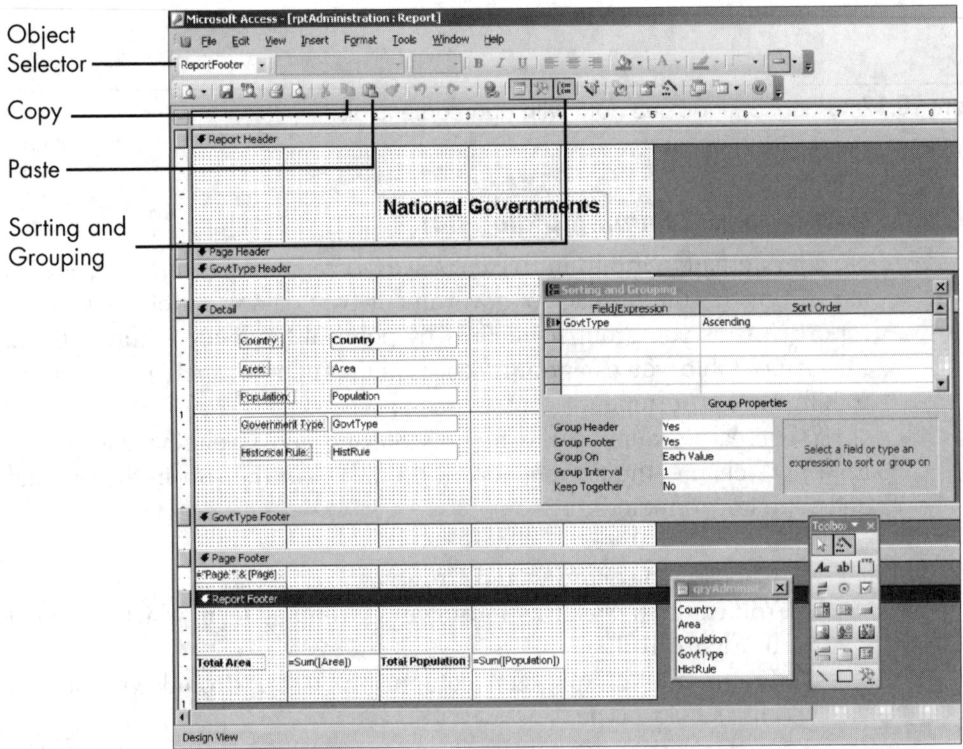

Figure 10.13 The `Administration` report in Design view. The `GovtType` field has been edited in the Sorting and Grouping window so that there is now a `GovtType` header and `GovtType` footer.

Q&A

Q: Okay, I can see that I somehow created a group in the dialog box. But I still can't figure out exactly which step did that. How can changing a property of some Access element create the element itself?

A: Your instincts are correct: You usually create, say, a field or control first and then assign properties to it. Grouping is different. When you select a field in the Field/Expression column, the mere act of editing either its `Group Header` or its `Group Footer` property to `Yes` changes the sort to a group and produces sections for that group in Design view of the report.

Click View and scroll through the first few pages of the report. Hmm, what's going on? The grouped report seems to be the same as the report without grouping, except that there's a little more empty space in it. Where are the group titles for each government type, such as those you saw for the `Left` and `Right` groups in Figure 10.11? Where are the aggregate statistics, such as `Sum`, for each group, as you saw in Figure 10.12?

Click View to return to Design view and scroll down the page. Take another look at the group sections. Yes, there is a `GovtType` header (a group header) above the Detail section, and, yes, there is a `GovtType` footer (a group footer) below it. But they're empty—there aren't any controls in them.

Here's the nasty little secret about creating groups in the Sorting and Grouping dialog box. It's like building an aquarium. When you create the group in the Sorting and Grouping dialog box, all you've done is buy a tank. You have got to put water, fish, and a plastic gazebo or two into it to make it into an aquarium. Ignoring the fishy metaphors, you must create the controls—labels, text boxes—to make the groups meaningful and informative.

Group Header

Fortunately, adding the controls is not hard. Because you now have a government type group, you don't need the `GovtType` field in the Detail section. You want to identify each group by government type, so you can use the same field in the group header section. Here are the steps:

1. In the Detail section, select the `Government Type` label and delete it.
2. Right-click the GovtType Header bar and select Properties. On the Format tab, edit the Height to `0.4"`.
3. Select the GovtType text box. Drag it to the GovtType Header section and drop it 0.5 inch from the left and two rows of dots from the top.

Are you having trouble moving the text box into the Header section? When you move the pointer to the top of the text box, make sure it changes to an open hand, not the pointing finger. If you still have trouble, here's an alternative method: Cut the text box, select the group section header bar, paste it, and then position it within the section.

1. On the Format tab of the `Text Box: GovtType` property sheet, edit the Width to `2"`, the Height to `0.2"`, and the Font Size to `12`. Close the property sheet.
2. In the Detail section, select all four text boxes. Choose Format, Vertical Spacing, Make Equal.
3. Right-click the Detail section bar, select Properties, and edit the Height of the Detail section to `2"` (see Figure 10.14). Close the property sheet.

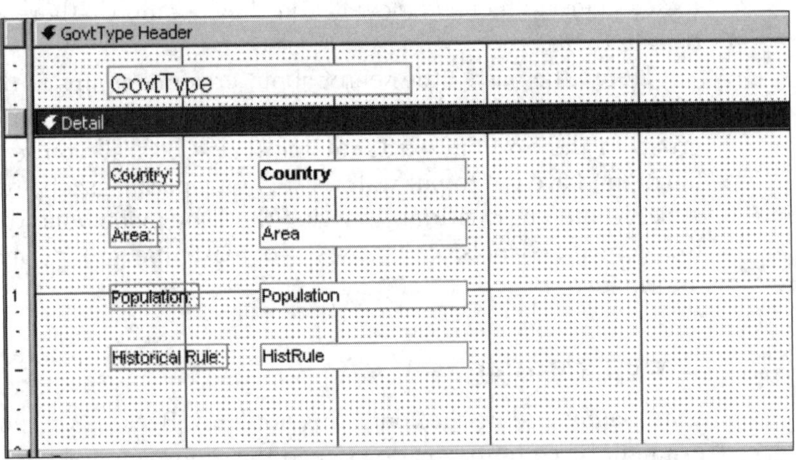

Figure 10.14 The Group Header and Detail sections in Design view.

Q&A

Q: These exercises are tiresome and tedious. Do you really think it's worth my time to go through all these steps for a report I will never want to create?

A: It's true that you're unlikely to have this exact set of controls and circumstances. But what you are doing here—changing fonts, resizing labels, moving text boxes—involves typical tasks for editing reports. You'll be able to build on this knowledge base for the design challenges you face.

Group Footer

A great advantage of grouping is including summary statistics for each group. These are usually created in the Group Footer.

You've already included summary statistics for the area and population fields in the Report Footer. A little cutting and pasting and some editing will give you the same aggregates for these fields by group:

1. Move your pointer to the 0.5-inch mark of the vertical ruler in the Report Footer section. When the pointer becomes a right arrow, click to select all four controls (see Figure 10.15).

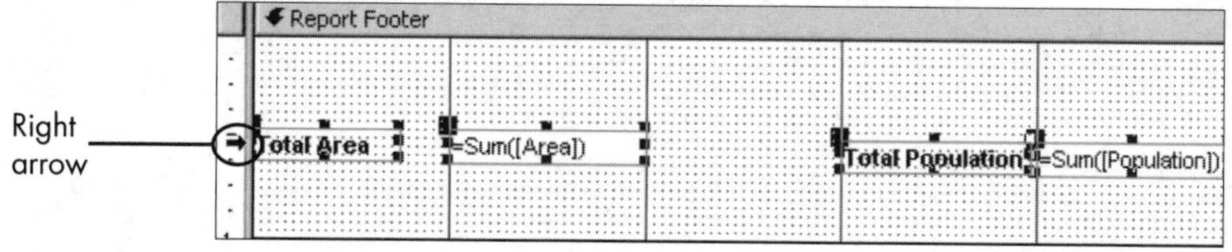

Figure 10.15 When the pointer is a right arrow, you can click to select all four controls.

2. Right-click any of the selected controls for a shortcut menu and choose Copy.
   You can use any Copy method—choose Edit, Copy; click the Copy button; or press Ctrl+C.
3. Right-click the GovtType Footer and click Paste.
4. Click anywhere outside any control so that no control or element is selected.
5. Right-click the `Total Area` label and choose Properties. On the Format tab, edit the `Caption` to `Group Area`.

6. Click the `Total Population` label to select it. On the Format tab of the property sheet, edit the `Caption` to `Group Population`. Close the property sheet.
7. Choose File, Save to save your changes. Click View to see the report.

One thing immediately strikes the eye: Within each group (such as Communist), the country names are not alphabetized. Let's alphabetize them.

1. Click View to return to Design view.
2. Choose View, Sorting and Grouping.
3. Click in the first empty row of the Field/Expression column. Open the drop-down list and choose Country. In the Sort Order column, leave Ascending as is. Close the dialog box.
4. Click View to see the report (see Figure 10.16).

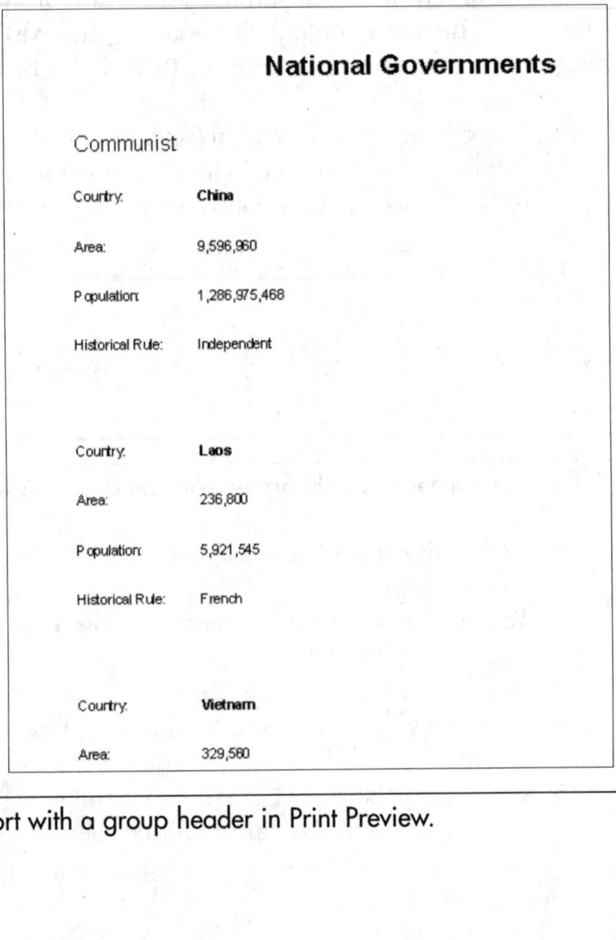

National Governments

Communist

Country: China

Area: 9,596,960

Population: 1,286,975,468

Historical Rule: Independent

Country: Laos

Area: 236,800

Population: 5,921,545

Historical Rule: French

Country: Vietnam

Area: 329,560

Figure 10.16 The report with a group header in Print Preview.

Now let's take a closer look at the report. At the end of the group, there are now group totals for area and population. The same expressions that calculated total area and population for all of Asia when they were used in the report footer section now calculate the group totals when used in the group footer section.

As for the rest of report, it's adequate, but it could be better. Forcing new pages before each group would give you an improved layout. You can also have the group's name appear again at the top of the next page when the group's records span more than one page.

You'll do those tasks in the case study at the end of the chapter.

Close the report and save your changes.

You can open the completed `rptAdministration` in `AsiaChap10End.mdb` and compare your own work with it.

Creating a Report Using the Report Wizard

Whew! If you've built all of `rptAdministration` from scratch, you can see why even Access pros like to use the Report Wizard, at least to get a running headstart. The wizard can create the same report (or one very similar to it) that took much work by hand, with just a few clicks of the mouse. But because our purpose is pedagogical, we'll go slowly through it and take a few detours so you can understand how the wizard works and what it offers.

Collecting Data

Because the Report Wizard works so seamlessly, it's difficult to see that you're accomplishing essentially two different tasks. First, you create a query; second, using the query as a record source, you build a report.

So let's begin to unveil the wizard's workings by taking a look at the Simple Query Wizard. This tool can be used to create single-table or multitable queries. I haven't talked about it much because it's a training-wheels tool that doesn't train you, and it won't save you much time in query making. But it's useful for understanding what the Report Wizard is up to.

In the Asia database, click the Queries button in the Database window. Double-click Create Query By Using Wizard. Open the Tables/Queries drop-down list. In this dialog box, you can choose fields from any tables or query to include in your query. Click Cancel.

Click the Reports button in the Database window, and double-click Create Report By Using the Wizard. Hmm, look familiar?

The point is that, however you create a report, you start by gathering data. Usually, that means creating a query. If you don't currently have a query for your report, you can use the wizard to assemble your data from different tables.

Assemble Your Data

You want a report with the same information as the one you built from scratch, so you could just select the query you created earlier in the chapter. But let's start from scratch and get the data you need from the various tables.

1. With the first dialog box of the Report Wizard open, open the Tables/Queries drop-down list and select tblCountries.
2. Select the `Country` field and click > to add it to the selected fields. Do the same for `Area` and `Population`.
3. Open the Tables/Queries drop-down list and choose tblGovernment. Add `GovType` to the Selected Fields pane.
4. Open the Tables/Queries drop-down list and choose tblHistory. Add the `HistRule` field to Selected Fields.
5. Click Next to go to the next dialog box.

Create the Groups

In this dialog box, Access selects a group for you, depending on the relationships in the underlying tables. Because you can customize groups the way you want them in the next dialog box, you can ignore this dialog box and click Next.

The main group you want is government type. Select `GovtType` in the available fields and click >. A hierarchy is set up with `GovtType` at the top level and all other fields at a second level.

Nesting Groups

In the report you created in Design view, there was just one grouping level: government type. But you can also nest groups—you can have groups within groups within groups. Why would you want to do that?

Let's say you work for an international consumer company, and you're creating a sales report for the vice president of sales. He wants to see a breakdown of sales by country, and within each country by region, and within each region by sales rep.

In this case, you would create three groups. The top level would be country data. Nested within the country group would be regional data. And nested within the region would be sales rep data.

TIP You'll want to limit the number of groups in your report, especially for readers who are unfamiliar with the data. Reports that have groups within groups ad infinitum can be confusing and can leave readers baffled about the overall flow of the report. The vice president of sales, however, is not likely to have problems understanding a breakdown with three or even more groups.

You can nest groups within the Asia database as well. Suppose that within each government group you want to add another level for the historical rule. In that case, you'd have the first group—say, Communist—and within the group, there would be additional groups for each historical rule (British, French, and so on). Then you'd have the second group, Constitutional Monarchy, and within this group, there would again be groups for each historical rule. (I included in your solution database `AsiaChap10End.mdb` an example of such a report. Its title is `rptAdministrationTwoGroups`, and you can view it at your leisure.)

1. At the left of the dialog box, select `HistRule` and click the right arrow.
   The report is now grouped first by government type and *then* by historical rule (see Figure 10.17). The `HistRule` group is selected in the scheme.

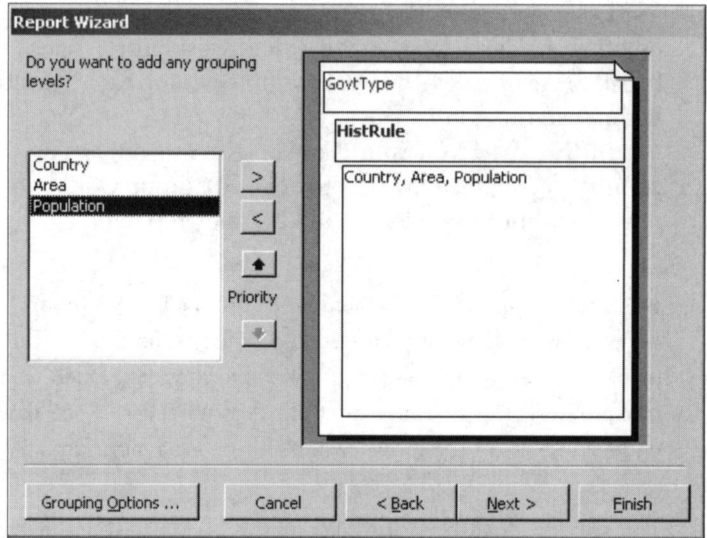

Figure 10.17 Two grouping levels in the Report Wizard.

2. In the dialog box, click the up arrow above `Priority`.
   Now your report is grouped first by historical rule and *then* by government type.
3. With `HistRule` selected, click < so your report is grouped only by government type.
4. Click Next to go to the next dialog box.

Sort the Records

Within each group, you can choose additional field sorts. Within each government type group, let's sort the records by country. Open the drop-down list and select Country.

Use an ascending sort to keep them alphabetized. (You can change the sort to descending by merely clicking Ascending.)

Q&A

Q: Why would I possibly want to add as many as four sorts?

A: Again, let's assume that it's a sales report for an international company. Assume that you have just one group, country. Even though you've decided that you have no particular need for summary statistics for subgroups, you still would like to sort the records by several fields so you can easily locate the detail records. Within each country you would sort records by region, within each region by city, within each city...well, you get the idea.

Summary Options

The wizard can add aggregate totals for you, for both the group and the entire report.

1. In the current dialog box, click Summary Options.
2. Click the Area and Population boxes under Sum to select them. This gives you sums for these fields for each government group, as well as grand totals for each at the end of the report. Because you want to see both records and totals, the Detail and Summary option should be selected.
3. Click OK and click Next to go to the next dialog box.

Layout

The dialog box for choosing a layout isn't terribly helpful, to say the least. Both the names and the graphical schemes are imprecise, and some are more confusing than anything else. If reports are central to your work, you'll want to try a few different layouts and see how they look. You might want to create a few reports using different schemes to see what they actually look like.

1. In the Layout section, select Align Left 1. In Orientation, Portrait should be selected.
   Many reports use landscape orientation, which turns the printed page sideways so you can fit more fields on each page, but fewer records. You designed the earlier report using a portrait orientation, so to make the comparison equal, use Portrait (it shouldn't make much of a difference with relatively few fields). Note that, within the report itself, you can choose the orientation by selecting File, Page Setup, Page tab.

2. Select Adjust the Field Width so all fields fit on a page.
   This choice can be catastrophic when you have many (say, 8 or 10) fields scrunched into one page, but you have relatively few here, so you should be okay.
3. Click Next to go to the next dialog box.

Style and Title

The style choice is your own. Only Casual is unsuitable for business purposes (and even that's questionable).

1. Select Corporate and click Next to go to the next dialog box.
2. Give your report the title **rptAdministrationWizard** and click Finish. Access builds your report (see Figure 10.18).
   You can compare your report with the completed `rptAdministrationWizard` in your solution database `AsiaChap10End.mdb`.

rptAdministrationWizard

GovtType *Communist*

Country	Area	Population	Historical Rule
China	9,596,960	1,286,975,468	Independent
Laos	236,800	5,921,545	French
Vietnam	329,560	81,624,716	French

Summary for 'GovtType' = Communist (3 detail records)

Sum 10,163,320 1,374,521,729

GovtType *Constitutional Monarchy*

Country	Area	Population	Historical Rule
Bahrain	665	667,238	British
Brunei	5,770	358,098	Multiple Rulers
Cambodia	181,040	13,124,764	French
Japan	377,835	127,214,499	Independent
Jordan	1,635	5,460,265	British
Kuwait	17,820	2,183,161	British
Malaysia	329,750	23,092,940	British

Figure 10.18 The report created from the wizard.

Comparing the From-Scratch and From-Wizard Reports

Let's compare the report you created from scratch (refer to Figure 10.16) with the report you made with the wizard (refer to Figure 10.18). If you view the two reports in Print Preview, you'll see that the data presented is the same. But there are obvious differences in the design.

It's a good idea to open both reports and tile them, as well as switch freely between Design view and Print Preview in each to see how the controls determine the display. Both reports are in your solution database `AsiaChap10End.mdb`.

This similarities and differences between the reports include the following:

- **Report header**—Both reports use labels to title the reports. You can easily edit the title in the wizard report by editing the label's `Caption` property on the Format tab.
- **Page header**—Both page headers are empty and contain no controls.
- **`GovtType` header and Detail**—The from-scratch report has a single control, a text box whose source is the government type field. It tells the name of each group (Communist, constitutional monarchy, and so on). The wizard report includes both a label (`GovtType`) and a text box that names the group. You could easily delete the label and move the text box left for a less cluttered look.
  The wizard report also has labels in the `GovtType` header for the country, area, population, and historical rule fields. The text boxes for these fields are in the Design section. In contrast, the from-scratch report uses a columnar format that has both the field labels and text boxes in the Detail section. The tabular format of the wizard report reduces the number of required pages by two-thirds. With a little work, you could move around the labels and text boxes in the from-scratch report to achieve the same tabular layout.
- **`GovtType` footer**—The from-scratch report has label/text box pairs for group area and population totals. In the wizard report, the tabular format requires only text boxes with expressions for these sums. (You might need to widen these just a tad to see the full total for all groups.) Although there are no field labels in the wizard report, there is a label of `Sum` on the far left for clarity.

The wizard report also includes a very long expression that tells you the number of records in the group. You might or might not find this information useful.

- **Page footer**—The from-scratch report has a text box that tells you the page number. The wizard report has the same, although the expression is a little more complex because it's in the "Page N of M" format.

  The wizard report also contains a control on the left with the expression `Now`, which tells you the current date.
- **Report footer**—As with the group totals, in the from-scratch report, there are area and population labels for the grand totals. The tabular format of the wizard dispenses with these labels, but it does include a label at the far left for `Grand Total`. In the wizard report, you might need to widen the text boxes just a bit to see the full totals.

Conclusion

In this chapter, you built reports both from scratch and using the wizard. Along the way, you learned about sorting and (especially) grouping, concatenation, calculated expressions, and various report tools. If you had trouble with some of the basics, such as moving and resizing controls, you'll find some help in Chapter 12, which discusses these topics in some detail.

CASE EXAMPLE

As this chapter has demonstrated, report creation involves many techniques and methods. This case example exposes you to a few more by making some improvements to `rptAdministation`.

In the Database window, open `rptAdministration` in Design view. Choose File, Save As and save the report as `rptAdminstrationCS`.

Cover Pages

Report headers are commonly used to create cover pages, which tell readers what's in the report, who originated the information, who created the report, the date of the report, and so forth.

The current title of `National Governments` really doesn't do justice to the material within and certainly could stand some explanation. We could dump it entirely, but let's just add a subtitle below it, along with pertinent data about the report:

1. Select the `National Governments` label and click after the letter *s*.
2. Press Shift+Enter to move to the next line.
3. Type **Key Political Data** and press Shift+Enter.
4. Type **CIA World Factbook**. Press Shift+Enter.
5. Type **John Doe**. Press Shift+Enter.
6. Type **January 1, 200X**. Press Enter.
7. Press F4 for the label's property sheet. On the Format tab, edit the `Font Size` to `12`. Close the property sheet.
8. Click View to see the report.

The title itself looks okay, but the data starts right after the last line of the title on the same page. Let's put things right.

NOTE Because the *CIA World Factbook* is in the public domain, the data is not copyrighted. Depending on the report and audience, you might need to include copyright notices in your report.

---

9. Click View to return to Design view. Right-click the Report Header bar and choose Properties.
10. On the Format tab, edit the `Force New Page` property to `After Section`. This leaves the title by itself on the cover page.
11. Edit the `Height` property to `6"`.
12. Select the label in the header. Edit `Top` to `4"`. Close the property sheet. Figure 10.19 shows the label at the bottom of the report header section.

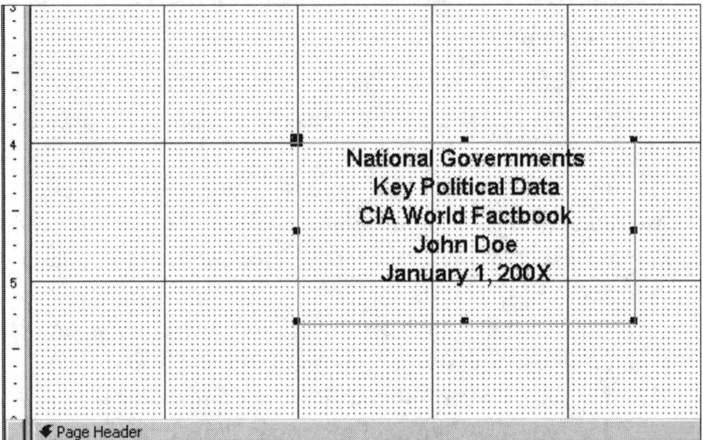

Figure 10.19 The report header section looks uncommonly long, but the extra space ensures that the report title will be on a separate page.

13. Click View to see the report.
    Much better—now the only extraneous item remaining on the page is the page number at the bottom. You could edit the expression in the control in the page footer so that no page number would print on page 1. But it's a lot easier to simply delete the control and create a new one using the Page Number dialog box.
14. Click View to return to Design view.
15. In Page Footer, select the page number control and press delete.
16. Choose Insert, Page Numbers.
17. In the Page Number dialog box, select a format of Page N of M, a position of Bottom of Page, and an alignment of Right. Deselect Show Number on First Page. Click OK.
18. Click View to see that there is no page number on the first page.

Separating Groups

If you don't mind lengthening your report somewhat, you can put the data for each group on separate pages. You use the same `Force New Page` property, except that the pertinent property sheet is that for the group header.

1. Click View to return to design view.
2. Right-click the GovtType Header bar and choose Properties.
3. Edit the `Force New Page` property to `Before Section`.
4. Click View to see the report. Review the Constitutional Monarchy group.

TIP The Constitutional Monarchy section extends over a few pages, beginning on or about page 3. But there is only a group title on the first page, not on succeeding pages. You can have the group's name appear again at the top of succeeding pages when the group's records span more than one page.

5. Click View to return to Design view.
   The GovtType Header property sheet should still be open.
6. On the Format tab, edit `Repeat Section` to `Yes`.
7. Click View and scroll through your finished report (see Figure 10.20).

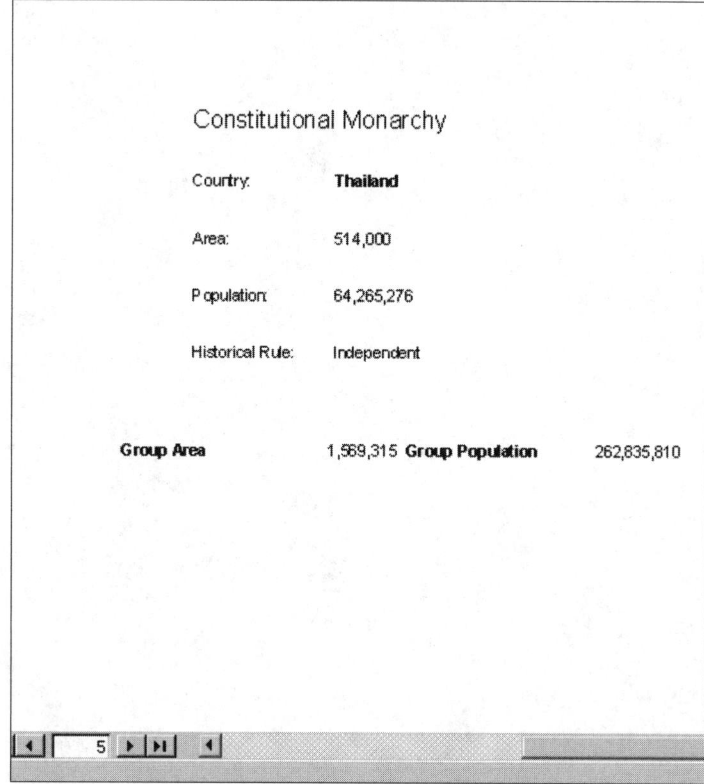

Figure 10.20 This is third and last page that has data about the group Constitutional Monarchy. The next group, Dictatorship, doesn't start until the following page.

8. You can compare your report with `rptAdministrationCS` in AsiaChap10.mdb. When you're done, save your work. Close the report and the database.

CHAPTER 11

Forms/Subforms

Forms are usually used for entering data and viewing it on your computer. Chapter 6, "Entering, Editing, and Displaying Data," introduced forms and explained various techniques for making data entry easier and more efficient. It also dealt with the key issue of how forms inherit field properties from the underlying table.

This chapter covers form construction. Compared with the serviceable but monotonous datasheet, the form employs a host of graphical elements to enter and display data. Form tools don't merely make your form aesthetically pleasing; they are devices for streamlining data entry and conveying information more effectively.

Some form-creation tools and techniques are the same as those you saw in Chapter 10, "Reports." The two objects have much in common, and the design issues that arise are often comparable.

But the two objects are also quite distinct. The primary purpose of a form is to enter and view data on a computer screen, while that of a report is to review information on paper. Design effects that look good on a computer might look terrible on a printout, and vice versa. Additionally, forms don't use grouping, from which so much of a report's raison d'être derives. Perhaps most important, the vast reserves of information on your computer and the Internet are easily accessible in a form. You can dedicate controls to storing Word documents, photos, hyperlinks, and so on.

This chapter focuses on creating form tools, including combo boxes, list boxes, option groups, and subforms. Similar to the previous chapter, although in less detail, I compare two forms with similar content, one produced from scratch and the other with the Form Wizard.

Form Overview

Let's first get an idea of the internal workings of a form before you start building any form objects.

The Nifty Lions Database

For this chapter, you'll use the Nifty Lions database that's among the files you downloaded. This database is for a small mail-order company that specializes in clothing, jewelry, novelty items, and other items with a lion motif.

Download `NiftyLionsChap11.mdb` to a convenient folder on your hard drive and open it. (`NiftyLionsChap11End.mdb` shows the database after all exercises in this chapter have been completed.) The database is modeled on the Northwind sample database and has most of the same tables and fields. But I hope the simpler names and fewer records make it a little easier to work with.

Let's briefly review its relationships, as shown in Figure 11.1. (For a more hands-on view, choose Tools, Relationships to open the Relationships window.) All tables are related to at least one other, with referential integrity enforced. Because one order can have many items, and one item can be in many orders, tblMerchandise and tblOrders have a many-to-many relationship. A third table, tblOrderDetails, has been created as a linking table to bring them together.

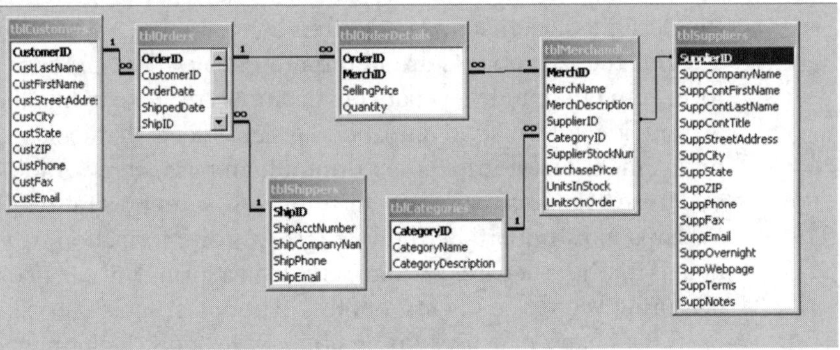

Figure 11.1 The relationships of the Nifty Lions database.

Understanding a Form/Subform

Forms are often accompanied by subforms. Let's take a closer look at the form/subform shown in Figure 11.2.

1. In the Database window, click the Forms button.
2. Right-click `frmOrders` and select Copy. Right-click anywhere in the Forms section of the Database window and select Paste.
3. Rename the copied form **frmOrdersPractice** and click OK. Open the form (see Figure 11.2).

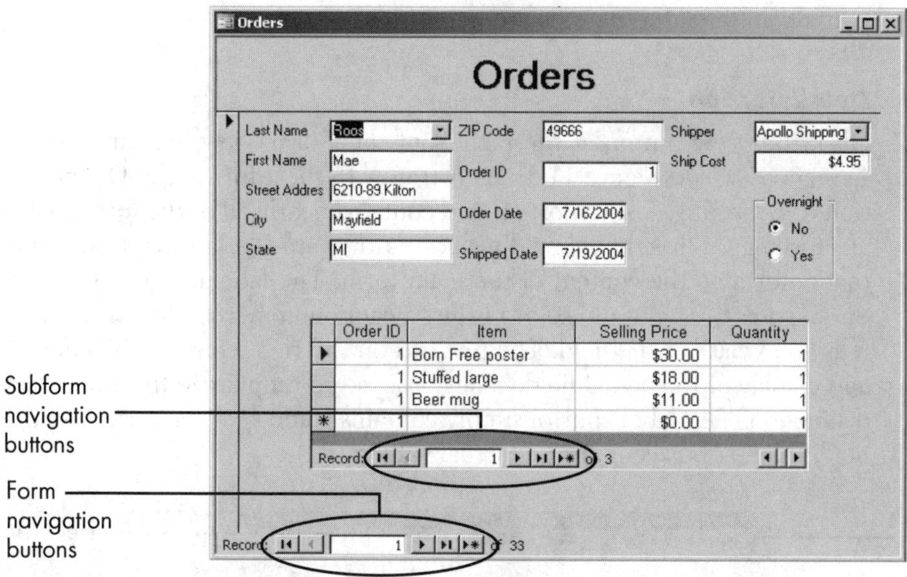

Figure 11.2 A form/subform created from several tables.

The form won't win any design prizes, nor does it have all the data you might want on an orders form. But it will be useful for exploring key form tools and functions.

The form combines data from several tables, including Orders, Customers, Shippers, and Order Details. As you'll see throughout the chapter, to combine fields from several tables in a single form robustly, the tables must be tightly bound through relationships. The scheme in the Relationships window demonstrates that such integration exists.

At the top of the form are fields that show the name and address of the customer, as well as key order data such as date shipped. At the bottom is a datasheet that shows the order details for each order. The datasheet is the subform. I use *form* to refer to the entire form (both form and subform), *main form* to refer to the fields on top, and *subform* to refer to the datasheet.

Note that there are two sets of navigation buttons. The buttons all the way at the bottom are for the form; they are used to move to specific orders. The navigation buttons in the middle of the form move the focus from record to record in the order details subform. This second set of navigation buttons is not overly useful here because each order has relatively few order detail records. But for longish datasheets whose records remain partially hidden, the buttons are helpful.

Detail Section

Click the View button at the far left of the Form View toolbar to go to Design view (see Figure 11.3). As is true with most forms, the Detail section is by far the most important and contains nearly all of the form's actual substance. Directly below the `Orders` title are the label/text box pairs that determine the content of the main form. The label on the left (`Last Name`, `First Name`, and so on) is just a caption, a mere string of text that tells you what's in the field. The text box on the right controls the content and display of the actual field values. Let me re-emphasize this important distinction: The label control simply contains static text that describes the field; the text box contains the actual values.

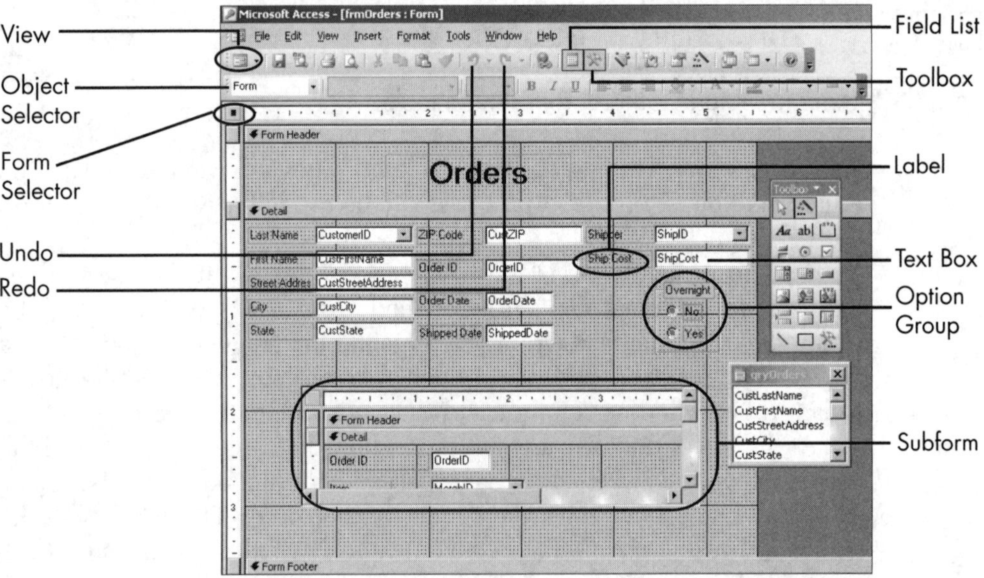

Figure 11.3 The `Orders` form in Design view.

The `Overnight` control is an option group, which I describe later in the chapter. Below the fields is the large `OrderDetails` subform control. Later in the chapter, you'll re-create it.

Form Header/Footer Sections

The Form Header appears once at the top of the form and is usually used for a title, as it is here. The Form Footer appears once at the end. Currently, it doesn't exist: Its height is `0` and, by extension, there are no controls. You might use the footer for command buttons or perhaps some general instructions on using the form.

The form header/footer always appear as a couple. They can be toggled on and off (that is, made to appear and disappear) by choosing View, Form Header/Footer. But if you select this command while the sections are in view, Access deletes both the sections and their controls (you will get a warning message before deletion).

Page Header/Footer

The mechanics of the Page Header/Footer are similar to those of the Report Header/Footer. They differ markedly in their content and objectives, however, as the following exercise demonstrates:

1. You should be in Design view. On the menu bar, choose View, Page Header/Footer.
   Page Header and Page Footer sections 0.25 inch long appear on your form. Both are currently empty.
2. Drag any field on the field list (say, `CustZIP`) and drop it anywhere in the Page Header section (see Figure 11.4).

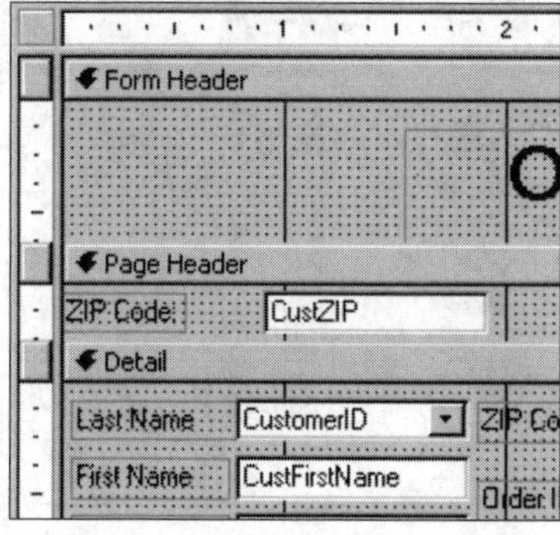

Figure 11.4 The `CustZIP` field has been added to the Page Header.

3. Drag the same field and drop it anywhere in the Page Footer.
4. Click View to switch to Form view and attempt to find the `CustZIP` data you just added.
   Hmm, where are these values? Controls in the Page Header and Footer appear only when you print the form. Many forms are printed only occasionally or never. Moreover, page numbers are less crucial in forms than they are in reports. You might find that you use the page header/footer infrequently in forms.
5. Click View to return to Design view. Choose View, Page Header/Footer and confirm the deletion.

The Data Source

In a form, controls have property sheets, sections have property sheets, and the form itself has a property sheet. You can find the data source of the form's records in, you guessed it, the form property sheet.

1. Double-click the Form Selector to view the property sheet (it's the small square at the very top left of the Form Design window—see Figure 11.3 if you need help locating it).
2. Click the Data tab and click in the Record Source property.
3. Click the ellipsis (...) button at the end of the property.
   As you see, the source for the form's records is the `qryOrders` query (see Figure 11.5), which itself was built from underlying tables. The Customers and Orders tables have been added to the query. Several fields from the Customers table have been added to the design grid. Use the horizontal scroll bar to move to the last column. It contains all the fields for the tblOrders table.

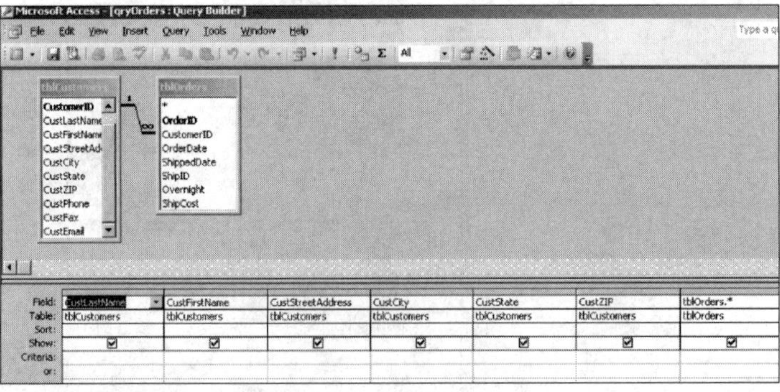

Figure 11.5 The Orders query in Design view.

4. From the Customers field list in the query, double-click `CustFax` to add it to the design grid.
5. In Design view of the form, find the field list and scroll to the end. (If the field list isn't in view, click the Field List button on the toolbar or choose View, Field List.)
   The `CustFax` field has been added and can be used to create additional controls.
6. Close the query and save your changes. Close the form property sheet.

Exploring Form Tools

With some background now underpinning the work, let's now focus on building the objects for more robust and effective forms.

Text Boxes and Accompanying Labels

Text boxes are the key control in forms. By now you're generally familiar with how they work; Chapters 6 and 10 can provide refreshers.

There are some wrinkles to adding and positioning text boxes and their accompanying labels. A common mistake is to forget to leave space for the label. Try this exercise:

1. Select the `CustFax` field at the end of the field list.
2. Drag it to the Detail area and drop it 0.5 inch from the left and two rows of dots below the `State` field (see Figure 11.6). A text box and its accompanying label are created.

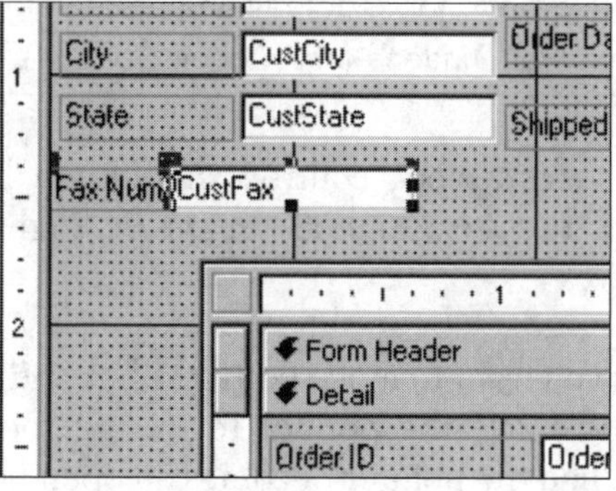

Figure 11.6 The `CustFax` field has been dropped.

3. Click View to see the form. The `Fax Number` controls are pushed too far to the left.
4. You could reposition the controls using a variety of techniques. But it's sometimes easier to have another go at drag-and-drop first.
5. Click View to return to Design view. The `CustFax` controls should already be selected. Press Delete.
6. From the field list, select `CustFax`. Drag and drop it so the left edge of the pointer is directly below the left border of the CustState text box (see Figure 11.7).

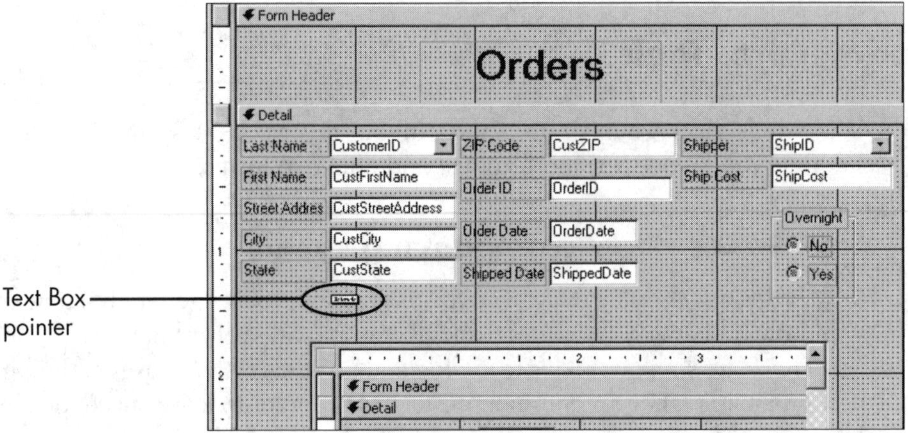

Figure 11.7 The CustFax text box is about to be dropped.

NOTE You can choose the Edit, Undo command to undo a single design action. You can also undo (or redo) a series of design actions by clicking the arrow on the Undo (or Redo) button (refer to Figure 11.3) and selecting the actions you want undone (or redone).

The `Fax Number` controls should now be about in the right spot, but the label, text box, or both might be slightly misaligned. Here are two alternatives:

- If you want to move both text box and label as a couple, select either and move the pointer to the top border of the selected control. When the pointer becomes an open hand, drag in any direction (see Figure 11.8).

Figure 11.8 Use the open-hand pointer to move both text box and label. Note that you want to position the pointer away from the upper-left move handle.

- If you want to move one control without the other, select the control you want to reposition and place the pointer at the move handle in the upper-left corner. When the pointer becomes a pointing finger, drag the solitary control where you want it (see Figure 11.9).

Figure 11.9 Use the pointing-finger pointer to move either text box or label alone. In this case, you want the pointer directly on the move handle.

> **TIP** Frequently you will want to add just a text box and dispense with the accompanying label. If you're adding just one or two boxes, it's easier to create the text box/label pair, select the unwanted label, and delete it. But if you're adding many fields, you'll want to change the default to create text boxes alone. In the toolbox, select the Text Box tool and choose View, Properties, Format tab. Edit the `Auto Label` setting in the Default Text Box property sheet to `No`.

Labels

You can create standalone labels for form titles, form instructions, and other text you want on your form, as follows:

- Select the label tool in the toolbox and drag the pointer to the appropriate section.
- With the crosshairs as your guide, click where you want the label and type your text in the box.
- Press Enter when you're finished.

You worked with labels often in the previous chapter on reports. They are a fairly easy topic, so I won't belabor them here.

Combo Boxes

The best way to introduce combo boxes, an extremely useful form tool, is to see one in action:

1. Click View to go to Form view.
2. Choose Data Entry on the Records menu.
3. Click the drop-down arrow in the `Last Name` field. Scroll down and choose Isaacs, Gloria from the list (see Figure 11.10).

NOTE When you select a name from the combo box, the other customer fields—`First Name`, `Street Address`, and so on—are automatically filled in. The existence of a combo box isn't the cause of this action, although it is built on the same principle of a one-to-many relationship between two tables with a field of matching data. You can learn more about this subject by reading the Access Help article "About AutoLookup Queries That Automatically Fill in Data (MDB)."

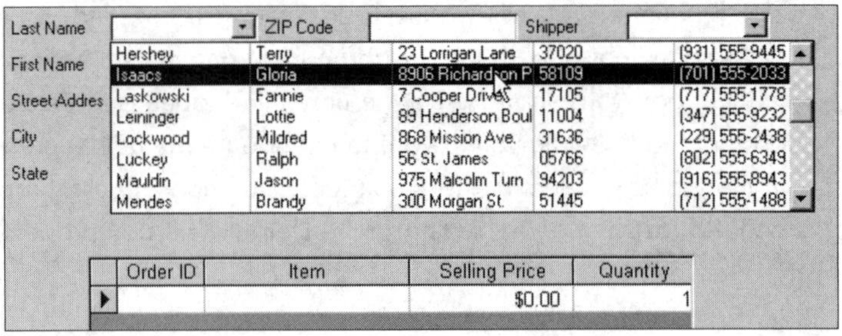

Figure 11.10 A combo box with several fields.

4. Press Escape and choose Records, Remove Filter/Sort to exit Data Entry mode.
5. Click View to return to Design view. Right-click the `CustomerID` control (it's to the right of `Last Name`) and choose Properties. As you can see from the title, this control is a combo box.
   A combo box stores the `CustomerID` field, which is the primary key of the Customers table and a foreign key in the Orders table. Access "looks up" the value of the `LastName` field in the Customers table and displays it. The other fields in the combo box columns that you saw in the drop-down list are there to help you select the correct record and are optional.

Now you'll re-create that same combo box:

1. Close the property sheet. With the `CustomerID` control selected, press Delete to delete the combo box and its label.
2. In the toolbox, make sure the Control Wizards button (see Figure 11.11) is selected. (If you don't see the toolbox, choose View, Toolbox.)

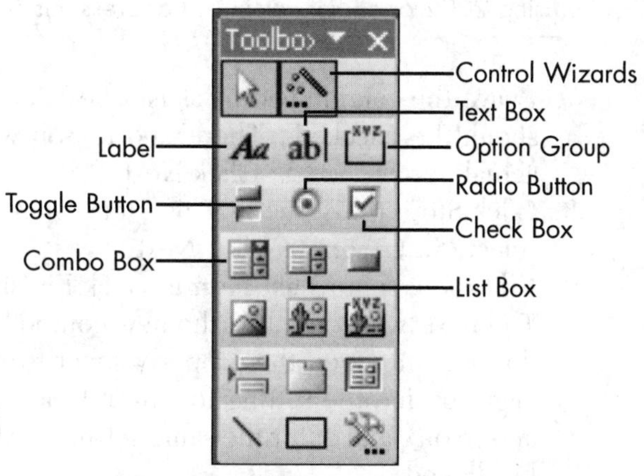

Figure 11.11 The toolbox can be displayed and hidden by choosing View, Toolbox.

3. Click the Combo Box tool and drag the crosshair so that it's one row from the top and a little less than 1 inch from the left.
   Don't worry if you don't get the position just right. You'll fiddle with the dimensions later so the combo box is in the same place it was previously.
4. In the first dialog box, choose the first selection, I Want the Combo Box to Look Up the Values in a Table or Query. Click Next.
5. Choose tblCustomers and click Next. Double-click the `CustLastName` field to move it from the Available Fields column to the Selected Fields column. Do the same for the `CustFirstName`, `CustStreetAddress`, `CustCity`, `CustState`, `CustZIP`, and `CustPhone` fields.
   The actual values you want to display are customer last names, which are in the first column. But to make sure you choose the correct last name, you want to have the other fields in view for verification.

6. Click Next. In this dialog box, you can sort by up to four fields. Open the first drop-down box and choose `CustLastName`. Open the second drop-down box and choose `CustFirstName`. You can keep the sorts at Ascending; for descending sorts, you would just click the button. Click Next.

NOTE Sorting in the Combo Box Wizard is a new feature in Access 2003. If you're using 2002 or earlier versions, I address this shortly.

7. Leave the column widths as is. The Hide Key Column check box should be checked. (There's no reason why you need to see the actual `CustomerID`.) Click Next.
8. Click Store the Value in This Field, open the drop-down list, and select `CustomerID`. Click Next.
9. Edit the label to **Last Name**. Click Finish.
   The next two steps align the new combo box controls. One way to do that is to open the property sheet for the control you want to align to, find the setting for the relevant property (`Left`, `Width`, and so on), and enter the same setting for the control that needs to be aligned.
   The text box below `CustomerID` is CustFirstName. The `Left` property for the CustFirstName text box is `0.7917"`. The control to the right of `CustomerID` is the `ZIP Code` label. Its `Top` property is `0.833"`. You will enter these settings in the property sheet.
10. With the `CustomerID` control selected, choose View, Properties, Format tab. Edit the `Left` property to `0.7917"` ; edit the `Top` to `0.0833"`. (If Access changes these numbers by a few thousandths, don't worry.)
11. Click the `Last Name` label. Edit the `Left` property to `0.0417"`. Close the property sheet. Choose File, Save to save your changes.
12. Click View and open the drop-down box to see your completed combo box. All the field columns are there as you entered them.

If you're using Access 2003, you're set. If you're using any earlier version, you'll need to sort the columns by name. Even if you're using 2003, I suggest that you look at the following steps. These will help you understand the underlying source of a combo box and enable you to add or adjust sorts as you like.

1. Click View to return to Design view. Right-click the CustomerID combo box and choose Properties.
2. Click the Data tab, click in the Row Source, and click the ellipsis button at the end of the row.
   The SQL statement window opens (see Figure 11.12). If you are using Access 2003, you will se ascending sorts in the CustLastName and CustFirstName columns. If you are using earlier versions, it's easy to add these sorts.
3. In the Sort row of the LastName column, type **a** for an ascending sort. Do the same in the FirstName column. Close the window and confirm your changes.

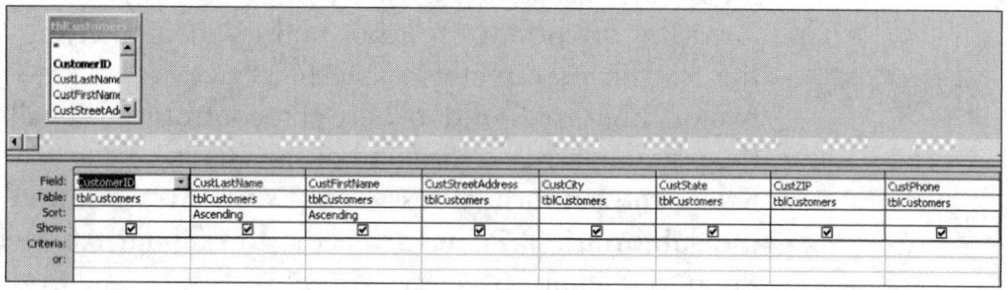

Figure 11.12 The SQL statement for the combo box.

NOTE In this example, you want to choose only customers that are in the combo box list. In other instances, however, you might want to set your combo box so that you can enter values that are not on the list by typing them directly into the box. In that case, you need to set Limit to List on the Data tab of the property sheet to No.

List Boxes

A relative of the combo box is the list box. This control displays all available values for the field at all times. The user clicks the value for that specific record; it becomes highlighted, distinguishing it from the other values. A different value can be selected by simply clicking it.

Let's create a list box for `ShipID`:

1. Click View to switch to Form view.
2. Click the down arrow in the Shipper field.
   As you can see, it's a combo box, albeit simpler than the one you just used. With only four values to choose from, it's a good candidate for a list box.
3. Click the drop-down arrow again to close the box. Click View to switch to Design view.
   Because you'll need some more room for a list box, you'll move the `ShipCost` controls and the `Overnight` option group (option groups are discussed later).
4. Drag the `ShipCost` text box and its accompanying label so that the text box is directly below the `ShippedDate` text box. Leave two or three rows of dots between controls. (You will fix the positioning of controls at the end of the chapter.)
5. Select the subform. Press Ctrl+Down Arrow several times until the subform is 2 inches from the top (about 0.5 inch below the `ShipCost` controls).
   Of course, there are other ways to position this control. The technique you just employed is "nudging," most often used to move controls a wee bit.
6. Click directly on `Overnight`. Drag the entire option group down to the 1.25-inch mark on the vertical ruler. Your form should look something like Figure 11.13.

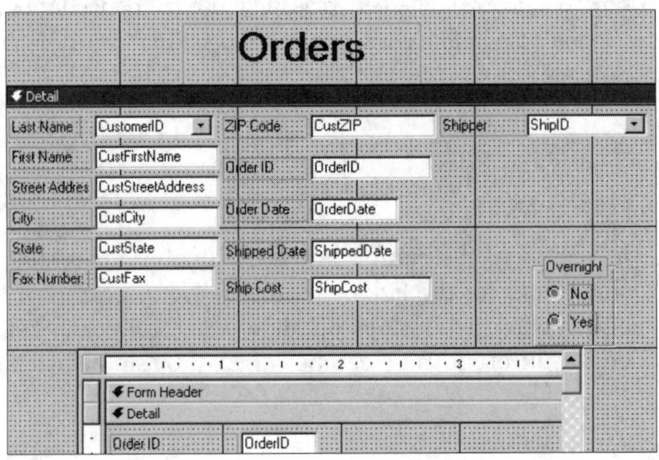

Figure 11.13 You can move controls to make additional room for list boxes and other tools.

7. Right-click the `ShipID` control. Choose Change To, List Box. Choose File, Save to save your changes.
8. Click View to switch to Form view.
9. The control now shows all fields, and the shipper for that specific record is highlighted (see Figure 11.14). Scroll through a few records to get a feel for how the list box works.

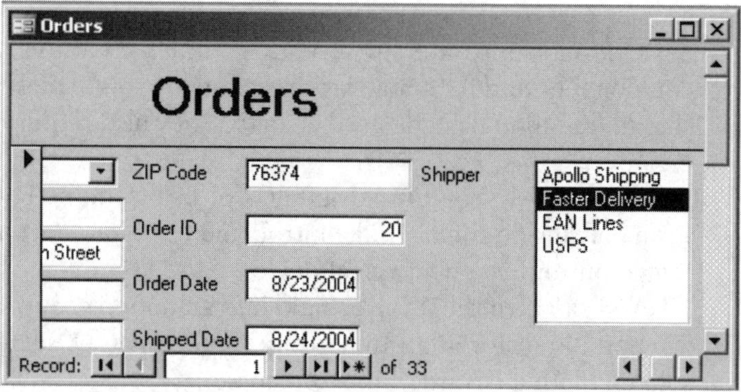

Figure 11.14 The Orders window has been resized to show the Shipper list box for the first record. All possible values are displayed, and the `Faster Delivery` value for the current record is highlighted.

To create a list box from scratch, you would use the List Box tool in the toolbox (be sure the Control Wizard button is selected; refer to Figure 11.11). It works nearly the same as the combo box, and if you understand that tool, you shouldn't have trouble using it. List boxes do take up space that can be saved with a text box or combo box, so it's usually best to use them when there are only a few values.

NOTE You don't have to use the control wizards to create combo boxes, list boxes, and other form tools. But usually they are the fastest, most convenient way to create these controls.

Option Groups

Another way to display values when there are just a few values to choose from is the option group. The `Overnight` control in the `Orders` form is an example (see Figure 11.15). The option group lets you use radio buttons, check boxes, or toggle buttons to designate the correct value.

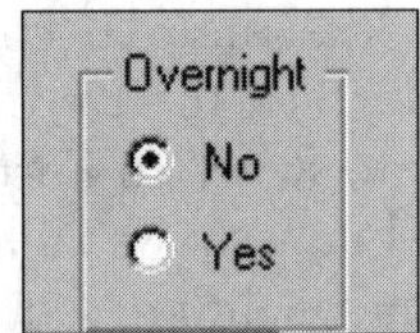

Figure 11.15 An option group is used for the `Overnight` field to display its values.

Option groups are surprisingly complex creatures. They have several components, and it's not always easy to figure out which property sheet you should edit to make a desired change. They also require a little thinking to create.

But you can see the advantages of using them: The `Overnight` title fits nicely inside the overall control, and the radio button (or check box, or toggle button) is a neat visual device.

You can turn the `ShipID` field into an option group. There's no Change To menu item for an option group, unfortunately, so you'll create it from scratch (with a wizard's help, of course):

1. Click View to return to Design view. Select the ShipID list box and press Delete.
2. The Options Wizard button in the toolbox should be selected. Click the `Option Group` control in the toolbox (refer to Figure 11.11 if you need help locating it). Drag the crosshair to the Design section and click 4 inches from the left and about two rows of dots from the top. The Option Group Wizard opens.
3. In the first dialog box, you enter the names of the shippers. Put them in ascending (alphabetical) order. Type **Apollo Shipping** and press the down arrow (do not press Enter). Type **EAN Lines** and press the down arrow. Type **Faster Delivery** and press the down arrow. Type **USPS** and click Next.
4. Click No, I Don't Want a Default. Click Next.
   Access has assigned values for each name. The number in the value column must match the primary key for each shipper in the label names column. Because you alphabetized the shipper names in the wizard dialog box, the labels `EAN Lines` and `Faster Delivery` are no longer in sync with the primary key (the `ShipID`) and need to be changed.
5. Edit the value for `EAN Lines` to **3**, and for `Faster Delivery` to **2** (see Figure 11.16). Click Next.

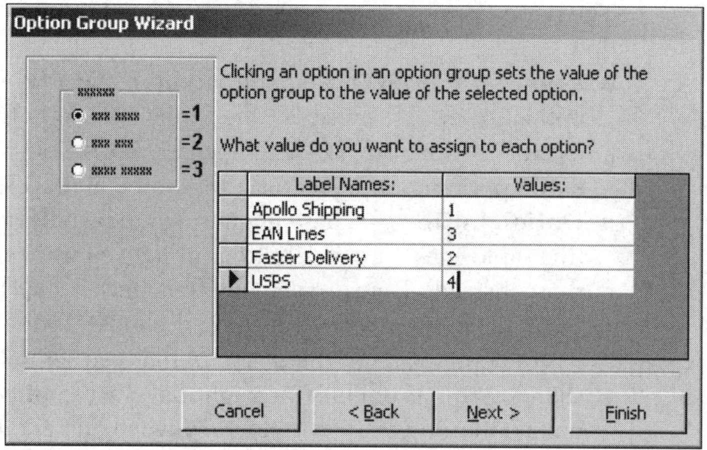

Figure 11.16 The values for `EAN Lines` and `Faster Delivery` have been edited so that `ShipID's` and shipper names match.

6. Click Store the Value in This Field. Open the drop-down list and select ShipID. Click Next.
7. In this dialog box, you choose the type of controls you want and the style. As you switch selections, the Sample in the dialog box changes to reflect your choices. Choose Option Buttons and Sunken style. Click Next.
8. Edit the caption name to **Shipper** and click Finish.
9. Click View to see the option group (see Figure 11.17).
   The shipper option group looks fine, but it's out of sync with the Overnight option group below it (Figure 11.19 shows the two groups in design view). You'll fix it at the end of the chapter.

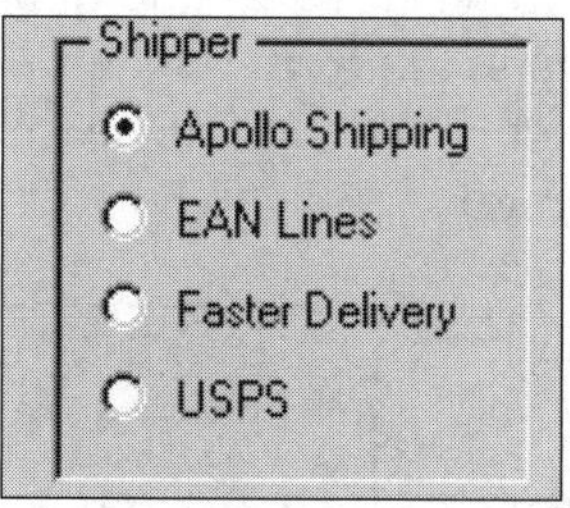

Figure 11.17 The option group in Form view.

10. Click View to return to Design view.

The option group (Figure 11.18) contains the following elements:

- **Frame**—Actually, the frame is not a separate element; it is the option group. If you select the frame and open the property sheet, its title is `Option Group`, not `Frame`. If you want to delete the entire option group, you click the frame and press Delete.
- **Option buttons**—These might seem to be only decorative elements (the same goes for check buttons or toggle buttons, if you had chosen those instead). But they actually contain the values for each record. Right-click any option button and choose Properties, Data tab. It has the option value (the `ShipID`) that you set in the wizard for that shipper. One problem you might have with option groups is a mix-up in option values. For example, if you hadn't edited the option values in the wizard, the EAN Lines button would mistakenly be selected whenever the order was delivered by `Faster Delivery`—and vice versa. You would need to edit this property for both option buttons to make sure it matches the `ShipID` (the primary key) in the underlying table. Primary key IDs and values in an alphabetized (or otherwise sorted) field often are not synchronized, so be on the lookout for mistakes in option values.
- **Value labels**—These are the shipper names `Apollo Shipping`, `EAN Lines`, and so on. These labels hold no data; they merely describe the option buttons.
- **Option group label**—This is the title of the option group, not the option group itself. If you delete this label, the rest of the option group still exists.

One final note about option groups might or might not be obvious: If you add a record (such as an additional shipper) to the underlying table, the option group in the form remains unchanged. To include the new shipper, your best bet is to delete the existing option group and use the wizard to build a new one.

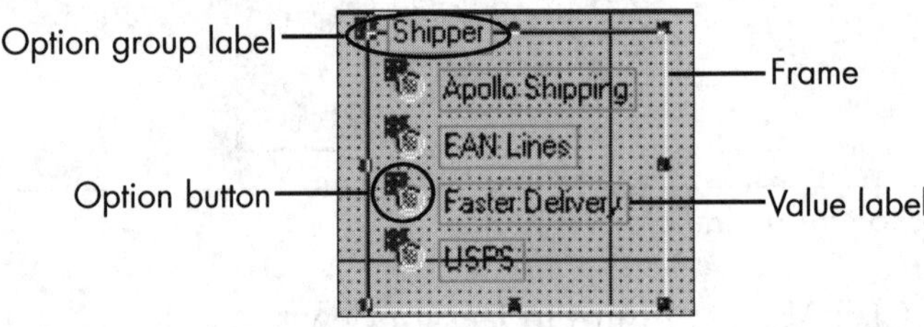

Figure 11.18 The option group in Design view.

Subforms

Compared with option groups, adding a subform to your form is relatively straightforward. There is one wrinkle: The main form must have a field that is on the "one" side of a one-to-many relationship, and the subform must have a field that's on the "many" side of the same relationship.

1. Choose Tools, Relationships to open the Relationships window.
   As you can see, the `OrderID` field in tblOrders is on the "one" side; the `OrderID` in tblOrderDetails is on the "many" side. Because the main form has the `OrderID` field from the Orders table, you shouldn't have any problem re-creating the Orders Details table as the subform.
2. Close the Relationships window. In Design view, click the border of the subform control to select it.
   Make sure you select the entire subform. As shown in Figure 11.19, the Object Selector should be tblOrderDetails.
3. Press Delete to delete the subform.

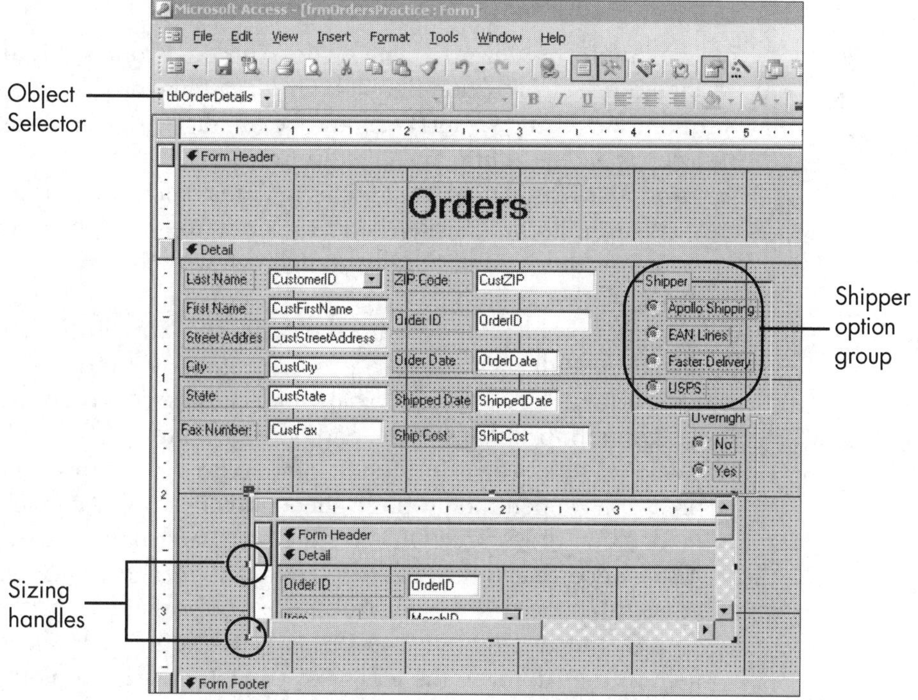

Figure 11.19 The Object Selector displays the currently selected form element.

4. At this point, only two Access windows should be open: the Database window and the `Orders` form. Choose Window, Tile Vertically.
5. In the Database window, click the Tables button and select the Order Details table.
6. Drag it to the Detail section of the `Orders Practice` form. Drop it 2 inches from the top and 1 inch from the left (see Figure 11.20).

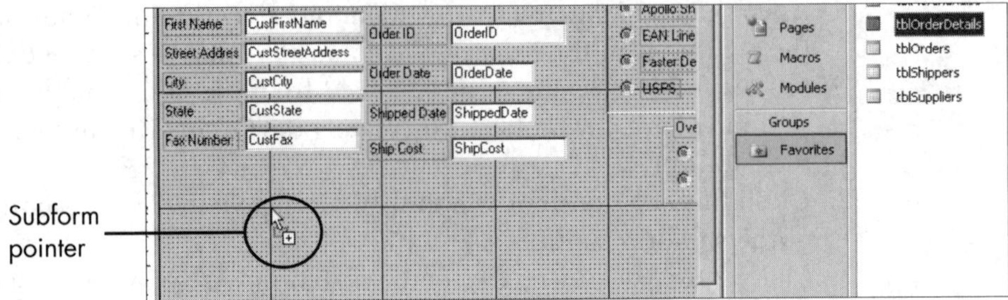

Figure 11.20 Drag the Order Details table from the Database window to the form. (It makes no difference whether the position of the two windows is switched.)

7. The Subform Wizard opens. The Choose From a List button should be selected, and Show tblOrderDetails for Each Record in qryOrders Using OrderID should be highlighted. Click Next.
8. Keep the default title and click Finish.
9. Minimize the Database window and maximize the form. Click View in the form to switch to Form view. You have the same subform you did before. Scroll through a few records to make sure that it works properly.
10. A couple problems exist with the subform. Not all the fields are displayed fully. A smaller problem is that there is a label `tblOrderDetails subform`, which is superfluous. You'll take care of both problems at the end of the chapter.
11. Click View to return to Design view. With the subform selected, press F4 to open the property sheet and click the Data tab.
12. Notice that the Source Object is the `tblOrderDetails` subform. Also notice that the `Link Child Fields` and `Link Master Fields` properties are set to `OrderID`, the field with matching data in the two tables. The `Child Fields` link is the linking field in the subform; the `Master Fields` link is the field in the main form. Each time you move to a new record in the main form (which has records from the table on the "one" side of the

relationship), the subform (which has records on the "many" side of the relationship) is revised to display the related records.

13. Close the property sheet. Save your changes and close the form. In the Database window, click the Forms button. Select the `tblOrderDetails` subform and open it.
14. This is the form that Access created when the subform was added. Note that it is a separate form in the Database window, and it can be used as a form on its own. If you edit the form, however, those changes will be reflected in the subform of the Orders Practice form.
15. Close the `tblOrderDetails` subform.

TIP Another way to add a subform is to use the Subform/Subreport tool in the toolbox. Click the tool, drag it to the Design section, and position the crosshairs where you want the upper-left corner of the subform.

Open `frmOrdersPractice` from the `NiftyLionsEndChap11.mdb` database that you can download. Your form should resemble it. You'll do some work on the form at the end of the chapter to fix it up a bit.

Using the Form Wizard

Let's turn now to the Form Wizard to see how you can use it in your work.

You might find the Form Wizard slightly less useful than the Report Wizard. With a report, it's great to let Access do all the grunt work, especially the arduous task of creating groups and their summary controls. Even if the final product is not exactly what you want, it's often good enough (with a little tweaking) for your intended audience—the information is all there.

A form, on the other hand, is something you might use every day to enter values. You want the controls, the tab order (discussed in Chapter 6), the design, and so on to be just right for easy data entry. An AutoForm is often fine for quick data entry, and you can always add a combo box or two to make life simpler. More advanced forms might require outside assistance from a database consultant who can automate your work by doing some programming. The Form Wizard might fall uncomfortably between these two ends.

But I could be wrong in this bias, at least for your own situation. As with the Report Wizard, the Form Wizard enables you to easily combine fields from different tables, add one or more subforms, and apply form styles.

To try the Form Wizard, let's try to create a form similar to the `Orders` form you've been using.

1. In the Database window, click Forms and click New. Select Form Wizard and click OK.
2. Open the Tables/Queries drop-down list and choose tblCustomers. Double-click `CustLastName`, `CustFirstName`, `CustStreet-Address`, `CustCity`, `CustState`, `CustZIP`, and `CustFax` to add them to the Selected Fields pane.
3. Open the Tables/Queries drop-down list and select tblOrders. Add `OrderID`, `ShippedDate`, `ShipID`, `Overnight`, and `ShipCost` to `Selected Fields`.
4. Open the Tables/Queries drop-down list and select tblShippers. Double-click `ShipCompanyName` to add it to `Selected Fields`.
5. Open the Tables/Queries drop-down list and select tblOrderDetails. Use the double-arrow button to add all four fields to `Selected Fields`.
   In this initial dialog box, the most logical choice would actually have been to select all the fields from `qryOrders`, on which the `Orders` form was built. But perhaps the main advantage of the wizard is that you can add fields from any table and have Access give you various options on how the data should be presented. To demonstrate this advantage, I had you add the fields separately from each table.
6. Click Next.
   In this dialog box, depending on the relationships among the fields you've chosen, Access offers various ways to present your data. The current selection is tblCustomers. If you choose to view your data by customer, the orders for each customer would be in a subform, and the order details for each order would be in a second subform. This makes sense: One customer can have many orders, and each order can have many detail records. So you have a hierarchy of one-to-many relationships. (If you find this confusing, when you're finished with the wizard, choose Tools, Relationships and review the relationships in the window.)

7. Click by tblShippers.
   Each shipper can handle many orders, and each order can have many order detail records. So you have another hierarchy of one-to-many relationships that can be displayed with a main form and two subforms.
8. Click by tblOrderDetails.
   The relationships in this table are always on the "many" side, so the form would just show all the fields together. This choice is unlikely because it doesn't organize your data meaningfully.
9. Click by tblOrders (see Figure 11.21).
   This displays the relationship you've been using in this chapter. Each order can have many order detail records, which are displayed in a subform.
   Note that you have a choice between Form with Subforms and Linked Forms. With linked forms, no subforms would appear on the form. Instead, there would be a button for you to open and view the related order detail records. If you think that you'll need to view the order details only infrequently, this choice would maintain the focus on the fields in the main form and save space.

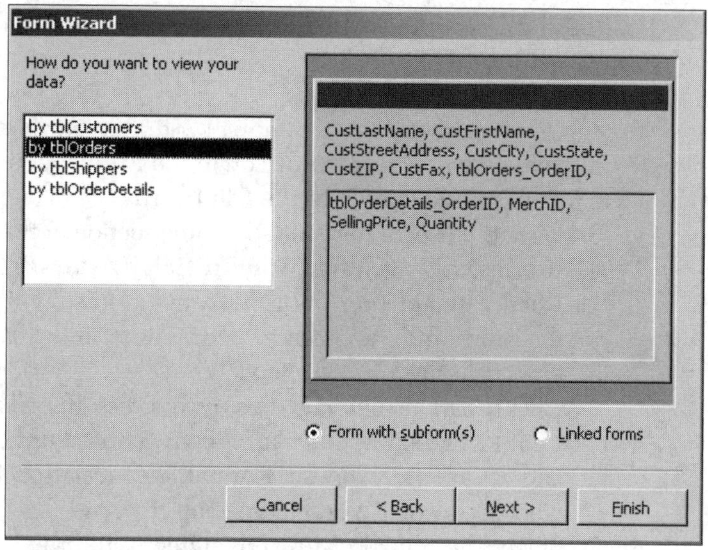

Figure 11.21 In this crucial dialog box of the Form Wizard, your choices for form/subforms derive from the relationships among the chosen tables.

10. With by tblOrders and Form with Subforms selected, click Next.
11. In this dialog box, you choose a layout for the subform. Keep the Datasheet selection and click Next.
12. In this dialog box, you choose a style. For comparison with the `frmOrdersPractice` form, use the same Standard style. Click Next.
13. Name your form `frmOrdersWizard`. Name the subform `frmOrderDetailsWizard Subform`. Leave the other options as they are, and click Finish.
14. Compare your form to `frmOrdersWizard` in the `NiftyLions-EndChap11.mdb` database.

    The form/subform you created resembles the `frmOrdersPractice` form/subform. It has the same fields in the main form, albeit in a different order than in `frmOrdersPractice`. However, it doesn't have the useful tools you added during this chapter—combo box, list box, option group—that would make the form more efficient to use.
15. Close the form and subform and save all your changes.

Refining Your Form

Let's finish the chapter by doing a little work on the `Orders Practice` form to get it into better shape.

1. Copy `NiftyLionsEndChap11.mdb` to your hard drive.
2. Select `frmOrdersPractice` in the Forms section of the Database window and copy it to the Clipboard.
3. Paste the copied form into the same section of the Database window.
4. Rename the form **frm[YourInitials]OrdersPracticeEnd**.

   I had you add your initials so you can distinguish your form from the solution `frmOrdersPracticeEnd` in the same database.
5. Open the form in Design view.
6. Click the CustomerID text box. Press the Shift key and select `CustFirstName`, `CustStreetAddress`, `CustCity`, `CustState`, and `CustFax`. Choose Format, Vertical Spacing, Make Equal. Choose Format, Vertical Spacing, Increase.
7. Select the ShipCost text box. Drag it and the accompanying label down so it is aligned with the `FaxNumber` control.
8. Click the CustZIP text box. Press Shift and select `OrderID`, `OrderDate`, `ShippedDate`, and `ShipCost`. Choose Format, Vertical Spacing, Make Equal.

   Your text boxes should look like Figure 11.22.

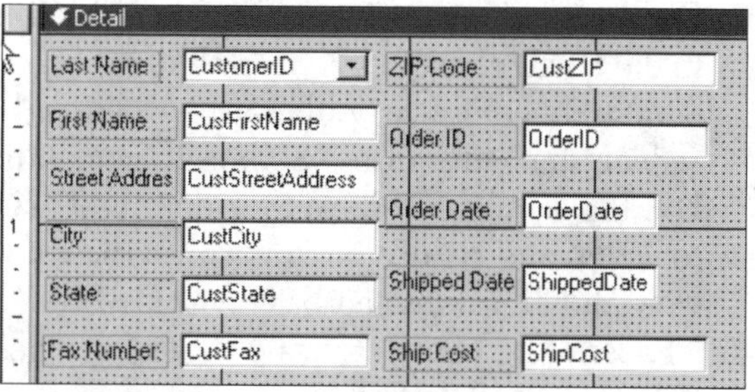

Figure 11.22 The label and text box controls after resizing and realignment.

Having two option groups on the right is a bit heavy. Now you'll change the `Overnight` option group to a check box.

9. Select the option group by clicking its frame. Press Delete. Select the `Overnight` field in the field list and drop it 4 inches from the left and parallel to `ShipCost`.
10. Select the `tblOrderDetails Subform` label (the label on top of the subform control) and delete it.
11. Select the subform. Move the pointer to the middle sizing handle on the right border. When the pointer becomes a double arrow, widen the control (see Figure 11.23) to the 4.5-inch mark.

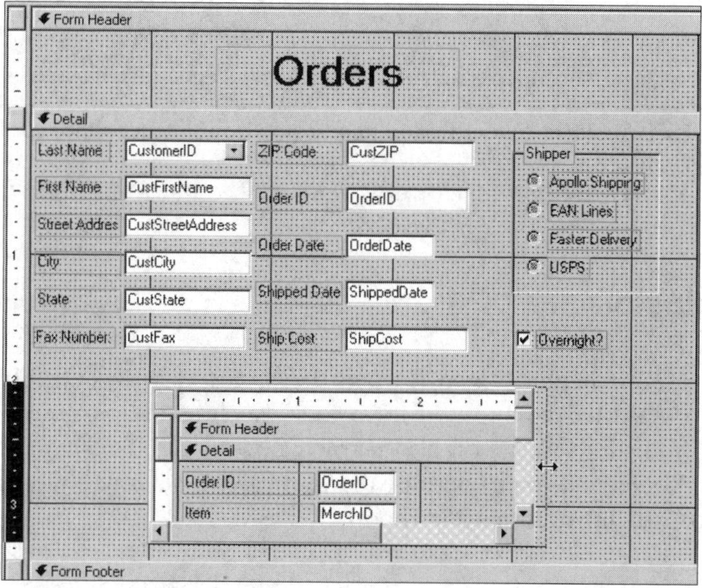

Figure 11.23 Use the double-arrow pointer to widen the control.

12. Click View to go to Form view. In the subform, move the pointer to the border between `Selling Price` and `Quantity`. When the pointer becomes a double-arrow with a bar (see Figure 11.24), reduce the width of the Selling Price column.
13. Use the same procedure to widen the Quantity column. Continue to widen and reduce columns until the column headings are in full view and all values can be seen.
14. Choose File, Save to save your changes. Open `frmOrders-PracticeEnd` and compare your work.

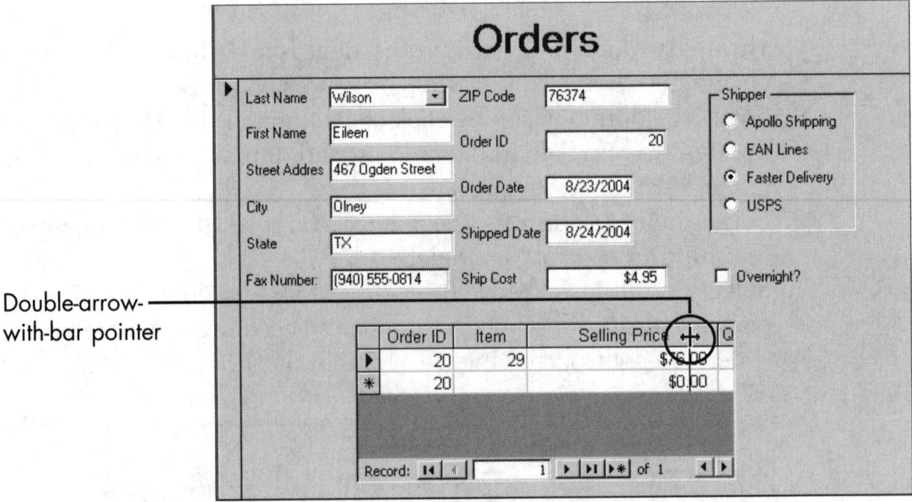

Figure 11.24 Subform columns often need some adjustment so that captions and values are in full view.

Conclusion

In Chapter 6, you learned the basics of form entry. In this chapter, you learned how to add form tools, such as option groups and subforms, in Design view; you also learned how to use the Form Wizard. In the next chapter, you'll continue to improve your skills in building the graphical elements of forms and reports.

CASE EXAMPLE

The frmMerchandise form includes all the fields in the Merchandise table, which contains data about Nifty Lions products. Combo boxes have been created for the CategoryID and SupplierID fields. In this example, you'll perform various tasks, including adding a subform, to improve the form.

1. Copy frmMerchandise to the Clipboard. Paste the form in the Forms section of the Database window. Name the form **frm[YourInitials]MerchandiseDetails**.
2. Open the form in Design view.
3. Choose View, Form Header and Footer. Lengthen the header so that its height is 1".
4. In the toolbox, click the Label tool. (If the toolbox isn't visible, click the Toolbox button on the toolbar.) Drag the crosshairs to the Form Header and click 2 inches from the left and anywhere from the top. Type **Merchandise Details** and press Enter.
5. Open the label's property sheet. Set the Top property at 0.375. Make the label 2 inches wide. Increase the Font Size to 16. Edit the Height to 0.25.
6. Choose Edit, Select All. Press Shift and click the label in the header to deselect it. Move all the controls in the Detail section down so that the top control ItemID is 1 inch from the top. (The Detail section lengthens when you move the controls.) Click anywhere outside the selected controls to deselect them.
7. Delete the CategoryName label. Move the CategoryID combo box so that it is two rows of dots below the Detail selector and aligned at left with the labels. Increase the font size to 14. Increase the width to 1.125 inches. Double-click the handle in the upper-right corner to lengthen the control for a better fit.
8. Select the SupplierID combo box. On the Data tab of the property sheet, click in the Row Source property and click the triple dots at the end of the line. Edit the SQL statement so that the supplier names are alphabetized. Close the statement and click Yes to save your changes. Close the property sheet.
9. Select the SupplierStockNumber, PurchasePrice, UnitsInStock, and UnitsOnOrder text boxes. Drag and drop them so that the text boxes are 4.5 inches from the left and 1 inch from the top.
10. Reduce the length of SupplierStockNumber to 6 inches. Decrease the width of the form to 6 inches as well (see Figure 11.25).

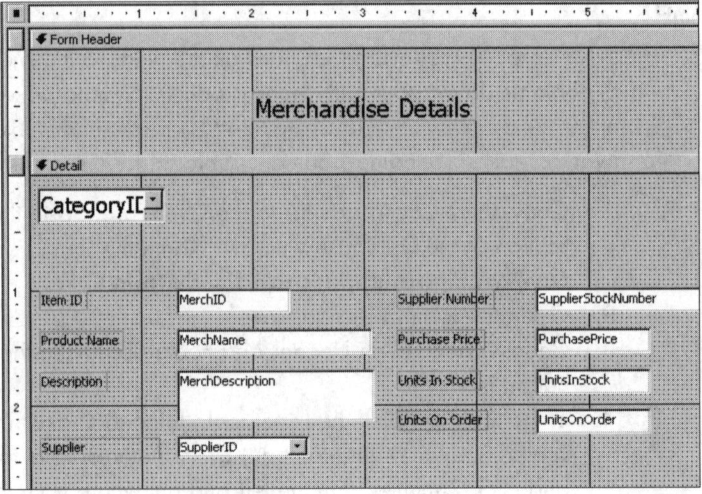

Figure 11.25 The text boxes and labels need to be aligned, and the space between them must be made equal.

11. Align the `UnitsOnOrder` controls to the `SupplierID` controls so all four controls are the same distance from the top.
12. Select the four text boxes in the second column of controls. Choose Format, Vertical Spacing, Make Equal.
13. Choose Tools, Relationships to open the Relationships window.
    The tblMerchandise table has a one-to-many relationship with tblOrderDetails through the `MerchID` field. Therefore, you can create a subform that shows order details for each product.
14. Close the Relationships window. Close the property sheet.
15. With the Control Wizards tool selected, click the Subform/Subreport wizard tool in the toolbox. Drag the crosshairs to the Detail section and click 3 inches from the top and 1.5 inches from the left.
16. In the first dialog box, choose Use Existing Tables and Queries. Click Next.
17. Open the Tables/Queries drop-down list and choose tblOrderDetails. Add all the fields from Available Fields to Selected Fields. Click Next.
18. Leave the current selections of Choose from a List and Show tblOrderDetails for Each Record in tblMerchandise Using MerchID. Click Next.
19. Name the subform `frmOrderInfo subform`. Click Finish.

20. Delete the label of the subform. Save your work.
21. In Form view, adjust the columns in the subform so that all column names are in view.
22. Apply an ascending sort to the Category combo box.
23. Inspect a few records to make sure the form is working properly (see Figure 11.26). Compare your form to `frmMerchandiseDetails` in `NiftyLionsChap11End.mdb`.

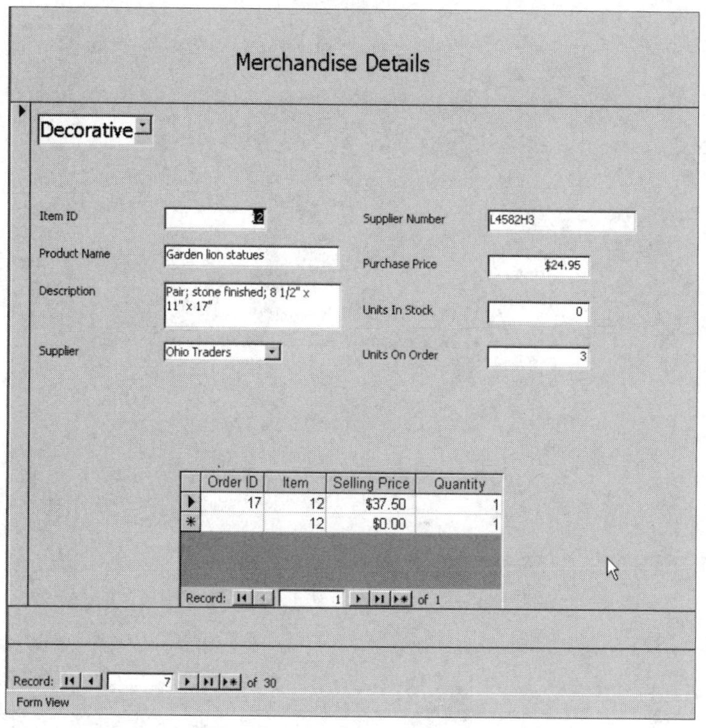

Figure 11.26 The completed form in Form view.

CHAPTER 12

Form/Report Design Elements

In Chapter 10, "Reports," you created a report from start to finish. In Chapter 11, "Forms/Subforms," you did a complete makeover of a form, step by step. I used this soup-to-nuts approach to give you a wide-lens view of how these objects work, a picture unobtainable when form and report creation is presented as a series of separate, piecemeal tasks.

There was a downside to this method, however: I didn't get to discuss many design features of forms and reports because they weren't specifically required by either project.

This chapter attempts to make amends for those shortcomings. I discuss techniques and features that forms and reports share, with the focus on adding pictures and other objects. I make some general comments about good design, including the use of special effects and fonts. And I take a look at several other design elements and features that are more specific to either forms or reports. These include switchboards, which are easy-to-use forms for selecting database tasks, and snaked column reports, which give you compact, efficient hard copy.

I also talk about macros. Access authors now tend to de-emphasize macros, arguing that nearly everything they do can be handled as well or better by writing Visual Basic for Applications (VBA) code. But for advanced beginner and intermediate users who don't want to learn application programming or database languages, macros often offer a workable alternative—especially for automatically executing simple tasks such as opening a form or printing a report at opportune moments.

Macros is a topic that requires many, many more pages than I've given it here. But as with my preparatory discussions of other tough-to-tackle topics, such as normalization or SQL, this brief introduction will at least give you a taste for how macros work in Access, as well as a few practical applications.

Adding Pictures and Other Objects

You can insert objects such as bitmap images, Excel spreadsheets, and Word documents into Access forms and reports. There are three important questions to consider:

- Should the control into which the object is inserted be bound or unbound?
- If the control is unbound, should you use an Image control or an Unbound Object Frame?
- Should the object be embedded or linked?

Significantly, both bound and unbound controls can be either embedded or linked. Given the various options of bound versus unbound, image control versus unbound object frame, and embedding versus linking, you might confront a sufficiently complex matrix of choices when attempting to answer all three questions that you might need some help.

Let's start by distinguishing bound and unbound controls and proceed from there.

Bound and Unbound Controls

Just as there are two kinds of egotists (those who admit it, and the rest of us), there are two kinds of Access pictures. Some change as you move from record to record, and some don't. Pictures that change from record to record are displayed in a bound control, which has a field in an underlying table as its source. Pictures that don't change from record to record are in an unbound control, which does not have a field in an underlying table as its source.

Bound Controls

The Northwind database provides ready-made examples of both types of controls. Let's first look at a bound control.

1. Choose Help, Sample Databases, Northwind Sample Database.
   I won't be asking you to make any changes to the database, so you should be okay if you use `Northwind.mdb` as is. But to be sure you have an unblemished Northwind file handy, it's always a good idea to make a copy. In Access 2003, you can make a backup by opening the database and choosing File, Back Up Database.

2. Open the Categories table in Design view.
   The table contains data about the various food categories into which Northwind's products are classified.
   Note that the `Picture` field has the data type `OLE Object`, which is used for storing images.
3. Click the View button at the far left end of the toolbar to go to Datasheet view.
   The `Picture` field shows the same entry for each record: `Bitmap Image`. Actually, each value is completely different, as you'll see presently.
4. Double-click Bitmap Image in the first row, the `Beverages` record.
   An image of beverages opens in a new window (see Figure 12.1). Close the window.

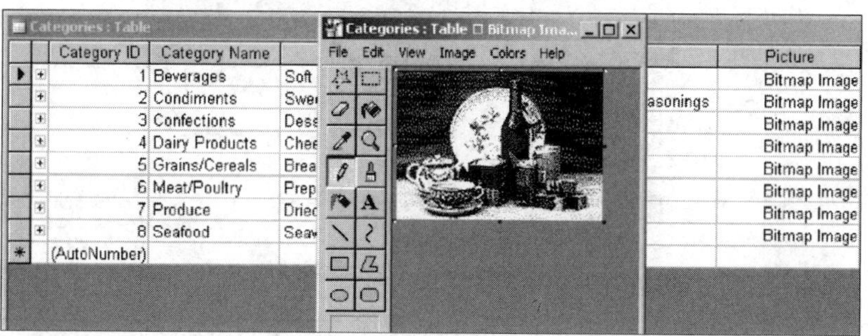

Figure 12.1 Although the values in the `Picture` field appear to be text, they are actually pictures.

5. Double-click Bitmap Image in the second row, the `Condiments` record.
   An image of condiments opens in a new window. Close the window.
6. Close the table. With the Categories table selected in the Database window, choose Insert, AutoForm.
   The new form has all the fields from the Categories table, including `Picture`.
7. Using the Next Record button in the navigation bar at the bottom of the window, view the first few records.

The picture changes from record to record to match the category. In the first record, you see an image of beverages; in the fourth record, you see an image of cheeses (see Figure 12.2). Although the images in the `Picture` field are stored in the table, within Access they can be displayed only in other objects, most notably a form.

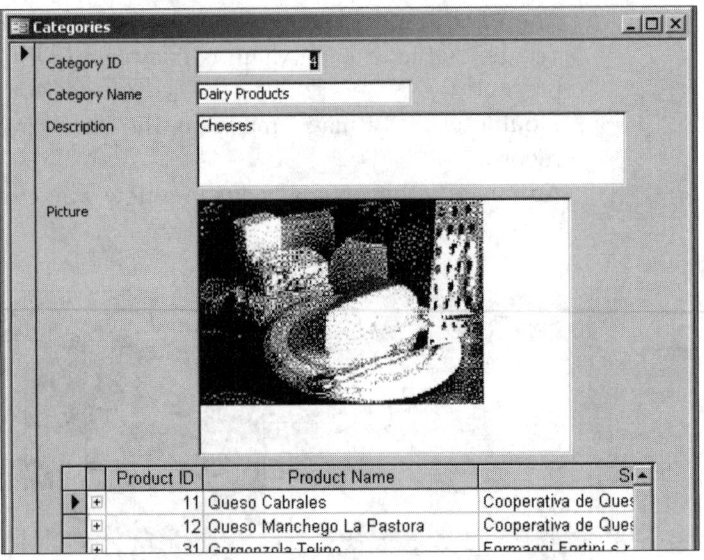

Figure 12.2 The pictures stored in the table can be viewed in a form. As you move from record to record, the picture changes to the image stored for that record.

8. Click View to go to Design view.
9. Right-click the rectangular box to the right of the `Picture` label and choose Properties.
   The title of the property sheet is `Bound Object Frame: Picture`. In a bound object frame, the data comes from a field in an underlying table.
10. Click the Data tab in the property sheet.
    The `Control Source` is `Picture`, which is the field in the underlying Categories table. In other words, `Picture` is a bound control that uses the `Picture` field in the Categories table as its source.
11. Close the form without saving it.

Q&A

Q: Okay, I understand how pictures are stored in a table. But how do I insert them in the first place?

A: In the appropriate record, click in the `Picture` field (which, because you're entering items into your database, is more likely to be in a form than a table). Choose Insert, Object and the dialog box shown in Figure 12.5 appears. When I discuss that dialog box a little later, I'll focus on other objectives; but you'll be able to use the same basic techniques to insert a picture in a field.

Unbound Controls

Now that you've seen how images in a bound control work, let's take a look at a picture in an unbound control.

1. In the Database window, click Reports.
2. Open the Catalog report.
   In the center of the report is the Northwind logo.
3. Click View to go to Design view.
4. Select the control with the Northwind logo. If necessary, choose View, Properties to open the control's property sheet.
   The title of the control is `Image: LargeLogo`.
5. View the Data tab of the property sheet (see Figure 12.3).

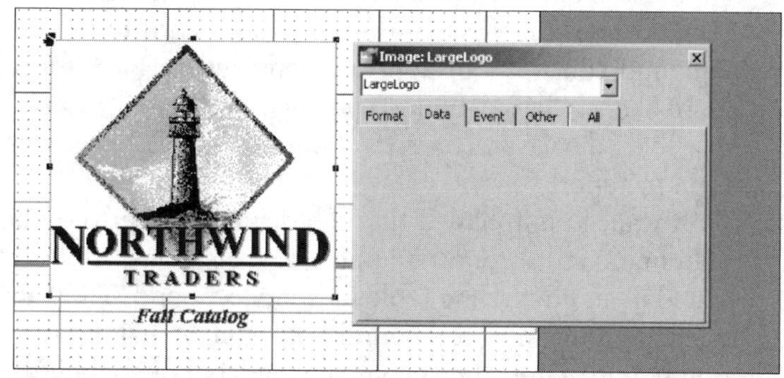

Figure 12.3 The logo in the unbound Image control is not stored in the field of an underlying table.

The Data tab is blank. Unlike the pictures in the previous example, the control isn't bound to a field in an underlying table.

6. Click the Format tab in the property sheet.
   In the `Picture` property, the setting is `(bitmap)`. An image has merely been inserted into this control to be displayed in the report; no image is stored in an underlying table.
7. Click in the `Picture` property. Click the ellipsis (...) button to open the Insert Picture dialog box.
   You use this dialog box to find and insert the picture file in the form.
8. Click Cancel in the Insert Picture dialog box.
9. Click in the `Picture Type` property. Open the drop-down list and note that there are two choices: Embedded and Linked. Embedded is currently chosen.
   I'll discuss embedding versus linking presently.
10. Close the property sheet, close the form, and close the database.

Comparing Bound and Unbound Controls

As you saw, you use a bound control when each image is specific to each record. The picture in the bound object frame changes from record to record to display the value from the underlying table—just as, say, street addresses in a text box of a `Customers` form would change from customer to customer.

An unbound control merely displays the image in the object and remains unchanged as you move from record to record. Both bound and unbound controls can appear in any section of a form or report. You're more likely to have a bound control in the Detail section, which is used primarily to display records. Unbound controls have uses throughout your form or report.

I want to emphasize that the distinction between bound controls and unbound controls doesn't apply only to images. Any control that is tied to a field in an underlying table or query is bound. Thus, text boxes that show the data from a field are bound. Any control that doesn't have a data source is unbound. Thus, the accompanying label of a label/text box combination is unbound, as is a label used as a title for a form or report. Graphical elements such as lines and rectangles are also unbound.

Image Versus Unbound Object Frame

In the previous example, you used an image control to display the picture as an unbound control. You can also add objects in an unbound object frame. What's the difference between them, and when do you each type of control?

The following example helps answer these questions. You'll insert a small Excel worksheet into a bare-bones form in the Nifty Lions database using an unbound object frame. You'll then display the same file in an Image control.

1. Copy the `NiftyLionsChap12.mdb`, `Surcharge_Chap12.xls`, `NiftyLionsOrders_Chap12.ppt`, and `Kenya_Money_Lion_Chap12.jpg` files to a convenient folder on your hard drive.
   You need only `NiftyLionsChap12.mdb` and `Surcharge_Chap12.xls` for this particular example; the other files you'll use later in the chapter.
2. Open `NiftyLionsChap12.mdb`. Click the Forms button and open `frmOrders` in Design view.
3. In the toolbox, click the Unbound Object Frame button (see Figure 12.4 for its location).

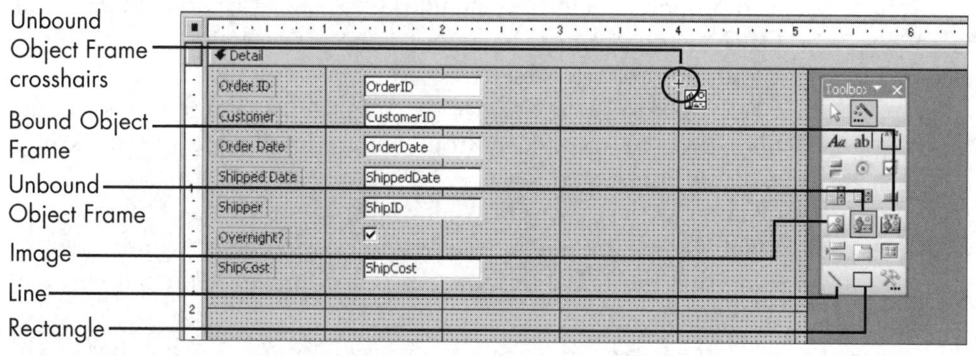

Figure 12.4 You can draw a rectangle for an unbound object frame, but it's probably easier to simply click where you want the top-left corner of the frame and do any resizing after you insert the object.

4. Drag the crosshairs 4 inches from the left and two rows of dots from the top (see Figure 12.4). Click to open the Microsoft Office Access dialog box (see Figure 12.5).

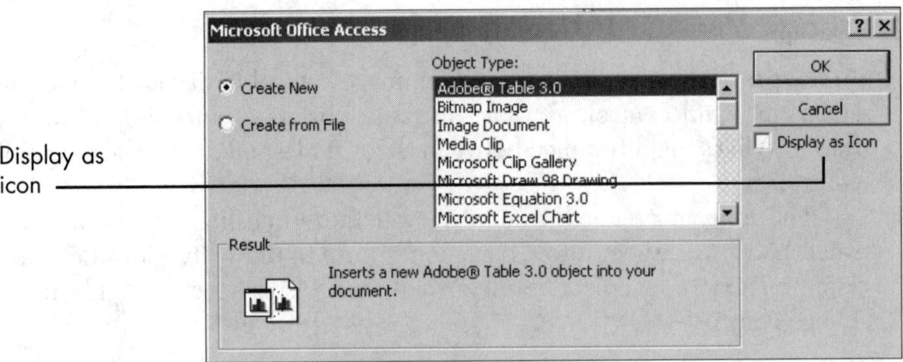

Figure 12.5 In the Microsoft Office Access dialog box, you can create a new object to insert or use an object stored in an existing file.

Notice that you can insert a wide variety of objects in an unbound object frame, including bitmap and Paintbrush pictures.

5. Select Create from File and click Browse.
6. Navigate to `Surcharge_Chap12.xls` and double-click it. Click OK.
7. Maximize the form window. Right-click the Excel worksheet and choose Properties. Click the Data tab.
   The property sheet title includes `Unbound Object Frame`. The OLE `Class` property includes `Microsoft Office Excel`.
8. Close the property sheet.
9. Click View to go to Form view. Scroll through a few records and note that, as you move from record to record, the worksheet remains unchanged.
10. Click View to return to Design view.
11. Double-click in the center of the unbound object frame.
    Note that the Excel formula bar is now in view. You can now edit the worksheet.
12. Click the `Overnight Surcharge` cell for Apollo Shipping. In the formula bar, edit the value to **$11.95** (see Figure 12.6). Press Enter.

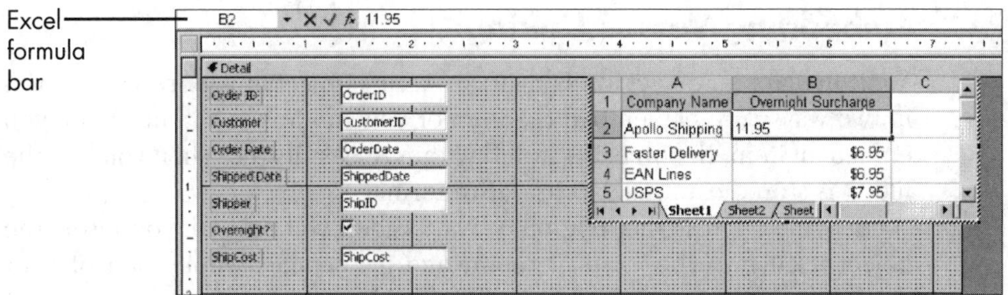

Figure 12.6 When you use an Unbound Object frame, you can edit the program in its native format. Here you can use the Excel formula bar to edit a value in an Excel spreadsheet.

13. Click anywhere outside the control to deselect it. Click View to see the change in the form, and click View to return to Design view. Save your changes and close the form.
14. Open the `Surcharge_Chap12.xls` file. Note that the edit you made is not reflected in the underlying file. Close Excel.
15. Open the `frmOrders` form in Design view.
16. Right-click the control with the Excel worksheet and choose Change To, Image. Click Yes to confirm.
17. Double-click in the middle of the control.
    Instead of opening the worksheet in Excel, only the Image Control property sheet opens. You cannot edit the spreadsheet in an image control.
18. Close the property sheet and press Delete to delete the control.

As you can see, an unbound object frame lets you edit the object—picture, Excel spreadsheet, and so on—within Access. An image control does not.

The obvious question: Why not choose the more flexible unbound object frame over an image control all the time?

The answer: Image controls load more quickly than unbound object frames.

The upshot: If you don't think need you'll need to edit the object, then use an Image control. For standalone pictures such as logos, an Image control makes sense.

But if you need to update the content of the object, use an unbound object frame. For an Excel worksheet whose numbers change frequently, an unbound object frame often makes sense.

Embedding Versus Linking

You can make an object available to an Access object in your report or form in two ways: You can embed the item or you can link the item. When you embed an item, the object is stored within Access itself. When you link the file, it is stored externally in its native format.

Let me express that one other way: When you embed, you insert the object itself into the form or report and it becomes wholly part of your database. When you link, you provide the location where Access can get the object when it needs it. When you embed the object and make changes to it, those changes are not included in the original file. When you link the file and edit it, however, you are also editing the underlying object; any changes you make in the underlying file will be reflected in the linked object.

Both embedding and linking have their drawbacks. Stored images in Access tend to take up a lot of room, resulting in database bloat. On the other hand, with a linked object, if you change the file's location, you need to tell Access where it has moved to. Determining the net trade-off between embedding and linking can help you decide which to choose.

Try this example that inserts a PowerPoint presentation in an Access form. (Don't worry if you know nothing about PowerPoint—the exercise requires minimal PowerPoint skills.)

1. In Design view of the `frmOrders` form, click Unbound Object Frame in the toolbox.
2. Drag the crosshairs 3 inches from the left and two rows of dots from the top. Click to open the Microsoft Office Access dialog box.
3. Select Create from File and click Browse.
4. Locate the `NiftyLionsOrders_Chap12.ppt` file you downloaded and double-click it. Click OK.
5. Click View to see the PowerPoint page and return to Design view.
6. With the control still selected, right-click and choose Properties. On the Data tab, note that the `OLE Type` setting is `Embedded`. Close the property sheet.
7. Right-click the control and choose Presentation Object, Edit.
8. Select Spring 2006 in the presentation and edit it to **Fall 2006**. Click outside the control to deselect it.
9. Open the `NiftyLionsOrders_Chap12.ppt` file. Note that the date has not been changed. Close the file and close PowerPoint.
10. Delete the control with the PowerPoint presentation.

11. In the toolbox, click Unbound Object Frame.
12. Drag the crosshairs 3 inches from the left and two rows of dots from the top. Click to open the Microsoft Office Access dialog box.
13. Select Create from File.
14. Click the Link check box to select it.
15. Click Browse. Locate `NiftyLionsOrders_Chap12.ppt` and double-click it. Click OK.
16. With the control still selected, right-click and choose Properties. On the Data tab, note that the `OLE Type` is `Linked`. Close the property sheet.
17. Right-click the control and choose Linked Presentation Object, Edit.
18. In PowerPoint, click Spring. Edit the date to **Summer 2006**.
19. Close PowerPoint and save your changes. The file itself has been edited.

    I think it's obvious that you just edited the actual file. But if you want, you can open `NiftyLionsOrders_Chap12.ppt` to confirm.
20. Switch to `frmOrders`. The control has been edited as well (see Figure 12.7).

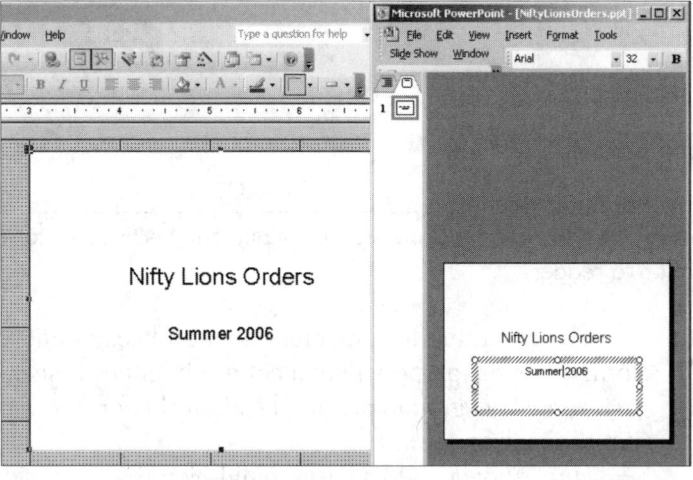

Figure 12.7 When you link, changes you make in an Access control are reflected in the underlying file.

21. With the control selected, right-click and choose Linked Presentation Object, Convert.

22. Click Display as Icon and click OK.
    You can save much space by displaying objects as icons.
23. Choose File, Save to save your changes.

Background Picture

Another type of graphic is the background picture, which places an image (such as a logo) behind the text in a form or report. I recommend taking a conservative approach to using background pictures: Sometimes they just make the text more difficult to read and serve no crucial purpose. But occasionally they are valuable, such as in a "confidential" warning displayed throughout a page so that there's no question the reader will see the warning (see Figure 12.8).

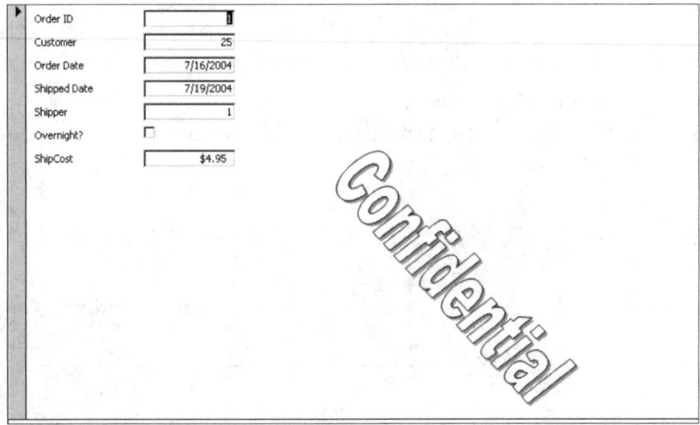

Figure 12.8 A background picture is occasionally an effective tool for communicating information to readers.

The key thing to remember about a background picture is that it's a form or report property, not a control in either object. So when you want to insert a background picture, head for the form or report property sheet, not the toolbox.

Here's how to add a background picture:

1. In Design view of the `frmOrders` form, choose Edit, Select Form. With the form now selected, choose View, Properties to open the form's property sheet.

2. On the Format tab on the property sheet, click in the `Picture` property.
3. Click the three-dot ellipsis on the right to open the Insert Picture dialog box.
4. Navigate to `Kenya_Money_Lion_Chap12.jpg`, the file you earlier copied. Double-click the file to insert it. Three properties should be set as follows:
   - Picture Size Mode: Clip
   - Picture Alignment: Center
   - Picture Tiling: No

   These properties are discussed in the next section.
5. Click View to go to Form view. Scroll through a few records to see the background picture in each record of the form (see Figure 12.9).
6. Click View to return to Design view. Choose File, Save to save your work.

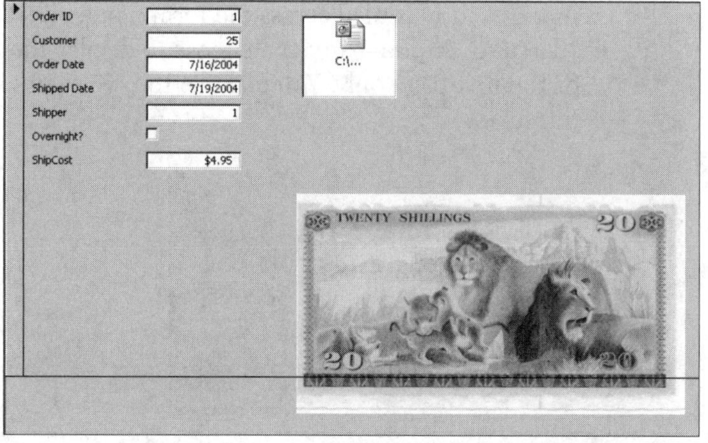

Figure 12.9 You can also use a background picture merely as a decorative element.

Picture Properties

Various properties change the placement and appearance of a background picture. Trial and error could be the wisest strategy for using them, but if you get confused about which property does what, these descriptions might help:

- `Picture Size Mode`—This property has three settings. Clip displays the image at its actual size (see Figure 12.10). If there isn't sufficient space for the image, it's truncated. Stretch fills the entire page with the image, but often at the cost of greatly distorting it (see Figure 12.11). Zoom manages to maintain the image's original proportions, but it can fill only the height or width of the available space, not both (see Figure 12.12).
- `Picture Alignment`—This property positions the image within the control. The settings include Center, Top Right, and Bottom Left. In forms you'll also have a Form Center setting. Choose this selection if you want the picture centered horizontally in relation to the width of the form and vertically in relation to the height of the form. All other settings, by contrast, are set in relation to the form window.
- `Picture Tiling`—When the setting is Yes, the picture is tiled across the entire form window or report. If `Picture Alignment` is set to Form Center and `Picture Tiling` is Yes, the background picture of a form is tiled across the form, not across the Form window.
- `Picture Pages`—You can choose to display the image on all pages or the first page only. You can use the No Pages setting to hide the image.

Figure 12.10 Clip.

Figure 12.11 Stretch.

Figure 12.12 Zoom.

TIP As you create forms, you might find that the property sheet continues to be visible in Form view. If you want the property sheet to be available in Design view only, in the Form property sheet, click the Other tab. In the `Allow Design Changes` property, change the setting to Design View Only.

Visual Elements and Tools

Whether you're discussing databases, dogs, or dirigibles, looks count. In the case of databases, attractive design is not merely a matter of making your reports and forms look pretty. A more aesthetically pleasing form or report often means greater efficiency and enhanced functionality.

Here are a few Access features to convey information more effectively or improve the appearance of your database objects. (The formatting toolbar is shown in Figure 12.13.)

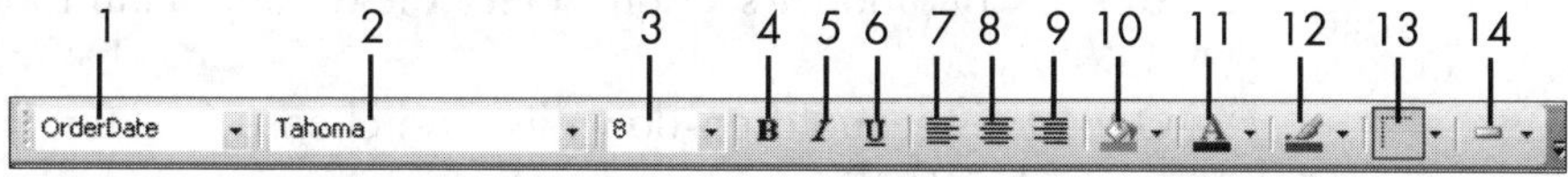

Figure 12.13 The tools of the Formatting toolbar.

1 Object Selector
2 Font
3 Font Size
4 Bold
5 Italics
6 Underline
7 Align Left
8 Center
9 Align Right
10 Fill/Back Color
11 Font/Fore Color
12 Line/Border Color
13 Line/Border Width
14 Special Effects

Datasheet Fonts

Usually there's little reason to change the default Arial 10-point font in tables. Although you can bold, underline, or italicize datasheet text, it usually serves little purpose. These fonts do not make your data easier to view. Conditional formatting can occasionally be helpful, as discussed in the next section.

If you do want to experiment with different fonts, avoid serif fonts (such as Times New Roman) for onscreen viewing. (A serif is a fine line projecting from the main stroke of a letter, such as that at the bottom of the letter *t*.) Instead, stick with nonserif fonts such as Arial.

Conditional Formatting

You can use conditional formatting in forms and reports to highlight specific numbers that meet conditions. You can apply a variety of special formatting, including bold, italics, and color.

Figure 12.14 shows the Conditional Formatting dialog box with the first drop-down list open to display three choices: Field Has Focus, Field Value Is, and Expression Is.

If you want to set a condition in the same field, use Field Value Is. For example, say you want values in the `ShipCost` field to be red whenever they're over $10. Follow these steps:

1. In Design view of the `frmOrders` form, right-click the ShipCost text box and choose Conditional Formatting (or choose Format, Conditional Formatting).
2. In the Condition 1 section, select Field Value Is in the first drop-down list.
3. Open the second drop-down list and choose Greater Than.
4. In the box to the right, type **10**.
5. In the same Condition 1 section, open the drop-down color palette on the Font/Fore Color button (see Figure 12.14) and choose a red swatch. Click OK.

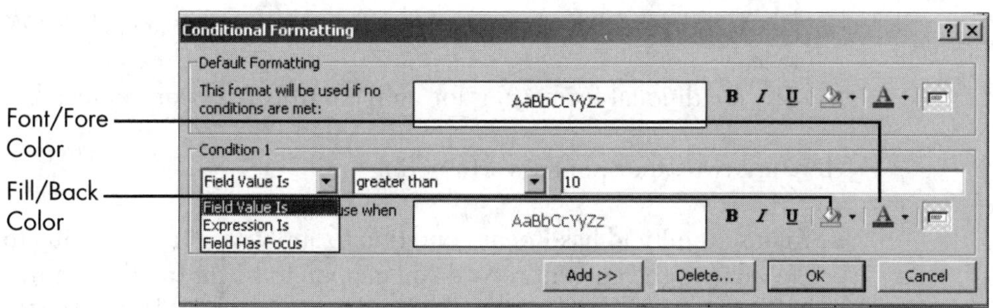

Figure 12.14 In the Conditional Formatting dialog box, use the Field Value Is setting to apply conditions in the same field.

6. Click View to go to Form view. Scroll through several records to see that values in the `ShipCost` field that are above $10 are now in red.
7. Click View to return to Design view.

You use the Expression Is choice when you want the formatting to change in one field when a condition is true in another field of the same record. For example, suppose you want the shipping date to be highlighted whenever the shipping cost is over $10. Here are the steps:

1. Select the `ShippedDate` control and choose Format, Conditional Formatting.
2. Open the drop-down list in the Condition 1 section and select Expression Is.
3. In the box to the right, type **[ShipCost]>10**.
4. In the same Condition 1 section, open the drop-down color palette on the Font/Fore Color button and choose a blue swatch. Click OK.
5. Click View to switch to Form view and scroll through several records. Whenever the shipping cost is above $10, the shipped date is in blue.
6. Click View to return to Design view.
7. With the ShippedDate text box selected, choose Format, Conditional Formatting.
8. Click Delete. Click the check box for Condition 1 and click OK twice.
9. Right-click the ShipCost text box and choose Conditional Formatting.

10. Click Delete. Click the check box for Condition 1 and click OK twice.
    The conditional formatting for both controls has been removed.

Here are two other points worth noting:

- You use the Field has Focus condition to apply special formatting to the value in the current record you happen to be in. In other words, let's say you move to a new record and the current field is `OrderID`. The value in the `ShipCost` field, which has a Field Has Focus condition of blue, looks the same as all other values in the record. When you click in the ShipCost text box, however, its value becomes blue.
- You can set up to three conditions. If none of the conditions is true, the existing formatting is maintained. If more than one condition is true, Access applies only the first true condition. So let's say the field contains the number of units in stock for various products. If condition #1 is for products with counts between 20 and 50, and condition #2 is for those with levels between 20 and 30, the 20 to 50 formatting will be used for all records.

Special Effects

Special effects usually work better onscreen than on paper—in other words, they have greater relevance for forms than reports. On paper, the layout of the material should be adequate to distinguish one type of information from another.

Figure 12.15 shows the various special effects available from the Special Effects palette on the Formatting toolbar in forms and reports. You apply them by selecting the control and clicking the effect. Here are some tips for working with them:

- Don't go overboard. In the world of special effects, a little goes a long way. In any one section of a form, use just one special effect.
- The effects themselves should be invisible. An effect should never call attention to itself. If a control shouts "Look at my beautifully chiseled frame!", remove the frame.
- Be careful about white backgrounds. Effects often don't show up well against light backgrounds. The gray of an Access Auto Form or Report usually works better.

- Use different frames for different elements. A raised frame helps draw the eye to a group of buttons. A sunken effect is better for check and option boxes.

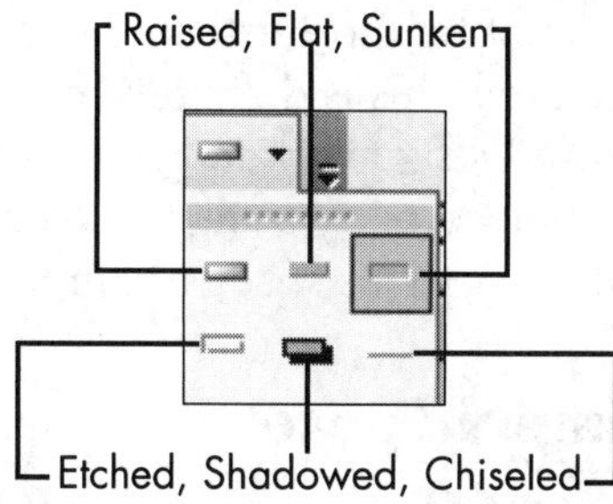

Figure 12.15 Special effects are occasionally useful for highlighting controls and improving appearance.

Can Grow, Can Shrink

Let's say you have a field that contains state abbreviations, such as AZ and CA. You know you'll need just two characters for all of the field's values, so you set the `Field Size` property for the `State` field in the table at `2`. When you create a form, that field size is inherited by the text box for the field. Therefore, you know exactly how much space the text box will take up on your form.

That's not the case for a field with a `Memo` data type whose contents are, say, the histories of countries. Then the amount of required space could vary radically from record to record. It's likely you'll want to enter many more words for China than for Chad.

In a form, you can have a scroll bar so that users can view the hidden text. But what do you do in a report? Because reports are usually printed, a scroll bar is no solution. If you need six times as much space for Italy as for Moravia, how can you make the report adapt to the changing space requirements?

The solution is the `Can Grow` and `Can Shrink` properties. When you set these properties to `Yes` in a report, the text box grows or shrinks to reflect the various space requirements.

What happens to the controls surrounding the Can Grow or Can Shrink text box? When a text box grows or shrinks, the entire report section grows or shrinks vertically. Adjacent controls move either up or down.

Also, note that a text box can't shrink to a height that's less than that of other controls on the same row. Let's say you have a text box with an accompanying label; the `Can Shrink` property in the text box is set to `Yes`. If there's no value in the text box, the label still appears, as does the text box, which cannot be shorter than the label.

As you can tell, this is definitely an area in which you'll want to switch frequently from Design view to Print Preview to see the impact of possible changes. Furthermore, try using test data of varying lengths to see how the controls adjust to various space requirements.

Reduce Empty Space

When you create a report, you'll sometimes find that it has a lot of empty space. Here are some things you can do to eliminate it:

- Decrease section height. You might have lengthened a section to include more controls and never used the additional space (see Figure 12.16). Check for stretches of empty space, especially between sections, in either Print Preview or Design view. Right-click the section's bar; choose Properties, Format tab; and edit the `Height` property.
- Reduce the width of controls. It makes no sense to have a 2-inch text box for a two-letter `State` field. Right-click the text box, choose Properties, Format tab, and edit the `Width` field. For labels, in which the required space does not change from record to record, it's easy to get a quick best fit: Double-click any handle except the move handle in the upper-left corner.
- Reduce the report's width. If there are no controls to the right of, say, the 5-inch mark on the horizontal ruler, you don't need a report that's 8 inches wide. Choose Edit, Select Report; then select View, Properties, Format tab. I recommend setting the `Width` at 5.5" just to leave a little extra room.
- Move controls closer together. The Report Wizard sometimes leaves too much space between labels and their accompanying text boxes. Use the move handle on either control to drag one closer to the other.

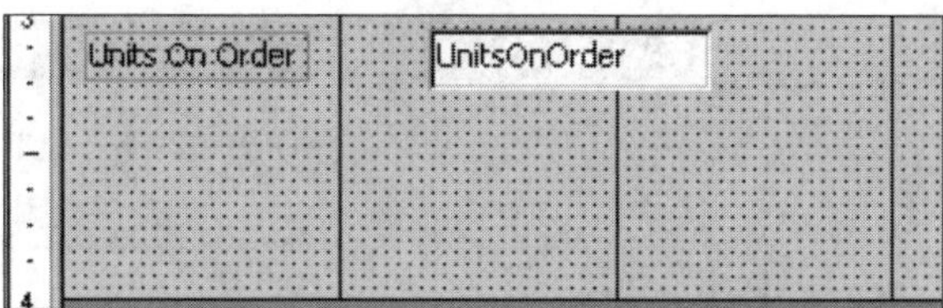

Figure 12.16 The vertical space between 3.5 inches and 4 inches has no controls and is unused space.

Lines

A line has both functional and decorative purposes. You can use a line to indicate areas with similar information (such as a line that separates a form from a subform). You can also use a line with some color or style to add visual interest.

The Line tool available in the toolbox is not difficult to use. I'll just make a few points that perhaps are not immediately apparent:

- For a straight line, press Shift as you draw the line.
- To lengthen or shorten an existing line, press Shift and tap the right or left arrow key.
- You can nudge a line up or down by holding down Ctrl and pressing the up arrow or down arrow key.
- For a straight, 1-inch horizontal line, click the Line tool in the toolbox, drag it to the Design area, and click anywhere on the form or report.
- Selecting a line can be difficult. Click the line at either end, or select the line from the Object Selector on the toolbar (refer to Figure 12.13).
- Finding lines in a form can also be difficult, especially when they are drawn right below a section bar (see Figure 12.17). One method to help spot it is to choose Edit, Select All, which shows the line's handles (see Figure 12.18).
- The Line/Border Width button (see Figure 12.13) controls the width of a line. It has seven settings, with Hairline the slimmest and 6 the heaviest.

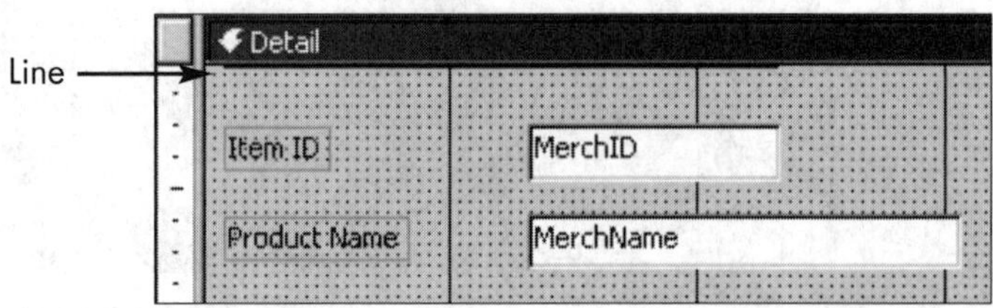

Figure 12.17 A line directly below a section bar is difficult to locate.

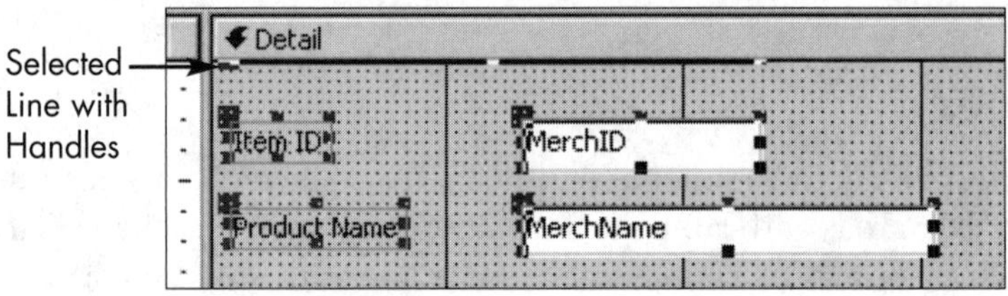

Figure 12.18 If you choose Edit, Select All, the handles on the line give you a better shot at picking it out.

Finally, you don't need to draw lines to separate different sections of a form. By default, the `Dividing Lines` property on the Format tab of the Form property sheet is set to Yes.

Rectangles

A rectangle, available from the toolbox, is one way to highlight or segregate a group of controls with similar data. Rectangles are not difficult to create, and I think you can make your way around the toolbar to find the Fill/Back Color, Line Border/Color, Line/Border Width, and Special Effects buttons that control their appearance (refer to Figure 12.13).

Manipulating Controls

Chapters 10 and 11 gave you substantial exposure to selecting, moving, resizing, aligning, and otherwise manipulating controls. Nevertheless, I thought it would be useful to summarize in one place the various techniques available to you.

Selecting

You select a control by clicking directly on it. The control displays a moving handle and sizing handles. If you select a text box with an attached label, the label's move handle also is displayed. If you select the label, the text box's move handle is visible (see Figure 12.19).

A selected control has several sizing handles. You use the sizing handles that border the control to resize it. You use the move handle in the upper-left corner to move the control.

You can also select any control from the drop-down list in the Object Selector (see Figure 12.19). If you haven't given the object a meaningful name, however, this method could prove difficult. To name a control, right-click it; choose Properties, Other tab; and type a name in the `Name` property.

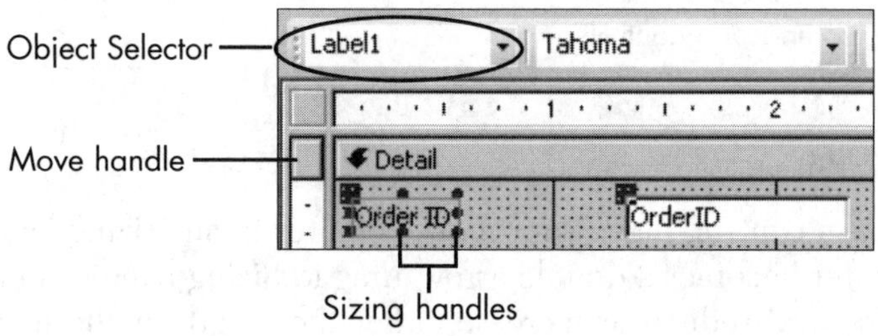

Figure 12.19 The currently selected object is the label, so only the text box's move handle is displayed.

To deselect a control, click outside it. Make certain you are not selecting any other element.

You can select several controls at the same time by these methods:

- Click the first control, press Shift, and click the other controls. You can use this method for controls that are either contiguous or far-flung. When you select text boxes, this method displays all handles of the text boxes and the move handle of the labels.
- Click anywhere outside the controls and draw a rectangle around them (the rectangle does not stay visible). This method displays all handles of all controls within the rectangle, not only the text boxes (see Figure 12.20).
- Move the pointer to the vertical or horizontal ruler. When it becomes a right or down arrow, respectively, click to select all the controls in the row or column (I'm speaking figuratively—there is no formally defined row or column). When you select text boxes, this method displays all handles of the text boxes and the move handle of the labels.

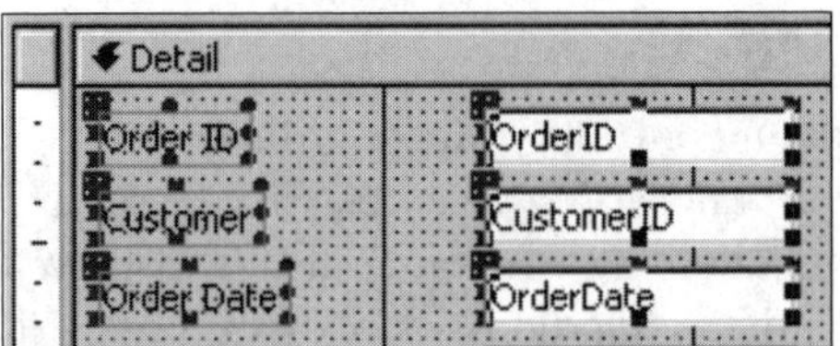

Figure 12.20 When you want to display all the handles of both text boxes and their accompanying labels, draw a rectangle around them and release.

NOTE You can group controls so that they stay together and can be resized as a group. Select the fields and choose Format, Group. If you use the Shift+click method, the text boxes are grouped; if you use the method of drawing a rectangle around them, both text boxes and labels will be grouped. Choose Format, Ungroup to ungroup controls.

Resizing

To resize a control, move your mouse pointer to any sizing handle. When the pointer becomes a double arrow, drag it. Sizing handles in the middle of the control reduce or increase either the length or the height. Sizing handles at the corners resize both dimensions at the same time.

NOTE As an alternative to using sizing handles, you can use the control's property sheet. Right-click the control and choose Properties, Format tab. Edit the properties for `Width` and `Height`.

You can use the Format, Size, To Fit command to get a best fit for the text string in a label. This command doesn't work in a text box, however, because its values vary in length.

You can resize a control grid line by grid line. Select the control and, while pressing Shift, tap the corresponding arrow key to lengthen, widen, or reduce dimensions.

Moving

To move a text box with an attached label, hover the pointer at any border, away from any handle. When the pointer becomes an open hand, drag the text box; the label follows (see Figure 12.21).

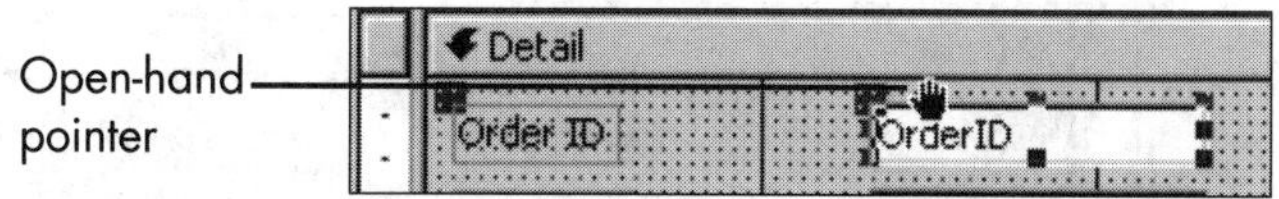

Figure 12.21 You use the open-hand pointer to move a text box and its accompanying label.

To move either the text box or the label separately, hover the pointer over the respective move handle. When the pointer becomes a pointing finger, drag the control (see Figure 12.22).

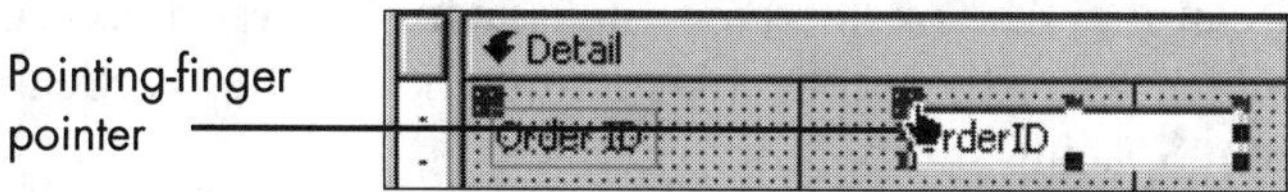

Figure 12.22 You use the pointing-finger pointer to move a label or text box alone.

You can also move a control grid line by grid line. Select the control and press the corresponding arrow key. If you want to nudge the control just a wee bit, press Ctrl while you press the corresponding arrow key.

Spacing

The Format menu also has commands that adjust horizontal and vertical spacing. In Figure 12.23, the three controls have unequal vertical spacing. In Figure 12.24, the three controls have been selected and the Make Equal command from the Vertical Spacing submenu of the Format menu has been applied. Note that the top and bottom label/text box pair has remained stationary, while the middle controls have moved upward.

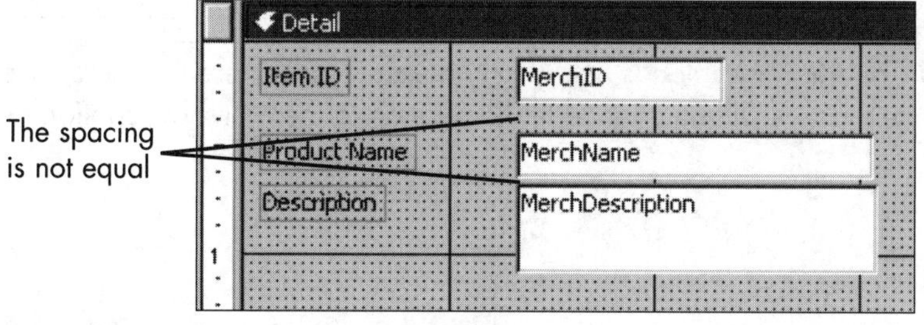

Figure 12.23 The three controls are not equally spaced.

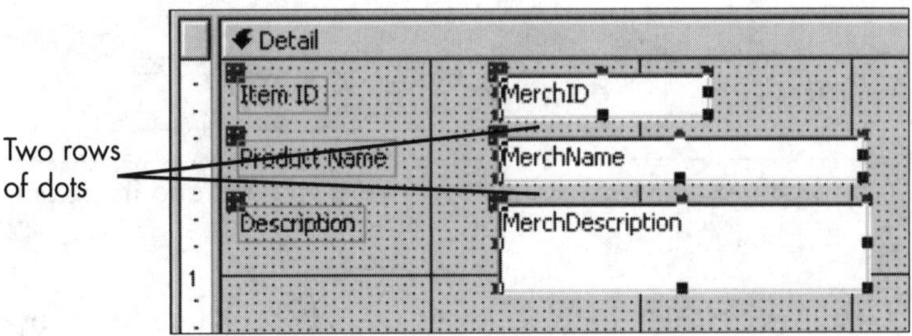

Figure 12.24 You use the Make Equal command to balance the spacing between controls.

You can increase or decrease the spacing between controls by selecting them and using the applicable command from the Vertical Spacing and Horizontal Spacing submenus.

Align

The Align command on the Format menu enables you to align controls to the left, right, top, or bottom. In each case, you must select two or more controls. You can think of the control to which Access aligns as the one with the "mostest." For example, if you select three controls and choose Format, Align, Left (see Figure 12.25), Access aligns two controls to the third that is leftmost (see Figure 12.26).

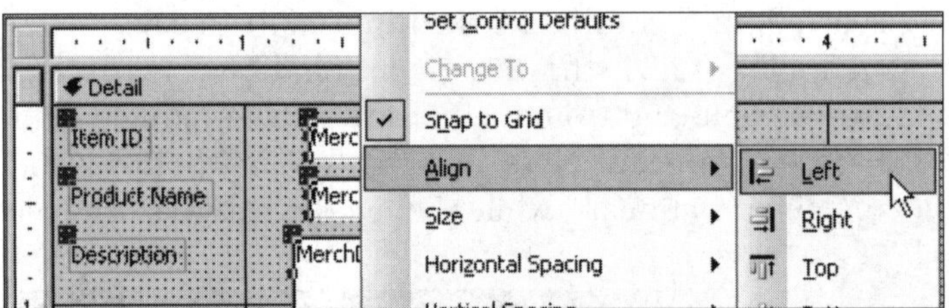

Figure 12.25 The Align commands help you line up controls. Here the MerchID and MerchName text boxes will be aligned left in relation to the MerchDescription text box.

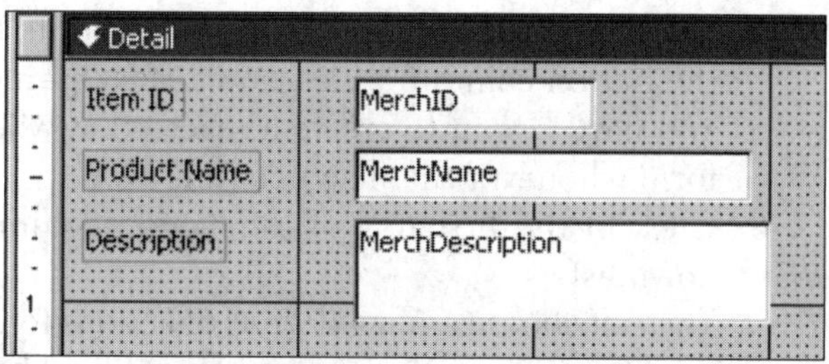

Figure 12.26 The MerchID and MerchName text boxes are now aligned left with the MerchDescription text box.

The Grid

In the background of the form and report design areas is a grid, a scheme of dots. The menu selection View, Grid toggles the grid on and off. New controls will be aligned to the grid, provided that Format, Snap to Grid (another toggle) is selected. Occasionally, you will want to turn off Snap to Grid so you can position controls exactly where you want them.

You can set the number of grid lines per unit of measurement (usually an inch) using the `Grid X` and `Grid Y` properties on the Format tab of the Form property sheet.

Macros

Let's shift gears a bit and take a look at macros.

A macro is an object that automates tasks. It is a set of one or more actions that perform specific operations. That definition, plagiarized from Access Help, gives you little idea of what macros are or how you can use them. Let's create a macro to get a better feel:

1. If the `frmOrders` form is still open, close it and save your changes.
2. In the Database window, click the Macros button and choose New. Unlike other Access objects, there is only this one view for a macro.
3. Press F11 to switch to the Database window. Click the Forms tab.
4. Choose Window, Tile Vertically.

5. Select `frmCustomers`. Drag and drop its icon to the first row of the Action column, which now reads `OpenForm`.
   You have begun to create a macro that will open the `Customers` form whenever the macro is run.
6. Click in the first row of the Action column and open the drop-down list.
   You can choose among dozens of actions to perform. Some of these might appear mysterious and forbidding, but others refer to easily understood actions, such as `PrintOut`, `OpenReport`, and `ShowAllRecords`.
7. Press Tab. In the Comments column, type **Opens frmCustomers**.
   The Comment column in a macro is like the Description column in Table Design view. It's used to provide information to the user, and it is entirely optional.
8. In the lower pane of the Macro window, click the `Form Name` argument.
   The lower pane contains action arguments, which might be (roughly) considered the macro's properties:
   - Form Name is self-explanatory.
   - View is also easy to understand; its drop-down list contains the possible views in which you can open the form.
   - Filter Name enables you to filter the form's records.
   - Where Condition lets you enter criteria that Access will use to select the records.
   - Data Mode determines what you can do with the data after you open it in either Form or Datasheet view. Its settings are Add, Edit, and Read Only.
   - Window Mode is both self-explanatory and difficult to explain. Click it and read the explanation at the right to get a better feel for the possible selections.
     Note that these actions are specific to opening a form, the action you entered in the first row of the top pane. Just as each field you enter in Table Design view has its own set of field properties, depending on data type, each action you enter in the top pane of a macro has its own set of arguments, depending on the action.
9. Click Data Mode and type **a** for "add."
   When the form opens, it displays a blank record and is ready for data entry.

10. Choose File, Save. Name the macro `mcrOpenfrmCustomers` and click OK (see Figure 12.27).
11. Choose Run from the Run menu. The `frmCustomers` form opens in Data Entry mode.
12. Close the `OpenfrmCustomers` macro. Leave the `frmCustomers` form open.

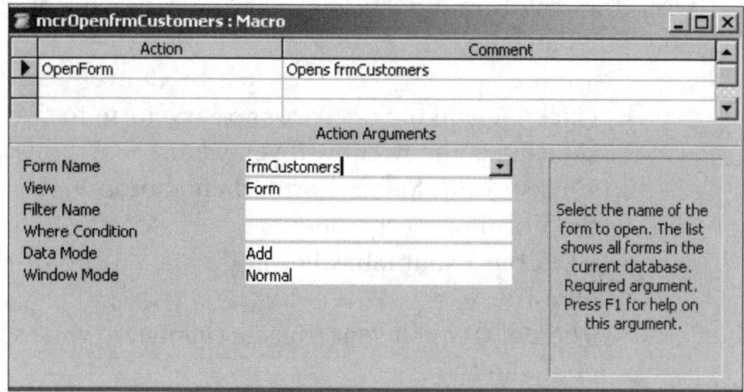

Figure 12.27 The `OpenForm` action with its arguments. (The macro has been resized for a better view.)

Understanding Macros

At this point, you might be thinking, "Great, I just spent 10 minutes doing something complicated that got a form to open. I can open a form with a 2-second excursion to the Database window."

But sometimes you don't want to open a form (or print a report or apply a filter) manually as a standalone action. You want to have a form open automatically when something else is going on: when you open another form, when a control gets the focus, when you exit a report, or when some other action is executed. In cases such as these, you can use the macro you just created to have `frmCustomers` open without your involvement. In other words, a macro is useful for automatically performing an action in a host of situations under varied circumstances.

You can run a macro automatically by assigning it to an event, an action that triggers a macro. A typical event is a mouse click. Whenever you click, say, a particular control, Access runs the macro and executes the operation (or, more often, operations). Other examples of events include opening a window, giving the focus, and pressing a key.

Understanding Events

Let's try an example using an event to trigger the macro. Suppose you'd like to print a `Customers` report whenever you exit the `Customers` form. You can use a macro to execute this two-step task. The first action is opening the report, and the second is printing a range of pages. If you have problems with the macro after completing all the steps, compare yours with the solution `mcrPrintCustRept` in the `NiftyLionsChap12 End.mdb` database.

1. Click View in the open `Customers` form to switch to Design view. (Maximize the window if you want.)
2. Choose Edit, Select Form; then choose View, Properties to open the Form property sheet.
3. Click the Event tab. Click in the `On Close` property and click the ellipsis.
   The `On Close` event triggers the macro you assign to it when you close the form.
4. In the Choose Builder dialog box, select Macro Builder and click OK.
   Choosing Macro Builder in a property sheet is another way of beginning the macro-creation process.
5. In the Save As dialog box, type **mcrPrintCustRept** and click OK.
6. Click in the first row of the Action column. Open the drop-down list and choose OpenReport.
   The drop-down list in the Action column contains the list of available actions. Note that it includes `OpenForm`, the action that Access selected for you in the previous example.
7. Press Tab. In the Comment column, type **Opens the Customers report**.
8. In the action arguments in the lower pane, click Report Name. Open the drop-down list and choose rptCustomers.
9. Click the `View` action argument. Open the drop-down and choose Print Preview.
   If you want to print the entire report immediately, choose Print instead. By selecting Print Preview, you merely open the report.
10. Leaving the second row of the top pane blank, click in the Action column of the third row. Open the drop-down list and choose PrintOut.

You can skip a row or two between actions, just in case you want to use more than one row for a comment. Skipping rows also makes the macro easier to read. Access is indifferent about blank rows: It performs the actions in the order they appear.

11. Press Tab. Type **Prints the Customers report**.
12. In the action arguments, click Print Range. Open the drop-down list and choose Pages.
13. Click in Page From and type **1**. Click Page To and type **1**.
14. Click in the Action column of the fifth row. Open the drop-down list and choose Close.
15. Press Tab. In the Comment column, type **Close the report**.
    This action closes the report after it prints the first page, so you don't have to close it on your own.
16. In the action arguments below, click Object Type, open the drop-down list, and choose Report.
17. Click Object Name, open the drop-down list, and choose rptCustomers (see Figure 12.28).

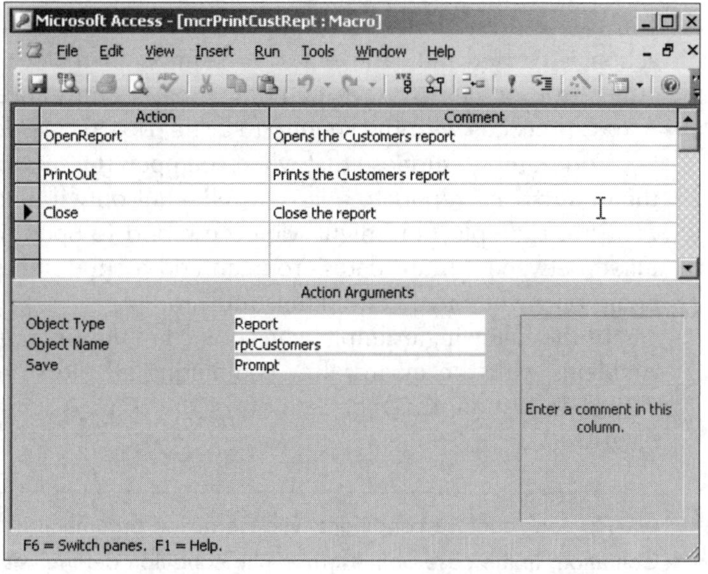

Figure 12.28 It's a good idea to leave a blank row or two between macro steps.

18. Choose File, Save and close the macro window.
19. In `frmCustomers`, choose File, Save.
    If you don't want to run the macro and print the page, skip the next step and the page won't be printed.

20. Click View to switch to Form view.
21. Close the form.

    Access opens the `Customers` report in Print Preview, prints the first page, and then closes it.

Q&A

Q: I don't understand why you're going through all this work to create a macro. I've used macros before. In Word, I turn on the macro recorder, perform the actions I want, and, bing, I've got a macro that runs whenever I press the shortcut key I've assigned to it. Isn't there some kind of feature in Access that lets you build a macro that way?

A: No, there isn't. When you create a macro in Access, you need to use the Macro window, as you just did.

Setting Conditions

You can also add a condition to the macro that determines whether an action is carried out. You enter an expression that can be evaluated as either true or false (or yes or no). If the circumstances are `True/Yes`, Access proceeds with the action; if `False/No`, Access does not.

For example, suppose that when you open the `Orders` form, you want the `Customers` report to open as well—but only if a certain condition is met. For example, you might want the report to open only if orders were made between certain dates. You can add a condition so that the report opens only when that condition is fulfilled.

In the following example, you set a condition in a macro. (If you have problems with the macro after completing all the steps, compare yours with the solution `mcrOrdersCust` in the `NiftyLionsChap12End.mdb` database.)

NOTE Don't confuse conditions with the action argument of the Where Condition. In the case of the former, the condition determines whether an action will be taken. In the case of the latter, you know that that an action will be taken. When the action is executed, the Where Condition limits the records retrieved to those that meet certain criteria.

1. In the Database window, open the tblOrders table and look at the `Order Date` field. Note that orders were made between July 16, 2004, and September 10, 2004. Close the Orders table.
2. In the Database window, click Macros and click New.
3. Click in the Action column. Open the drop-down list and choose OpenForm.
4. Press Tab. In the Comment column, type **Opens the Orders form**.
   Remember, a comment is only "for your information"; it does not affect the action, and it is not required.
5. In the action arguments below, click Form Name, open the drop-down list, and choose frmOrders.
6. Choose View, Conditions. The Condition column is displayed.
7. Click in the third row of the Condition column and type the following expression: **[Forms]![frmOrders]![OrderDate] Between #16-Jul-2004# And #10-Sep-2004#**.
   This expression is comprised of the following components:
   - `[Forms]![frmOrders]![OrderDate]` is the identifier for the field that the expression applies to. I briefly mentioned identifiers in Chapter 7, "Find and Filter." Note its syntax. `[Forms]` is a general identifier for forms and is followed by an exclamation point. `[frmOrders]` is the form name, also followed by an exclamation point. `[OrderDate]` is the name of the text box or the control that contains order date values.
   - `Between...And` is the operator that finds a range of numbers, dates, and so on.
   - The dates of `16-Jul-2004` and `10-Sep-2004` are literal values that are enclosed in pound signs.
8. Press Tab. Open the drop-down list in Action and choose OpenReport.
9. Press Tab. In the Comment column, type **Opens only if the Orders form has records between certain dates**.
   This comment will still be true if you decide later to edit the dates in the condition.
10. In the action arguments below, click Report Name, open the drop-down list, and choose rptCustomers.
11. Click in the View argument, open the drop-down list, and choose Print Preview.

12. Choose File, Save and save the macro as `mcrOrdersCust`. Close the macro.
13. In the Database window, click Macros and double-click `mcrOrdersCust`. The form and report open.
14. Close the form and report.
15. Open `mcrOrdersCust` in Design view.
16. Click in the condition you wrote. Press Shift+F2 to open the Zoom window.
17. Edit the first date in the condition to **7/18/2004** (see Figure 12.29).

    Remember, the form contains records from July 16, 2004, so the condition is now `False`.

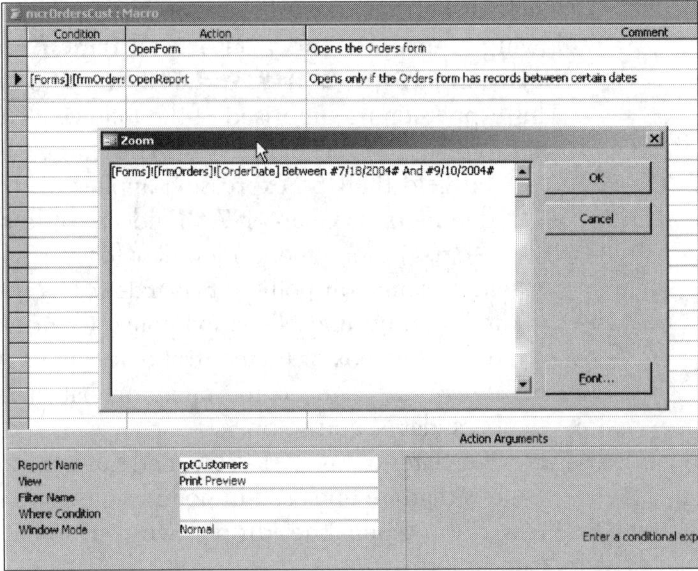

Figure 12.29 You can add a condition to a macro so that an action is run only if the condition is true.

18. Click OK. Close the macro and save your changes.
19. Double-click `mcrOrdersCust` to run it.

    Because the condition for opening the report is `False`, only the `Orders` form opens, not the report.
20. Close the `Orders` form.

Macro Groups

A macro group comprises several related macros, each with its own name. Bundling macros in a group is a good way to organize them so they can be easily found and used. Otherwise, building macros with macro groups is the same as building macros. The case example at the end of the chapter has an extended example of how to use macro groups.

Single Step Tool

Finally, let's take a look at a tool Access provides to troubleshoot macros. It's inevitable that you'll create macros that won't work on your first, second, or even eleventh try. Not only must you be painstaking in entering the various conditions and arguments for each action, but you must also be sure to include every action, in the proper sequence. At some point, you're going to assume that Access just knows that an action needs to be performed—you have to open the report before you print it, right?—and you won't bother to include specific instructions. But Access knows no such thing. It won't perform any action unless it is explicitly told to do so.

Here's where the Single Step tool becomes invaluable. As the name implies, it takes you step by step through each action so you can spot the error(s) you've made.

There's no error in `mcrOrders`, which matches the macro `mcrOrdersCust` macro you created earlier. But you can use the Single Step tool to go through it and see how the tool works:

1. Click Macros in the Database window.
2. Select `mcrOrders` and click Design.
3. Click Single Step on the toolbar and click Run on the toolbar. The Macro Single Step dialog box is displayed (see Figure 12.30).
   The action name is `OpenForm`, the first action. Note that the condition is `True`, even though you didn't enter a specific condition for the `OpenForm` action. This merely means that the action can be executed.
   The Halt button is self-explanatory, but how does Step compare with Continue? Use Step to run the current action and move to the next action. Use Continue to cancel Single Step and run the entire macro without stopping.

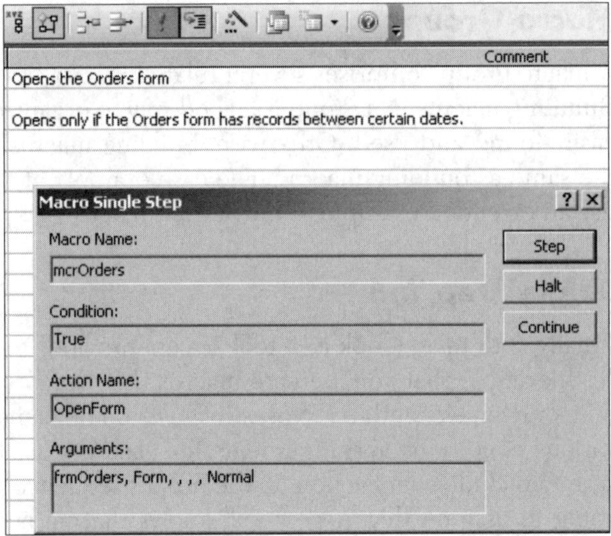

Figure 12.30 The Single Step tool can help you find out why your macro doesn't work.

4. Click Step.
   Access opens the form. The details for the next action of `OpenReport` are displayed. Because the condition is `False` (the report includes records before 7/18/2004), the next action will not be executed.
5. Click Continue to end Single Step. Close the macro and close the form.

Multipage Forms

Sometimes a single form comprises two or more groups of data that you'd like to segregate in some fashion. There are several ways to accomplish that objective. Often design tools, such as a rectangle or a line, can be used successfully to divide data.

In other cases, you'll want to take more radical steps and divide the form into separate pages. The less interesting and more mundane method is to include page breaks in the form. The more innovative technique is to use a tab control that accomplishes the objective of creating separate pages without actually creating any additional pages.

I don't want to imply that tabbed controls are necessarily better than page breaks. Each has its uses, and, depending on your form design, you might be better served by a page break. For example, you can use page breaks to create multiscreen forms on which each page is the same size and each window shows only one page at a time. But I think that tabbed pages can often accomplish the same objectives more efficiently.

Page Breaks

A page break forces a new page in a form or report. Let's assume that your form has two pages so that each record is presented in two pages. You're in the first of the two pages. When you press Page Down, the text immediately following the page break appears at the top of your screen. Note that a page break is in effect only in Form View when the `Default View` property (which is on the Format tab of the Form property sheet) is set to Single View.

To create a page break, click the Page Break control in the toolbox, drag it to the form, position the crosshairs, and click. The page break will be selected; click anywhere away from it to see the page break (see Figure 12.31).

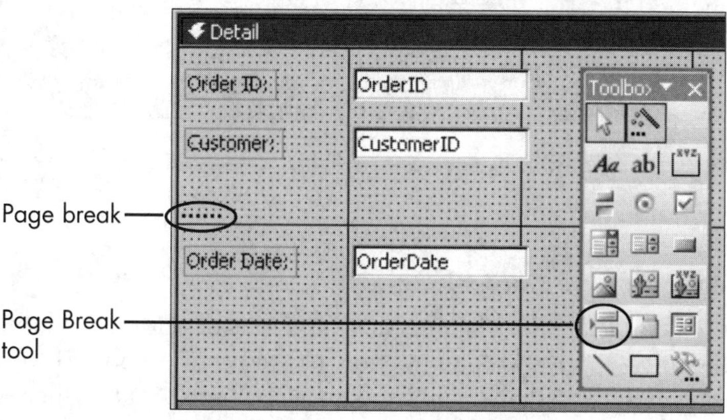

Figure 12.31 You can use page breaks to create multipage forms.

Tab Controls

Tab controls are an efficient method of segregating and presenting lots of data in a relatively small area. The `Employees` form in the Northwind database is a good example of the effective use of a tab control (see Figure 12.32). The Company Info page contains fields such as `Hire Date` and `Reports To`; the Personal Info page has fields such as `Home Phone` and `Birth Date`. As you will have guessed, you switch pages by clicking the tabs. The tabbed pages usefully separate different types of data, efficiently using the available space.

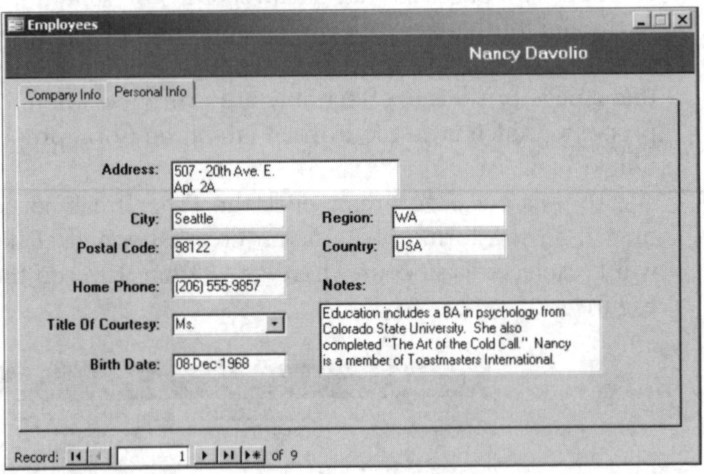

Figure 12.32 The `Employees` form uses a tab control to present employee data in two tabbed pages.

Creating a Tab Control

You can add tabs by clicking the Tab Control button in the toolbox and dragging it to the Design section (see Figure 12.33). If you click and release at the crosshairs, you'll create a tab control that's 2 inches by 2 inches and that has two tabbed pages. More likely, you'll want to position the crosshairs where you want the top-left corner, and then click and drag across and down for tab pages with dimensions that suit your needs.

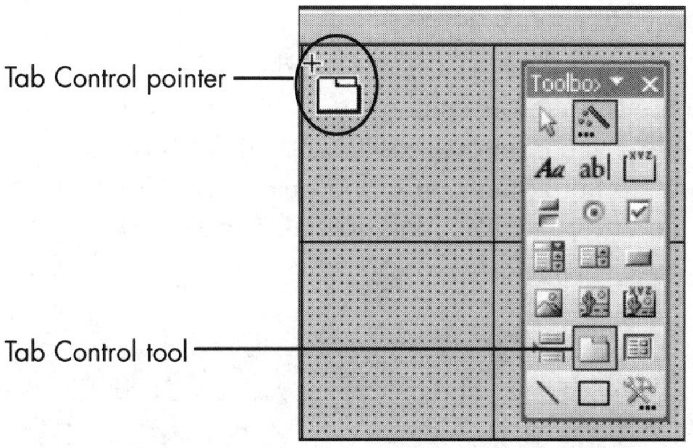

Figure 12.33 A tab control is initially created with two tabbed pages.

Although it's less complex than the option group you met in Chapter 11, a tab control has a number of separate elements, each with its own property sheet. Specifically, each page has its own property sheet, and the tab control as a whole has a property sheet. When you want to choose a page, click directly on its tab. When you want to choose the tab control, click to the right of the tabs (see Figure 12.34). As always, make sure you're using the correct property sheet by checking the title.

You can easily replace the numbered page name (such as Page1) on the tabs by right-clicking the tab and selecting View, Properties, Other tab and typing a new name (see Figure 12.34). If you'd like a caption on the tab separate from the name, use the `Caption` property on the Format tab.

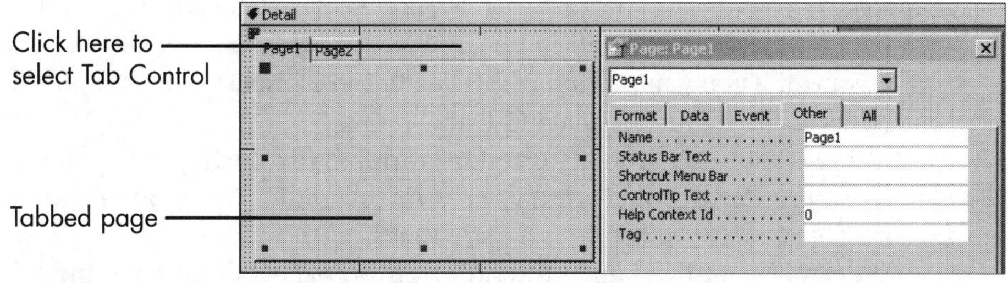

Figure 12.34 The Page1 tab page (not the tab control) is selected. You can create a new name for the tabbed page by using the `Name` property in the property sheet.

Adding Controls to Tab Pages

To add a field to a tab page, just drag and drop it onto the tab page. You can also use the tools in the toolbox.

One problem you might have with adding fields is that, by default, grid lines and dots do not appear on tabbed pages. But that situation is easily rectified: Select the tab control and open its property sheet. On the Format tab, edit the `Back Style` to Transparent (see Figure 12.35).

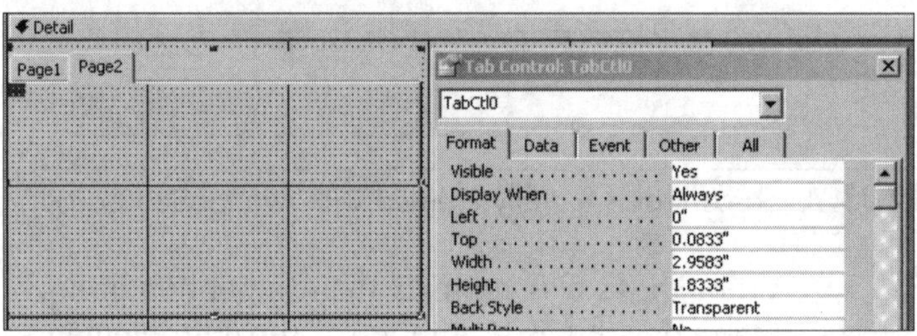

Figure 12.35 You can add grid lines and dots to the tabbed pages.

Other Tab Tasks

It's unfortunate that in Access the same word can have a variety of meanings. One such word is *groups*: You have groups in the Database window, groups of controls, groups in reports, and so on. Another example is *tab*. When you right-click the tab control, there's a command for Tab Order. This is the same dialog box that's available from the View menu, and it has nothing to do with tab controls (see Figure 12.36). Instead, you use the command to change the order in which Access moves the focus from control to control when you press the Tab key (a topic discussed in Chapter 6, "Entering, Editing, and Displaying Data").

From the same right-click (or, more formally, context) menu, you can choose Insert Page to add a new page to the right of the other pages. Choose Delete Page to delete the page that is currently selected.

You can also easily change the order of the pages. Right-click the tab control and choose Page Order. Use the Move Up and Move Down keys to change the sequence of the pages.

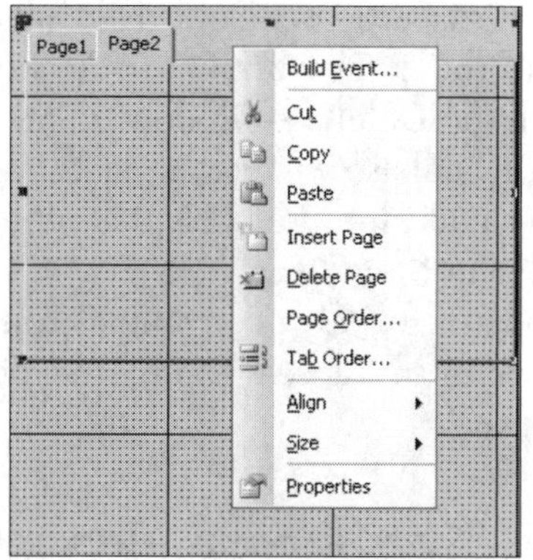

Figure 12.36 The context menu offers a variety of commands.

Switchboard Manager

When you open the Northwind sample database, the first thing you see is the switchboard shown in Figure 12.37. (I've assumed you've already told Access not to show the Welcome window again.) A switchboard is a fast way to perform your most common and useful Access tasks. As in the Northwind database, you usually want to display a switchboard at startup so you can get right to work. (I show you how to get Access to do that in the upcoming section "Displaying the Switchboard at Startup.")

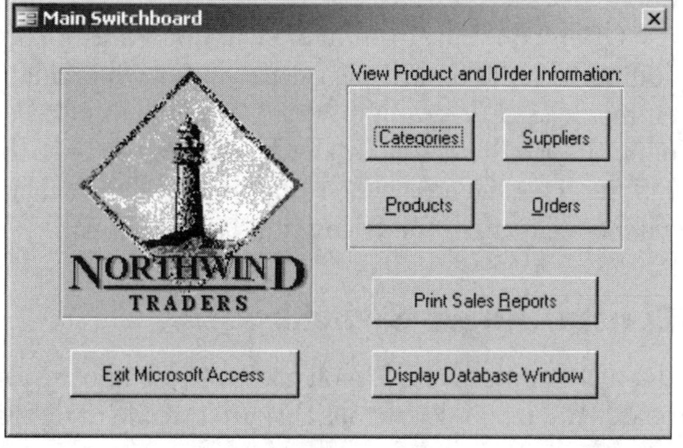

Figure 12.37 A switchboard is an easy-to-use form for performing Access tasks.

Switchboards are especially helpful for new users who have little knowledge of the inner workings of Access and have no desire or need to contend with the Database window. In fact, if you have a switchboard, you can hide the Database window altogether. It's not the best form of security; but it does make it more likely that other users will work with only those objects you want them to.

Switchboards are also convenient timesavers for experienced Access users. They offer fast access to objects you use most often so you can get to work quickly.

Using the Switchboard Manager

From a construction point of view, a switchboard is a form composed almost entirely of command buttons that run macros. In early versions of Access, you had to build a switchboard from scratch, but now you can use the Switchboard Manager, available from the Tools, Database Utilities menu. For the most part, you can create your switchboard just by selecting options in its dialog boxes. A little knowledge of some simple macros is helpful in building switchboards.

From a theoretical or conceptual standpoint, the Switchboard Manager is not difficult to use. But it is can be confusing, and it's easy to get lost in it. As you work through the steps in the following example, pay special attention to the titles of the various dialog boxes; they can help you fix your position in the switchboard-making process. I've included notes after many of the steps, to let you know why you're doing what you're doing.

Often you'll use the main switchboard as a launch point for creating additional switchboard pages; the latter will contain the buttons for executing tasks. For example, the Main Switchboard could have a button to open the Products switchboard, where you could then open the Products report. (Don't worry if you don't understand what I'm talking about—it will become apparent as you build a switchboard.)

Constructing a Switchboard

In the following example, you add two switchboard pages to the main switchboard. You then add buttons that are specific to the switchboard page.

1. In the `NiftyLionsChap12.mdb` database, choose Tools, Database Utilities, Switchboard Manager. Click Yes when the Switchboard Manager asks if you'd like to create a switchboard.

2. Click New in the Switchboard Manager dialog box.
3. In the Create New dialog box, type **Customers** and click OK.
   You've created the first of two switchboard pages that will be accessed from the main switchboard.
4. Click New. Type **Orders** and click OK (see Figure 12.38).

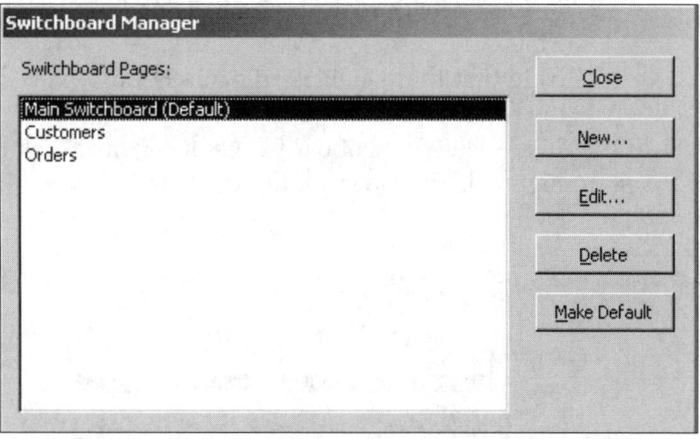

Figure 12.38 In the Switchboard Manager dialog box, you see all of your switchboard pages.

   You've created the second of two switchboard pages that will be accessed from the main switchboard.
5. With Main Switchboard (Default) selected, click Edit.
6. In the Edit Switchboard Page dialog box, click New.
   You are now adding buttons to the Main Switchboard that will send you to the Customers and Orders pages.
7. In the Edit Switchboard Item dialog box, enter **Edit/Print Customer Data** in the Text box. Keep the Go to Switchboard command. At Switchboard, open the drop-down list and choose Customers. Click OK.
   You've created a button on the Main Switchboard that says Edit/Print Customer Data. When you click it, the Customers page appears.
8. In the Edit Switchboard Page dialog box, click New.
9. In the Edit Switchboard Item dialog box, edit Text to **Edit/Print Order Data**. Keep the Go to Switchboard command. At Switchboard, open the drop-down list and choose Orders. Click OK.

You've created a button on the main switchboard that says Edit/Print Order Data. When you click it, the Orders page appears.

Now you'll create buttons on each of the subsidiary switchboard pages to perform tasks.

1. In the Edit Switchboard Page dialog box, click Close.
2. In the Switchboard Manager dialog box, select Customers. Click Edit.
   Note that the switchboard name is Customers. You're working on the Customers page.
3. In the Edit Switchboard Page dialog box, click New.
   Figure 12.39 shows all three dialog boxes you have been working with.

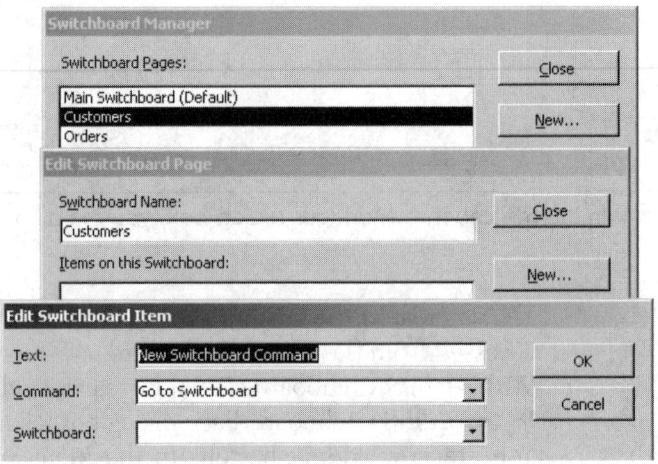

Figure 12.39 When you create a switchboard, keep a careful eye on which dialog box you're working in; it's easy to lose your bearings.

4. In the Text box, change the text to **Edit Customer Data**. At Command, open the drop-down list and choose Open Form in Edit Mode. At Form, open the drop-down list and choose frmCustomersSwitch.
   You created a button on the Customers page that will open the `frmCustomersSwitch` form so you can edit customer records.
5. Click OK. In Edit Switchboard Page, click New.
6. Edit Text to **Return to Main Switchboard**. In Command, keep Go to Switchboard. Open the drop-down list for Switchboard and choose Main Switchboard.

The Go to Switchboard command is convenient for returning to switchboards from other switchboard pages.

7. Click OK. Click Close in the Edit Switchboard Page dialog box.
8. In the Switchboard Manager dialog box, select Orders. Click Edit. Now you'll add buttons to the Orders page.
9. In the Edit Switchboard Page dialog box, click New.
10. At Text, type **Edit Order Data**. For Command, select Open Form in Edit Mode. For Form, select frmOrdersSwitch. Click OK.
11. In the Edit Switchboard Page dialog box, click New.
12. Edit Text to **Print Order Data**. For Command, select Run Macro. For Macro, select mcrPrintOrdersReport.
    The `mcrPrintOrdersReport` macro is a simple macro that opens and prints the first page of the `Orders` report. If you've read the previous section on macros, you should have no trouble understanding it. For our immediate purposes, simply note how you attached this macro to a button.
13. Click OK. In Edit Switchboard Page, click New.
14. Edit Text to **Return to Main Switchboard**. In Command, keep Go to Switchboard. Open the drop-down list for Switchboard and choose Main Switchboard.
15. Click OK. Click Close in the Edit Switchboard Page dialog box. Click Close in the Switchboard Manager dialog box.
16. Click Forms and double-click Switchboard to open it (see Figure 12.40). Assuming you haven't renamed the database, your own title will be NiftyLionsChap12.

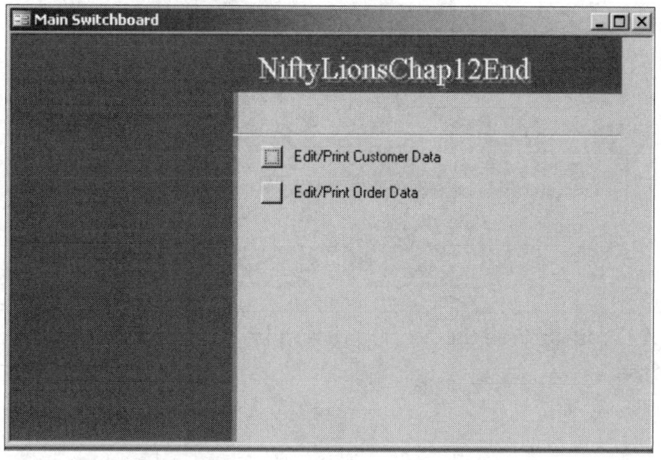

Figure 12.40 The main switchboard of the switchboard you created.

17. Click Edit/Print Customer Data.
18. Click Return to Main Switchboard
    You can see the usefulness of including buttons that return or send you to other switchboards.
19. Click Edit/Print Order Data.
20. If your printer is set up, click Print Order Data.
    The first page of the `Orders` report prints.
21. Close the `Orders` report and close the switchboard.

NOTE When you create a switchboard, you also acquire a Switchboard Items table. For the most part, you can ignore it, and it shouldn't otherwise interfere with your work. But don't be surprised by its presence.

Displaying the Switchboard at Startup

The Startup dialog box, available from the Tools menu, controls how Access looks and acts when you open it. The options apply only to the current database.

You can use the Startup dialog box to display the Switchboard when Access opens (see Figure 12.41). From Display Form/Page, you open the drop-down list and choose Switchboard. If you want, you can also deselect Display Database Window.

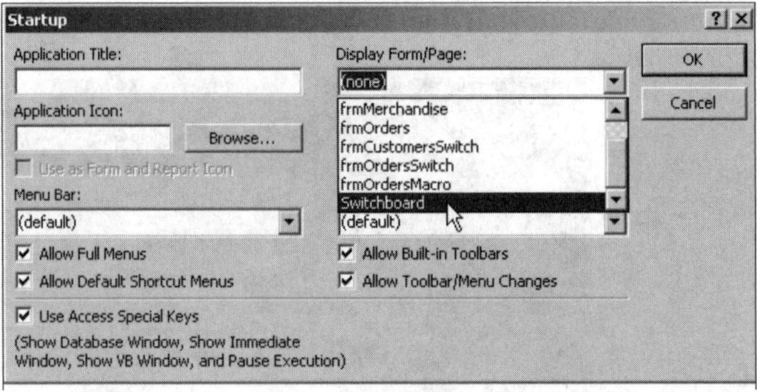

Figure 12.41 You can use the Startup dialog box to open the switchboard when you open the database.

NOTE There's another way to open a form and execute other actions when you open an Access database. Create a macro and include any actions you want performed in that particular database at startup. Save the macro and name it `AutoExec`. When you open the file, Access runs this macro. Note that the `AutoExec` macro runs after the Startup options have taken effect, so be careful about using both. If your only goal is to have the Switchboard displayed at startup, I think it's easier to use Display Form/Page in the Startup dialog box.

Other Report Types

The Label Wizard and snaked column reports are two Access report features that are worth spending some time on. Let's look at how they work.

Label Wizard

The Label Wizard is a handy device for quickly creating mailing labels. It's easy to use, and I'm not going to drag you through the many options in its dialog boxes; either they are self-explanatory or their mysteries can be unraveled with some trial and error.

But one dialog box might cause you some problems, at least initially. This is the "construction" dialog box where you actually create the label (see Figure 12.42).

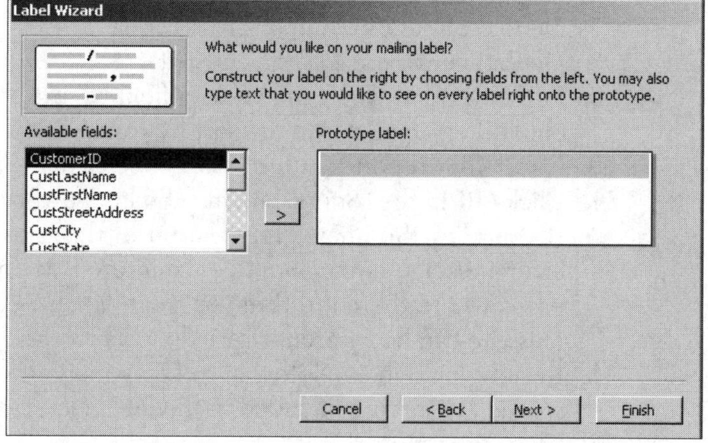

Figure 12.42 In this dialog box, you build a prototype label that uses your contact data.

Besides the fields (first name, street address, and so on) that you include in the label, you'll almost always need to include some spaces or a little punctuation, such as a comma. Here's what you need to remember: Access assumes nothing. If you want a space between first and last names, you have to put it in there—you need to press the spacebar. If you want a comma, you must press the comma key. Access won't do it for you. You can also include in the label a text string—say, `Attention:`—by typing it in on your own.

Out of context, that probably doesn't make much sense. The following example should make things clearer:

1. In the Database window, select tblCustomers. Choose Insert, Report.
2. In the New Report dialog box, select Label Wizard and click OK.
3. Keeping the default selections in the first two dialog boxes, click Next twice to reach the dialog box asking "What would you like on your mailing label?" (refer to Figure 12.42).
4. Double-click CustFirstName to include it in the `Prototype` label. Tap the spacebar once to leave a space. Double-click `CustLastName`. Press Enter.
5. Double-click `CustStreetAddress` and press Enter.
6. Double-click `CustCity`. Type a comma and press the spacebar once.
   Actually, the U.S. Postal Service doesn't require or even recommend a comma after the city in postal addresses. I've included it simply to show you how you can include characters in the label.
7. Double-click `CustState`. Press Enter.
8. Double-click `CustZIP`. Click Next.
9. In this window, you can choose a field to sort by. Click Next without adding any fields to the sort by pane.
10. Name your report `rptCustomerLabels` and click Finish.
11. Click OK in the "Some data may be lost" error message.
    If you click the Show Help button in this message, it says "This error message is commonly encountered when printing to label pages where there are three or more labels per row. Usually this message can be ignored." Let's do what Access suggests.
12. Review your labels. Note that the punctuation you entered and the spaces you left are included in the label (see Figure 12.43).
13. Close the report.

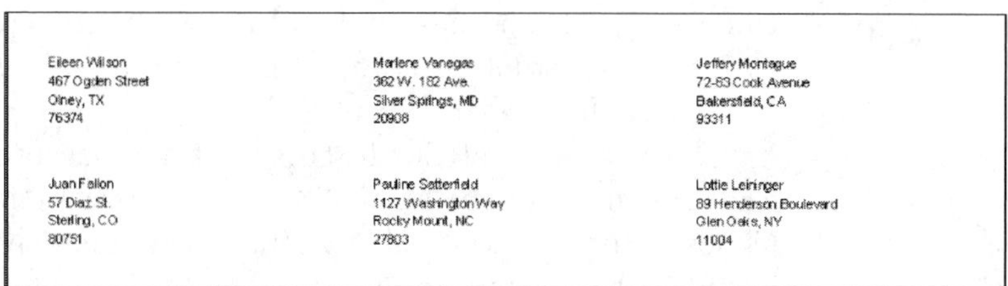

Figure 12.43 The labels include the data from the fields in the underlying table, as well as any text you entered yourself.

Snaked Column Reports

The columnar report that Access produces when you select AutoReport has just one column at the left of the page. That's fine if you want extra room for writing notes or scribbling doodles. But often the empty space is left unused, which leaves your report with a lopsided look. It also wastes paper.

You can often add one or more columns to the page for greater symmetry and efficiency. These multicolumn reports are called "snaked" (for reasons that will soon become obvious, if they are not so already). Snaked column reports require a little know-how and some patience for the trial and error necessary to get the columns in the right proportions. But after you gain some experience, you shouldn't have much trouble creating or editing them.

First, let's create a report whose data you can snake:

1. In the `NiftyLionsChap12.mdb` Database window, click Reports and click New.
2. With Design view selected at the top, open the drop-down list and select tblCustomers. Click OK.
3. Maximize the Report Design window.
4. Choose View, Page Header/Footer to eliminate these two sections.
5. Select `CustLastName` in the field list. While holding down the Shift key, click `CustZip` to select these two fields and all in between.
6. Drag and drop the six selected fields 1 inch from the left and two rows of dots from the top.

7. Choose View, Properties. In the Multiple Selection property sheet, click the Format tab. Edit the `Left` property to 1". Edit `Width` to 1.5". Close the property sheet.
   I had you widen all the text boxes a bit because the `Street Address` and (perhaps) `Last Name` fields were a little narrow.
8. Choose Format, Vertical Spacing, Increase. Choose Format, Vertical Spacing, Increase again.
9. Click outside the controls to deselect them.
10. Select all the accompanying labels.
    Try using the "pointer in the ruler" method you learned in this chapter for selecting controls in a column. (Alternatively, just click each label while holding down the Shift key.)
11. Press F4 to open the Multiple Selection property sheet. Edit the `Left` property to `.04"`. Close the property sheet.
12. Choose File, Save. Name your report **rptSnakedColumn** and click OK.
    Your design window should look like Figure 12.44.
    Click View to see your records.

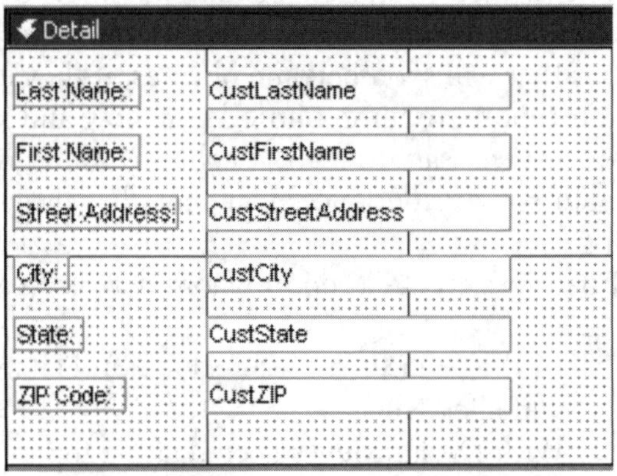

Figure 12.44 You can use a variety of methods to add and align controls.

Now you'll snake the report:

1. Choose File, Page Setup, Margins tab. All the settings should be 1 inch.
2. Click the Columns tab.

The settings don't require much explanation. Let me just emphasize that Row Spacing is the amount of space between rows, and Column Spacing is the amount of spacing between columns. The Column Spacing setting is not available unless the number of columns is greater than one.

3. Edit the number of columns to 2, the row spacing to 0.3" and the column spacing to 2".
4. In the Column Size section, deselect Same as Detail. Edit the width to 2"; the height should be 2".
5. You can "snake" the records either across or down, or down and across. Let's use the Across, then down selection.
6. Click OK. The report now has two columns (see Figure 12.45). Note that only the contents of the Detail section of the report are snaked. Page Headers and Footers are not.

   If you want, print a page of the report to test your work. Close the report and save your changes.

Last Name:	Wilson	Last Name:	Vanegas
First Name:	Eileen	First Name:	Marlene
Street Address:	467 Ogden Street	Street Address:	362 W. 182 Ave.
City:	Olney	City:	Silver Springs
State:	TX	State:	MD
ZIP Code:	76374	ZIP Code:	20908

Figure 12.45 You can save space and often create a more handsome report by using snaked columns.

With a little more work, and if you were willing to let a few values be truncated slightly, you could get three columns on the page. (Another possibility would be to decrease the font size of the controls so you could reduce the width of the columns.) To fit more columns, you reduce the sizes of Column Spacing and Width.

TIP Actually, the best strategy for fitting in more columns would be to get rid of the labels. The contents of most or all of the fields are obvious, so labels are unnecessary.

Conclusion

This chapter covered a wide range of topics to help you create more effective forms and reports. Form and report creation might seem like a tedious affair, at best, but over time, many of the tools and procedures will become second nature to you. Access features and wizards have made form and report creation extremely efficient. Instead of attempting to edit an object that has significant problems, it is often easier to give yourself a fresh start by using a wizard or a blank form.

Case Example

Earlier in this chapter, you learned how to automate actions by using macros. In this example, you'll use a macro group to help you create command buttons that open sets of records in a form. Specifically, you'll create buttons on an orders form to filter for regular delivery and overnight orders. This exercise also exposes you to creating and using command buttons. I haven't discussed command buttons separately, but (as you'll see) you shouldn't have any trouble figuring them out on your own.

First, let's create the macro group:

1. In the Database window, click the Macros tab and click New.
2. Choose View, Macro Names. The Macro Names column is displayed. You toggle the Macro Names column on and off by choosing View, Macro Names.
3. In the first row of the Macro Names column, type **yes**. Press Tab.
4. In the Action column, open the drop-down list and choose ApplyFilter. Press Tab.
5. In the Comment column, type **Filter** for overnight clients.
6. In the Where Condition of the action arguments, type **[Overnight]=yes**.
   This is an expression that creates criteria for the action. It tells Access to select those records whose value is `Yes` in the field `Overnight`.
7. In the third row, click in Macro Name and type **no**. Press Tab.
8. In Action, open the drop-down list and choose ApplyFilter. Press Tab.
9. In Comment, type **Filter** for regular delivery.
10. Click in Where Condition. Type **[Overnight]=no**.
11. In the fifth row, click in Macro Name and type **all**. Press Tab.
12. In Action, type **sh** to choose ShowAllRecords. Press Tab.
    Note that no action arguments are available for this action.

13. In Comment, type **Shows both overnight and regular delivery records**.
    Your macro should look like Figure 12.46.
14. Save the macro group. Type **mcrDeliveryMethod** and click OK.
15. Close the group macro.

Macro Name	Action	
yes	ApplyFilter	Filter for overnight clients
no	ApplyFilter	Filter for regular delivery
all	ShowAllRecords	Shows both overnight and regular delivery records

Figure 12.46 A group macro contains several macros, each with their own names.

Now you'll create command buttons on the form to filter for regular delivery and overnight orders. You'll also include a button to show all records.

1. Open the `frmOrdersMacro` form in Design view.
2. Click the Command Button tool (it's in the last column and fourth row of the toolbox). Move the pointer 3 inches from the top and 0.5 inch from the left, and click.
3. In the Command Button Wizard, click Miscellaneous in the left pane. Click Run Macro in the right pane. Click Next.
   In this dialog box, you determined the action of the command button.
4. Choose mcrDeliveryMethod.no and click next.
   In this dialog box, you selected the appropriate macro. The macro name comprises the group macro name and the individual macro.
5. Click Text. Highlight Run Macro and type **Regular**; click Next.
   In this dialog box, you put text on the button to identify it in the form.
6. Name the button **RegularDelivery**. Click Finish.
   Now you'll create the two other buttons for retrieving orders.
7. Click the Command Button tool. Move the pointer 3 inches from the top and 1.5 inches from the left, and click.
8. In the Command Button Wizard, click Miscellaneous in the left pane. Click Run Macro in the right pane. Click Next.
9. Choose mcrDeliveryMethod.yes and click Next.
10. Click Text. Highlight Run Macro and type **Overnight**. Click Next.
11. Name the button **OvernightDelivery**. Click Finish.
12. Click the Command Button tool. Move the pointer 3 inches from the top and 2.5 inches from the left, and click.
13. In the Command Button Wizard, click Miscellaneous in the left pane. Click Run Macro in the right pane. Click Next.
14. Choose DeliveryMethod.all and click Next.

15. Click Text. Highlight Run Macro and type **All Orders**. Click Next.
16. Name the button **AllOrders**. Click Finish.
17. Choose File, Save to save your changes. Your Design window should look similar to Figure 12.47.

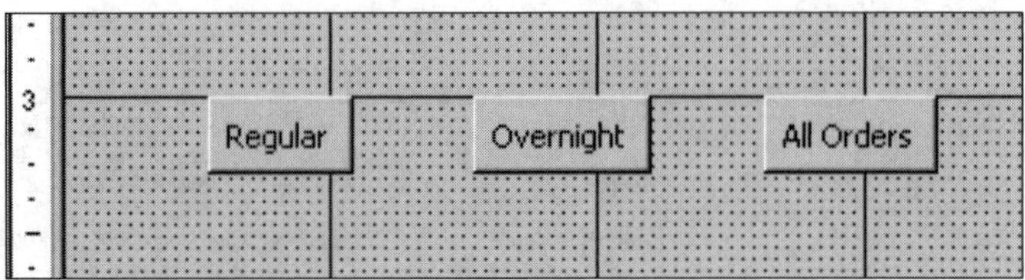

Figure 12.47 The command buttons in Design view.

18. Click View to switch to Form view.
    Try out the various filter buttons you created. The Overnight records should have a check in the Overnight check box. There are 33 total orders, of which 2 were shipped overnight.
19. Choose Records, Remove Filter/Sort to remove any filters you applied.
20. Close the form and close your database.

You can compare any of the objects you created in this chapter to those in `NiftyLionsChap12End.mdb`.

CHAPTER 13

Importing and Exporting

When you create an Access database, it's possible (perhaps even likely) that much of your data already exists in electronic form. It could be in another Access database or a database of another software maker. It could be in another Office program, such as Word or Excel. Or it could be on the Internet or in some other computing environment.

It's equally possible that, although you store and manipulate your data in an Access database, you will ultimately use the data in some other milieu. The final destination could be in another program on your own computer, such as a mail-merge document in Word. Or it could be an external audience, such as a client who will look at your billings only if they're in Excel.

In this chapter, I discuss ways of making external data available to an Access database, and making data in an Access database available to non-Access users and outside environments. That's a long-winded way of saying that this chapter discusses importing and exporting. But it's also more precise because I describe linking as well, which occupies some middle ground between those two activities. You were already exposed to linking in Chapter 12, "Form/Report Design Elements," where I discussed how it compares with embedding objects in forms and reports. But here the emphasis is linking external data sources as tables so they become active parts of an Access database.

Import/Export Overview

Just as import/export firms have different methods for transferring goods (air, rail ground), as an Access importer and exporter, you can choose among various transport methods. As always in Windows, cut and paste is a simple, powerful, and convenient device for moving data and objects between two Access databases or Access and an external environment. Drag-and-drop can sometimes be an alternative to copy-and-paste. The

Office Links command from the Tools menu is an excellent way of quickly sending Access data to Word and Excel. Perhaps most often, however, you'll work with Access import and export wizards, whose dialog boxes make it relatively easy to move data in and out of Access files.

As in international trade, exporting and importing in Access are not truly separate actions, but rather opposing halves of the same activity. Exporters of, say, machine tools, pharmaceuticals, and foodstuffs have to work closely with importers to make sure their products are compatible with local laws, tastes, and customs. Similarly, you'll be a more successful Access exporter if you have a good knowledge of the target program. Importing data into Access goes much more smoothly if you diligently perform preliminary spade work in the source program to make sure the data complies fully with Access rules. These rules include both Access conventions and specific field and table properties.

Another important question in this area is whether you should begin the import/export process from the external program or start the transfer in Access. Because this is an Access book, I focus on Access as the initiator in both exporting and importing. But by no means is this emphasis rigorously applied. The ultimate goal is to make your computing work easier, so some exercises are partially or even primarily performed in other Office programs—notably, Word and Excel.

NOTE After completing an exercise, I often ask you to save the file. You can then compare your work to the solution file of the same name that you downloaded. However, none of the exercises depends on another, so you can ignore saving the file and still complete all other exercises.

Move Access Data to a Word Processor or Text Editor

You can easily send Access records to a word processor (most notably, Microsoft Word) or a text editor. Sometimes you want the records in a file type such as RTF or DOC, to preserve table formatting. Other times you want the records to be in TXT files, which contain no formatting so they can be easily manipulated or re-exported to another program or computing environment.

Perhaps the most important way Access and Word are used together is in a mail merge to create form letters. (The term form letter is often used pejoratively, but here I simply mean letters with similar content sent to a number of recipients.) The increasingly automated mail-merge tool in Microsoft Word has made form letters easier than ever to create. But the process is still not completely intuitive, so I have provided an extended exercise on mail merges in the Case Example at the end of the chapter.

In this section, I focus on the various ways you can move Access records to word-processing and text files.

Cut and Paste

Sometimes you want to move just a few records from Access to Word. An easy way to do that is copy and paste. If you paste records into Word, you can do a plain-vanilla paste or use the Paste Special command to modify the formatting.

Plain Vanilla

Let's try a plain-vanilla copy and paste first.

1. Download the `NiftyLionsChap13.mdb` file from the companion website and open the database.
2. From the Database window, open the tblCustomers table.
   Note that the First Name column is rather wide for the relatively short values it holds.
3. Select the first four records.
4. Right-click and choose Copy.
5. Open Word. Right-click and choose Paste to insert the records.
   Access pastes the records as a table that includes the table name and field names. You can easily delete these elements, as described in the next step.
   Also note that the column widths have been resized to fit the available space in Word.
6. In Word, highlight the first two rows, which contain the tblCustomers title and field names. Right-click and choose Delete Rows (see Figure 13.1).
7. Save the Word document as `PasteCustomers.doc`. Close the document.

1	Wilson	Eileen	467 Ogden Street	Olney	TX	76374	(940) 555-3753	(940) 555-0814
2	Vanegas	Marlene	362 W. 182 Ave.	Silver Springs	MD	20908	(227) 555-8237	(227) 555-1211
3	Montague	Jeffery	72-63 Cook Avenue	Bakersfield	CA	93311	(661) 555-0248	
4	Fallon	Juan	57 Diaz St.	Sterling	CO	80751	(970) 555-7532	(970) 555-4485

Figure 13.1 A simple cut and paste of Access records into Word.

NOTE You could have accomplished the same task by using drag and drop. Open Word and then select the records in the tblCustomers table. Move the mouse directly below any column selector. When the mouse pointer becomes a white arrow (see Figure 13.2), drag the rows to the Word button on the Windows taskbar. Windows switches to Word, and you then can drop the selected records into the document. Alternatively, you can tile Access and Word windows, and then drag the records from Access to Word. Overall, I think copying and pasting is easier.

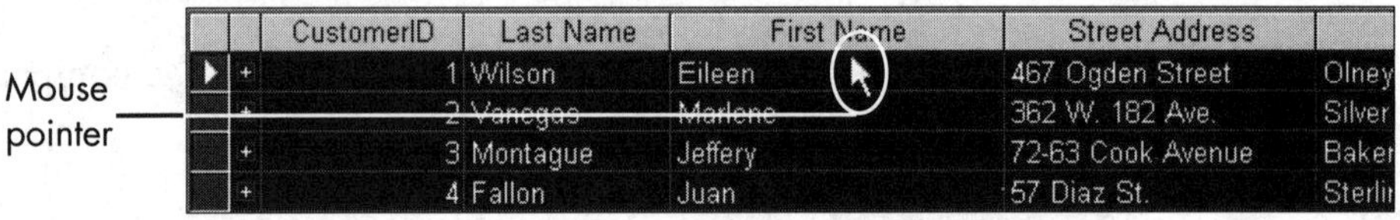

		CustomerID	Last Name	First Name	Street Address	
▶	+	1	Wilson	Eileen	467 Ogden Street	Olney
	+	2	Vanegas	Marlene	362 W. 182 Ave.	Silver
	+	3	Montague	Jeffery	72-63 Cook Avenue	Baker
	+	4	Fallon	Juan	57 Diaz St.	Sterlin

Figure 13.2 To drag and drop records, look for the white arrow pointer.

Paste Special

Now let's take a look at the choices offered by the Paste Special command in Word.

1. If you haven't done so yet, open the tblCustomers table and select the first four records.
2. Right-click and choose Copy.
3. Switch to Word and choose Edit, Paste Special (see Figure 13.3).

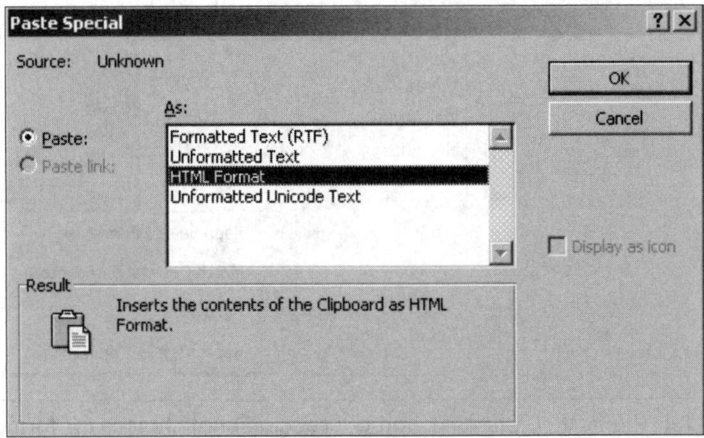

Figure 13.3 The Paste Special command gives you more flexibility than a simple Paste.

You have the following choices:

- **Formatted Text (RTF)**—This choice pastes the rows with the same formatting and column widths as those in the original table. The table title is not included.
- **Unformatted Text**—The records are pasted as plain text, not as a table. All formatting (such as italics) is dropped. Tab stops separate the values in the fields.
- **HTML Format**—The records are pasted with HTML formatting. Columns are resized to fit the width of the document.
- **Unformatted Unicode Text**—Similar to the Unformatted Text option.

4. Click Formatted Text (RTF) and click OK.
   The records are pasted with the original column widths.
5. Save the file as `PasteSpecialWord.doc` and close it. Close the tblCustomers table.

NOTE In Microsoft Office 2002 and 2003, you can also use the formatting commands on the Paste Options button, shown in Figure 13.4. (If the Paste Options icon is not displayed after you paste, in Microsoft Word, choose Tools, Options, Edit tab and select the Show Paste Options Buttons check box.) Unraveling their mysteries is beyond my scope, but you can experiment with them to see if they help you deal with Word formatting issues.

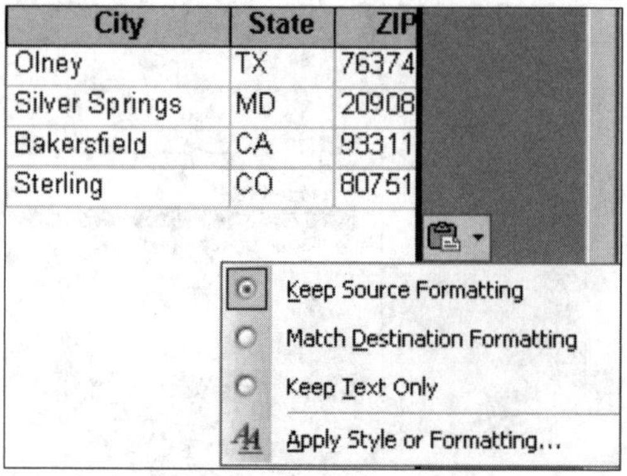

City	State	ZIP
Olney	TX	76374
Silver Springs	MD	20908
Bakersfield	CA	93311
Sterling	CO	80751

Keep Source Formatting
Match Destination Formatting
Keep Text Only
Apply Style or Formatting...

Figure 13.4 The Paste Options button offers additional choices for formatting pastes of Access records.

Office Links

A quick and easy way to export records to Word is to use the Office Links command. The records are exported into a new RTF file, which maintains the formatting of the original file.

Let's try an example that exports an Access table.

1. In the Database window, select tblOrders, but don't open it.
2. Choose Tools, Office Links, Publish It with Microsoft Word.
3. The table opens in a new file with the table name and an RTF extension.
4. Close the `tblOrders.rtf` document.

By default, the file is stored in your `My Documents` folder.

Export Wizards

The most robust tool for exporting Access data is, naturally enough, the Export command, available from the File menu in the Database window. When you issue the command, it initiates a wizard that takes you through the export process.

As with Office Links, you export an Access table to Word as an RTF file instead of as a DOC file (a Word document). But that's not really a problem: You can always save the RTF file as a DOC file. Notably, many word processors can handle documents with the more flexible RTF format.

New computer users quickly learn to distinguish between rich-text (RTF) files and plain-text (TXT) files. A rich-text file keeps the formatting included in an Access table; a plain-text file strips it away. Sometimes you might find this to be a distinction without a difference; you merely want to get Access values into some kind of word processor or text editor. Afterward, you can change the formatting to fit your needs.

But exporting to a rich-text file and exporting to a text file are two quite different things because, as you'll see, their purposes are different. Let's export a table, first as an RTF file and then as a TXT file.

Export a Table as an RTF file

To export a table as an RTF file, simply do the following:

1. In the Database window, click Tables and select tblOrderDetails.
2. Choose File, Export.
3. Select a convenient folder to store the new file, or just leave the default setting of My Documents.
4. In *Save As Type*, open the drop-down list and choose Rich Text Format (.rtf).
   The selection is near the bottom of the list.
5. In the File Name box, change the suggested name to **tblOrderDetailsExport.rtf** and click Export.
6. Open the file to see your results, and then close it.

The RTF file you created gives you the same results obtained using Office Links. When you use the Export command, however, the file doesn't open automatically.

NOTE You can use the same basic steps to export to an HTML file. In step 4, open the drop-down list and choose HTML Documents (*html;*htm,).

Export a Table as a TXT File

You usually export an Access table as a text file so that the records can then be easily imported into some other program or environment. The absence of formatting in text files eliminates one headache in importing because the content contains no formatting characters or instructions to deal with. On the other hand, the absence of formatting means you must use some other means to distinguish records and fields from another.

Distinguishing one record from another is handled easily enough: A different record appears on each line. To separate columns, you either include a delimiter or choose fixed-length columns. Delimited text files are more common (and I think easier to work with), so I focus on them.

What is a delimiter? It's an uncommon word for some common bit of punctuation, such as a comma or semicolon. In an Access table with fields for last name, first name, address, and so on, the punctuation mark separates last name from first name, first name from street address, and so on (see Figure 13.5).

```
5,"Satterfield","Pauline","1127 Washington Way","Rocky Mount","NC","27803","2525557531",
6,"Leininger","Lottie","89 Henderson Boulevard","Glen Oaks","NY","11004","3475559232","3475550061"
7,"Luckey","Ralph","56 St. James","East Middlebury","VT","05766","8025556349","8025555295"
8,"Paschal","Jesse","211 19th Avenue","Kiowa","CO","80117","3035557668","3035556682"
9,"Laskowski","Fannie","7 Cooper Drive","Harrisburg","PA","17105","7175551778","7175557472"
10,"Cotto","Justin","67 West 246 St.","Van Nuys","CA","91316","5675555482",
```

Figure 13.5 In this delimited text file, the commas separate one value from another, and the text qualifier of quotation marks encloses each value.

What happens if that bit of punctuation, such as a comma, appears within the values themselves? In other words, how do you distinguish between a comma that separates street addresses from cities and a comma such as the one in the book title *Captain Newman, MD*? For the commas in values, you need a text qualifier (such as quotation marks) that maintains the value as a single text string (as in `"Captain Newman, MD"`). The text qualifier also keeps the entire value together, spaces and all.

My discussion makes delimited text files sound more complicated than they are. An example will you show much more readily how they work.

1. In the Database window, choose tblMerchandise.
2. Choose File, Export.
3. Navigate to a convenient folder on your hard drive. In Save As Type, choose Text Files (*.txt; *.csv; *.tab; *.asc). Keep the filename of tblOrders. Leave the Save Formatted option unchecked.
4. Click Export.
5. In the first dialog box of the Export Text Wizard, the Delimited selection should be chosen. The Sample export format box shows the values that will be exported.
6. Click the Advanced button to open the Export Specification dialog box (see Figure 13.6). Key settings include these:

   - **Field Delimiter**—You can choose which character separates values in a record.

- **Text Qualifier**—This is the character that keeps text strings together.
- **Date Order**—Open the drop-down list to see the various choices you have for `Date/Time` fields.

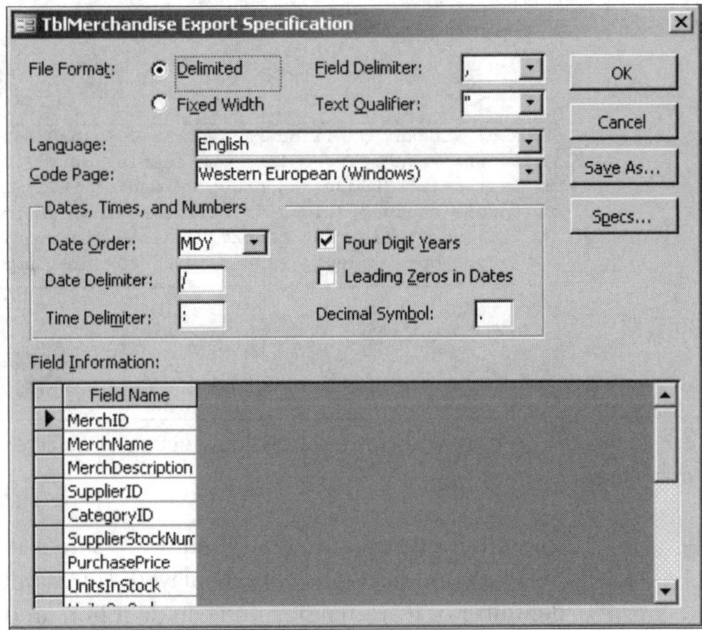

Figure 13.6 In the Export Specification dialog box, you can choose a delimiter and a text qualifier. These settings can be saved for future use in exporting and importing.

7. Keep the default settings. Click Save As.
   You might want to use the same settings for future exports (and imports of delimited text files as well). You can save the set of specifications you just made for future use.
8. Keep the suggested title in the Save Import/Export Specification dialog box and click OK.
9. Click Specs.
   In the Import/Export Specification dialog box, you see the name of the specifications you just saved. In future exports or imports of delimited text, you can apply the same setting by selecting it and clicking Open.
10. Click Cancel. Click OK in the Export Specification dialog.
11. Click Next. You see the dialog box in Figure 13.7.

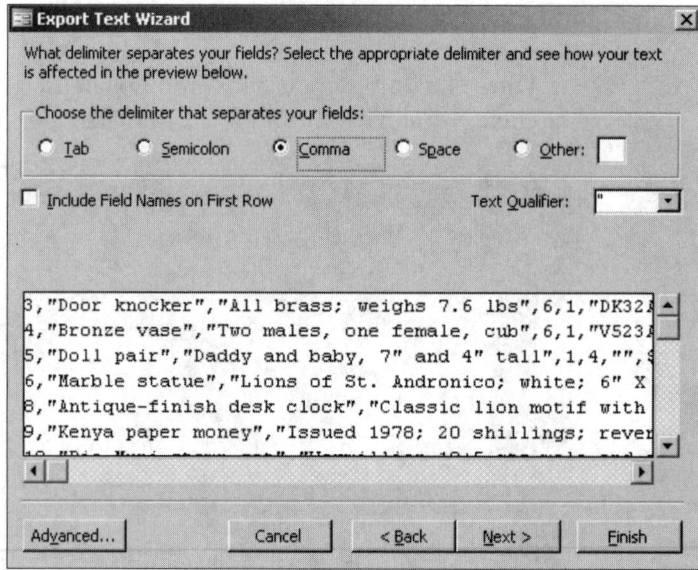

Figure 13.7 In this dialog box, you can see how the values will be affected by choosing various delimiters.

The delimiter and text qualifier selected in the Export Specification dialog box are displayed. If you only want to choose a delimiter or text qualifier, you can do it here and ignore the Export Specification dialog box. You can also choose to include the field names by selecting this option.

12. Click Next and click Finish. Click OK. Open the text document `tblMerchandise.txt` to see your data (see Figure 13.8).

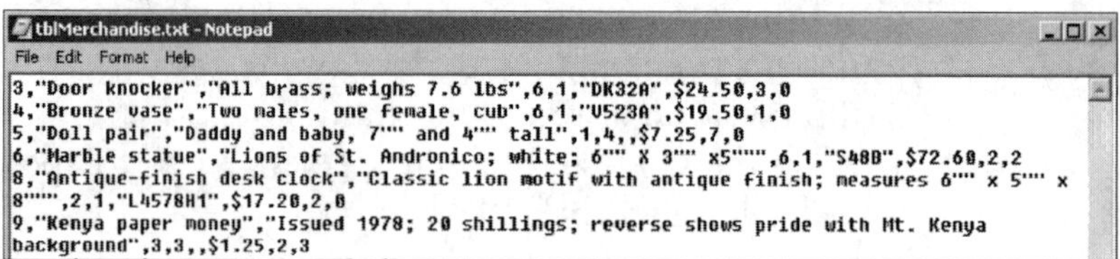

Figure 13.8 Access exported the table with the comma delimiter between fields; quotation marks are used as text qualifiers.

Zeroing Out the Zeroes

When you export values in fields with the `Date/Time` data type to a delimited text file, both the dates and the times are exported. But often in a `Date/Time` field, the values just indicate dates—the times are inconsequential or irrelevant. If there are no times accompanying the dates, you have a problem: Access attaches a string of zeroes, shown as 0:00:00, to each `Date/Time` value (see Figure 13.9).

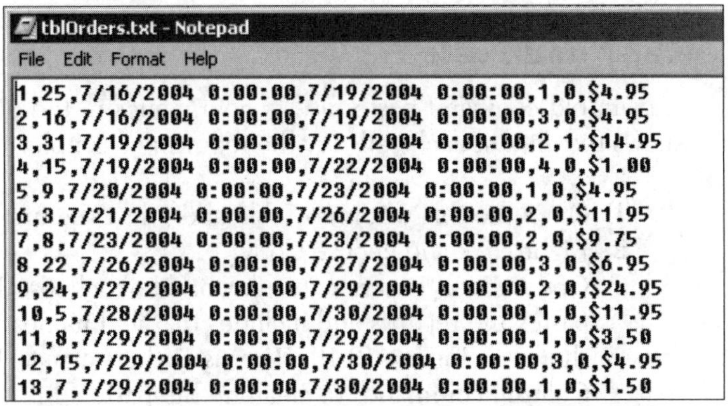

```
tblOrders.txt - Notepad
File Edit Format Help
1,25,7/16/2004 0:00:00,7/19/2004 0:00:00,1,0,$4.95
2,16,7/16/2004 0:00:00,7/19/2004 0:00:00,3,0,$4.95
3,31,7/19/2004 0:00:00,7/21/2004 0:00:00,2,1,$14.95
4,15,7/19/2004 0:00:00,7/22/2004 0:00:00,4,0,$1.00
5,9,7/20/2004 0:00:00,7/23/2004 0:00:00,1,0,$4.95
6,3,7/21/2004 0:00:00,7/26/2004 0:00:00,2,0,$11.95
7,8,7/23/2004 0:00:00,7/23/2004 0:00:00,2,0,$9.75
8,22,7/26/2004 0:00:00,7/27/2004 0:00:00,3,0,$6.95
9,24,7/27/2004 0:00:00,7/29/2004 0:00:00,2,0,$24.95
10,5,7/28/2004 0:00:00,7/30/2004 0:00:00,1,0,$11.95
11,8,7/29/2004 0:00:00,7/29/2004 0:00:00,1,0,$3.50
12,15,7/29/2004 0:00:00,7/30/2004 0:00:00,3,0,$4.95
13,7,7/29/2004 0:00:00,7/30/2004 0:00:00,1,0,$1.50
```

Figure 13.9 In the delimited text file, zeroes have been attached to each date/time value.

Simply setting the `Format` field property in the table to `Short Date` or some other setting that eliminates the time display won't solve the problem. You need to create a query using the fields from the tables, and then export the query to the text file. Instead of using the original date field, you'll create a calculated field in the query that wipes out the zeroes. For example, for an `OrderDate` field, you can use this expression:

```
OrderDate2: Format([OrderDate],"mm/dd/yy")
```

where:

- `OrderDate2` is the name of the column.
- `Format` is the function.
- `OrderDate` is the field.
- `"mm/dd/yy"` is two-digit month, day, and year formatting.

When you export the query, there won't be any `0:00:00` strings in the `OrderDate` field.

Move Access Data to Excel

Many Microsoft Office users prefer working in Excel instead of Access. Sometimes the reasons are excellent (for example, calculations are often more easily and robustly performed in Excel). Sometimes the reasons are less admirable (users don't want to learn Access).

Regardless, if your boss or client wants to see data in Excel, you'll want to deliver it in XLS format.

Copy and Paste

A plain old copy-and-paste inserts field names in the first Excel row and shows the data in each cell. Try the following example.

1. Open the tblCustomers table and select the first four records.
2. Right-click and choose Copy.
3. Open Excel. In a new blank workbook, choose Edit, Paste. Excel pastes the records and includes the field names in the first row, as shown in Figure 13.10. (I've used the Format, Row and Format, Column commands to clean up the paste a bit.)

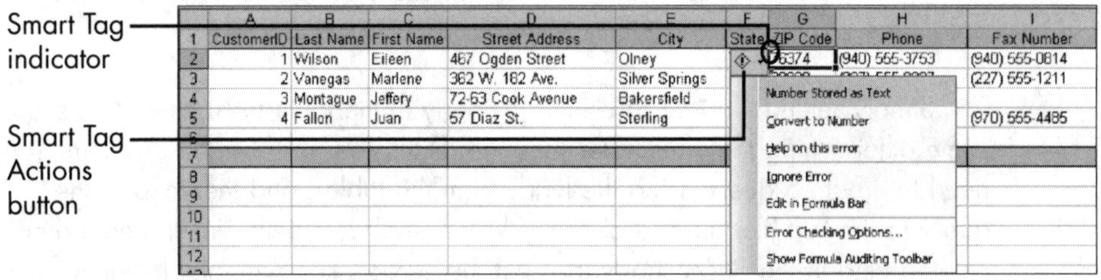

Figure 13.10 Excel pasted the records beginning in the first row. You can also click a cell and Excel will begin the paste there.

If you have Smart Tags turned on, you will see tiny green triangles in the upper-left corner of each cell in the ZIP column. Excel regards this ZIP column with suspicion. If these are all five-digit numbers, why have they been formatted as text?

You can open the drop-down list beside the Smart Tag to deal with this issue (see Figure 13.10). You can also avoid the problem entirely by choosing among the options in the Paste Special dialog box, as follows:

1. Click the Sheet2 tab for a new worksheet.
2. Choose Edit, Paste Special.
   Most of these choices you've seen in the Paste Special dialog box in Word. The others include the Comma Separated Value (CSV) file format and Binary File Format (BIFF5).
3. Select Text and click OK. The records are pasted as plain text without formatting.
4. Save the file as `PasteExcel.xls` and close it. Close the tblCustomers table.

NOTE You can copy and paste whole tables into Excel. The procedures are the same, except that you choose the table in the Database window.

Office Links

You can use the Office Links command to create and open a file of Access data in Excel. Try this exercise:

1. In the Database window, select the tblOrderDetails table.
2. Choose Tools, Office Links, Analyze It with Microsoft Office Excel.
3. Access creates a new file with the table name and an XLS extension.
4. Close the file and close Excel.

NOTE If you want to delete this file or others created by Office Links commands, by default, the files are placed in your `My Documents` folder.

Export Command

You can also use an Export wizard to export data to Excel.

1. In the Database window, choose the tblOrders table.
2. Select File, Export.
3. In the Export Table dialog box, open the Save As Type drop-down list and choose Microsoft Excel 97-2003 (*.xls).
4. ClickExport. Access exports the table, using the first row for field names.

TIP You might want to import from Excel instead of exporting from Access, especially if you have strong Excel skills. The Import External Data command in Excel, available from the Data menu, has numerous options and is a more robust tool than the Access Export feature.

E-mail an Access Object

In both Outlook and Outlook Express, you can cut and paste a set of Access records or a table directly into an e-mail message. In Outlook, make certain that the Message Format box on the E-mail toolbar is set to either Rich Text or HTML. In Outlook Express, Rich Text (HTML) should be selected from the Format menu.

It's also easy to send a table, query, form, or report as an attachment. In the Database window or in the open object itself, choose File, Send To, Mail Recipient (as Attachment). Access displays the various formats that are available (see Figure 13.11).

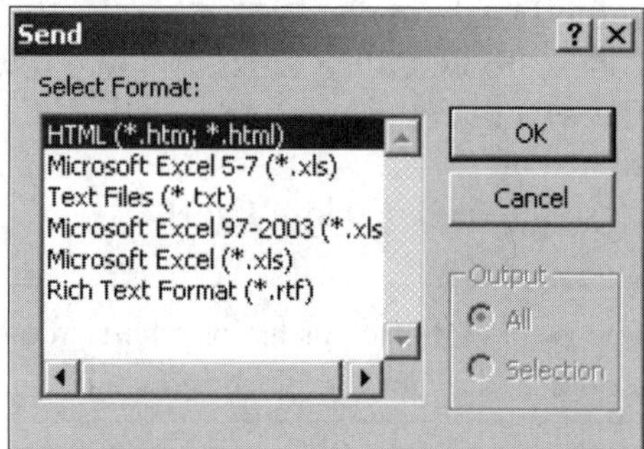

Figure 13.11 You can attach an Access object to an e-mail in a variety of formats.

For a report, you'll notice an additional choice: Snapshot Format. A report snapshot is a file that contains an exact copy of each page of a report, preserving its layout, graphics, and embedded objects. A Snapshot file has an SNP extension and can be read with Snapshot Viewer software. Microsoft Office users shouldn't have a problem reading a snapshot. Non-Office users can include a link in the e-mail message for users to download the Snapshot Viewer at the Microsoft site (www.microsoft.com/downloads). Depending on the audience, a snapshot might fit the recipient's specific needs or simply cause more hassle than using HTML and other widely used formats.

Import Access Data into Outlook

If you have contact data in Access that you'd like to transfer to Outlook, your best bet is to use the import tools in Outlook, as follows:

1. Select View, Navigation Pane and click Contacts.
2. Choose File, Import and Export.
3. Select Import from Another Program or File.
4. Choose Microsoft Access.
5. Follow the instructions in the rest of the wizard.

I know this last instruction is feeble, but I don't think you'll have difficulty with the wizard. The only interesting dialog box is Map Custom Fields, shown in Figure 13.12. Here you match the fields in the table (say, `CustLastName`) with the fields in your address book (say, `Last Name`) by dragging the Access field in the left pane to the Outlook field in the right pane.

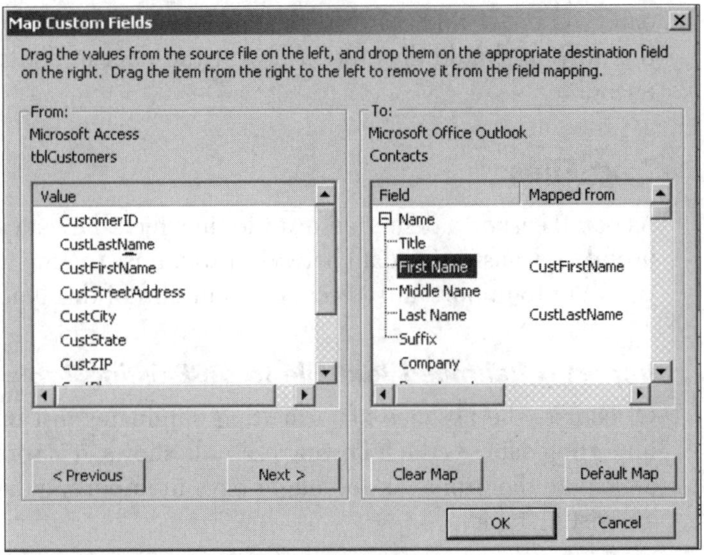

Figure 13.12 The Map Custom Fields dialog box matches Access and Outlook fields.

Importing Data into Access

Importing data into Access can be like trying to re-enter the United States after traveling overseas. Sometimes the process goes so smoothly you wonder what you were worried about. Other times, there seems to be an officious agent standing at the gateway of your Access table, making it as difficult as possible to let any data in.

But there's good reason for the intrusive inspection. When it comes to the domestic security of any nation, it doesn't make sense to worry exclusively about internal threats and be indifferent about who is entering your country. Similarly, it makes little sense to put tremendous effort into maintaining data integrity for values you enter directly into Access yourself while waving through any piece of data from an external source. Indeed, data from outside your computer could be especially likely to break validation rules, exceed field sizes, have the wrong data type, and otherwise breach data integrity.

Thus, it's essential to do a through review of the external data before you import it into Access. Even with a careful inspection of the source data, you might find that you have problems importing it. The exercises in this section should illustrate a few of the data integrity issues you might encounter.

Text Files

As noted earlier, a delimited text file (in which the data is not formatted) is useful for transferring data between programs. You might find that the data you want to import into Access exists in files of this type.

Import a Delimited Text File to an Existing Table

Of course, the absence of formatting eliminates just one of the issues in importing data. As the following example shows, it is sometimes difficult to anticipate the problems you might have in importing data into Access into an existing table.

1. Copy (i.e. download) `DelimitedFieldNames.txt` and `DelimitedAllDigits.txt` to a convenient folder on your computer.

NOTE I ask you to copy other files at various points in this chapter. You might want to copy all of them at this point: `Assets.xls`, `ShipperErrors.xls`, and `EmployeesLink.xls`.

---

2. Open `DelimitedFieldNames.txt`. Review the data and note that that there are three rows of customer contact data, beginning with a row for ID `32`.
3. Open the tblCustomers table and review the data. Note that the last row in the table has ID `31`. Switch to Design view and review the fields. Compare the table and the text file (see Figure 13.13). Everything seems in place for an easy import. Both files have the same number of columns. The field headings match nicely, and all your data in the text file is in the same format as the table.

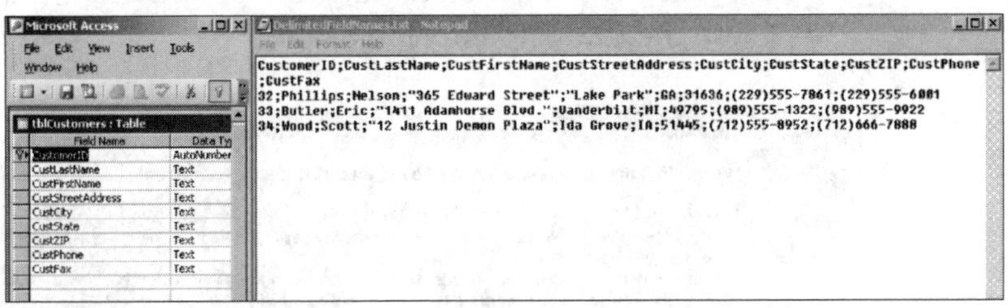

Figure 13.13 The tblCustomers table and the `DelimitedFieldNames.txt` file have the same number of columns with the same names.

4. Close the tblCustomers table and the text file.
5. With tblCustomers selected in the Database window, choose File, Get External Data, Import.
6. In the Import dialog box, select Text Files (*.txt; *.csv; *.tab; *.asc) in Files of Type. Navigate to the DelimitedFieldNames.txt file and double-click it.
7. In the first dialog box, Delimited should be selected. Click Next.
8. In the next dialog box, make the following selections:
   - Semicolon should be selected as the delimiter.
   - Check the First Row Contains Field Names check box.
   - Open the drop-down list for Text Qualifier and choose double apostrophes (`"`).
9. Click Next.

10. Click In an Existing Table. Open the drop-down list and choose tblCustomers.
11. Click Next. In Import to Table, keep tblCustomers. Click Finish.
12. A message appears that not all the data was imported (see Figure 13.14). Click Yes, then OK.
13. Open tblCustomers and look at the last row. None of the rows was imported.
14. Click View to go to Design view.
15. Click in the `CustPhone` field.
    Note that the field's validation rule is `Like "##########"`. Although the numbers are formatted in Datasheet view to include non-numeric characters that make the values appear as telephone numbers, the value that is stored has 10 numbers and no other characters. In Figure 13.13, note that telephone numbers in the delimited text file include the normal formatting characters.
16. Close the tblCustomers table.

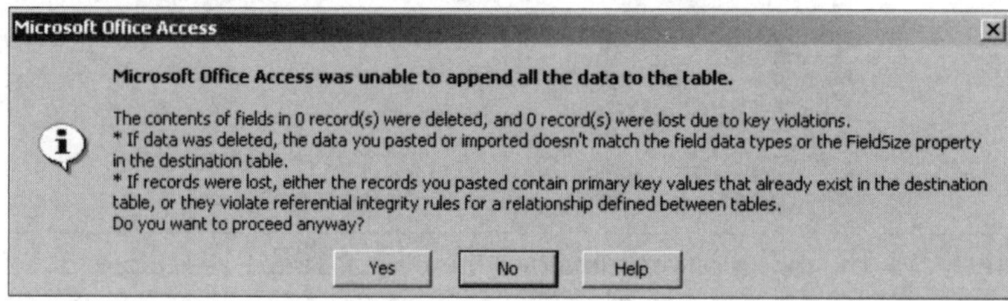

Figure 13.14 The complex error message that tells you the records weren't added. Even though the message might indicate otherwise, none of the records was added.

Modify the Source File

When you discover why Access won't import the data, you can modify the source file accordingly. Let's try to import the same data, which has been modified to meet the validation rule.

1. Open `DelimitedAllDigits.txt` and review the data (see Figure 13.15).
   This file is the same as `DelimitedText.txt`, except for one thing: The customer phone numbers (but not the fax numbers) have 10 digits and no other characters.

DelimitedAllDigits.txt - Notepad

File Edit Format Help

```
CustomerID;CustLastName;CustFirstName;CustStreetAddress;CustCity;CustState;CustZIP;CustPhone;CustFax
32;Phillips;Nelson;"365 Edward Street";"Lake Park";GA;31636;2295557861;(229) 555-6001
33;Butler;Eric;"1411 Adamhorse Blvd.";Vanderbilt;MI;49795;9895551322;(989) 555-9922
34;Wood;Scott;"12 Justin Demon Plaza";Ida Grove;IA;51445;7125558952;(712) 666-7888
```

Figure 13.15 The CustPhone column now includes only 10 digits and no other characters.

2. Close `DelimitedAllDigits.txt`.
3. Choose File, Get External Data, Import.
4. In the Import dialog box, double-click the `DelimitedAllDigits.txt` file.
5. In the first dialog box, Delimited should be selected. Click Next.
6. In the next dialog box, make certain that…
   - Semicolon is the delimiter.
   - First Row Contains Field Names is selected.
   - The Text Qualifier is a double apostrophe (`"`).
7. Click Next.
8. Click In an Existing Table. Open the drop-down list and choose tblCustomers.
9. Click Next and click Finish.
10. Click OK. Open the tblCustomers table and scroll to the bottom. The fields have been imported.
11. Close the tblCustomers table.

Import to a New Table

You can also import a text file as a new table. This process might go more smoothly because you don't have existing fields and field properties to worry about. Still, you need to make certain that the data in tables is consistent. Access reviews the first few records to assign data types, but you can always change these selections after importing in Design view.

Here's an exercise that creates a new table from `DelimitedFieldNames.txt`, the file you previously had difficulty importing into an existing table.

1. Choose File, Get External Data, Import.
2. Double-click `DelimitedFieldNames.txt`.
3. Delimited should be chosen. Click Next.

4. In the next dialog box, make the following selections:
   - Semicolon should be selected as the delimiter.
   - Select First Row Contains Field Names.
   - Open the drop-down list for Text Qualifier and choose double apostrophes (`"`).

   It's a good idea at this point to scroll through your data to make sure that the fields and columns look OK.
5. Click In a New Table. Click Next. Click the Advanced button.
6. In CustomerID, click Skip.

   Because it's a new table, you can start the primary key from `1` (as you know, though, there would be no problem using ID of `32`, `33`, and `34`). You can choose to create a primary key in the next dialog box.
7. Click in the Data Type column of the CustZIP row. Open the drop-down list and select Text.

   Using the first several rows of data, Access does its best to select data types for the new tables. Selecting a `Number` field data type (that is, `Long Integer`) for CustZIP makes sense from Access's viewpoint. But, of course, you want a `ZIP` field to be `Text`.
8. Click OK to close the Import Specification dialog box with your changes, and click Next.
9. Let Access Add Primary Key should be selected. Click Next.
10. Name the table **tblContactInfo** and click Finish. Click OK in the message.
11. In the Database window, open tblContactInfo (see Figure 13.16).

tblContactInfo : Table

	ID	CustLastName	CustFirstName	CustStreetAddr	CustCity	CustState	CustZIP	CustPhone	CustFax
▸	1	Phillips	Nelson	365 Edward Str	Lake Park	GA	31636	(229)555-7861	(229)555-6001
	2	Butler	Eric	1411 Adamhors	Vanderbilt	MI	49795	(989)555-1322	(989)555-9922
	3	Wood	Scott	12 Justin Demo	Ida Grove	IA	51445	(712)555-8952	(712)666-7888
*	(AutoNumber)								

Figure 13.16 The CustZIP field has been imported as text, not as a number, and a primary key has been assigned in the first column.

Access had little problem importing the table. In Design view, you can inspect and modify field properties. For example, you could assign captions to each field so that the columns are easier to read.

12. Close tblContactInfo.

Create a New Table Using Excel

You can similarly import files from Excel. Let's try an example in which you create a new table.

1. If you haven't already done so, copy `Assets.xls` to an appropriate place on your hard drive. Open the file.
   This simple spreadsheet contains columns with a variety of data, including `text`, `dates`, `numbers`, `dollar amounts`, and `true/false entries`.

TIP As shown in the Depreciable? column, if you want Access to identify the data type of `Yes/No` fields correctly, edit the values to `True` and `False`; don't use `Yes` and `No` or `-1` and `0`.

---

2. Close `Assets.xls` and close Excel.
3. Choose File, Get External Data, Import.
4. Navigate to `Assets.xls`. Double-click the file to import it.
5. In the first dialog box, select Show Worksheets and Sheet1.
   If your Excel file contains more than one worksheet or range, Access asks which you would like to import.
6. Click Next. First Row Contains Column Headings should be checked.
7. Click Next. The In a New Table button should be checked.
8. Click Next.
   In this dialog box, you should be able to click on any column and modify its field name, index, and data type. Unfortunately, a bug in Office 2003 might prevent you from doing so. You might also find that the Data Type drop-down list is grayed out and inaccessible. I ignore any fixes here because the workaround is simple enough. After Access creates the table, review and modify field properties as necessary. At the same time, you can review data types in Table Design view.
9. Click Next. Click Let Access Add Primary Key and click Next.
10. Name the new table **tblAssets**. Click Finish. Click OK in the message.
11. Open tblAssets in Datasheet view and briefly review the records.
    The columns and data appear reasonable. In the `Depreciable?` field, which has a `Yes/No` data type, the values are correctly stored

as `-1` and `0`. If you want, you can change to an easier-to-understand text display (such as `Yes/No`). In Design view, click in the Depreciable? row and edit the `Format` property.

12. Click View to switch to Design view (see Figure 13.17).

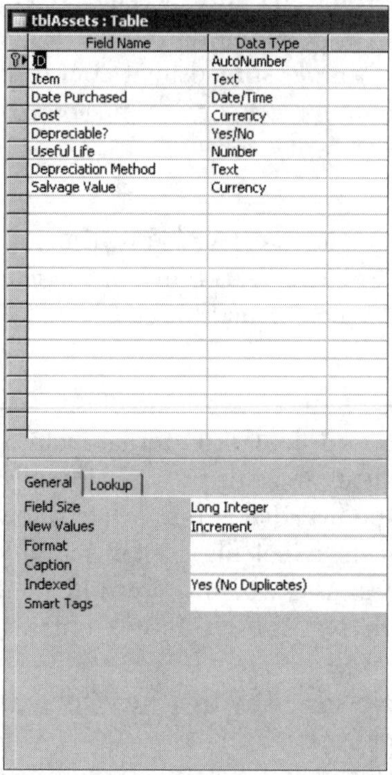

Figure 13.17 Access has successfully guessed the data types of all fields based on its inspection of the first few rows of data.

Access did a good job of figuring out the data types. As I suggested earlier, you'll want to review all field names, data types, field properties, and so on to make sure they meet your needs.

13. Close the table.

Q&A

Q: When I import data from Excel, I sometimes get an extra row in Access. It has an ID number but no other data. What's going on, and how do I fix it?

A: In Excel, you probably entered something in a row below the data. Whatever you entered is now gone, and the row is vacant. But Excel remembers that the row has been used and extends the range of the worksheet. The cure is to delete the last few blank rows in the Excel worksheet before importing.

Add Excel Rows Using Copy-and-Paste

Sometimes the best way to add rows from Excel to an existing Access table is to copy and paste. As with all imported data, Access rejects any values that violate data integrity. You'll find that Access often allows some records to be appended but blocks others. The rejected rows are pasted into a new Paste Errors table that can be accessed from the Tables section of the Database window. You can modify these values and paste them into the table. Sometimes it's easier, however, to modify the records in the source document and copy and paste them again.

Access might decide not to paste records for a variety of reasons. You've already seen one example in this chapter: a violation of a validation rule. Other causes include wrong data type, values that are too long and thus violate the `Field Size` property, and duplicate values in primary keys.

The following exercise illustrates several problems you might encounter in appending Excel records to an Access table.

1. Open tblShippers in Design view. Briefly review the information. If you have not already done so, copy `ShippersErrors.xls` to your hard drive. Open the file.
2. Minimize all other windows besides tblShippers and `ShipperErrors.xls`. Right-click on any open area of the toolbar and choose Tile Horizontally (see Figure 13.18).

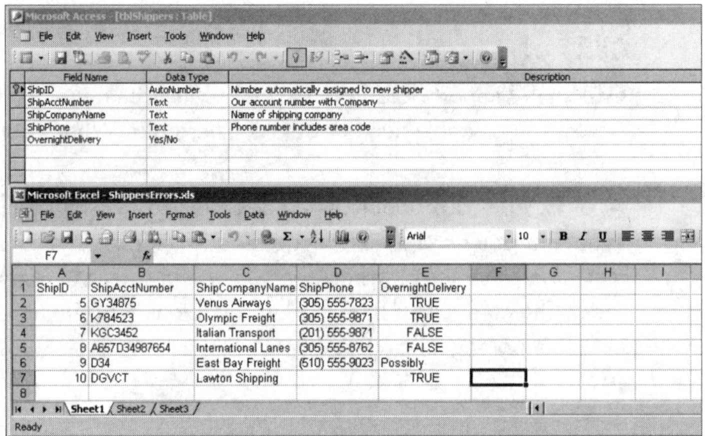

Figure 13.18 The columns in the table and spreadsheet match.

If you can't get the windows to tile successfully, don't worry about it; you can just switch between windows using the taskbar.

3. Compare the field names in tblShippers and the column names in `ShipperErrors.xls`.

   The field names and column names match exactly in number, order, and name, so Access shouldn't have any problems lining up the data correctly.
4. In `ShipperErrors.xls`, select the rows for ShipID5, ID6, and ID7, and copy them to the Clipboard. Click anywhere in tblShippers and click the View button at the far left of the toolbar to switch to Datasheet view.
5. Select the New Record row (the bottom, empty row). Choose Edit, Paste to paste the records. Confirm the paste.

   Access had no problem pasting the records. There might or might not be a gap in the ID numbers between the new records and the existing ones. As you know, if there is a gap, it's irrelevant.
6. Switch back to Excel. Copy row ID#8.
7. Select the New Record row in tblShippers. Paste the row.

   You get the error message in Figure 13.19. Click OK. You get another message that the record has been pasted into a Paste Errors table.

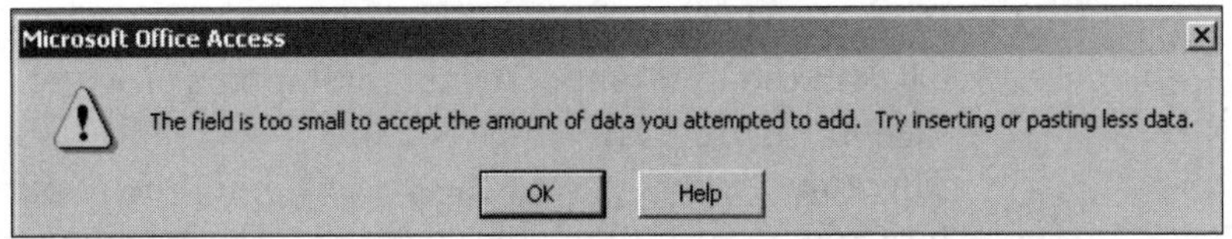

Figure 13.19 The error message tells you the field size is too small.

8. Click View to switch to Design view. Click in the ShipAcctNumber row. In the lower pane, note that the field size is 10.
   Access couldn't paste the record because the field size couldn't accommodate the account number.
9. Edit the field size to **20**. Save the change and click View to switch to Datasheet view.
10. Select the New Record row and paste the row.
    The record pastes with no problem.
11. Select the ID#9 row in `ShipperErrors.xls` and copy it to the Clipboard. Select the New Record row in tblShippers and paste. You get the error message in Figure 13.20. Click OK. You get another error message; click OK in that message as well.

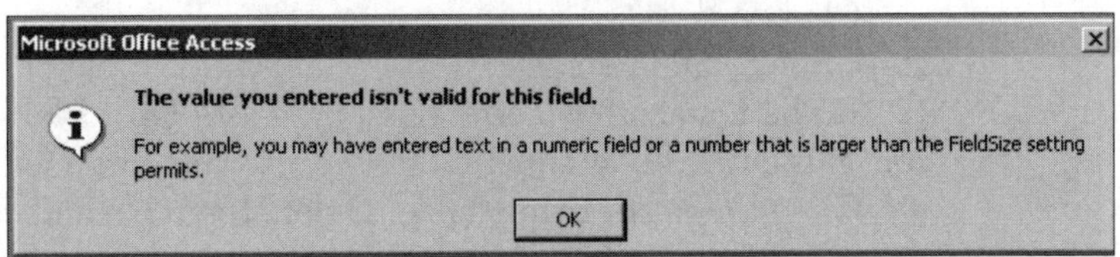

Figure 13.20 The error message tells you that the data isn't valid for the field, which indicates an error in data type.

12. Click View to switch to Design view. Note that the `OvernightDelivery` field is a `Yes/No` field. Review the ID#9 record in the Excel spreadsheet.
    In the OvernightDelivery column, the entry is `Possibly`. This is not a value that is accepted in a `Yes/No` field.
13. In `ShipperErrors.xls`, edit `OvernightDelivery` for ID#9 to False. Copy the row again.
14. In the table, switch to Datasheet view. Paste the ID#9 row as a new record.
    This time you had no problem pasting the record.

15. Copy the ID#10 row in the spreadsheet and paste it in tblShippers. Click in the next empty row in tblShippers. You get the error message in Figure 13.21.
    This time Access pasted the record, but when you moved to the next row, you were unable to save it. The upshot is the same: The record is unacceptable. `ShipPhone` cannot contain a null value.

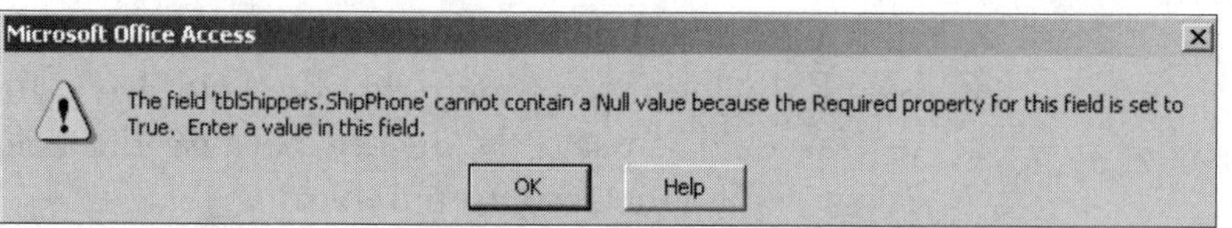

Figure 13.21 `Phone` is the only field with a null value, so you must either change the field property or enter a phone number.

16. Click OK. In tblShippers, click in the `ShipPhone` field for the record you just pasted. Enter the telephone number **(212) 555-1876**. Press Tab twice; Access has saved your record.
17. Close `ShipperErrors.xls`. Click No when you are asked to save your changes. Click No if you are asked to save copied data to the Clipboard.
18. Close tblShippers.
19. In the Database window, open the Paste Errors table.
20. This table is now superfluous because you corrected all the errors.
21. Close the Paste Errors table. Delete the table and confirm.

Usually when you paste records, you don't step through it as we did in the example. Access pastes the records it can, gives you a series of error messages of why other records weren't pasted, and then throws all the problem rows into the Paste Errors table. The lesson is clear: If you do the spade work of reviewing data before you paste records, you'll save yourself an awful lot of trouble.

Importing Access Data

Because data imported from one Access database to another is already in Access formats, these transfers usually go relatively smoothly.

Copy and Paste

The easiest way to move data between Access databases is to copy and paste tables, as follows:

1. Right-click the table in the source database and choose Copy.
2. Switch to the target database and paste the table.
   The dialog box in Figure 13.22 appears. If you click Structure Only, the new table will contain the fields of the original table but none of its data. Structure and Data pastes the entire table. Append Data to Existing Table is self-explanatory; for Table Name, instead of naming a new table, you supply the name of the table to which you want to add the records.

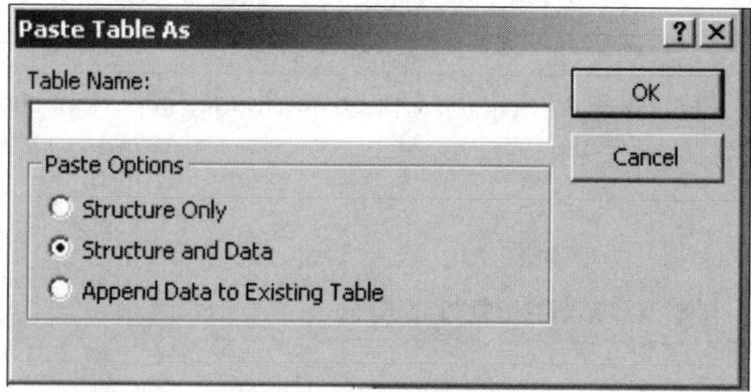

Figure 13.22 Copy and paste is an easy way to move Access tables from one file to another.

Use the Import Wizard

The Import Wizard is the more robust way of importing Access data.

1. Choose File, Get External Data, Import.
2. In the Import dialog box, navigate to any of the Nifty Lions databases from earlier chapters that you've copied to your hard drive (`NiftyLionsChap12.mdb` is fine). Select it and click Import.
3. On the Table tab of the Import Objects dialog box, choose tblSuppliers.

4. Click Options.
   You see the selections in Figure 13.23. In the Import Tables section, I frankly don't know why the word *definitions* is used here instead of the term *structure*, which is used when you paste; they appear to mean the same thing. It is important to note that if you select two or more tables (don't use the Ctrl or Shift keys to select them—just click each one), you can also import their relationships.
5. Click OK. The table is imported.

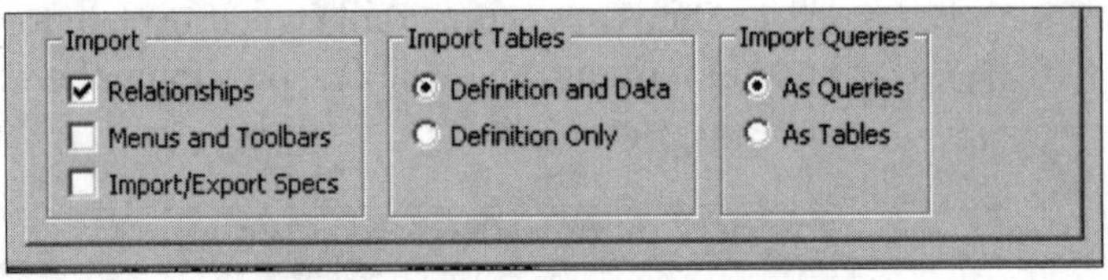

Figure 13.23 Remember to click the Options button for important choices that define your import.

Linking Versus Importing

You can work in Access with data from other programs in two ways: You can import it or you can link it.

When you import a table, as you just did, you are awarding it full Access citizenship. In other words, it becomes indistinguishable from any other table in your database. The source document, whether residing in another Access database or an external environment such as Excel, is left untouched and unaffected by any changes you make in your new Access table.

By contrast, a linked table attains only expatriate status in Access—it remains a citizen of its native program. You can view and edit the data of the linked table and even create a query based on it. However, you can't alter how the table and its fields are defined in its home environment. It naturally follows that, although you can delete the linked table in Access, you have no control over its longevity in its native program.

You can set certain field properties for a linked table, but these affect how the data is displayed, not its inherent traits. Specifically, you can change the field's format and give it a caption, but you can't change important properties such as `Validation Rule` and `Required`. Even a default value is prohibited.

Importing data obviously offers you more flexibility than linking. It also speeds performance. Linking is useful, however, when you or other users are also updating the data in another program.

Here's an exercise that links an Excel spreadsheet to an Access database.

1. If you haven't already done so, copy `EmployeesLink.xls` from the download file to your hard drive.
2. Open the file and briefly review its fields. Close the file and close Excel.
3. In the Database window, choose File, Get External Data, Link Tables.
4. In the Link dialog box, set File of Type to Microsoft Excel (*xls). Navigate to the folder where you downloaded `EmployeesLink.xls` and double-click the file.

   The Link Spreadsheet Wizard opens.
5. With the First Row Contains Column Headings option checked, click Next.
6. Edit the table name to **tblEmployees**. Click Finish and click OK in the message.
7. In the Database window, select tblEmployees.

   Note that there is an arrow next to tblEmployees, indicating that the table is linked (see Figure 13.24).

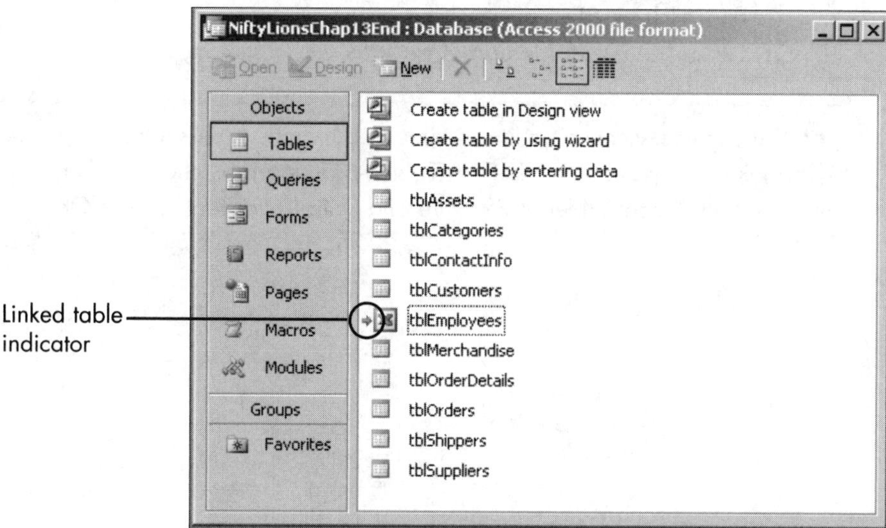

Figure 13.24 Linked tables are prefixed by an arrow in the Database window.

8. Click Open. Review the fields in the table.
   The table has the same data and headings it did in Excel.
9. Click View to switch to Design view.
   You get a warning message that, because the table is linked, some properties can't be modified.
10. Click Yes. Click in the Birth Date row of the Field Name column.
    The message in the lower pane tells you that the property (the field name) cannot be modified.
11. Press Tab to move to the Data Type column.
    The message at the right half of the lower pane tells you, "This property [i.e., the field type] cannot be modified in linked tables."
12. In Field Properties in the lower pane, click Format.
    The message at the right tells you that you can edit the property. Because Format affects only appearance, not the underlying data, there is no problem changing the setting.
13. Using the down arrow key, move from property to property to see which properties can be modified and which cannot.
    `Format`, `Input Mask`, and `Caption` can all be edited, whereas most other properties cannot.
14. Click View to switch to Datasheet view. In ID 5, edit the Last Name from **Wood** to **Woodbridge**.
15. Close the table. Open `EmployeesLink.xls`.
16. The change you made in the table has also been made in the spreadsheet file.
17. Close the Excel file and close Excel.

TIP You can easily convert a linked table to a regular Access table. Copy the linked table and paste it. In the Paste Table As dialog box, choose either Structure Only (Local Table) or Structure and Data (Local Table). Click OK.

Conclusion

In this chapter, you learned how to export data from Access and how to import and link it. You can compare the objects in your `NiftyLionsChap13.mdb` to those in the solution database `NiftyLionsChap13End.mdb`. One area I did not cover was how to export/import data to other notable database programs, particularly dBASE and Paradox. My sense is that in the current environment, most readers will not need to transfer data from or to this software.

Note, however, that in Access 2003, you can continue to export and import from these programs. The export and import of data from dBASE and Paradox are covered, with varying degrees of detail, in Access Help.

CASE EXAMPLE

In the following example, you create a query with contact info and use it in a mail-merge Word document. The finished letter is shown in Figure 13.30.

1. In the Database window, select tblCustomersSalutation.
2. Choose Insert, Query. With Design View selected in the New Query dialog box, click OK.
3. In the field list, click `CustSalutation`. Press Shift and click `CustZIP`. Drag the seven fields to the design grid and drop them.
4. Click in the Criteria row of the `CustState` field and type **ca**. This limits the recipients to only those customers who live in California.
5. Choose File, Save. Name the query **qryCaliforniaCustomers** and click OK. Click View to see the records. Close the query.
6. In the Database window, click Queries.
7. Select qryCaliforniaCustomers. Choose Tools, Office Links, Merge It with Microsoft Office Word.
8. In the first dialog box of the Mail Merge Wizard, check Create a New Document and then link the data to it. Click OK.
9. If necessary, maximize the Word window. With Letters selected in the Mail Merge pane at the right, click Next, Starting Document.
10. In Select Starting Document, Use the Current Document should be selected. Click Next, Select Recipients.
11. In Select Recipients, Use an Existing List should be selected.

As shown in the Use an Existing List section, the recipients are selected from `qryCaliforniaCustomers` (see Figure 13.25).

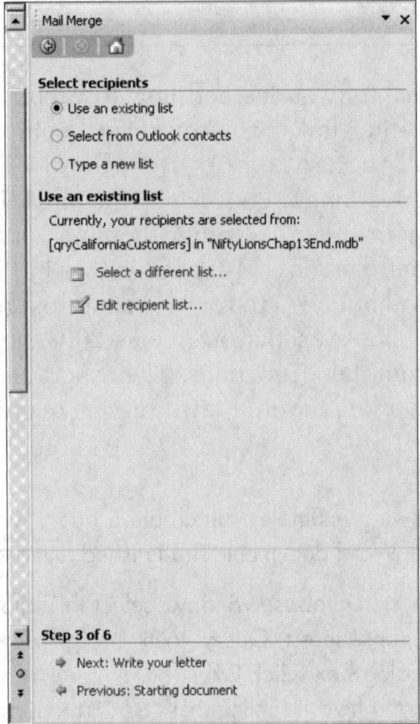

Figure 13.25 The Mail Merge Wizard makes it relatively easy to create form letters.

12. Click Edit Recipient List.
    You can make changes to the recipient list in this dialog box, which is self-explanatory except for the Validate button. If you want to validate addresses, you need to download address-validation software from the Microsoft Office website.
13. Click OK in the Mail Merge Recipients dialog box. Click Next, Write Your Letter.
14. Press Enter five or six times to leave room for the letterhead.
15. Choose Insert, Date and Time. Click the date in the usual month/day/year format for a date in a letter, as in `August 17, 2005`. Click OK.
16. Press Enter twice.
17. Click Address Block in the Mail Merge pane. Insert Company Name should be deselected. Other settings should match those in Figure 13.26.

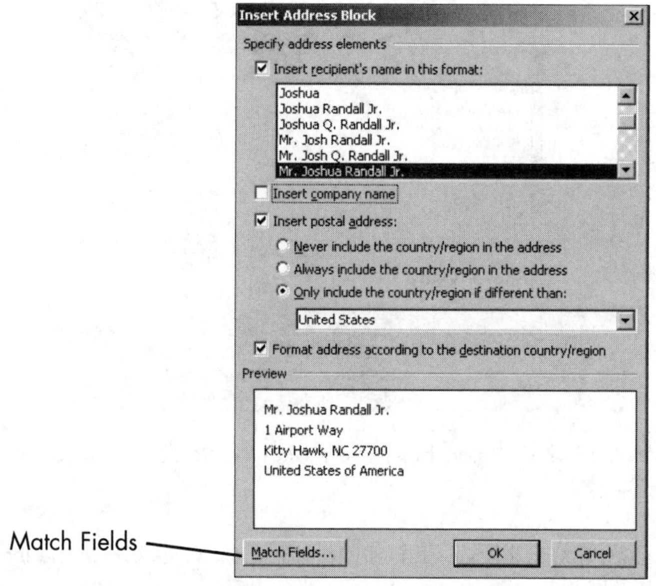

Figure 13.26 In early versions of Microsoft Office, you needed to add fields one by one for a mail merge. Later versions let you add whole sections of the letter, such as the address.

18. Click the Match Fields button (refer to Figure 13.26). In the Match Fields dialog box (see Figure 13.27), open the drop-down lists for the following items in Required Information and match the fields as follows:
    - `Last Name` *`CustLastName`*
    - `First Name` *`CustFirstName`*
    - `Courtesy Title` *`CustSalutation`*
    - `Address1` *`CustStreetAddress`*
    - `City` *`CustCity`*
    - `State` *`CustState`*
    - `Postal Code` *`CustZIP`*

Scroll down the list to see what other items are available in Optional Information.

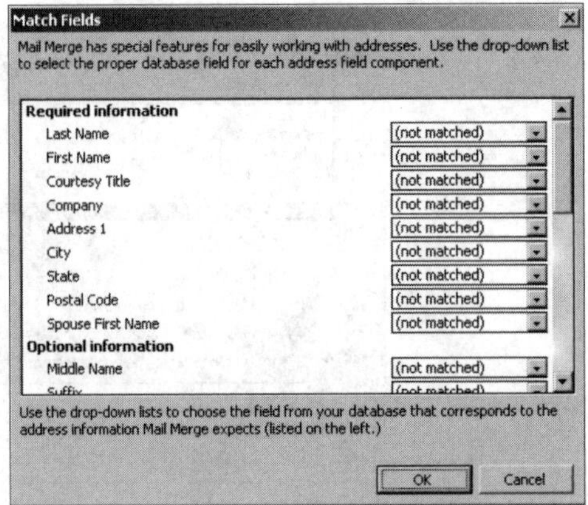

Figure 13.27 In the Match Fields dialog box, you match the fields in your query to the fields in the Address Block.

19. Click OK in the Match Fields dialog box. Click OK in the Insert Address Block dialog box. Press Enter twice.
20. In the Mail Merge pane, click Greeting Line. Review the dialog box (see Figure 13.28), leave the settings as they are, and click OK.

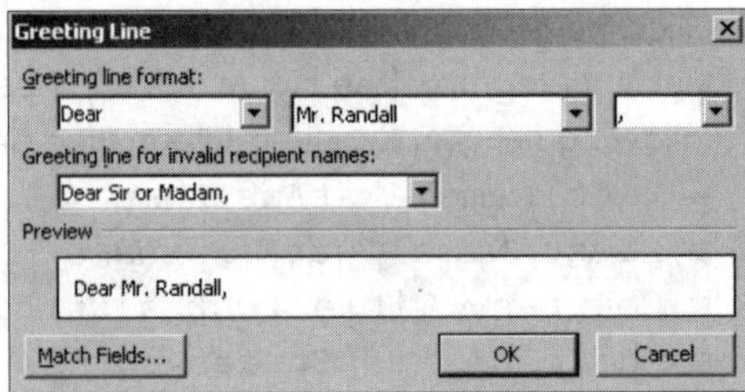

Figure 13.28 The Greeting Line dialog box.

21. Type the rest of your letter. A sample letter is displayed in Figure 13.29.

NOTE You can add fields in the body of the text. Click where you want to insert the field and then click More items in the Mail Merge pane. Select the field and click Insert.

July 20, 2004

«AddressBlock»

«GreetingLine»

New California tax law adds a 10% sales tax surcharge on all FUGASI (pronounced fu-GAY-see, ie, Future Garage Sales Items). We have reviewed our product list and found that all of our merchandise is subject to the new regulations. We are therefore implementing a 10% across-the-board price increase.

Thank you for your understanding.

Sincerely,

Augustus Pinot

Figure 13.29 The sample letter includes the Address Block and Greeting Line, as well as the body of the letter.

22. Click Next, Preview Your Letters.

    You can scroll through the letters by clicking the double-arrow keys in Preview Your Letters. Figure 13.30 shows the third letter in the merge.

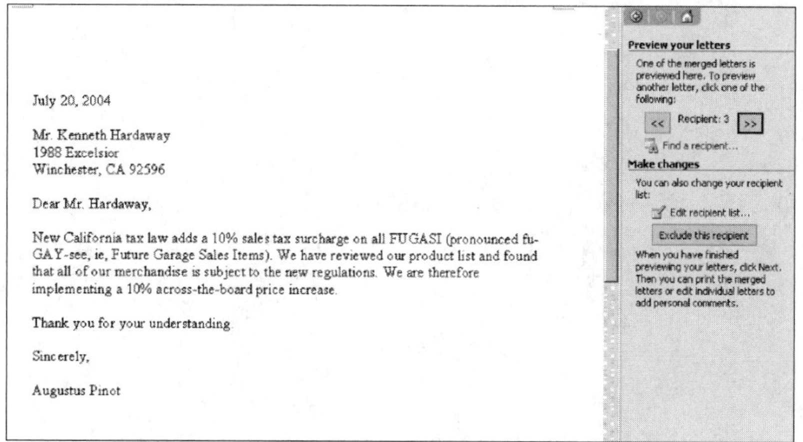

July 20, 2004

Mr. Kenneth Hardaway
1988 Excelsior
Winchester, CA 92596

Dear Mr. Hardaway,

New California tax law adds a 10% sales tax surcharge on all FUGASI (pronounced fu-GAY-see, ie, Future Garage Sales Items). We have reviewed our product list and found that all of our merchandise is subject to the new regulations. We are therefore implementing a 10% across-the-board price increase.

Thank you for your understanding.

Sincerely,

Augustus Pinot

Figure 13.30 A completed letter with address and greeting line data.

23. Click Next, Complete the Merge.
    You can click Print to print all your letters, or Edit Individual Letters to merge the letters in one document.
24. Click Edit Individual Letters. In the Merge to New Document dialog box, with All selected, click OK.
    The letters are merged into one document, which you can save or discard as you choose.

NOTE One final note: Remember that the mail-merge document depends on data from the underlying table or query. Any changes in the underlying object could affect your mail merge.

CHAPTER 14

PIVOT TABLES AND PIVOT CHARTS

In Chapter 9, "Queries, Part II," you learned about crosstab queries; in this chapter, you learn about pivot tables. Both summarize data in two-dimensional matrixes. But pivot tables are much more powerful than crosstab queries: They add extra levels of detail for more in-depth analysis. They are extremely flexible, so you can "slice and dice" your data in many ways. They make it easy to find all kinds of totals, such as sums, counts, and averages, for many sets and subsets of data.

And pivot tables are fun. Yes, they do entail a learning curve. There's a lot going on in a pivot table, and you can set many properties that affect both substance and appearance. But when you know how pivot tables work, you'll find yourself pivoting like crazy. Pivot tables are useful for managers who want to view and analyze data from many standpoints. You can quickly move from finding the average monthly revenue of the Wilmington office for the third quarter to finding the total number of orders for the Dayton branch last year. Extended analysis can be a substitute for action, but more frequently, the powerful analytical tools that pivot tables offer will help you make better decisions.

The term *pivot table* itself is a little deceptive. True, *pivot* is an apt adjective for the kind of data gymnastics it enables you to perform. And it is a *table* in the broadest sense of the word: The end product is a grid with a lot of values and sums, as you might expect from a feature that has its origins in Excel. (Until the most recent Access versions, pivot table creation in Access was executed through an embedded Excel object.)

But a pivot table is not another type of Access table (the term I'll use for the tables you've been working with all along). When you create a table, there is no pivot table selection in the New Table dialog box. A pivot table is not a full-fledged object, but rather a view, as in Datasheet view. Although it enables you to examine data in meaningful ways, you cannot add or edit records in PivotTable view. (I use the Access spelling of *PivotTable* when appropriate, but otherwise I prefer the simpler *pivot table*.)

Furthermore, you'll usually build a pivot table based on a query, not a table. That makes sense if you think of a pivot table as a crosstab query's big brother. In both, you usually combine data from several tables so you can break down and sum the data for analysis. It's unlikely that all the data you need will be in a single table because tables are organized by subject, not mission objective.

As with a pivot table, a pivot chart is a dynamic view of data that can be quickly changed to examine different data from different standpoints. As a chart, of course, the perspective is graphical instead of textual. Pivot tables and pivot charts are close cousins, but not necessarily kissing ones. Design and data changes in one are reflected in the other. But if you want to build a pivot chart, you just go ahead and do it—you don't need, or even necessarily want, to build a pivot table first.

NOTE In earlier versions of Access, the Pivot Table Wizard was central to creating pivot tables. With the introduction of views, however, the wizard has lost much of its value, although it remains a selection in the New Form dialog box. Similarly, you can continue to use Microsoft Graph to create charts in Access, but I think you'll prefer pivot charts when you learn how to build them.

Getting Started with Pivot Tables

Any table or query can be given a PivotTable view by selecting it from the View drop-down list (see Figure 14.1). But this is merely the launch point for creating a pivot table; your work is just beginning. The virgin PivotTable view in Figure 14.2 can be compared to the Design view that greets you when you build a new form from scratch—but with one vital difference. With a form, you build in Design view, but the display is in Form view. With a pivot table, you build in PivotTable view and display in PivotTable view. The main building blocks of a pivot table are the fields in the field list, which you drag and drop onto specific areas of the table.

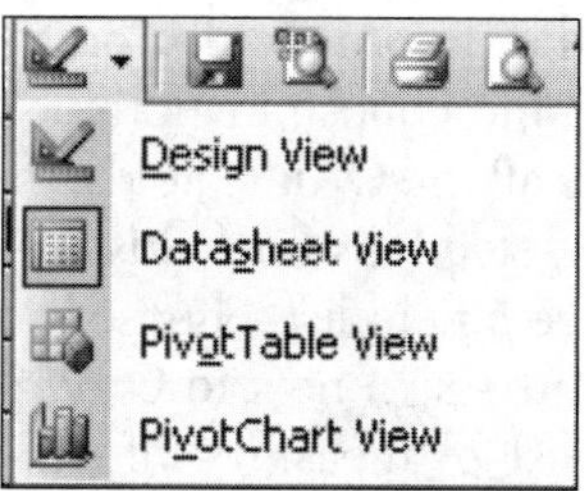

Figure 14.1 PivotTable and PivotChart are views in a table, form, or query; they are not separate objects in the Database window.

These areas correspond to the four key elements in a pivot table: row, column, filter, and totals/detail (see Figure 14.2). These elements, particularly column and detail, work together slightly differently than they do in an Access table. A simple example is the best way to get a feel for how a pivot table works.

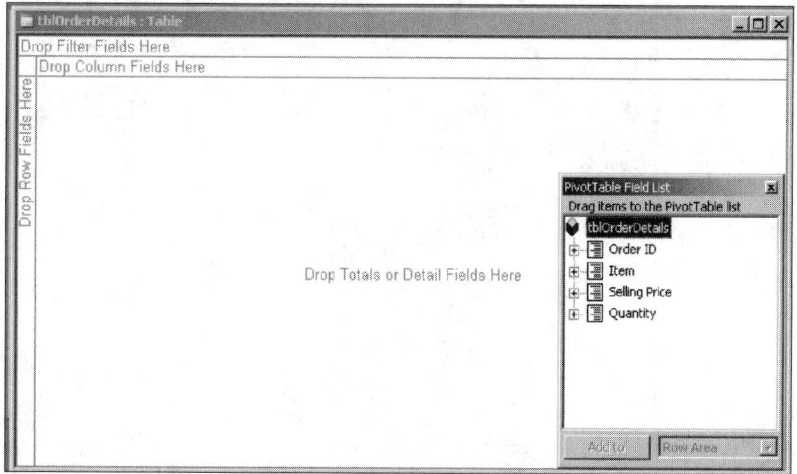

Figure 14.2 The Order Details table in PivotTable view before any fields have been added. (The field list has been moved and the table has been resized for a better picture; your screen will look slightly different.)

1. Copy the `NiftyLionsChap14.mdb` database to your hard drive.
2. Open the tblOrders table and briefly familiarize yourself with the data.
   Note that all the orders were made in the third quarter of the year. Also note that `Overnight?` is a `Yes/No` field.

3. Open the drop-down list on the View button at the far left of the toolbar and choose PivotTable View.
   Besides all the Orders fields, the field list includes By Week and By Month selections for fields with the `Date/Time` data type. (If you don't see a field list, choose View, Field List.)
4. Click the + sign next to Order Date by Month.
   A full list of measures of time is displayed, including Years and Quarters.
5. Select Years, and drag and drop it onto Drop Row Fields Here.
   In the list, note that Order Date by Month Field and Years Field now appear in bold.
6. Click the + sign next to 2004 to expand the tree.
   Only Qtr3 is displayed because all orders were made in that period. If orders were made in all quarters, all would be displayed.
7. Click the + sign next to Qtr 3 (see Figure 14.3).

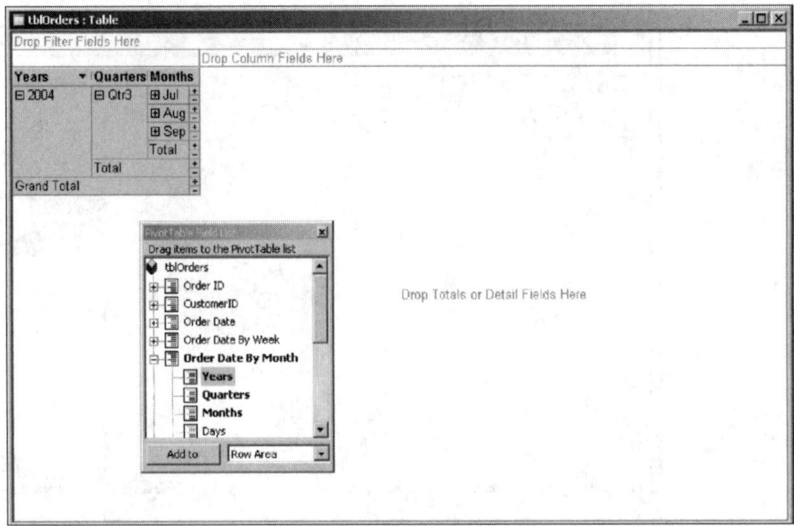

Figure 14.3 You can expand or collapse pivot table items by clicking the + or – buttons.

The months are displayed. You could similarly expand the tree to display days, hours, minutes, and seconds (if the times had been entered with such specificity).

8. Click Shipper in the field list. Drag and drop it onto Drop Column Fields Here.

Note that dropping fields in the Column (or Row) section does not add values to the detail area. Instead, it gives you the column (or Row) headings.

Also note that the table displays the `ShipperID`, the actual ID stored in the Orders table. If you built a query and included supplier company names on the design grid, you could then display the names in the pivot table.

TIP When you select fields for columns, they should contain only a few different values. In other words, the fields can have lots of records, but the data in them should be highly repetitive, not highly unique. Otherwise, you'll find yourself with hundreds or even thousands of columns, and your PivotTable will be difficult to manage and interpret.

---

9. In the field list, click `ShipCost`. Drag and drop it anywhere on Drop Totals or Detail Fields Here.

   The values from the underlying table are displayed.

10. Right-click `ShipCost` in the first column in the Detail area. Choose AutoCalc, Sum.

    The freight costs are summed by shipper and quarter (see Figure 14.4).

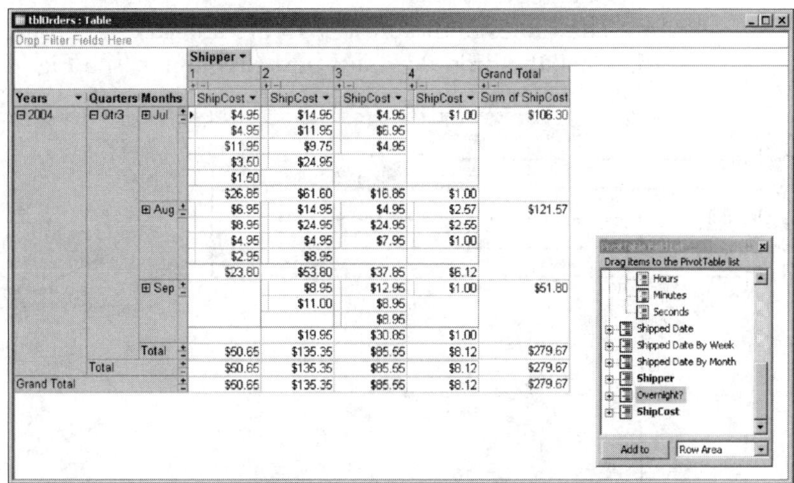

Figure 14.4 Totals can be quickly added to the table using the AutoCalc command on the shortcut menu.

TIP If the field list disappears, click anywhere in the table. You can also click View, Field List once (or twice) on the Pivot Table toolbar.

---

11. Click `Overnight?` in the field list. Drag and drop it onto Drop Filter Fields Here.
    You can use the Filter area for fields you might want to use as a filter but don't want to include on the table itself. For example, you might want to filter the records by customer state, but you don't want any state totals in the table.
12. Click the Overnight? drop-down button.
13. You select and deselect the check boxes to specify the values you want. The All choice shows all records. You can use the same method to filter from a row or column field, but you cannot filter from a totals/data field.

TIP As you can see, the filter tools in a pivot table are limited. One workaround is to create a filter with your usual methods (such as Filter by Selection) in Datasheet or Form view and then switch to PivotTable view.

---

14. Deselect Yes to show only those records sent by regular freight. Click OK.
    The values in the pivot chart are adjusted accordingly.
15. Click the drop-down list next to Shipper (see Figure 14.5).

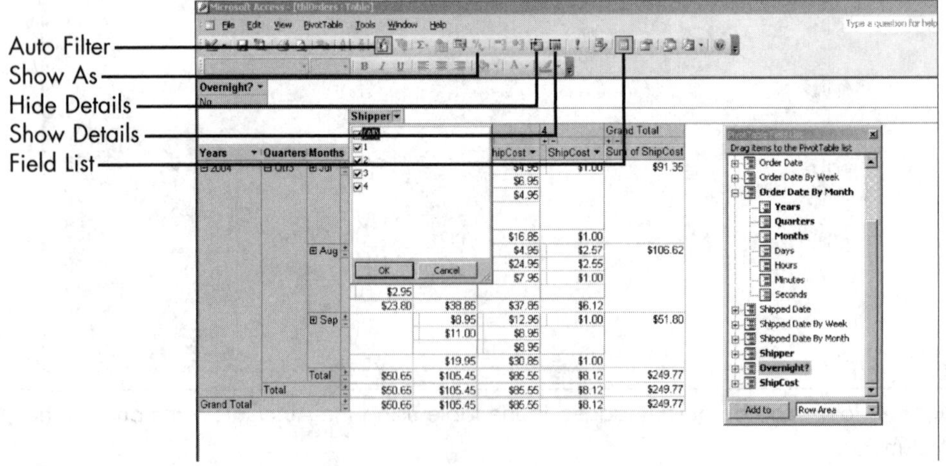

Figure 14.5 You can filter records using row, column, or filter fields.

You can filter the Shipper records by similarly selecting and deselecting the records you want.

16. Click Cancel. Close the table. Click Yes to save the layout changes.

Details and Totals

Let me spend a moment discussing the Hide Details and Show Details commands, which are important.

In a pivot table, you have two ways to present data. You can show the details, which are the actual values from the underlying table(s). You can also show totals, which includes sums, counts, and other aggregates.

When you drop a field onto the Drop Totals or Detail Fields Here area, the values (the details) are displayed. If you want to show totals instead, you can right-click the field name and choose an aggregate from the AutoCalc menu. (The Q&A in the upcoming section "Another Pivot Table Example" describes an additional method for calculating aggregates.)

When you don't want to see the actual field values, you can choose the Hide Details command from PivotTable menu; you can display them again by choosing the Show Details command.

Pivot Table Commands

As is often the case in Access, there are several ways to perform tasks. Here are a few of the more useful buttons on the Pivot Table toolbar (refer to Figure 14.5):

- **AutoFilter**—Lifts the filter and displays all records. If you click AutoFilter again, the filter is restored.
- **Hide Details**—Displays only totals.
- **Show Details**—Displays both values and totals.
- **Show As (Percentage)**—Displays numbers as various percentages of others.
- **Field List**—Shows the field list.

Pivot Tables Using Queries

Occasionally, all the fields you need for a pivot table will be in a single table. But it's more likely that you will want to use fields from several tables. Thus, you will usually want to begin a pivot table by creating a query. In the following example, you create a query and then use it to learn more about the various features and functions of pivot tables.

Suppose that as the Nifty Lions sales manager, you want to get a sense of what kind of merchandise is selling best in each state, as well as which of your suppliers are providing this merchandise. To do this analysis, you need to know the category (for type of merchandise), the customer's state, the merchandise in each order, and who supplies which product. Table 14.1 shows the fields you need.

Table 14.1 The Fields Necessary for the Analysis

What You Need to Know	Field	Table
Type of merchandise	CategoryName	Categories
State of customer	CustState	Customers
Merchandise in order	MerchName	Merchandise
Supplier	SuppCompanyName	Suppliers

In the Database window, choose Tools, Relationships. The Categories, Suppliers, and Merchandise tables are all related. You can join the `Customers` and `Merchandise` fields by adding linking tables—namely, the Orders and Order Details tables. (If you have problems understanding this paragraph, review Chapter 9.)

Create the Query

To create the query, simply do the following:

1. In the Database window, click Queries and choose New. With Design View selected, click OK.
2. Add the tables in the Show Table window in the following order: tblSuppliers, tblCategories, tblMerchandise, tblOrderDetails, tblOrders, and tblCustomers.
   If you want to see all the relationships, drag the Categories field list down slightly, as shown in Figure 14.6.

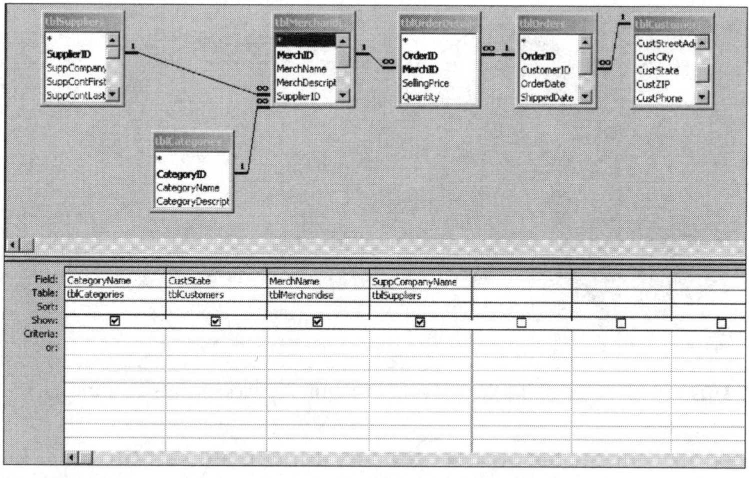

Figure 14.6 The `Orders` and `Order Details` fields have been added only to provide a join between the Customers and Merchandise fields.

3. Add the following fields from the following field lists:
   - `Categories` *`CategoryName`*
   - `Customers` *`CustState`*
   - `Merchandise` *`MerchName`*
   - `Suppliers` *`SuppCompanyName`*
4. Save the query as **qryPivotProducts**.
5. Click View to see your records.

With the data collected, let's create a pivot table.

1. Choose PivotTable View from the View button drop-down list.
2. Click `Category Name` in the field list. Drop it on Column Fields Here.
3. Click `Product Name`. Drop it on Drop Totals Or Detail Fields Here.
4. Click `CustState`. Drop it on Drop Row Fields here.
5. Choose PivotTable, Hide Details.
6. In the pivot table, right-click `Category Name`. Choose AutoCalc, Count.
7. Right-click `CategoryName` on the pivot table and select Hide Details.

   Your pivot table should look like Figure 14.7. You can see the count of products by category and state. Note that this merely counts the number of times the product name is mentioned; it does not reflect the quantity of each product ordered.

Drop Filter Fields Here

	Category Name					
	Clothing	Decorative	Jewelry	Novelty	Toys	Grand Total
CustState	Count of Category Name	Count of Category Name	Count of Category Name	Count of Category Name	Count of Category Name	Count of Category Name
AK		1		1		2
AZ				1		1
CA	1	1	1	2	2	7
CO	1	1			1	3
GA			1			1
IA		1		3	1	5
IL		1			1	2
KY	1	1	1			3
MI				2	1	3
MS				1	1	2
NC		1				1
ND	1	2		2		5
NV				1		1
PA	1	1		1		3
TX			1			1
VT		1			1	2
WA			1			1
WV				1	2	3
Grand Total	5	11	5	15	10	46

Figure 14.7 A pivot table makes it easy to quickly add totals to the grid.

8. Click `Company Name`. Drag it all the way to the left. When you see the heavy blue line, drop it to the left of `CustState`.
   Now you can see the merchandise ordered broken down by supplier and further broken down by customer state.
9. Click `Company Name` on the pivot table (to the left of `CustState`). Drag it to the left of `CategoryName`. When you see the heavy blue line (see Figure 14.8), drop it.
   This gives you counts broken down first by supplier and then by category.
10. Save your query and close it.

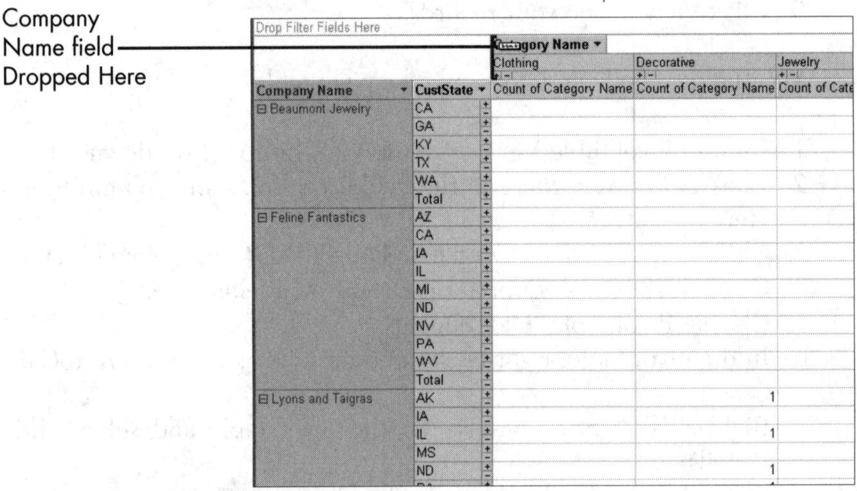

Figure 14.8 One of the many advantages of pivot tables is that you can easily switch fields to a different axis. Here the `Company Name` field is just about to be dropped to the left of `Category Name`.

TIP Because pivot tables are so flexible, it is tempting to throw lots of fields into the query, just in case you want to include another element. But I suggest that you decide beforehand what information you want the pivot table to show and use only the data you need for each query. You can always create another query or add fields to an existing one, if you need to.

Another Pivot Table Example

As you can see, the pivot table gives you excellent capabilities to break down data in different ways. Let's try one more example, in which you'll analyze Nifty Lions freight costs by shipper.

1. In the Database window, click Queries and choose New. With Design View selected, click OK.
2. From the Show Table window, add the tblCustomers, tblOrders, and tblShippers field lists. Close the dialog box.
3. From the Shippers table, add the `ShipCompanyName` field. From the Customers table, add the `CustState` field. From the Orders table, add the `ShipCost` and `Overnight` fields.
4. Save the query as **qryPivotFreight** (see Figure 14.9).
5. Click View to switch to Datasheet view and review your records.
6. Click the View drop-down button and choose PivotTable View.
7. In the field list, click `Company Name`. With `RowArea` selected at the bottom of the field list, click the Add To button next to it.
   You might find this method of adding fields to the pivot table easier than dragging and dropping.
8. Click `CustState`. With `RowArea` selected at the bottom of the field list, click Add To.
9. Click `Overnight?`. Open the drop-down list at the bottom of the field list and select Column Area. Click Add To.
10. Click `Ship Cost`. Open the drop-down list and select Detail Area. Click Add To.
11. Right-click either occurrence of `ShipCost` in the Detail area. Select AutoCalc, Sum.
    You now have shipping costs, broken down by company and then by state. The freight costs are also divided between regular and overnight orders (scroll down a bit to see the data in Figure 14.10). The pivot table also shows the total shipping costs for each shipper.

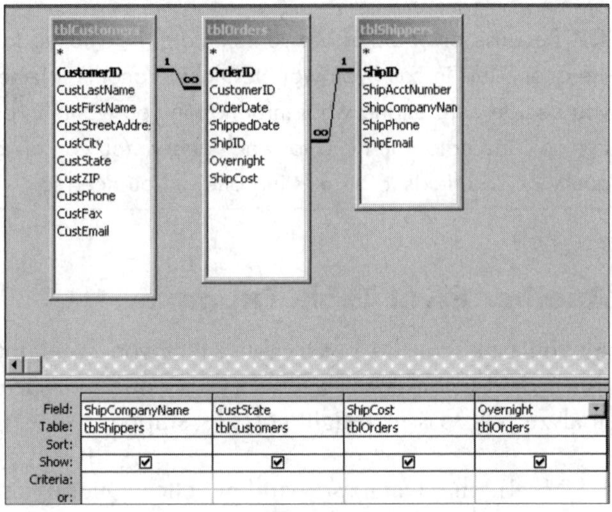

Figure 14.9 The `PivotFreight` query in Design view.

Drop Filter Fields Here

		Overnight?		
		No	Yes	Grand Total
Company Name	CustState	ShipCost	ShipCost	Sum of ShipCost
		$17.90		
	ND	$24.95		$24.95
		$24.95		
	NV	$4.95		$4.95
		$4.95		
	PA	$8.95		$8.95
		$8.95		
	Total	$85.55		$85.55
⊟ Faster Delivery	AK	$24.95		$24.95
		$24.95		
	CA	$11.95		$11.95
		$11.95		
	CO	$9.75	$14.95	$24.70
		$9.75	$14.95	
	IA	$11.00		$11.00
		$11.00		
	IL	$8.95		$8.95
		$8.95		
	TX	$4.95		$4.95
		$4.95		
	VT	$24.95		$24.95
		$24.95		
	WA		$14.95	$14.95
			$14.95	
	WV	$8.95		$8.95
		$8.95		
	Total	$105.45	$29.90	$135.35
⊟ USPS	CA	$2.55		$2.55

Figure 14.10 In the field list, you can use the Add To button to place fields in the various sections of the pivot table.

12. Save your changes and close the query.

TIP To remove a field from the pivot table, right-click it and choose Remove.

Q&A

Q: I've been using pivot tables a bit, and there's one thing I don't get. A lot of the time I get a bunch of empty columns that say No Details (see Figure 14.11). Why is this happening? How do I stop it? Do I want to stop it?

A: I was afraid you were going to ask me that. Let me try to explain what's going on.

In the drop-down list next to the Add To button you'll find a Detail Area selection (which I used in the previous example) and a Data Area selection (which I didn't). When you choose Detail Area, you add the actual values to the table. When you choose Data Area, you add only totals, not the actual values.

The totals you can create using Data Area are specific and limited (although common and useful). If the field has a `Number` or `Currency` data type, the totals will be sums. If the field is non-numeric (such as `Text`), the totals will be counts.

Suppose you want to compute any other aggregate (for example, average) or view the actual values and not just the totals. In these cases, you must first add the actual values (either by dragging and dropping the field or by using the Add, Detail Area button) and then choose the AutoCalc command.

Here's the crux of the matter: If you use Add, Data Area to add totals and then choose the Show Details command, you're going to get a bunch of columns that say No Details. Why? Because you haven't added the actual values; you've added only the totals.

I don't want to tell you to avoid the Data Area selection because it is fast and convenient. But be aware of how it works and its limitations. And remember, you can always use the AutoCalc method as an alternative.

	Overnight?		
	No	Yes	Grand Total
Order ID	No Details	No Details	Sum of Ship Cost
11			$3.50
Total			$3.50
21			$8.95
Total			$8.95
22			$4.95
Total			$4.95
1			$4.95
Total			$4.95
10			$11.95
Total			$11.95
5			$4.95
26			$2.95
Total			$7.90
13			$1.50

Figure 14.11 The pivot table with empty No Details columns.

Pivot Table Properties

Pivot tables come with an array of features that either enhance your analytical power or simply make life easier and more pleasant. On the mundane side, you can change fonts and supply captions. On the much more interesting analytical side, you can create group items and filter for top (or bottom) values. Most of the fine-tuning is performed in the Properties dialog box, which is available from the context (shortcut or right-click) menus. The properties in the dialog box, as with those in the property sheet in a form, depend entirely on which element of the table you select.

Using the Top Values Property

As you might recall from Chapter 8, "Queries," you use the `Top Values` property to show the best, the worst, the highest, the lowest, and so on. You can set top and bottom limits for values in a pivot table as well.

You might initially have some trouble deciding which field has the top values you want to see. The temptation is to choose one of the `Detail` fields because that's where all the data is. But as the following example shows, the solution lies elsewhere.

1. From the Database window, open `qryPivotFrieghtTopValues`. This is the same query as `PivotFreight`, with one more column: I've added the `OrderID` field.
2. Open the View drop-down list and select PivotTable View. The Order ID column is the third row field, after CustState. Because orders have only one freight cost, the subtotals in the ShipCost column are unnecessary (see Figure 14.12). You can easily hide the subtotals by using the Subtotal toggle on the shortcut menu.

Subtotals

			Overnight?		
			No	Yes	Grand Total
Company Name	CustState	Order ID	ShipCost	ShipCost	Sum of ShipCost
⊟ Apollo Shipping	⊟ CA	16	$6.95		$6.95
			$6.95		
	⊟ CO	11	$3.50		$3.50
			$3.50		
	⊟ GA	21	$8.95		$8.95
			$8.95		
	⊟ IA	22	$4.95		$4.95
			$4.95		
	⊟ MI	1	$4.95		$4.95
			$4.95		
	⊟ NC	10	$11.95		$11.95
			$11.95		
	⊟ PA	5	$4.95		$4.95
			$4.95		
		26	$2.95		$2.95
			$2.95		
	⊟ VT	13	$1.50		$1.50
			$1.50		
	Total		$50.65		$50.65
⊟ EAN Lines	⊟ AZ	25	$7.95		$7.95
			$7.95		

Figure 14.12 The subtotals in the ShipCost columns are superfluous and can be easily eliminated.

3. Right-click Order ID. Click Subtotal to eliminate the subtotals.
4. Right-click either occurrence of `ShipCost` for a shortcut menu. Note that the Show Top/Bottom Items selection on the menu is grayed out and unavailable. Because `ShipCost` is a detail field and not a row or column, you cannot show the top values.
5. Right-click Order ID and choose Show Top/Bottom Items, Show Only the Top, 5. The pivot table hides all but the five orders with the highest freight costs. Notice that a little filter symbol now appears in the Order ID column (see Figure 14.13).

Drop Filter Fields Here

Filter symbol

			Overnight?		
			No	Yes	Grand Total
Company Name	CustState	Order ID	ShipCost	ShipCost	Sum of ShipCost
⊟ EAN Lines	⊟ ND	23	$24.95		$24.95
			$24.95		
		Total	$24.95		$24.95
	Total		$24.95		$24.95
⊟ Faster Delivery	⊟ AK	9	$24.95		$24.95
			$24.95		
		Total	$24.95		$24.95
	⊟ CO	14		$14.95	$14.95
				$14.95	
		Total		$14.95	$14.95
	⊟ VT	17	$24.95		$24.95
			$24.95		
		Total	$24.95		$24.95
	⊟ WA	3		$14.95	$14.95
				$14.95	
		Total		$14.95	$14.95
	Total		$49.90	$29.90	$79.80
Grand Total			$74.85	$29.90	$104.75

Figure 14.13 The Top/Bottom Values command hides all orders except those with the highest freight cost.

6. Right-click Order ID. Choose Show Top/Bottom Items, Show All.
7. Close the query and save your changes.

Grouping Records

Sometimes you want to group records by intervals. For example, you might want to group the records by `OrderID` number.

1. From the Database window, open `qryPivotFreightGrouping`. This is the same query as `PivotFreightTopValues`, but I've deleted the company name and customer state fields from the pivot table.
2. Click the View drop-down list and choose PivotTable View.
3. Right-click Order ID in the row area and choose Properties.
4. Click the Filter and Group tab.
5. In the Grouping section, open the Group Items By drop-down list and choose Numeric Interval.
6. Edit the interval to **5**.
   In the Properties dialog box, note that you could have also supplied a range of orders.

7. Close the Properties dialog box. The `OrderIDs` are now grouped in units of five (see Figure 14.14).
8. Close the query and save your changes.

Drop Filter Fields Here

	Overnight?		
	No	Yes	Grand Total
Order ID	ShipCost	ShipCost	Sum of ShipCost
1 - 5	$4.95	$14.95	$30.80
	$4.95		
	$1.00		
	$4.95		
	$15.85	$14.95	
6 - 10	$11.95		$65.55
	$9.75		
	$6.95		
	$24.95		
	$11.95		
	$65.55		
11 - 15	$3.50	$14.95	$29.85
	$4.95		
	$1.50		
	$4.95		
	$14.90	$14.95	
16 - 20	$6.95		$41.97
	$24.95		

Figure 14.14 Grouping is just one of many properties you can set in the Properties dialog box. Here the `OrderIDs` have been grouped in intervals of five each.

Creating Pivot Charts

Microsoft defines a pivot chart as a "practical interface that allows users to view comparisons, patterns, and trends in data in a visually appealing manner." That might or might not be more useful than saying that a pivot chart is a lot like a pivot table, except that it's a chart.

Pivot charts and tables are closely entwined in some ways, yet separate in others. If you create a table in PivotTable view, you will see a graphical representation of it in PivotChart view. In fact, the data source for the chart is the pivot table. Any changes you make in PivotTable view will be reflected in PivotChart view, and vice versa.

On the other hand, for the most part, there's no need to bother with an underlying pivot table if your only objective is to create a pivot chart. You can create the chart directly in PivotChart view. Moreover, when you create a pivot chart, you can choose among numerous chart types, each of which presents data graphically in its own way. So when your objective is a pivot chart, I advise doing all your work in PivotChart view and ignoring PivotTable view entirely.

NOTE This general rule has some exceptions. If you want to display aggregate functions besides `Sum` and `Count`, you'll need to create them first in PivotTable view. They will then be available in the pivot chart's field list, and you can add them to the chart.

Figure 14.15 shows a pivot chart that contains no fields. As with pivot tables, you drag and drop fields from the field list onto the chart. Where exactly you drop the fields is of utmost importance.

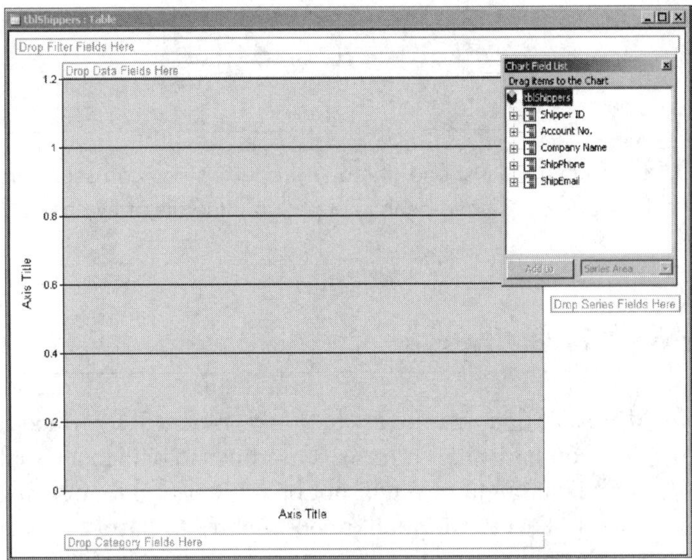

Figure 14.15 A blank pivot chart. The scale at the left is purely a template view and will change to reflect the values in your chart.

Pivot Chart Elements

Describing the various data components of a pivot chart might not be particularly useful. A little experimenting will tell you how each element affects the chart and how the various components interact with each other.

Still, in the interest of completeness, here is a description of each element:

- Category fields represent one point of each data series. In most charts, the categories are represented along the x-axis (horizontal axis) of the chart. Category fields correspond to the Row Fields area of the pivot table.
- The series fields are represented in the chart by data markers—a bar in a bar chart, a slice in a pie chart, and so on. Each data item in the series is defined in the chart legend. The data points are usually plotted on the y-axis (vertical axis) of the chart.
- The data fields contain the values that will be summarized in the chart. You will almost always use other drop areas as well, but the data area is the only area that must have at least one field. The Data Fields area corresponds to the Totals or Details area of a pivot table.
- The filter fields can be used to filter data. As with a pivot table, however, the filtering method is not robust. To filter the records, it's best to filter first in Datasheet or Form view.

Create a Pivot Chart

You can use PivotChart view in any table or form. But as with pivot tables, often you'll want to create a query first so you can use fields from different tables. First you'll create a new query; then you'll design the pivot chart.

Suppose you want to get a picture of your inventory situation. Specifically, you want to know how many units you have on hand of each item. Additionally, you want to see the supplier for that item. You also want to be able to tell quickly what kind of product it is—novelty, jewelry, and so on.

1. In the Database window, click Queries and click New. In the New Query dialog box, click Design View and click OK.

2. In the Show Table dialog box, click tblCategories, press Ctrl, and click tblMerchandise and tblSuppliers. Click Add to add the three field lists to the design grid. Close the Show Table dialog box.
3. In the Categories field list, double-click `CategoryName`. In the Merchandise field list, double-click `MerchName`, `UnitsInStock`, and `UnitsOnOrder`. In the Suppliers field list, double-click `SuppCompanyName`.
4. Save the query as qryMerchandiseUnits.
5. Click View to see and review your records in Datasheet view.
6. Click the View drop-down arrow and choose PivotChart view.
7. Click `Category Name` in the field list and drop it onto Drop Series Fields Here (if you can't find Drop Series Field Here, refer to Figure 14.15 for its location).

   Because you have only five types of product, this will work nicely as a series. You'll be able to use the legend to quickly distinguish one category from the next.
8. Click `Company Name` and drop it onto Drop Category Fields Here.

   Let's think about the relationship between suppliers and products for a moment. Each supplier sells several products, and each product has only one supplier. If you want to see which products are supplied by which supplier, it's best to put suppliers first (on the outside) and products second (on the inside).
9. Click `Product Name` and, in the Drop Category Fields Here area, drop it to the right of `Company Name`.
10. Click `Units in Stock` and drop it onto Drop Data Fields Here. Units in stock is the data you want to measure. The scale at the left tells you how many units are in stock for each product.

    Take a look at the chart. There are some problems. First, where's the legend that tells the product type (jewelry, novelty, and so on)? You can easily display it.
11. On the PivotChart toolbar, click Show Legend (see Figure 14.16).

    The next big problem is that listing suppliers and products along the x-axis makes them difficult to read.

    Perhaps if you used another chart type, the chart could be read more easily. Instead of a column chart, use a bar chart that will measure the units along the x-axis instead of the y-axis.

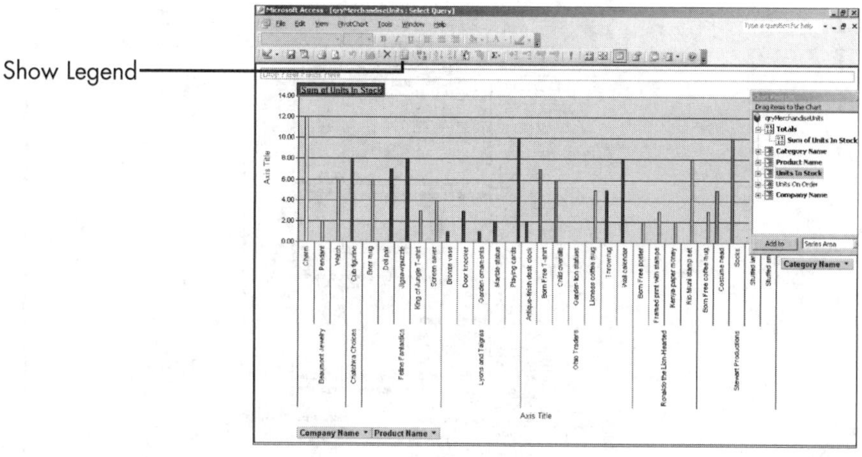

Figure 14.16 A pivot chart built from a query. It has the data you need, but its presentation could be improved.

12. Click any empty space in the chart, away from any element. Choose PivotChart, Chart Type. Click the Type tab. Click Bar. In the first row, select the first bar (see Figure 14.17). The axes are switched and the chart is easier to read. Close the Properties dialog box. Figure 14.18 shows your work (I've closed the field list chart for a better view).

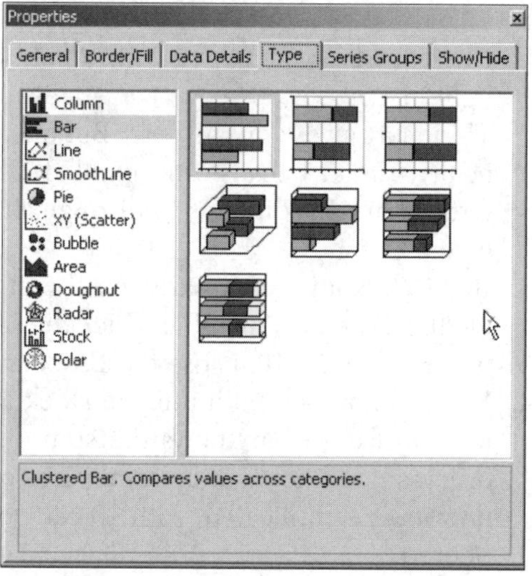

Figure 14.17 In the Properties dialog box, you can choose another chart type. Click the type of chart in the left column, and choose a chart on the right.

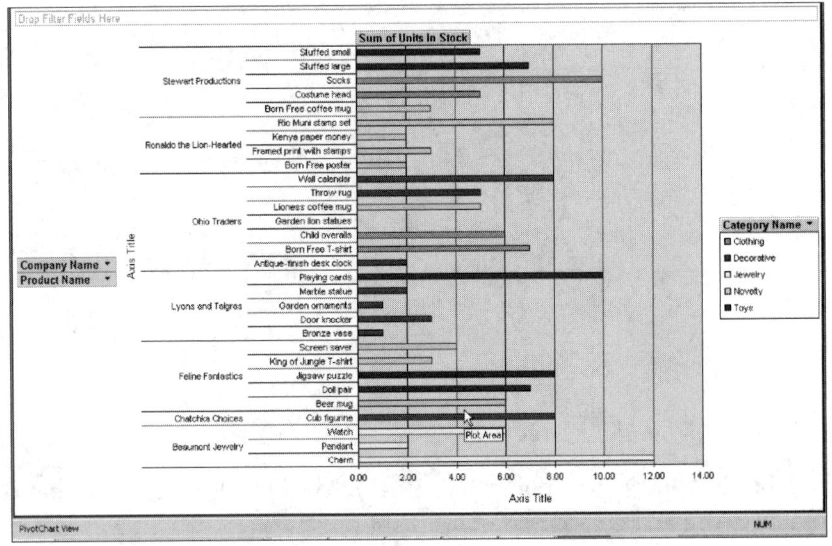

Figure 14.18 The bar chart shows the number of units in stock for each product by supplier, as well as the product category. It still needs some work, however: You can add axis titles, eliminate the decimal places on the scale, and more by using the Properties dialog boxes described in the next section.

Suppose you also wanted to show the `Units On Order` for each product. Let's add it to the chart:

1. Click `Units On Order` in the field list. Drag and drop it to the right of `Sum of Units in Stock`.
2. This chart gives you the data. But on smaller screens, it will be difficult to read because the parallel Units In Stock and Units On Order bars are difficult to distinguish. Let's choose another chart type.
3. Right-click any empty area on the chart and choose Chart Type. On the Type tab, click Bar. Click the second sample in the first row (see Figure 14.19). Close the Properties dialog box.
4. You can now see both units in stock and units on order. The total length of each bar shows the sum of units in stock and units on order, an additional and useful piece of information. The legend is now a bit complicated, with 10 categories, but it can still be deciphered.
5. Save your changes and close the query.

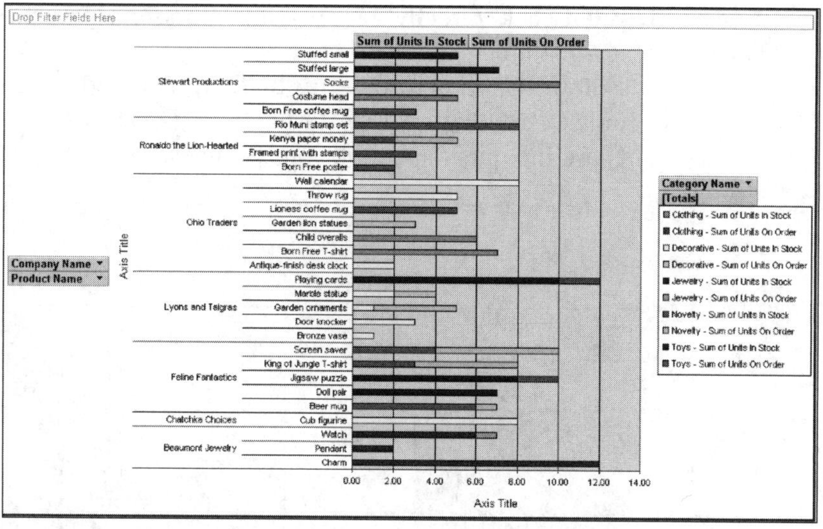

Figure 14.19 This bar chart includes both data fields on the same bar.

Multiple Plot Charts

Sometimes you might prefer to break the data into two or more charts for comparison purposes. The `PivotChartFreight` query shows the total freight of orders, broken down by shipper and state. One of the fields is `Overnight`, a `Yes/No` field that tells you whether the order was shipped by regular freight or overnight delivery. You can have separate charts for overnight and regular delivery of orders.

1. Open the `PivotChartFreight` query. Open the View drop-down list and choose PivotChart view.
2. Choose PivotCharts, Multiple Plots.
   In the middle of the chart, Multi-Chart appears.
3. Click `Overnight?` (either in the field list or on the chart) and drag and drop it onto Drop MultiChart Fields Here.
   The chart on the left is for regular delivery (`NO`, not overnight); the chart on the right is for overnight delivery (`YES`, overnight).
4. Right-click directly on No and choose Properties. Click the Format tab.
5. Edit the Caption to **Regular Delivery**. Close the property dialog box.

6. Right-click directly on Yes and choose Properties. Click the Format tab.
7. Edit the Caption to **Overnight Delivery**. Close the property dialog box (see Figure 14.20).
8. Close the query and save your changes.

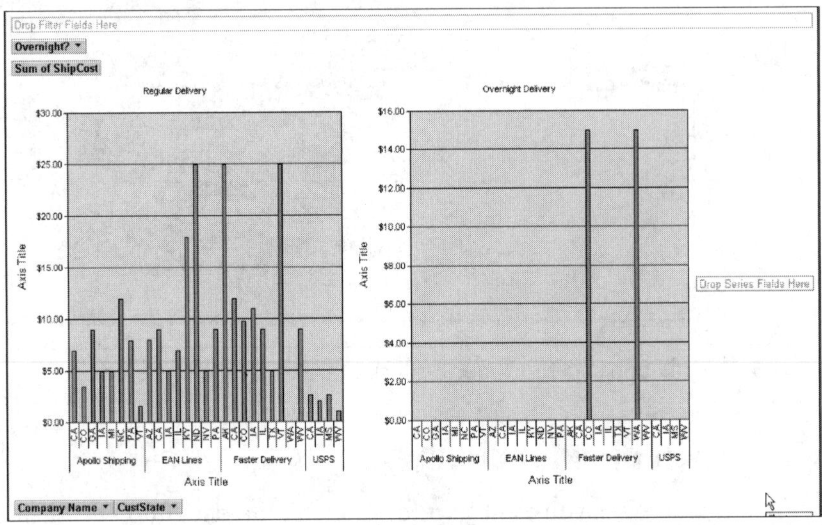

Figure 14.20 You might want multiple charts to segregate presentations of different data elements.

Chart Properties

As with pivot tables, you can set a host of properties for each of the many elements in the chart. Editing chart properties can get confusing because there are so many choices and so many parts. Choosing the correct element is crucial—the properties you edit depend completely on the element chosen. But finding the right place to click is a task unto itself. Look at the element name in the Select box in the General tab of the Properties dialog box to make certain you've chosen the one you need.

One possible (but by no means foolproof) solution is to select the element you want from the General tab in the Properties dialog box. Even a simple chart has a host of elements, however, and figuring out which element is which from their names can be difficult (see Figure 14.21).

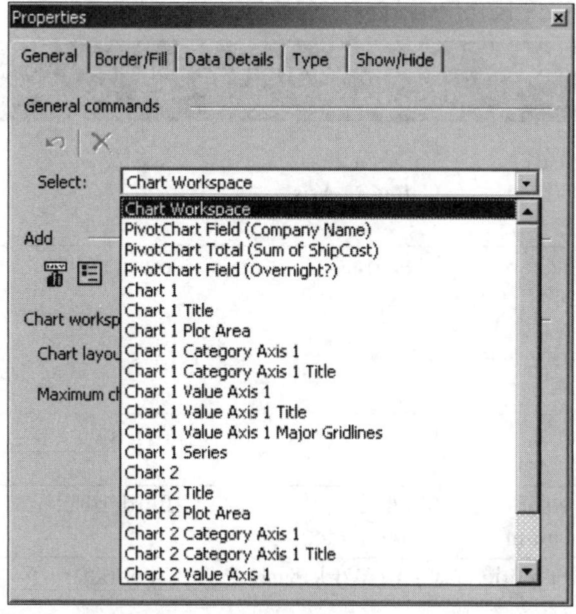

Figure 14.21 You can select chart elements directly on the chart or on the General tab of the Properties dialog box. With so many chart elements, neither method is certain, so carefully check your changes after editing properties.

Table 14.2 shows you how to edit several key items in the various properties dialog boxes.

Table 14.2 Editing Chart Properties

If You Want To...	Select Properties for the...	Click This Tab...	And Do This...
Show the field list by default	Chart Workspace	Show/Hide	Select the Field List
Show the scale in a different format (e.g., percent or currency)	Value Axis	Format	Open the Number drop-down list and select a format
Change the units on the scale	Value Axis	Scale	Edit Custom Major Unit

(continues)

Table 14.2 Editing Chart Properties *continued*

If You Want To...	Select Properties for the...	Click This Tab...	And Do This...
Include vertical/ horizontal gridlines	Value or Category Axis	Axis	Select Major Gridlines and Minor Gridlines
Dress up the chart with a pattern	Plot Area	Border/Fill	Select Picture/ Texture in Fill Type, open the Preset drop-down list, and choose a pattern
Flip the chart	Plot Area	General	Click one of the flip icons
Change the color of one bar or column	Single bar, column, etc.	Border/Fill	Select a color from the palette
Give the chart a title	Chart Workspace	General	Click the Add Title icon
Group items	A category field	Filter and Group	Edit Group Items By and Interval settings
Display top or bottom values	A category or series field	Filter and Group	Edit Filtering settings

Conclusion

In this chapter, you learned the basics of pivot tables and pivot charts. Hopefully the discussion was useful, but I'm certain that for some readers it was simplistic. The examples I used didn't include any calculated expressions, which are often integral to data analyses. For example, extensions of quantity and unit price (such as `7 units @ $3 = $21`) would be handled by a calculated expression.

An excellent place to learn about the use of calculated expressions in pivot tables/charts is a Microsoft Support WebCast on the topic; in fact, it's a good introduction (or, at this point, review) of the entire area. The webcast is for Access 2002, but nearly all of it is still applicable for Access 2003. You can find it as Microsoft Knowledge Base Article 324695. Both the full webcast (sound and PowerPoint presentation) and the printed transcript are offered.

CASE EXAMPLE

In Chapter 11, "Forms/Subforms," you learned how to create a form/subform. The subforms you created were in Datasheet view, but they could have also been displayed in PivotTable view or PivotChart view. As you move from record to record in the main form, the subform's pivot table or pivot chart changes to correspond to the main record.

In the following example, you'll use the Form Wizard to create a form with a subform. You'll then design the pivot chart.

1. In the Database window, click Forms. Double-click Create Form by Using Wizard.
2. Open the drop-down list and select Table:tblOrders. Add all the fields to the Selected Fields pane.
3. Open the Tables/Queries drop-down list and select Table:tblOrderDetails. Add the `OrderID`, `SellingPrice`, and `Quantity` fields to the Selected Fields pane.
4. Open the Table/Queries drop-down list and select Table:tblMerchandise. Add the `MerchName` field to the Selected Fields pane.

By selecting `MerchName` from the Merchandise table instead of `MerchID` from the OrderDetails table, you'll be able to see the actual product name instead of the relatively meaningless merchandise ID.

5. Click Next. View your data by tblOrders and Form with Subform(s). Click Next.
6. Choose PivotChart for the layout of the subform. Click Next.
7. Select the Standard style and click Next.
8. Name the form **frmOrders** and the subform **frmPivotOrderDetails subform**.
9. Click Finish.

Access creates your form, with the subform in PivotChart view (see Figure 14.22). Let's get to work on the subform.

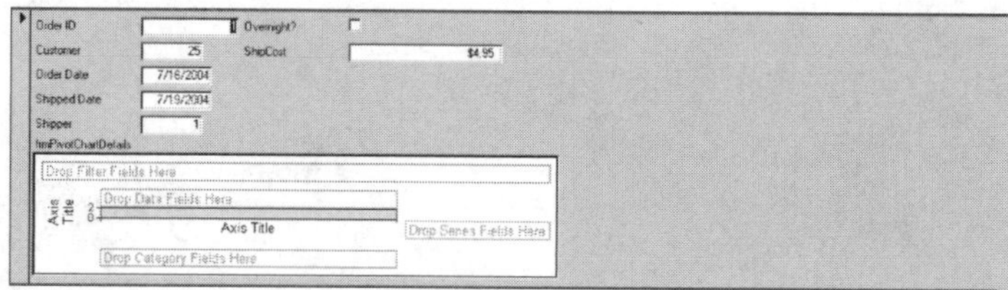

Figure 14.22 The new form/subform in Form view. You still have much work to do on the pivot chart.

1. Click View to go to Design view (see Figure 14.23).

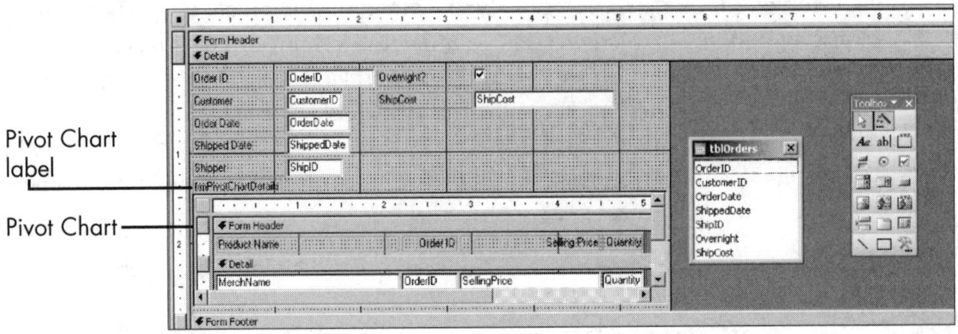

Pivot Chart label

Pivot Chart

Figure 14.23 The form/subform in Design view.

2. Delete the unnecessary label `frmPivotOrderDetails` (refer to Figure 14.23).
3. Select the pivot chart (refer again to Figure 14.23).
4. Press Alt+Enter for the property sheet. Make sure the title is Subform/Subreport frmPivotChartDetails Subform.
5. On the Format tab, edit the Height to **4"**. Close the property sheet.
6. Click View to go to Form view. Click any empty space on the pivot chart to select it.

   Be sure to select the entire chart, not just the data area. If you want to make sure you've selected the entire chart, choose View, Properties. In Select on the General tab, Chart Workspace should be selected.

7. Choose View, Field List.
8. Click `Quantity` and drop it onto Drop Series Fields Here (see Figure 14.24).

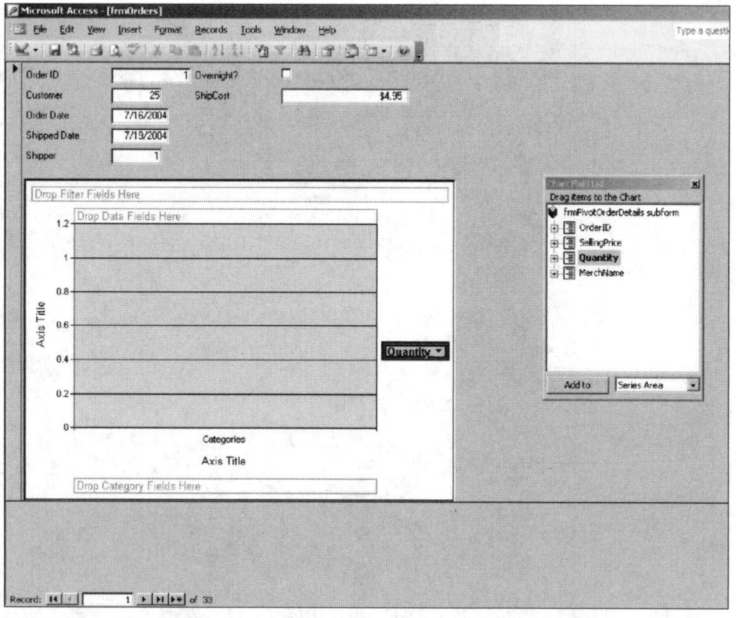

Figure 14.24 The pivot chart has been selected, so only the Form View toolbar is in view. The `Quantity` field has just been dropped onto the chart from the field list.

9. Click `Selling Price` and drop it onto Drop Data Fields Here.

   Don't be misled by the title `Sum of Selling Price`. Because each item in any individual order in the Order Details table has only one selling price, the columns in the chart represent actual prices, not totals.

10. Click `MerchName` and drop it onto Drop Category Fields Here.
11. Right-click in an empty space in the chart and choose Properties. If necessary, open the Select box on the General tab and choose Chart Workspace.
12. On the General tab, click the Add Legend icon (see Figure 14.25).

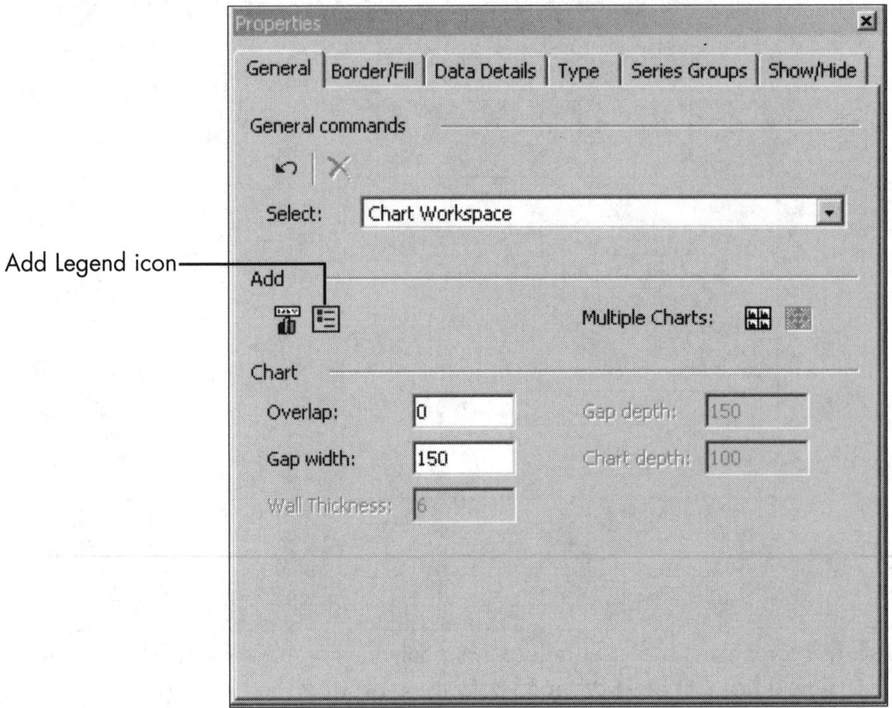

Figure 14.25 The Properties dialog box for the Chart Workspace and the Add Legend icon.

13. Right-click Axis Title on the x-axis. If the Properties dialog box isn't still open, choose Properties. Click the Format tab. Edit the caption to **Merchandise**.
14. With the Properties dialog box still open, click Axis Title on the y-axis. Edit the caption to **Price**.
15. Close the property sheet. Click in any empty space to deselect the y-axis title.
16. Edit the Record Selector box to **16** (see Figure 14.26).

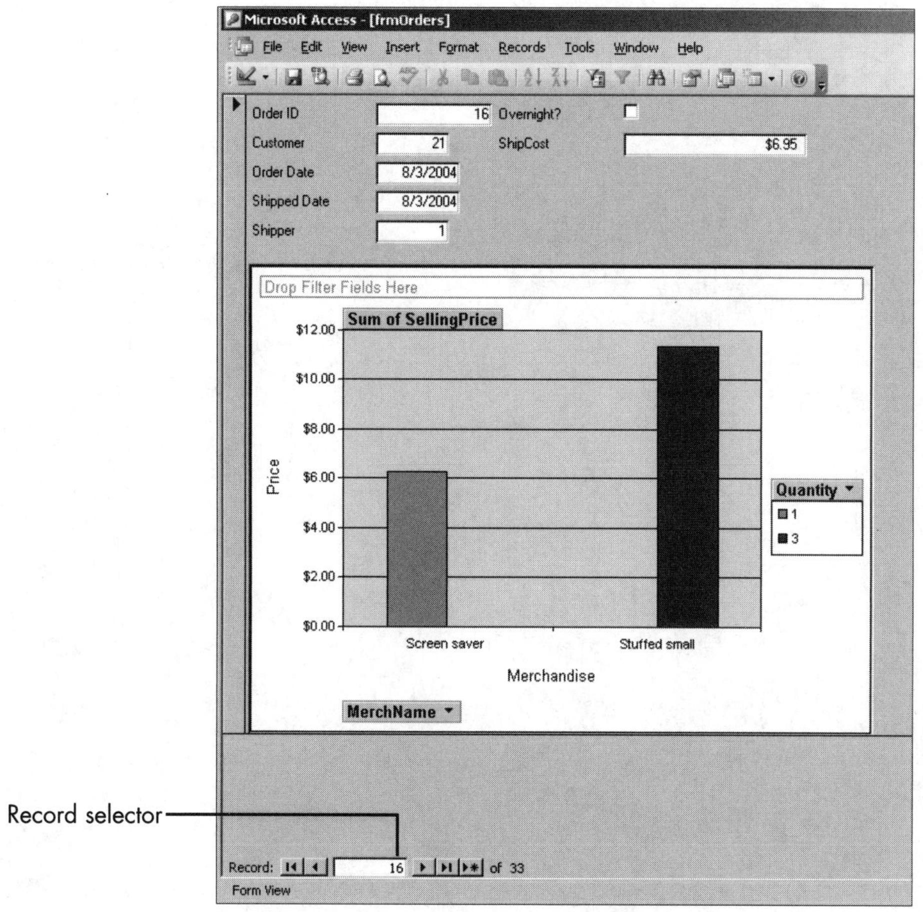

Figure 14.26 The final pivot chart, with captions for the axis titles.

The pivot chart tells you that `OrderID` 16 included one screen saver at a price a little above $6 and three small stuffed lions at a price a little above $11.

17. Close the form and save your changes.

GLOSSARY

NOTE Some definitions have been taken or adopted from the Microsoft Access 2002 glossary available online at http://office.microsoft.com/en-us/assistance/HA010562951033.aspx.

action query A query that copies or changes data. (Compare with *select query*.)

aggregate function A function such as `Sum`, `Count`, or `Avg` used to calculate totals.

alternate key A candidate key that is not used as a primary key.

arithmetic operator A symbol (such as `+` or `-`) that tells you to perform an arithmetic operation.

artificial primary key A key created solely for the purpose of serving as a primary key. In Access, artificial primary keys usually have an AutoNumber data type.

`AutoNumber` A data type usually used as a primary key. By default, each new record in the field stores a unique number that is one higher than the previously entered record.

bound control A control used in a form or report to display a field in an underlying table.

business rules Restrictions on the values that can be entered in a database based on the needs of an organization. Business rules are often enforced through the use of validation rules.

calculated field A field that displays the results of an expression.

candidate key A field whose values can be used to uniquely identify a database record. A primary key is selected from the available candidate keys.

combo box A control used on a form that enables you to either type a value or click the combo box to display a list and then select an item from it.

command button A button that performs an action when clicked.

comparison operator An operator that compares two values, such as `>` (greater than) and `<` (less than).

composite primary key A primary key that includes more than one field.

concatenation A way to tie together various elements in an Access expression. The symbol for concatenation is an ampersand (`&`).

constant Value such as `Yes`, `No`, `True`, and `False` that do not change.

control An object such as a textbox, check box, or option group used to display data or choices, perform an action, or make the user interface easier to view.

criteria Limits placed on a query or advanced filter that enable you to retrieve and view the specific records you want to work with.

crosstab query A query that calculates a sum, average, count, or other type of total on records, and then groups the result by two types of information, one down the left side of the datasheet and the other across the top.

currency A data type that is useful for calculations involving money.

current record The record that currently has the focus.

data integrity A set of rules that ensures the validity, consistency, and accuracy of the data in a database.

data tables The main tables in a database where most of your data is stored.

data type A characteristic of a field that determines what kind of data it can store.

datasheet Data in a table, form, or query that is displayed in a row-and-column format.

default value A value that is automatically entered in a field or control when you add a new record. You can either accept the default value or override it by typing a value.

delimited text file A text file that contains values separated by commas, tabs, semicolons, or some other punctuation. A delimited text file is a useful format for transferring data to or from Access.

detail section The main section of most forms and reports. It usually contains controls bound to the fields in the record source, but it can also have unbound controls, such as labels that identify a field's contents.

embed To insert a copy of an OLE object from another application. The source of the object can be any application that supports object linking and embedding. Changes to an embedded object are not reflected in the original object.

event An action taken by a user that Access can recognize.

export To output data and database objects to another database, spreadsheet, or file format so another database or program can use the data or database objects.

expression Any combination of operators, constants, functions, and names of fields, controls, and properties that evaluates to a single value.

field A column in an Access table.

field list A window in Design view that lists all the fields in the underlying record source, such as a table or query.

field selector A small box or bar that you click to select an entire column in a datasheet.

filter A set of criteria applied to data to display a subset of the data or to sort the data.

fixed-width text file A file containing data in which each field is a constant width.

flat file A database system contained in a single table and without structured relationships.

focus Wherever your next action will take place, as indicated by the cursor or highlighting.

foreign key The field on the "many" side of a one-to-many relationship that contains matching data.

formatting The way values are displayed or printed, as opposed to the way they are stored.

function A procedure that returns a value based on a calculation.

grid (Datasheet view) Vertical and horizontal lines that visually divide rows and columns of data into cells in a table, query, or form. You can show and hide these grid lines.

grid (Design view) An arrangement of vertical and horizontal dotted and solid lines that helps you position controls precisely when you design a form or report.

identifier Element in an expression that refers to the value of a field, control, or property.

import To copy data from a text file, spreadsheet, or database table into an Access table. You can use the imported data to create a new table, or you can add it to an existing table that has a matching data structure.

index A structure that speeds up sorting and searching for data.

inner join A join in which records from two tables are combined in a query's results only if values in the joined fields match.

input mask A template that commonly contains parentheses, periods, hyphens, and other marks and helps you control where data can be entered in a field, the kind of data that can be entered, and the number of characters allowed.

join An association between a field in one table and a field of similar data type in another table. Records that don't match can be included or excluded, depending on the type of join. See also *inner join* and *outer join*.

join table A table that resolves a many-to-many relationship between a pair of tables.

key A field that plays a specific role within a table

label A control that displays descriptive text, such as a title, a caption, or instructions, on a form or report. Labels might or might not be attached to another control.

landscape The orientation of the printed page when the width is greater than the length. A landscape orientation includes more fields but fewer records than a portrait orientation.

legacy database A database that has been in existence and used for an extended period of time.

linked object An object created in a source file and inserted into a target (or destination) file, while maintaining a connection between the two files. The linked object in the target file is updated when the source file is updated, and the source file is updated when the linked object in the target file is updated.

linking table See *join table*.

list box A control that displays a list of values you can choose from.

literal values Names, dates, numbers, and so on that Access evaluates exactly as they are written.

lookup field A field that displays values "looked up" from a field in another table.

lookup table See *validation table*.

macro An action or set of actions you can use to automate tasks.

macro group A collection of related macros that are stored together under a single macro name.

main form The primary form that contains one or more subforms.

many-to-many relationship A relationship between a pair of tables in which a single record in the first table can be related to many records in the second table, and a single record in the second table can be related to many records in the first table.

memo A data type used for large amounts of text.

multipart field A field that contains more than one type of value.

multivalue field A field that stores more than one value in each row.

natural primary key A field that already exists in a table because it defines a specific trait and is designated as the primary key.

navigation buttons The buttons that you use to move through records, located in the lower-left corner of datasheets, forms, and reports.

normal form A set of rules that can be used to test a table structure to ensure its soundness.

normalization To minimize the duplication of data in a relational database through effective table design. The process involves breaking down tables with redundant data into smaller tables.

null value A missing or unknown value. See also *zero-text string*.

number A data type used to store values on which you will want to perform arithmetic.

object selector A box on the Formatting toolbar in Design view of a form or report that you can use to select the various elements within it.

OLE (Object Linking and Embedding) Processes that permit the sharing of files and objects between applications. For example, OLE permits you to link or embed a Microsoft Excel spreadsheet in a form or report.

OLE object A data type used for linking and embedding objects in Access, such as spreadsheets and pictures.

one-to-many relationship A relationship between a pair of tables in which a single record in one table can be related to many records in a second table, but a single record in the second table can be related to only one record in the first table

operator Symbol that tells you what action to perform in an expression.

option group A frame that can contain check boxes, toggle buttons, and option buttons on a form or report. An option group presents all alternatives, from which you choose a single value.

outer join A join between two tables in which all the records from one table and only those records with matching data in the joined field in the second table are included in the query's results.

parameter query A query that, when run, displays one or more dialog boxes that prompt you for criteria for retrieving records.

portrait The orientation of the printed page in which the length is greater than the width. A portrait orientation includes more records but fewer fields than a landscape orientation.

primary key One or more fields that uniquely identify each record in a table.

property A characteristic of an item.

property sheet A window used to view or modify the properties of various objects, such as tables, queries, fields, forms, reports, and controls.

RDBMS (relational database management system) A software program used to create and modify a relational database.

record A row in a table.

referential integrity A system of rules that Microsoft Access uses to ensure that relationships between records in related tables are valid and that you don't accidentally delete or change related data.

relational database A type of database that stores values in tables.

relationship An association between two tables that have fields with matching data.

select query A query that retrieves a set of records from one or more tables and displays them in a datasheet. Compare with *action query*.

snaked column report A multicolumn report that "snakes" data up and down the page.

SQL (Structured Query Language) A database language used to create and modify relational databases.

subform A form contained within another form or a report.

subform control A control that displays a subform in a form or a subform.

subset table Data tables that contain fields that describe a specific subject and, thus, are better suited to their own tables.

switchboard A form that consists almost entirely of buttons that initiate tasks and help you get to work quickly.

tab control A control that contains several pages, each with a tab, and each containing controls such as text boxes. When you click a tab, that page becomes active.

text box A control used to display data from a record source.

text qualifier Punctuation, such as quotation marks, used in a delimited text file that maintains values as single text strings.

text string An array of characters.

toggle button A control used to provide on/off options on a form or report. It can display either text or a picture.

toolbox The set of tools available in Design view to add controls to a form or report.

truncated text Text that has inadvertently been shortened because of a lack of space.

unbound control A control that is not connected to a field in an underlying table or query. An unbound control is often used to display descriptive text or decorative pictures.

update To accept changes to data in a record.

validation rule A property that defines the values that can be entered in a field or record. Validation rules are often created to enforce business rules.

validation table A table used to validate data entered into other tables.

value Data entered at the intersection of a row or column.

VBA (Visual Basic for Applications) A programming language built into Microsoft Office that allows automation of tasks and creation of new features.

wildcard A character used in an expression that acts a placeholder for other characters.

Yes/No A data type that has only two possible values, `Yes` and `No`. These values can also be expressed as `True` and `False`, or `-1` and `0`.

zero-length string A string that contains no characters. You can use a zero-length string to indicate that you know there's no value for a field. You enter a zero-length string by typing two double quotation marks with no space between them (`" "`).

INDEX

Symbols

A

D

E

F

N

O

Q

R

S

W

X-Z